MAN, OH MAN!

Man, Oh Man!

Writing Quality M/M Fiction

Josh Lanyon

JustJoshin Publications

Man, Oh Man!
Copyright © 2013 Josh Lanyon

Cover art by L.C. Chase

The moral right of the author has been asserted.

Published by JustJoshin Publications

ISBN: 978-1-937909-41-3

JustJoshin
3053 Rancho Vista Blvd.
Suite 116
Palmdale, CA 93551
www.joshlanyon.com

Typesetting services by BOOKOW.COM

ACKNOWLEDGEMENTS

The second-and greatly revised-edition of *Man, Oh Man!* has been made possible due to the generous effort and enthusiasm of a number of people who I wish to sincerely thank. In addition to the many authors, editors, reviewers, and publishers who agreed to be interviewed, several people contributed essays, including Kari Gregg, Nicole Kimberling, Jordan Castillo Price, and Aleksandr Voinov. I think these essays alone make the book worth the price of admission.

Special thanks to the authors who took part in the roundtable discussions in the new genre fiction sections. In alphabetical order: Tamara Allen, Astrid Amara, Alex Beecroft, P.A. Brown, Charlie Cochet, Charlie Cochrane, Lynn Flewelling, L.B. Gregg, Ginn Hale, Nicole Kimberling, Elliott Mackle, Ava March, Jordan Castillo Price, AM Riley, Abigail Roux, KZ Snow, Andrea Speed, Marshall Thornton, Aleksandr Voinov, Haley Walsh.

Absolutely indispensable was the help of my wonderful editor, Sasha Knight.

As ever, thank you to my wonderful Virtual Assistant, Janet Sidelinger who, among other things, gathered and double-checked data on publishers, reviewers and contests.

As with the first edition of *Man, Oh Man!*, by the time this book reaches you, almost certainly something will be out of date. And, as before, I'll have thought of a half-dozen things I should have included, people I forgot to interview, materials I neglected to include. That's the nature of writing guides. However, the bulk of this book is devoted to the art and craft of writing itself, and quality writing does not go out of date. I hope you will find this book both entertaining and of practical use.

CONTENTS

NOT THAT THERE'S ANYTHING WRONG WITH THAT

INTRODUCTION

It's startling to realize that the first edition of *Man, Oh Man!* was significantly outdated within three years of publication. It wasn't surprising that the market info should rapidly prove useless, but what *was* surprising was the significant change in the relationship between the M/M writing community and the gay literary community. Even more unpredictable were the earthshaking changes which occurred in the world of publishing, especially regarding self-publishing.

In the original introduction, I wrote: *This book is a writing tool, plain and simple. It's designed to help those who wish to write for the M/M market figure out the best way to do that—and, ideally, help those already working in this genre hone their skills.* That is all certainly true, and to that end you will find updates on choosing publishers and using social media; expanded sections on writing within the particular subgenres of M/M mystery, speculative fiction, and historical fiction; and new segments on etiquette, reviews, and self-publishing.

What this book is *not* about: Although there's a clear link between slash fan fiction and the rise of original Man on Man fiction—as well as a direct correlation between the Internet and e-publishing, and the mainstreaming of M/M fiction—the intention here is not to trace the history of M/M writing as a commercial enterprise. Nor is this an effort to analyze or justify M/M writing. It is not an attempt to figure out what M/M literature means for gay letters in general. This is not a scholarly work or a philosophical treatise.

If you're familiar with the first edition, you'll notice that a number of the old interviews were removed. Or, more precisely, replaced with new interviews or panel discussions. Also missing is the section on why women read gay or male/male fiction. Partly, that section is missing because the question can be answered in a single sentence: *There are as many and varied reasons women enjoy male/male fiction as there are types of women.* The other reason it is missing is that I've come to find the question tiresome in its implication that there is something peculiar, something requiring explanation, in a woman choosing to read about gay characters.

Should women only read stories about women? Should white people only read stories about white people? Should gays only read stories about gays?

The question is not merely academic. Over the past few years, one of the hottest topics of debate in the larger gay literary community has been the question of exactly what gay fiction is and who should be allowed to write it. There isn't much debate over who should be allowed to *read* it—writers never object to selling books—and therein lies the crux of the argument.

The unanticipated popularity of male/male romance has created the unusual, even possibly unique, paradigm whereupon outsiders of a sometimes oppressive majority can make more money writing fiction about a marginalized people than the insider members of that minority can.

It's not—to put it mildly—an ideal situation.

Accordingly, there has been a great deal of understandable resentment and frustration in some corners of the gay community, playing out in things like gender witch hunts, Boys Only book clubs, and redefining (and then redefining again) the criteria for the prestigious Lambda Literary Awards.

A frequent refrain goes something like this: *I want to read about gay men's real experience, not a straight woman's fantasy about a gay man's experience.*

Some of those concerned fear that all these happy endings present a misleading and confusing portrait for young or naïve gay readers. Some are concerned with the fetishizing of gay men. Some are concerned that gay men and their real-life experiences are being written out of their own literary culture. Some are concerned with a combination of these things. Some, unsurprisingly, are concerned that it's hard enough to compete for bookshelf space without having to compete against a bunch of straight women who don't know what they're writing about anyway.

All of these concerns are understandable. But male/male fiction is a bit of a publishing and cultural anomaly. It does not, for the most part, pretend to portray any recognizable reality. It is genre fiction—and romance fiction at that. It is a subgenre of romance. And it is largely marketed to a romance-reading audience. Which means, whether your male/male romance is written by straight women or gay men, **it's all make-believe.** Looking to M/M romance fiction for real-life advice or insight into gay relationships makes as much sense as looking to mystery fiction for training as a police officer or Age of Sail novels for learning to handle a boat.

This is not to say that readers are not entitled to read and enjoy the authors they choose, or should not support GLBT authors whenever possible, but let's be honest in our biases and not pretend that *all* gay men write more realistic romance fiction about gay men than *all* straight women who do their homework and use their experience and imagination to fill in the blanks.

NO human experience is so exclusive or so unique that it cannot be thoroughly researched and then reproduced as believable fiction by a conscientious and skilled writer. We all want to believe our human experience is original and singular, but the simple truth is, humans are all pretty much the same the world over—and have been since the beginning of time.

Storytelling is universally revered even within vastly different cultures and societies: good fiction can move us, can teach us, can inspire us. But, fiction is not reality. Fiction is merely a symbol of reality. To reiterate, you do not need to be a thing to write about a thing. You just need to do your homework.

Also missing is the section on editing your own work. This is not because editing is no longer an issue in this genre. Far from it. Frankly, the problem—and the topic—is too big for inclusion in this book. It requires a book of its own, and happily there are many good books on self-editing and excellent online courses as well, including Carina Press Editorial Director Angela James's Before You Hit Send b4youhitsend.com.

While each section of this book builds on the previous section, you'll find that we're often doubling back or leaping ahead to other facets of the M/M story. That's because, in writing, it all works together. No single element stands on its own. Characterization intersects with plot, plot dovetails with theme, theme often leads back to characterization, which leads to point of view...

The majority of excerpts I use to illustrate my points are taken from my own work—published or soon-to-be published. This isn't just to appease my fans or even because I'm an egomaniac; it's a practical consideration as well. How do you know you want to take my advice if you have no idea what kind of writer I am? These excerpts serve as my credentials. If you don't like my style or the techniques I use in any given writing component, then you know what to ignore. The deliberate choices you make, the conscious decisions of *how* you will tell your stories, is all part of honing your craft. The best writing is usually not the product of a happy accident.

A lot of writers and even aspiring writers are irritated by the notion of some-one telling them what to do. I know because I'm one of them. Please keep in mind that I'm not trying to give you one definitive answer to any single question. Frankly, that's not the reality of writing or publishing. I wouldn't have included all these essays and quotes from other learned folks if I wanted you to sit unquestioningly at my feet while I bounce pearls of wisdom off your noggin.

By the time you finish this book you should have an understanding of the steps involved in getting published—and the different options open to you. You'll almost certainly have a better, more realistic understanding of how this business—and it is a business—works.

Equally important, you should have a refined appreciation for what consti-tutes good M/M writing—yep, as I define it. We're going to examine the elements necessary to any work of fiction, but our focus will be how these elements apply specifically to M/M writing. There are plenty of wonderful, useful writing books out there (and I'll be sure to recommend some of my favorites), but the M/M genre has its own requirements, and those are the gist of this book.

I hope that no matter where you are in your publishing career, you'll take away a few tips and tricks to improve your own work. I admit that this is a self-serving motive. Like most fiction writers, I'm first and foremost a lover of stories, and the more wonderful M/M books there are to read, the happier I'll be.

My sole qualification for writing this book is that I'm a skilled and successful author of gay and M/M fiction. I win awards. I write bestselling books. I can probably give you some useful advice. But don't look to me for answers to the secrets of the universe because I'm still trying to figure those out myself.

Alex Beecroft: I personally would also like to see a bit more "realism"—a bit more awareness that life is sometimes rough, particularly if you're GLBT, and that it isn't all swooning into the arms of some hard-muscled chap who will solve all your ills with his magic penis. Or at least that and the werewolf/vampire bite which will magically mean you instantly lose a stone in weight, never age, and stay beautiful and soul-bonded forever.
Author of *False Colors, Captain's Surrender,* **etc.**

You'll notice that there's no separate chapter on romance or relationship. That's because M/M fiction is, by definition, romance fiction. Every element that we're going to discuss ultimately works as a building block toward the goal of writing an effective M/M romance. Regardless of subgenre, every M/M romance is the same in as much as it contains a central homoerotic relationship: two men falling in love against the odds. As such, it is genre fiction.

By genre fiction, we mean fiction that falls into distinct literary categories: mystery, fantasy, westerns, military, paranormal, science fiction, historicals—and, of course, pure (or impure) romance. The M/M titles that initially broke out (all things being relative) were almost exclusively genre fiction: *Swordspoint* by Ellen Kushner, *The Fire's Stone* by Tanya Huff, the historical novels of Mary Renault, just to name a few well-known examples. M/M itself is kind of an umbrella term for a strong gay or male-male romantic plot (or subplot) in what could well be a genre novel. Is Lynn Flewelling's Nightrunner series fantasy or M/M or both? The answer really depends on who you talk to and what they love about her books.

Genre or escapist fiction is not the same thing as Fiction for Dummies, and just because a novel is a fantasy or a western or a mystery needn't mean it has nothing of importance to say. Genre fiction often provides an entertaining framework on which to hang a story with an ultimately serious message.

Genre fiction is also referred to as commercial fiction. This is important to remember for later.

Our challenge is to write an entertaining book that will appeal to a lot of readers, both male and female, and perhaps have something meaningful or memorable to say about life and love.

Think about the novels that have moved you—made you laugh or cry or even managed to change your mind—think about the novels that inspired you to want to write your own stories.

For me that book was *The Charioteer* by Mary Renault.

On one level the novel is a wartime love story among three men, but it's also an exploration of sexuality, identity and disability, power dynamics within romantic relationships, the role of the individual in society, etc. I read *The Charioteer* in college. It genuinely moved me, reassured me, changed my mind about a number of things, and set me on my own course to write gay fiction and male/male romance.

This is not to say that every work of M/M fiction needs to change someone's life. Unlike gay fiction proper, M/M fiction is commercial fiction. But there's nothing wrong with providing someone a little amusement at the end of a hard day's work. It is a reminder, though, that an erotic novel can be more than a stimulus for masturbation.

While it's important to familiarize yourself with what's been done within any genre in which you hope to write, it's equally important to anticipate what need has not yet been filled by those of us already working in the field. Remember, when you check out what's available at your bookstore or on the cyber shelves of Amazon *et al*, you're seeing what editors and publishers were buying *one to two years ago*. Chances are good they aren't still buying those kinds of stories: the need for them has been met. It's a little different with e-publishing, but even so, you want to be ahead of the curve, not behind it. The best way to anticipate what editors will be looking for next is to study the industry and stay current with developments within the genre and publishing in general.

By the way, it's hard to write the kind of books you don't like to read.

If you want to know what editors will be publishing next, *listen to readers.* I don't mean your friends and your mom and the pals who beta or critique your fiction; I mean listen to readers in general. Take a look at what's hitting the bestseller lists on the publishers you're submitting to. Listen in on reader discussion forums. Check out what's hot in mainstream publishing.

When I first mentioned to friends that I was thinking of putting together a book on writing M/M fiction, reader and aspiring writer Lise Y. wrote me and said, "I think you should open the book with a note similar to the one you sent me once: that the writer's objective is to weave a cocoon of make-believe around the reader and keep them totally engaged in the story—and that every bit of advice you give will be to make sure that end is achieved."

Keep that advice in mind, my friends, and you don't need to read the book!

Is There A Difference Between M/M And Gay Romance?

Short answer: yes.

Long answer: all M/M fiction is, by strictest definition, gay fiction. But all gay fiction is *not* M/M fiction.

To start with, M/M fiction is genre fiction. It is commercial fiction. Much of gay fiction, including gay romance, is literary fiction. Commercial fiction is primarily intended to amuse and entertain. It is considered light. Literary fiction is considered heavy or serious. Literary fiction is supposed to be of literary merit. Its purpose is to explore ideas and push the boundaries of craft. Literary fiction can be entertaining, just as commercial fiction can be of literary merit, but you get the idea.

The essential definition of M/M fiction is that regardless of the genre—mystery, military, paranormal, historical—the romantic relationship between the two male protagonists is going to be the main story. The romance is the foundation. The superstructure is whatever genre you choose to build on that foundation. So you can have an M/M mystery or an M/M paranormal or an M/M contemporary romance, and the story will have to meet all the requirements of that genre *plus* it will have to meet the requirements of an M/M romance.

Because M/M is genre or category fiction, there are inherent expectations. Some people refer to this as "formula." Call it what you like, every genre is defined by its structure, conventions, and tropes. An obvious example in romance would be The Happy Ending or HEA (Happily Ever After).

This is not to say that if you write a love story about two gay men it has to have a happy ending. Gay fiction has no genre requirements. It does not require a happy ending. But if you are going to label your story "M/M Romance" in the hope of getting better sales, then it damn well better have a happy ending. Or at least a hopeful ending. You are not obliged to write happy endings or M/M romance. You *are* obliged to label your work correctly.

Now, having made a big point of all that, the trend in ebook publishing is moving away from the M/M label. More and more publishers are simply labeling male/male romance as GLBT. I honestly don't know if this is ultimately a good thing or not. It does simplify everything, but it's also liable to exacerbate frustrations in the gay literary community.

Is there a difference between M/M romance novels and gay romance novels? I'm going to generalize here and say yes, there is. Usually. Not always. Usually gay romance novels are going to make an attempt at exploring (a personally experienced?) reality. There is no such burden on M/M romance, which is why you see a lot more stories about hot cowboys and hot vampires and hot spies in M/M romance than you do in gay romance.

M/M romance also has an emotional tenor, and a distinct sensibility—regardless of whether it's written by male or female writers. In fact, there are male M/M writers who pen some of the most sappy, saccharine stuff out there. In effect, M/M is about gay men in love and making love (frequently) versus gay men figuring out who they are and maybe just fucking. You don't see a lot of experimenting or infidelity in an M/M novel—any more than you would in a heterosexual romance novel.

Overall, there is WAY more sex in an M/M romance than a gay romance. Not only is there more sex, the sex is different, and that difference has to do with sensual and evocative details. It's about the choice of language. It's about emotions rather than mechanics. Perhaps it's a more sentimental and romantic approach to love and sex than you might find in a gay romance novel—let alone gay porn.

That's my take, but this is a question that cannot be answered to everyone's satisfaction. As more and more gay men flood into M/M as both authors and readers, the genre continues to change and redefine itself. What I do know, and what you need to know, is that you must understand and appreciate who *your* audience is. Essentially what we're doing here—and I apologize in advance for wiping the fairy dust off—is creating a product. In effect, you're in the business of producing stories to sell to specific readers, the audience for male/male romance. So you need to write the kind of stories *that* audience will want to read.

Regardless of whether you feel you're writing gay romance or M/M romance, chances are you will choose to distribute your work through a middleman, also known as a publisher.

There are numerous publishers, especially e-publishers, of M/M or gay genre fiction. *Way* more publishers than when we put together the first edition of this book, so that section has been completely revamped. I've also added a section on self-publishing written by Jordan Castillo Price of JCP Books. I predicted in 2008 that we were in our growth phase with no signs of slowing: *It's a great time to be writing M/M fiction; however it's important to be aware that any time a market experiences this kind of explosive growth, a flood of inferior, second-rate product is in the offing and will soon swamp readers in derivative mediocrity. And what happens then is that readers grow jaded and bored with the genre as a whole and move on to something new.*

But despite the hundreds of new M/M titles published each and every week, I still believe that the best writers survive regardless of market fluctuations. Yes, you have to work harder, and marketing and promotion play a greater role than ever before. But if you've concocted original and well-written stories and nurtured your loyal readership by consistently providing them with quality fiction, you'll weather any eventual glut. Respect your readers and constantly strive to improve your craft, and you're investing in the best insurance policy a writing career can have.

YOU GOT A BETTER IDEA?
COMING UP WITH A STORY CONCEPT

New and aspiring writers have a tendency to wonder if they are doing it right. We're talking writing here, by the way.

Anything that helps you get that first rough draft down on paper is the right way of doing it.

I get questions about whether I write in longhand or at the computer (I started out in longhand and I now write directly to my laptop); whether I outline (sometimes); whether I work on more than one project at a time (yes); whether I listen to music when I write (that's changed and is now a yes); whether I think critique groups are a good idea (usually); whether I do what Stephen King does (what are we talking about here?); whether it's okay to write during a full moon (if you can type with furry paws, go for it).

Anything that helps you get that first rough draft down on paper is the right way of doing it. Period.

Does it help if I confess that every time I start a new project I have moments of genuine panic. Moments when I wonder if it's always this hard, if it's going slower than usual, and whether I always feel like this?

Writing is hard work; don't kid yourself. We keep writing because we love the stories. We love finding out what happens next.

Every story starts with an idea. A hook.

What Is A Hook?

No, it's not some kinky sex toy gay guys use.

The hook is the distilled essence of your story. In TV and film it's known as the tagline. It's your one-minute elevator pitch. It's the second paragraph in your query letter. It's the first paragraph of the blurb on the back of your book. It's the foundation of your ten-minute pitch to publishers at writing conferences.

The hook is what the story is about: who, what, when, where, why, and how. It's the characters and their conflict. But most importantly, it's what sets your book apart from everyone else's.

Every story must have a hook.

You should be able to recite your story's hook in your sleep—in twenty-five words or less.

Okay, fifty words or less. But if you can't explain what your book is about in a couple of sentences, you've got a problem.

Ideally, the hook should be strong and original. It should be commercial. It should convince a publisher that she or he wants to invest time and money in you and your work.

Fifty years ago a glamorous Hollywood party ended in murder—the only clue a bloody tarot card. Timothy North is trying to find out what happened that long ago summer's night, but when a tarot card turns up pinned to his front door, the only person Tim can turn to for help is his ex-lover, Detective Jack Brady.

Cards on the Table by Josh Lanyon (JustJoshin Publishing, 2012)

(Uh, now that I think about it, fifty-*eight* words is perfect for the hook.)

Coming Up With Great Commercial Ideas

I don't think coming up with ideas is the hard part for most aspiring authors. I think ideas are plentiful. Great ideas are a little more scarce. Great *original* ideas are hard as hell to come by. Don't worry about it.

Seriously. I'm sure you've heard the saying, *nothing new under the sun.* It's essentially true. There are no new ideas. In fact, according to Ms. Matsukado, my tenth-grade creative writing teacher, there are only seven basic literary plots:

- man vs. nature
- man vs. man
- man vs. society
- man vs. machines/technology
- man vs. the supernatural
- man vs. self
- man vs. god/religion

And I've seen that condensed to Joseph Campbell's monomythic Hero's Journey.

If you have no idea what I'm talking about, again, don't worry about it. I'm just hoping to convince the kids in the back of the class that I know what I'm talking about.

What makes an idea original and fresh—or commercial—is in the execution. A big part of execution is your writing. Your skill as a writer. Your voice, your facility with language, your sense of humor—or ability to create gut-wrenching angst—your psychological or social insights. Writing skills have to do with a lot more than mechanics and a grasp of basic grammar.

The other part of execution has to do with stage trappings or motif. The framework of your story is where the commerciality comes in.

Here's an example of how you take an ordinary plot and make it topical and commercial.

Let's start with a basic tried-and-true story idea: hero rescues his lover from danger.

We've got a million possibilities (and at least five of the seven basic literary plots at our disposal), and how we decide to spin this yarn will determine whether publishers, reviewers, and readers will find it fresh or not.

What we do is take some hot elements in M/M fiction—ex-lovers, foreign lands, and the military—and combine them with what's newsworthy or currently selling well in mainstream fiction and—pay attention—*nonfiction*. Like…the war in Iraq.

So the new-and-improved plot is: the leader of a Special Operations force is sent into the wilds of Iraq to rescue his missing ex-lover, a Navy SEAL.

Lots of potential there for both internal and external conflict—and that's crucial. You want strong ideas that support a meaty story. Ahem. And in romance, conflict equals plot. We'll talk more about that later.

Our Special Ops protag rushing to the rescue of his ex-lover has lots of potential for action and adventure—there's nothing like shared danger to bring two guys together—and what's sexier than Navy SEALs or Special Ops? Just looking at that tagline I'm wondering why these guys broke up, and why did the Navy SEAL's mission fail, and will he be glad to see his ex-lover or will it be too tough on his ego having his ass saved by his ex? Is the SEAL injured? Who dumped whom?

There's a story here—lots of story. It's hot, it's topical, and it's commercial.

But how do you know what's currently selling in mainstream publishing? Visit your bookstore. Check out Amazon's bestseller lists. Check out *Publishers Weekly*. Even better, subscribe to *Publishers Lunch* through Publishers Marketplace: www.publishersmarketplace.com

In fact, our soldier-sent-to-rescue-his-ex-lover scenario was based on a couple of deals I saw in *Publishers Lunch*.

The first was a U.S. Marine captain's *Band of Brothers* account of his platoon in Iraq "showcasing how love and faith prevail even in the darkest hours of the war." The second was for another nonfiction memoir by the leader of a Special Operations force sent to rescue a missing Navy SEAL in Afghanistan.

Now, while it's true that much of our work in M/M fiction is never going to appear on the mainstream publishing radar, I'm not advising you to steal your concepts and ideas wholesale. Obviously, you would need to tweak such ideas, make them your own. Change the names and faces and setting and military rank to protect the innocent.

Still, military rescues are not news in the history of the world. Soldiers have been sent to retrieve missing comrades since man first started crunching heads with handy dinosaur bones—we've all read the books and seen the movies—everything from *Gunga Din* to *Saving Private Ryan*. It's not a new idea, but there are ways to make it fresh. Turning it into an M/M love story is one of them, but in itself not enough.

Again, when you're looking for a concept or motif for your story, pay extra attention to the elements that are selling well in nonfiction. For example, flipping through my current copy of *Publishers Weekly*, I'm seeing books out on underwater photography, an Italian-American pastry chef with a bestselling book on desserts, and the story of two male slaves who escaped to freedom in the 1800s.

That's some good, workable stuff. Although there's been some improvement since the first edition of this book, there's still a need for realistic ethnic and minority M/M stories; underwater photography hasn't been done much, if at all; and chefs, cooking, and all things culinary are trendy right now. Just check out *Love's Evolution* by Ally Blue, *Stirring Up Trouble* by Z.A. Maxfield, or Poppy Z. Brite's New Orleans series.

Read the newspaper, watch the news, scan the Internet for those goofy, offbeat tidbits. These are all good sources for timely and interesting plot ideas.

What Are You Tired Of Seeing In Submissions For M/M Or Gay Fiction?

Angela James, Carina Press: I think the number one thing is submissions from authors who think male/male means it must be 75% sex and 25% story/plot.

Deborah Nemeth, Carina Press: I'm tired of seeing authors rush to publish without taking the time to fully flesh out their stories and polish their manuscripts. And receiving erotic M/M submissions that don't contain enough plot, conflict, and character development.

Irene Williams, Loose Id: I like M/M stories to have a more male POV, even if much of what we get is still female fantasy.

Sasha Knight, Samhain Publishing: I'd love to never see a submission again where one of the men in the relationship might as well be a woman with a penis. Men are different from women. I don't want to read a book marked as M/M when it seems like the author just took a het romance and changed one of the names and the subsequent body parts. That doesn't work for me, or for readers.

Aleksandr Voinov, Riptide Publishing: Probably the same thing everybody is tired of seeing: flat characters, weak writing, and the thought that sex is enough to engage an audience. We love sex, but it has to further the plot and character development. We're possibly the only publisher that cuts sex scenes if they don't add anything. Also, two members of our staff are BDSM lifestylers, and they do not like inauthentic or wrong BDSM. Similarly, as a trained historian, historical fiction should have a solid grounding in research and reality (as we know it). Also, importantly, we don't like women-bashing in our submissions. If the only woman in the cast is an evil bitch and all gay men are long-suffering saints, that leaves an odd aftertaste in a genre populated with many female readers and writers.

Trace Edward Zaber, Amber Quill Press: At this point in time, there is no subgenre we are tired of seeing. However, we cannot express strongly enough that emotion and drama, whatever the story, are key factors. We only publish manuscripts that contain a firm storyline—in other words, an endless string of meaningless sexual encounters based around a flimsy plot will not interest us in the least. The stories we publish must be able to stand on their own, even if an author were to remove all the actual sexual content—take it off-screen, so to speak. Therefore, when we see a story with absolutely no plot or character development or emotion, we consider it a firm reject. Adding sex for the sake of sex might work at some publishers, but not at AQP. Each story must justify its content.

Margaret Riley, Changeling Press: Honestly, nothing. I don't ever want to read another F/F written by a guy who thinks he's not only welcome to watch but hopes to join in, but if it's M/M and fits our guidelines, bring it on.

Tina Burns, Liquid Silver Books: So far I'm not sick to death of any M/M themes. Just more.

Nicole Kimberling, Blind Eye Books: Heroes with no apparent personal interests or goals larger than getting in some other guy's pants. Unrelenting ass-ramming. Endless crying. I dislike angst extremely.

Because something doesn't click for one editor, doesn't mean it won't work for another. Cut down on your chances of rejection by paying attention to the writer's guidelines that all publishers offer. This is so basic it shouldn't need to be said, but if a publisher indicates they don't accept stories with underage characters, rape, incest, adultery, or M/F/M pairings, then either don't send that submission or don't whine when—best-case scenario—you're asked to make some changes.

The other thing to remember is that, for the most part, neither publishers nor reviewers are sick of particular plots or concepts *per se*. Most of their complaints have to do with characterization and execution and structure—that's all fixable stuff. So if you're burning to pen the story about an adulterous werewolf, and it's well-written enough, likely someone will be willing to publish it.

What Would You Like To See More Of?

Simmer down, class, we're talking about submission ideas.

Angela James, Carina Press: We're still extremely interested in M/M, both by authors new to the genre and from veteran authors. Quite a number of my editors love this genre, as do our readers. I want to continue to see more developed male/male stories, with well-drawn, realistic characters, a great plot and a well-thought out storyline. The sex is a bonus (even in an erotic romance—and I love erotic romance!).

Deborah Nemeth, Carina Press: I particularly enjoy historical M/M fiction and M/M suspense. I'd also love to acquire an M/M mystery series, whether in a contemporary, historical, steampunk, or space opera setting.

Sasha Knight, Samhain Publishing: I'd like to see more well-developed characters and worlds. I'd like authors to step away from gay clichés to write stories where men, acting like men, fall in love. I'd love to see an epic sci-fi, space-opera series where the main character is gay, and over the course of his adventures and many books, falls in love. I'd also love to see an apocalyptic or post-apocalyptic series similar in vein to The Walking Dead, where the hero finds love while figuring out how to survive in this new world.

Aleksandr Voinov, Riptide Publishing: Plotty romances, where people do stuff, develop as people and as a couple and also kick ass in some fashion (aka: an external plot). We have big soft spots for speculative fiction (steampunk, fantasy, horror, and sci-fi), and we also like romcoms and funny stories. I would also like to see more historicals and thrillers. Like normal readers, we like to be excited and wowed.

Nicole Kimberling, Blind Eye Books: Real plots—any kind. Science fiction. Substantial themes—again, any kind.

By the way, if you don't enjoy vampire stories, don't try to write a vampire story simply because vampires sell well. And don't *not* write about shapeshifting pirates because there are so many shapeshifting and/or pirate stories out there. (Actually, there aren't that many pirate stories out there, which is surprising considering how popular pirates are in the mainstream media these days.)

Jot down a note to self: *You need to write the kind of thing you enjoy reading.* Otherwise, it shows in the writing. You're just kidding yourself if you think it doesn't. If you're planning to write M/M fiction because you think it's a sure moneymaker, take it from me, there are easier ways to make money.

Any Thoughts On Trends In M/M Or Gay Genre Fiction? Any Feel For What Might Be The Next Big Thing?

Asking a publisher to identify The Next Big Thing is really sort of a joke because by the time a trend has been recognized, it's already cresting—which means the market is about to get hit with tsunami-like waves of more of the same. More paranormals fulfilling readers' fantasies. More military men falling in love. More college romances between roommates, between teammates, between coaches and players, between professors and students. You get the idea. We *all* get the idea. Making the idea your own is what matters.

Still, for the record, here's the word from our panel of editors and publishers.

Angela James, Carina Press: I think some of the genre's early rise (sorry, no pun intended) did come about through erotic romance, but I'm now seeing an increase in readership for non-erotic male/male. I think we're going to see a continued increase in sales for non-erotic, story-driven gay fiction. I'm also noticing an interesting increase in the number of men writing, submitting, and publishing male/male, and I wonder if we'll see more male/male written by men for men, versus by women for women.

Sasha Knight, Samhain Publishing: As for what's the next big thing—I think M/M fiction is going to be more widely accepted. With New York Times bestselling authors writing M/M books—Suzanne Brockmann and J.R. Ward, in particular—as well as mainstream publishing starting M/M romance lines, it seems that New York is ready to see how this genre will be accepted, which will get more readers interested in M/M romance.

I'm also seeing more M/M romances with lower heat levels being submitted, and I think those are great gateway reads for those new to gay romance who aren't ready to delve into explicit stories.

Aleksandr Voinov, Riptide Publishing: Looking at pure sales data, contemporary M/M books outsell everything else. I don't see that changing, though I think the niche genres at least seem to be growing, if slower. An author can grow a respectable readership even outside the best-selling genre, though it can feel like an uphill battle. I think readers are getting more critical of sloppy editing (from content to punctuation), and with Amazon allowing them to return ebooks, that's something a publisher ignores at their own peril.

Rachel Haimowitz, Riptide Publishing: As gay rights continue to advance, gay fiction will follow apace. M/M might be a slightly harder sell for people who've never considered the possibility before, but strong gay genre fiction with romantic plots or sub-plots will make for great gateway reads. Over the next five to ten years, I expect to see more and more people willing to consider the next great YA dystopian with a gay lead, or a new set of cozy mysteries being solved by a husband-and-husband team, or a military thriller that also explores how its gay protagonist and his team are adjusting to a post-DADT service.

We're also seeing mainstream houses—traditional NY and even Big Six imprints—starting to dip their toes into the M/M waters. Primarily with digital-first, but not always; think JR Ward's Lover at Last. How that book is received will probably rather disproportionately influence how the rest of the genre is received for the next year or two, but it's clear that even publishers who operate on very large scales are starting to see both the literary merit and the commercial value in M/M romance and gay fiction. Their marketing machines and distribution presses will help to "normalize" those genres. So will publishing houses like Riptide: small specialty presses with a relentless focus on quality, broad distribution, and LGBTQ activism. In a perfect world, ten years from now, LGBTQ romances and thrillers and mysteries will be shelved right next to straight romances and thrillers and mysteries—not separated out into an LGBTQ section—and your average reader won't think twice about the sexual orientation of the protagonist(s) when making their choices. It's a vision I think all the LGBTQ presses share, and certainly one we'll be fighting to help make happen.

Trace Edward Zaber, Amber Quill Press: In actuality, overall M/M fiction is the current big thing, regardless of subgenre. We are in the middle of the explosion, but it will be anyone's guess what will be the next hot ticket on the horizon. There's truly no predicting. Several years ago, customers could not get enough of vampire erotic romance, but these days, you can't even give those books away. Trends change, fast, and without warning, depending on the influx of new books within the genres…in other words, it depends on how many companies jump on the bandwagon to flood the market. Once customers grow tired of a trend, they will certainly look for something else, but unfortunately, no one possesses a crystal ball to predict what it will be.

Tina Burns, Liquid Silver Books: Trends are hard to track as it's very reader based. I think the erotic romance industry was a bit surprised at the enthusiasm for M/M from a mostly female readership. Our policy is if it's a good story, well written, and smokin' hot, we'll add it to our library. Of course, those are very loose criteria.

Love never goes out of style. Romance still controls the lion's share of the popular fiction market. Classic plot dynamics are as reliable and serviceable as that little black dress of yours, but you have to…er…accessorize…to keep that classic from seeming faded and overworked. Sex sells, but as reviewer "Water Nymph" AKA Kimberly Swan points out, it's **very important if there's a new or growing romance, but it has to work in the overall plot, not just be** thrown in. Gratuitous sex scenes aren't going to make a book, but love scenes, even if they're spontaneous and wild, can definitely add to a good plot."

By the way, I'm sure you've noticed that the opinions of publishers/editors often contradict each other—not to mention me. No book is right for every reader, and that's important to remember when you start getting rejections—or reviews.

The wonderful thing about storytelling is that no matter how many times a tale has been told, if you can tell it in a fresh and exciting way—if you can make it your own—someone, somewhere, will want to read it.

Margaret Riley, Changeling Press: Ya know, they've gotten pretty good at predicting the weather these days, but that's as far as I'd venture—we never try to predict what people will buy, because any hot trend is going to be yesterday's news way too fast. Werewolves, vampires, cats…again, it's the quality of the writing that makes the most impression on sales.

Truer words, etc. Genuinely original ideas are easier to sell, but the strength of any idea ultimately relies on your ability and execution. Almost any element can work if you can figure out a way to…er…"romanticize" it.

Publishers don't know what will be the next hot thing any more than you do. Remember that. The best ideas are the ones that fill you with enthusiasm. The ones you can't wait to work on. The ones that almost seem to write themselves.

Write your passion.

Where Do You Get Your Ideas?

The question "Where do you get your ideas?" is one of the big clichés on the writer's circuit. But so many people ask it, I guess a lot of beginning writers persist in thinking there must be some mystery or trick to it.

Z.A. Maxfield: I get my ideas everywhere, from every single thing I observe during the day. The best ideas are so insistent I can't sit still until I make a brief outline of a story. I never lack ideas, I only lack time to flesh them all out. It's simply essential to observe everything around you all the time. You never know when your nosiness will result in a great story.
Author of *Crossing Borders*, the St. Nacho's series, etc.

K.A. Mitchell: They attack me randomly, while watching a movie, seeing a person walk, hearing a couple fight, listening to a lyric in a song, or staring out at the road as I drive. The idea attacks and I have a frozen moment where I feel what a character is experiencing. I have tons of ideas locked in a folder. (If I don't write them down, they keep attacking. They have sharp enough teeth and claws to jerk me out of sleep.) The problem with the idea comes when I let it out and start turning it into a story someone wants to read. At that point they stop attacking and run away, making me chase them and wrestle them into submission. Slippery little suckers.
Author of *Regularly Scheduled Life, Collision Course*, etc.

Scott Sherman: Like most authors, my ideas come from a variety of places, including my life, TV shows, other books, news stories, and some dark part of my subconscious I'm afraid to peer into.

I do find it essential to read a lot of different kinds of books. It stimulates the creative process and exercises a part of the mind only triggered by the act of reading. I find myself unintentionally analyzing stories as I read them, examining what works, what doesn't, and what I could learn for my own writing.

A funny story—as my first series was about a male prostitute, I got many questions about whether or not I had worked as a rent-boy in my real life. The closest I ever got was when I was a teenager hanging out in Times Square, waiting for a Broadway show to begin. A rather shabby-looking fellow approached me and asked if I were interested in making any "spare change."

"Spare change?" I asked him. "Really?" Even as an adolescent, I felt I was worth more.

Author of the Kevin Connor mysteries, *Wild Talents*, etc.

Rhys Ford: Wow. Usually they simmer into being on their own. A lot of time I'll hook on to a concept or an idea and build up from there. Music or a situation will strike me, or I'll see a character trait in someone else and think, that's got to be built on. I usually start off with a character then create a conflict around that person.

Things shift. I'll start off one place and then flow to another before going back to tighten up an idea. Even then, I leave myself some wiggle room to maneuver around.

Author of *Dirty Kiss*, *Sinner's Gin*, etc.

Scott Pomfret and Scott Whittier AKA The Romentics: Mostly from everyday life. That is another advantage to being a gay male couple. We live openly gay lives and go to gay resort towns for vacation. Any person we meet, location, or situation can spark an idea. Romance can be created out of most any concept. It's just exaggerated, dramatized, and focused on the relationship. We have based characters on friends and relatives, but by the time we've turned it into a romance they are no longer recognizable. We have also taken simple facts of gay life, like coming out or online dating, and created entire romance novels around them.

Also, there is an opportunity to take classic themes and turn them into gay romance because it hasn't been done to death as in the

straight market. We have done gay twists on Romeo and Juliet, city mouse/country mouse, rags to riches, amnesia thrillers.
Authors of *Hot Sauce, Razor Burn*, **etc.**

I'm glad Scott—and Scott—brought that up. Another really, really easy way of coming up with ideas—in fact, it's so easy you should be ashamed of yourself if you have to resort to this—is lifting the plots of old heterosexual romance novels.

On the surface it probably looks like a viable idea, especially given the issues so many M/M writers have with plot and pacing. Here's the problem. The inherent conflicts and power dynamics between men and women are simply not the same as between two men. And if you think they *are* the same, you've been reading too much M/M romance and need to get out and meet some real guys. To try and lift wholesale the plot from a heterosexual romance and slap it on an M/M story is not going to simplify the plotting process, it's going to complicate it.

But since I know you're going to nod obediently and then go off and do it anyway the minute my back is turned, let's take a practical look at ripping off Old Masters. Here are a couple of book blurbs from dusty and tattered Harlequin Romances:

> When her father mysteriously disappeared searching for the Lost City of the Incas, Charley was set on finding him. And, infuriatingly, she needed the help of Braden Quest, the brilliant anthropologist.

> *Bittersweet Pursuit* by Margaret Mayo (Harlequin, 1988)

Okay, this one actually isn't too bad a match. How hard is it to change Charley to Charles, and Braden Quest (*Braden Quest???*) to Jack Martin, brilliant archeologist/explorer/kidnap expert? The father becomes Charlie's partner—hell, it could be his brother or best friend or mother, for that matter. Just shake up the dynamic. Now Charles and Braden are rivals and competitors. Equals. Move the locale. Now the partner/mother/brother is searching for the legendary Arabian city of Ubar—or Atlantis. Actually, please not Atlantis. That's been overused, though possibly not in M/M fiction.

But keep in mind that M/M fiction doesn't exist in a vacuum. Most of our readers read other things as well. When M/M was a novelty, they were more patient, tolerant of the clichés. That's changing because there's so much to choose from. Remember, readers vote with their PayPal accounts. You need their votes.

> Everything was going wrong for Alison. Her job was in jeopardy, and she was going to have to sell her beloved family home to a stranger. As if that wasn't enough, Niall MacBain had come home; Niall, her arch-enemy, whom she had not seen for nine years but for whom she still felt nothing but hatred.

Black Niall by Mary Wibberley (Harlequin, 1977)

Provided no marriage of convenience is required, I guess this could work. Alison becomes Andrew, struggling to keep the failing family business afloat and facing having to sell to hated corporate raider (and maybe ex-boyfriend) Scott Harper.

> "Fear not the desert, nor the destiny you deny," the sand diviner told Melissa when she came to Morocco in search of her missing sister. But Melissa feared the dark arrogant Raoul Germon even more. And he was the only man who knew the truth behind her sister's disappearance.

The House of the Amulet by Margery Hilton (Harlequin, 1971)

Huh? What the hell is a sand diviner?

Anyway, Melissa becomes Mark, now searching for his twin brother who disappeared during a photo shoot on the Navajo Reservation. Raoul Germon becomes Ralph Goodeagle, tribal police officer. Ralph is rumored to have started an affair with the missing man shortly before he vanished.

So…yes. I guess in theory this also could work. Still. A word of caution.

If you're lifting heterosexual romance plots, it's crucial that you make these stories unique and masculine in every detail. The characters—and their goals and motivations—must be male. Please God, no secret babies. No forced "marriages." No cowboys. Okay, okay!! Yes, cowboys are fine. Just remember, if you're doing it right, the final story should bear little if any resemblance to its previous incarnations. If you're doing it right, you'll probably work harder changing the original into something new than you would have worked just creating something new to begin with.

Tara Renee, Two Lips Reviews: Some books look like first-time efforts that haven't been well developed or thought out. Some recent books I've come across feel like the story came out of one of the NY publishers and just changed the gender of the characters—no originality to distinguish the work from others.

It's important to remember that not every idea is a good idea. The best ideas are the ones that seem to write themselves both because of the enthusiasm you feel for the story, and the complexity and possibilities within that plot.

Also, I want to point something out that shouldn't need saying, but I'll say it anyway. It's one thing to crib an idea and make it your own. It's something entirely different to plagiarize another writer's work. Don't do it.

Also to be avoided: filing serial numbers off fan fiction and publishing it as original fiction. Yes, there are fanfics so cracky, so unique, so AU that it's impossible to recognize their origins. But that's going to be the minority. Not only are there legal and ethical ramifications, a lot of readers resent being charged for what was previously offered as a free read. If you're going to publish your own fan fiction, you better plan on doing some serious rewriting and expanding.

Some ideas are better suited to a shorter format. A novel (50,000 + words) requires a lot of plot—and several subplots. A novella (20,000 - 50,000 words) usually requires a plot and a subplot. My personal preference is for the twin plots of mystery and romance. A novelette (10,000 - 20,000 words) or longish short story (5,000 - 10,000 words) may not require anything more than a complicated love story. But make no mistake; the short story is a demanding art form. You don't have room to wander or ramble. Regardless of length or format, every story requires some kind of conflict—or there is no story. The exception is flash fiction (usually under 1,000 words) which merely requires the ability to write memorable (often erotic) scenes with the suggestion of a backstory.

Ideas are where you find them. This afternoon I happened onto a blog about disability. The title was "Lord Chatterley Abandoned Once Again," and the writer was talking about how contemporary reviewers of the recent French film *Lady Chatterley's Lover* simply took for granted the traditional premise that because Lord Chatterley was disabled and in a wheelchair he was no longer a sexual being.

I thought that was an interesting point, and I started thinking about how poor Clifford Chatterley might have amused himself while his good lady was romping with the gamekeeper. Like…what if Lord Chatterley was gay? What if he got rid of that female nurse and had his own virile and earthy manservant to tend to all his needs?

Reasonably original, and it has the advantage of being historical, featuring a disabled protagonist, and using a famous literary character, which is very hot in mainstream publishing right now.

Basically that's how I come up with my ideas. I browse around and something catches my eye, and then I start thinking about the characters. I always start with characters, and then I think…*what if?*

The late, much beloved Bobby Michaels wrote, "I love writing male/male romance because, despite what is believed in society about females, I think that males are far more romantic. They just have greater difficulty in expressing it. That's how I write. I develop two male characters in my mind and then think up a difficult situation for them and see what happens. I also love the feedback that I get from males who find themselves, without expecting it, crying over my stories. That is one of my major goals in writing is to touch my reader's deeper emotions. I treasure one email that was sent to me about one of my very romantic novels. All the email said was, 'I've got a hard-on and I'm crying. What do I do now?'"

Don't you hate it when that happens?

Take your time picking the right idea. It'll save you trouble and grief later.

GENTLEMEN, START YOUR ENGINES
THE WRITING PROCESS AND OUTLINES

That Thing You Do—Finding Time To Write

It's always hard to keep my mouth shut when someone says, "Someday, when I have the time, I'm going to write a book."

Yeah. Whatever. When I had a day job, I worked sixty hours a week and still managed to do a book a year. Granted I also shot my blood pressure through the roof and nearly gave myself a nervous breakdown, but…the point is, writers write.

If you really want to *be* a writer, then sooner or later the writing must become one of your priorities. It doesn't have to be the entire focus of your life, but it does have to be in the Top Five Things to Do Today list.

I used to write before work, on my lunch, and after work. I usually managed to cram in about four hours per sleep-deprived day that way. And I used to average about a thousand words daily.

When I first moved to writing full-time, my schedule got a little out of control. It started out sensibly enough. I'd wake up at five, stumble into my office and do email for an hour, then go do yoga or tai chi, work in the garden for an hour, then have breakfast, then write straight through—no interruptions allowed—to five or six o'clock. Then I'd work out, have dinner, and, depending on how well the day's writing went, I'd either relax a bit, read, blog, spend time with the guy I'm married to—or get back to work. I was producing about one to three thousand words a day.

That quickly went to hell in a handbasket.

For one thing the "busyness" of writing increased exponentially with each new story. For another, the pressure of having to earn my livelihood as a freelancer, the fear that I had gambled everything on something as precarious as writing fiction for a living, led me to accept every possible project that came my way—and these things combined led to working an average of twelve hour days every day for the next six years. That's right. For six years I didn't take a weekend off, let alone an actual vacation. The closest I got to time off was my annual bout of the flu.

Unsurprisingly, these lousy work habits led to carpal tunnel, a host of other ailments, and a serious case of burnout. So serious that I needed to take a year off just to be able to sit at my laptop without experiencing an anxiety attack.

Now I'm back at work, but I'm trying to stick to eight hour days. I try to take weekends and holidays off. In fact, I try to make time for the occasional lunch with friends or a movie with the SO or a swim with the nieces and nephews.

I still work longer hours than almost anyone I know—anyone who isn't a writer, anyway. I'm self-employed, and my business is writing. I have to take it seriously; my financial survival depends on it. I happen to love my job, I think I'm incredibly lucky to be able to do what I love for a living, but it's still hard work and I get bored and frustrated like anyone else. So, yes, I do occasionally play hooky or have sick days—and I sure as heck plan to have a vacation this year. And every year from now on.

There are a couple of things about my schedule I want to bring to your attention. The first is that I try very hard to avoid doing email during the day. I also try to avoid Goodreads, the blog circuit, Facebook, Twitter, discussion lists, or any of the other fascinating Internet playgrounds. This is because these things will eat up your writing time like Pac-Man on a rampage.

The other thing to note is the physical activity I once more try faithfully to work in. Sitting on your butt all day is really hard on your body. What you might not be aware of is that it's also hard on your mind. Breaking up the writing day with physical activity is good for all your muscles, including the creative ones.

I'm reasonably productive, but I'm not in the Nora Roberts class. Heck, I'm not even in the Laura Baumbach class.

K.A. Mitchell: My writing day has frequently evolved. I have been writing to escape the boredom of reality as long as I can remember, but on my quest to make a living at it, here's how it went. At first, I gave up sleep on weekends and wrote from 8 PM through 6 AM on Fridays and Saturdays. That book took 3 years and is a steaming pile of...words. Then I wrote 8 PM-12 AM every day and got a pace where I could finish a book in a year. When I finally started earning money, (still with my day job) that shiny bit of motivation had me writing roughly the same schedule but much faster. As soon as I could afford it, I went part-time at my day job. Since I've always been more alert at night, I took a 10 AM-3 PM shift. I would get up at 8 AM, read over what I'd written the night before and make changes, then nap after the day job so that I could write from 8 PM-2 AM.

Now that I write full-time, my schedule is roughly that of an office worker of 9-5, but I often start earlier and finish later. I think it's better to have a page or word count goal rather than an hourly one. Find your prime time and write during that time. Save the drudgery for when you're naturally sluggish (for me 3 PM-7 PM). Something else in your life (TV, video games, unicorn hunting) has to give if you want to write, whether full-time or part-time.
Author of *Regularly Scheduled Life, Collision Course*, etc.

Z.A. Maxfield: I started writing while I was a stay-at-home mom, so I write full-time. My situation is only applicable to those who write full-time. I start before my first cup of coffee in the morning, and most days, I expect to get two thousand words. That means seven days a week, by the way, although there are days I take a break out of necessity or because the brain isn't working. I keep a very cheap, old-time paper calendar, and I write the word count at the end of the day in silver sharpie. I have contracts for work through October. It's a full-time job.

If I didn't require myself to produce a specific, easily achievable number of words per day, I wouldn't do them. If I opened my email before I gathered my work thoughts together, or spent my day searching the web for interesting Tumblr tidbits to share with my daughter (which I am guilty of some days), I would not be able to complete my books. It's a simple matter of treating your writing job like any other. Grab your coffee, sit at your desk, and work.
Author of *Crossing Borders*, **the St. Nacho's series, etc.**

Rhys Ford: Coffee. Lots and lots of coffee. I focus at least three hours or so on writing. Early mornings or late nights are the best for me. Sometimes I even break it in half so I can log in a few thousand words. I do break my writing up into chapters or scenes and will go until that is complete. I try not to leave a scene halfway because it's hard to recapture the feeling of where I was going when I first sat down to it. I mean I do go get coffee or let the dogs out, but all in all, I at least want to finish that scene.

Day job flows around that. It's just time management in chunks, really. There are some days when it's instant dinner of some kind, although I do love cooking. There are some days when it's going to be a scrambled-eggs-and-rice day because I want to finish what I'm working on.
Author of *Dirty Secret, Sinner's Gin*, **etc.**

Scott Sherman: As a full-time employee and a single father of two, the idea of a "writing day" is as foreign to me as life on the moon. I have more like "writing moments," some of which are more productive than others.

My most enduring philosophy of writing is simply to focus on production. Getting words onto the page (or, more accurately, the screen) is the ultimate measure of success. It's easy and tempting to spend days and weeks endlessly revising that first page or chapter, but it kills your productivity.

Like many of life's challenges, I believe storytelling must be faced with a relentless determination to keep moving forward. There will always be time to edit and polish, but the fastest possible first draft is a necessity for me. For that reason, when I'm working on a manuscript, I keep an Excel spreadsheet that holds me to a 500 or 1,000 words/day rate of production. I know that doesn't sound very artistic, but, believe me, even Michelangelo wasn't paid to ponder the Sistine Chapel—he was commissioned to paint it.

You can create something terrific, but not by thinking about it or spending a year worrying over one sentence. There's a tremendous sense of relief that comes when you type "the end," even if you know it's really only the beginning of several weeks or months of revision.

In terms of scheduling, the first draft is hammered out in the time I have between putting the kids to bed and falling asleep myself, a lunch hour here and there, and on the occasional weekend when the kids are otherwise occupied.

Author of the Kevin Connor mysteries, *Wild Talents*, etc.

As you see, we've all got different writing styles and schedules, but we all manage to do one thing: we steadily and consistently produce publishable-quality work. Doing that requires writing every day—or as close to every day as you can get.

The main lesson to take away from this section: *Write Every Single Day—or as close to it as humanly possible.*

Remember, if you only wrote one page a day, at the end of a year, you'd have completed roughly 91,250 words. That's a complete novel—or two novellas—or a slew of short stories. Of course, if you're Sarah Black, you'd have completed *all* of those and you'd be working on some flash fiction just to keep your hand in.

To Outline Or Not To Outline?

Like I said earlier, anything—any *process*—that enables you to get the rough draft down on paper, is the right approach to writing. All the same, I'm repeatedly asked whether I outline or not.

For a novel-length work, yes, I do outline. Sometimes I wait to outline 'til I'm halfway through and things are getting complicated, but I think it's ideal to outline before you start writing. Especially if you're inexperienced.

I don't outline for novellas or short stories. However, if I find myself getting stuck, I stop, chart out the rest of the book as I envision it, and that usually solves the problem.

I tossed the question "Do you outline?" to the usual suspects:

K.A. Mitchell: Such words as "outline" and "synopsis" cause me to twitch and shudder, but the fact is, if you're going to be working with publishers, you will probably sell on proposal and that means an outline. I use one after I've learned about my characters to see what growth they need and how they'll affect each other. I keep the details about the external elements (they're in a bakery when an explosion of custard forces them to realize...) to a minimum and stick to the important turning points in the romance. I strive for an outline that leaves out enough to appease my ADD so I can keep writing, while at the same time gives an editor enough information so that I can get a contract and a date on a publishing schedule. Now and then, an outline helps when I get very much off track, but recognizing that usually comes from a gut sensation rather than an outline that tells me I should have taken a left at Albuquerque. **Author of** *Regularly Scheduled Life, Collision Course,* **etc.**

Scott Sherman: I've read many books and articles extolling the virtues of outlining, but it's a process I've never found helpful.

For me, writing is a process of discovery. I can never predict what characters will come alive for me until I place them in a scene and start putting words in their mouths. Likewise, a plot reveals itself as I go along. For example, I wound up switching the killer from my original intent on two out of three murder mysteries. In both cases, the story took twists I hadn't anticipated, and my ultimate choices seemed more interesting, surprising, and fun than my first instincts.

Proponents of outlining will tell you that a strong structure would prevent you from making that kind of "mistake," in which you write too much without knowing where you're going. However, for me, that is the benefit of writing a fast first draft. You can always go back and tweak dialogue, plant clues, and rework scenes to serve your final outcomes.

What works for me is having a few—five or six—big scenes or reveals I know will form the basis for my story. I may have separate notes, research, and character sketches. With those on the screen (I very much like the writing program Scrivener for keeping track of these bits and pieces) I just start writing. Within the first few thousand words, I find I've wandered into places I hadn't anticipated and met characters who deserve more time than I expected. Of course, the reverse is also true.

That being said, I have attempted outlines and mind maps of my stories. They've been helpful to a point, but they feel more like "work" than the actual writing. I want to tell fully fleshed out stories—building the skeletons feels tedious to me. I'd rather course correct than draw a map.

Author of the Kevin Connor mysteries, *Wild Talents*, etc.

Z.A. Maxfield: I used to be more of a seat-of-my-pantster, and then I started contracting books in advance. That's where the rubber meets the road of outlining. If you're writing on contract, you need to be able to create a book on time, every time, regardless of what's going on in your life. Say your house burns down… Hey. It happens. You need to be able to create in a reliable way, even though creativity isn't very quantifiable.

The problem, of course, is not everyone likes planning, and not every type of outline works with every type of writer. Thankfully, I finally found what works for me. It's an outline that makes it possible to see the components of the story and the progress I've made with respect to the storyline. The simple outline style of essays, all those roman numerals and subheadings, doesn't work for me. Even bullet points, which I used to use, don't work. I require a spatial outline, like a timeline with major plot points and the character arc drawn out in a more right-brain way, I guess. Find what works for you, but never forget the outline isn't written in

stone (unless that's how you like it). You can diverge from your outline, change it as you write. The magic is what happens when you work; the trick is to work smart.
Author of *Crossing Borders*, the St. Nacho's series, etc.

Rhys Ford: I would say I framework more than outline. I do break the story up into chapters based on a timeline. Say Chapter One is Monday morning and I list what's going on there and then if the character drives to the next scene, I make sure to mark the time shift. Mostly I do this to keep track of time and to ensure that my character doesn't instantly teleport down the 405 during rush hour.

The framework has key points, but I don't sketch out scene by scene. Sometimes the story will change midway, and I want to have that freedom. Especially if I decide to kill someone off when I hadn't planned to. Some people just need killing.
Author of *Dirty Secret*, *Sinner's Gin*, etc.

So obviously opinion is pretty evenly divided on whether to color within the lines or fly by the seat of your pants.

Judging by the letters I get from perspiring—er—aspiring writers, I'm going to guess that most newbie writers don't outline—which could be why most first novels don't get finished. And why most first novels that *do* get finished don't get published. Maybe I should amend that. We do see a number of first novels get published here in M/M fiction. We also see a number of authors learning their craft in front of their audience. That's not the way you want to do it. Very often you have one shot at winning over a reader. You don't want that shot to be your lame-ass first effort that, had you only known then what you know now, would still be sitting in your bottom desk drawer.

Consider your outline to be a kind of roadmap. I don't know about you, but I don't jump into the car and start driving across country before I've decided where I'm going and the best way to get there. Like the prudent motorist I am, I pick my destination, and I decide on the various scenic spots that I want to see along the way. I figure out how long the trip's going to take and how to pace myself—and *then* I start driving like a maniac and running slower cars off the road.

I hear writers complain that they want to keep the writing process spontaneous and joyful. Speaking for myself, I'm plenty joyful when I finish a project right on schedule—or even ahead of time. And, to belabor a metaphor, using a TripTik doesn't mean I can't go off-roading or take a short cut when required. Writing is an organic process; once you start, things begin to happen. Plans change. That's part of the fun. Part of the magic. Better ideas replace the original plan. But having the original plan helps you decide whether any given side trip is really going to enhance your travel experience or merely end with you lost in the woods chewing on your tires while the snow drifts quietly, quietly down.

Not that I'm trying to tell you what to do.

Oh. Wait a minute, yes I am. I strongly suggest that if you are inexperienced enough to be in doubt about whether you should outline, you *should* outline.

Another reason you should outline is because the basic manuscript proposal to a prospective agent or publisher consists of three sample chapters and your outline. Once you've worked with a publisher for a while you'll actually sell stories based on proposals, so learning to outline is a useful skill indeed.

And because beginning writers always fret about this stuff—don't. Other than the bare basics: one-inch margins all around, single-spaced, error-free, 12-point Courier or New Times Roman font on one side of three to fifteen pages of *white* paper, there is no one definitive outline style or form. Agents and editors are used to seeing a variety of formats. They're looking to see that you've worked out a competent, complete, and commercial plot with a satisfying resolution, that you appear to understand structure, pacing, character arcs—in short, that you've got more to offer than three great opening chapters. The decision to see the rest of your manuscript will be based on those three chapters and the outline. Yes, yes, I know it's unfair, and no one can truly appreciate the genius of your work without reading the entire manuscript, but that's the way the game is played—and, by the way, there's no crying in publishing.

What does an outline contain? Well, it needn't contain bullet points, subheadings, or Roman numerals unless you like that kind of thing. It can be as simple as a timeline or as complicated as an abridged, barebones version of the first draft.

One thing it contains is the ending to your story, so don't get coy and say something like, "And to find out how it all ends, you'll just have to read the rest of the book!" Your outline will have the ending, and all the clever twists and turns—all the very best bits of the story laid out in black and white. You're going to cover all the highlights. All the main points of the story, starting with the pivotal opening scene.

Yeah, that's the first thing: your story should begin at a pivotal point in the main character's life. Don't build up to the story. Catch the wave and ride it in. Think up a great opening line or a great opening scene. Start strong.

And give a little thought to the ending. Yes, right now, while you're starting the story. Plan ahead, think it through. Your ideas may change—they'll almost certainly change—by the time you're tying up the loose ends, but chances are the *essentials* will stay the same. Put some thought into the ending because it's the final impression a reader takes away from the book. How many great stories are spoiled by a weak ending? Too many.

Of course, you also need a really strong *middle*, but I don't want to throw too much at you at one time. At the very least, for the purpose of your outline, you'll need to know what the climax or turning point of your story will be. Then, start filling in all the scenes that have already occurred to you—plug them in where you think they should fall in the story timeline. Don't worry, you'll think of additional scenes, you'll cut some of the ones you first thought of, you'll move things around—that's fine. That's how it works. The outline is a tool for you to use. Make it work for you.

I've included a couple of samples—the synopsis and the original outline for *The Hell You Say*—in the resources section. I usually start by writing out a synopsis of the story as I envision it, and then I break it down into a rough chapter-by-chapter outline. I outline knowing it's going to change, and if you're familiar with the novel, you'll notice that the outline did change a bit from what I'd originally planned, although the ending stayed the same in spirit.

Remember, you're not chiseling any of this into a stone tablet. Laptop, paper, index cards, crayons, or storyboard, I don't care what you use to outline.

Just remember that you can—and should—cut and paste as necessary. Your working outline is flexible. New and better ideas may well replace the original ideas. The outline is your plan, your roadmap, not a contract signed in blood and mailed to the Devil. *That* paperwork only gets filed once the manuscript is complete.

WHOSE LIFE IS IT ANYWAY?
POINT OF VIEW

While you're putting together a breakdown of the important scenes and story highlights, give some careful thought to who is telling the story. Whose story is this? As your characters take form in your mind, so should the point of view—POV in authorspeak.

POV is one of the most important decisions you'll make regarding the telling of any story. And here's a tip: If you're finding it difficult to nail your main character's voice, or find the focus of the story, try writing from a different POV.

You have several options for POV: first-person, second-person, third-person omniscient and third-person limited (also called tight third). Each has its advantages and disadvantages. There is no one method better than another, it all depends on the requirements of the work and your skill as a writer. Whichever one you choose, remember that your aim is to get deep inside the character's head. You want a subjective and personal viewpoint. The more your readers can see, taste, smell, feel, hear what your characters do, the better.

First person: A character within the story narrates. A surprising number of readers don't like this technique, and when it's done badly, it's distancing, but when it's done well, it creates a sense of immediacy and empathy with the main character. The disadvantage here is the story is limited to those scenes and events where the narrator is actually present or which are related to him through dialogue with other characters. This is especially tricky in writing crime and mystery novels, although it can be fun creating an unreliable narrator.

First person is especially good for developing character voice, and I've seen it recommended to new writers for that very reason. At the same time I've heard editors say this is tricky for beginners.

Example of first-person narration:

> "We're lost."
> Luke came up behind me. I pointed, hand shaking, at the cross carved into the white bark of the tree.
> "We're going in goddamned circles!"
> He was silent. Beneath the drone of insects I could hear the even tenor of his breathing although we'd hiked a good nine miles already that autumn afternoon—and no end to it in sight. My head ached and I had a stitch in my side like someone was jabbing me with a hot poker.
> I lowered my pack to the ground, lowered myself to a fallen tree—this time not bothering to check for ant nests or coiled rattlers—put my face in my hands, and lost it. I mean, lost it. Tears…oh, yeah. Shoulders shaking, shuddering sobs. I didn't even care anymore what he thought.

> *In a Dark Wood* by Josh Lanyon (JustJoshin Publishing, 2011)

You've got the immediate first-hand sensory experience of the main character, you're privy to his thoughts and reactions, and you've got a strong sense of his voice.

Second person: You see this used a lot in poetry, speeches, letters, and how-to books like this one. It's rarely used in prose fiction because it's extremely stylized and usually comes off as a bit artificial. An unknown reader or listener is being addressed by the narrator, rather as in a Choose Your Own Adventure novel. The idea behind it is to create reader identification with the character of *You.* The advantage is it's chatty and informal, which can work well when you're trying to impose your iron will on unsuspecting aspiring writers. The disadvantage for fiction is it's noticeable; it puts focus on your writing itself, and unless you're quite good, you may not want to turn a magnifying glass on your literary gymnastics.

Example of second-person narration:

Cops before breakfast. Before coffee even. As if Mondays aren't bad enough.

After last night it's not a total surprise.

Oh, but first things first. You are a thirty-two-year-old Los Angeles bookstore owner. You're reasonably successful despite the fact that these are hard times for indie bookstores, and you recently sold your first novel *Murder Will Out* to a small press. That's about it for your professional life. Your personal life…well, you don't have a personal life, let's face it.

Your college sweetheart walked out years ago because you've got a bum ticker and he didn't want to take a chance on getting saddled with, well, you. Not that he didn't love you and everything.

Did I mention you are gay?

Anyway.

Cops. Standing outside Cloak and Dagger Books at this very second—crowding the welcome mat and leaning on the buzzer. For God's sake. It's not even seven in the morning. Whatever this is, it's not good news.

Stranger Things Have Happened by Josh Lanyon (JustJoshin Publishing, 2013)

Third-person omniscient: Most M/M fiction is now divided fairly evenly between first-person, third-person limited, and head hopping. The head hopping is written by authors who fondly imagine they're writing something known as third-person omniscient. Third-person omniscient permits an all-knowing narrator to comment on events, characters, etc. This technique, Gentle Reader, is still very popular in historical fiction. Most modern narrators are expected to keep mum and restrict their omniscience to what the characters think and feel. The advantage to third-person omniscient is obvious. The narrator is only limited by what he chooses to reveal to the reader. This can be a lot of fun in a romance where the reader is privy to each of the protagonists' (that would be your two heroes') innermost thoughts about each other. There is no real disadvantage, but you have to watch for awkward POV changes within scenes. In fact, a roving POV and omniscient commentary is very out of favor these days. Probably because it's hard to pull off. For an example of a romance writer who did it very well indeed, check out any of Georgette Heyer's historical novels. While Heyer didn't write overtly gay characters, the masculine friendships within her novels could inspire many a slash fic.

Example of third-person-omniscient narration:

> The bite of spade on stone rang hollowly in the excavation site. This was followed by an equally ringing silence—and then shouts of dismay. From what Major Valentine Strange, late of the Emperor of Alba's 21st Regiment of Benhali Lancers, discerned, a nest of baby cobras had been discovered in the bowels of the ancient temple. Just one of any number of unpleasant surprises that had been laid bare as the bones of the old building were picked clean.
> It was less than an hour's ride from the noise and bustle of the capital city of Harappu to the Great Temple and the eerie green silence of the jungle where the ruins of the ancient tombs had lain buried for centuries. Unsettling really, were Strange a fanciful man, to note how fast the jungle moved in to reclaim its own once life had departed.
> Sometimes before life had departed.
>
> *Strange Fortune* by Josh Lanyon (Blind Eye Books, 2009)

Rather than being deep within any particular character's POV, here we have an impersonal narrator observing what's going on, observing the main character and relating his thoughts—but not actually being within that character's brain. The one-step-removed narrator is commenting on the main character as an observer would, not as the main character himself would. So we might easily get some amusing commentary on Strange or the scene, but again, it would be from this objective viewpoint, rather than the direct feelings of an actual participant in the story.

Third-person limited: This is also known as tight third POV. Though told in third person, the story viewpoint is as limited as first person, and can be as unreliable (in a good way). There are some advantages in that the author can describe the character in less-intrusive ways than can be done if we're actually in the character's head. No need to trot him over to a mirror or have someone else comment on his looks. The author can simply state how terrifically good-looking he is. How terrifically good-looking the *character* is, I mean. Again, there are no real disadvantages to tight third POV, except that there can be absolutely no switching POVs and no author insight or commentary. If you are going to switch POVs, it needs to be following a scene break or a chapter break.

Example of third-person-limited narration:

> Situation defused, Nick thought. Rack time at last. "I guess that's it," he said. "I guess I'll say good night too."
> Foster's head jerked his way. "You're going?"
> "Yeah." Nick was elaborately casual in response to the note he didn't want to hear in Foster's voice. "It's all clear here."
> Foster was a frail-looking kid. He lived on his own and presumably held a job, so he couldn't be fourteen, though that's how old he looked. His wrists were thin, and bony knees poked out of the holes of his fashionably ripped Levi's. There were blue veins beneath the pale skin of his hands. Nick thought of the Fruit Loops cereal and the asthma chart on the refrigerator.
> Hell.
> "Thanks," Foster said huskily. "I know you probably think I'm nuts too, so I appreciate your helping me."
> "I don't think you're nuts." Actually he had no idea if the kid was nuts or not. "I think you saw something. But whatever it was, it's gone now. It's over." Nick thought of the shoe with the hole in it. Someone had switched shoes after he left. Someone had swabbed down the tub and the floor. Someone had balls of steel. But it was not Nick's problem. It was not his job to save the world. Not anymore.

> *The Ghost Wore Yellow Socks* by Josh Lanyon (JustJoshin Publishing, 2012)

You can still get a strong sense of character voice through a limited third-person POV because, done correctly, we're right there in the POV character's head. You'll notice that Perry is called *Foster* in this scene. That's because we're looking at him through Nick's eyes, and Nick thinks of, and refers to Perry, by his last name.

One additional thought on omniscient or alternating POV. Though a lot of readers profess to like it, it does lessen the romantic tension—the suspense—if your reader has access to both protagonists' thoughts and feelings. You and your reader play a little game; the reader pretends uncertainty as to whether these men will end up together. If there's nothing left in doubt, no question of what each man is feeling, you take away a large part of the fun. We don't have access to each other's minds in real life, which is one of the reasons that falling in love feels so exciting and perilous.

My personal preference is for first person or limited POV, but in all cases I make sure I don't give everything away. I try to preserve a little mystery, a little suspense. Not everyone—writer or reader—feels the same. Choose the POV you're comfortable with and which best suits the story and the characters.

Editor and author K.M. Frontain: Some of the worst M/M I've read has really awkward use of pronouns and names. The story ideas can be wonderful, but the pronoun usage destroys the reading experience. There's no reason for such clumsiness. It marks the author as someone who hasn't sufficiently learned the tools of the craft. Just because a story has two male characters in any given scene does not justify the laziness with pronouns I've seen in some currently published books.

Read a non-M/M book written by a best-selling, published author who has more than two male characters acting in a scene. Examine how the author uses pronouns referring to these two characters. How does that author make certain the reader does not become confused?

If you've created vivid, believable characters with distinct voices, there should rarely be confusion in the reader's mind as to who is speaking or thinking within any given scene—even during a scene of intimacy when the characters are, as it were, as one.

And yet, even when the POV is unchanging, without the familiar romance tags of *she said* and *he said*, authors—let alone readers—can get tangled up

43

in pronouns and descriptives. The best approach is a simple and clean one. Of course, that's easy for me to say. I usually write in first-person POV.

The rule of thumb is that you reinsert the reminder proper noun or name after a couple of uses of the pronoun. When I do write in third-person POV, I try to work it so that my pronoun will refer to the character who last spoke or acted. Obviously that isn't going to always work, but it's what I aim for.

"Suit yourself," Will said. "You usually do." He picked up his canteen and wiped the mouth of it, ignoring Taylor's taut silence. He put the canteen to his lips and drank.

Now, I guess Will *could* be putting the canteen to Taylor's lips, but probably not—and certainly not within the larger context of the scene.

The bottom line is, yes, it's a little more complicated when the two protagonists are male, but avoid straining or overcomplicating your scenes. Don't overthink this stuff. To some extent you can rely on the internal logic within the action being described. A sentence is read much faster than it is written, and there's less likelihood of confusion because of it. While you agonize over three *he*s within one line, the reader absorbs it without difficulty.

> It was a gentle kiss because Nick was thinking what a stupid thing this was to do, and that Perry, being inexperienced, probably expected songbirds and firecrackers.
>
> He tasted like hot chocolate and something warm and young and male. It was unexpectedly erotic. He responded sweetly, opening right up, and Nick's heart turned over in his chest, his hands sliding down Perry's back, feeling delicate bones and tension, warm nakedness beneath too many clothes. And without thinking any more, his hands went to Perry's waistband. He was amused and aroused at the feel of Perry's hands mimicking the motions of his own. The kid's knuckles felt ice cold against Nick's belly as he tugged on Nick's belt.
>
> Nick yanked Perry's pajama bottoms down, and he had a fleeting, uncomfortable impression that he was robbing the cradle.
>
> Perry was having a harder time with Nick's Levi's, so Nick just

scooped him up over his shoulder. Perry burst out laughing, head dangling down at Nick's waistband. He tried to raise up, and Nick smacked his ass, carrying him into the bedroom and flinging him down on the bed.
Perry was still laughing, a kid's untroubled laugh. There was trust in the hazel eyes gazing up at him. It pierced Nick right through a vulnerable piece of his anatomy there was really no name for.

The Ghost Wore Yellow Socks by Josh Lanyon (JustJoshin Publishing, 2012)

Basically you only want to use names when it would be otherwise unclear who's doing what. Keep it simple and specific. Avoid awkward and complicated workarounds like "the slim, green-eyed agent said" or "his taller, dark-haired partner laughed." Occasionally you can get away with a *the other man* or *the kid*, but these phrases stand out more than given names or pronouns do. Use them sparingly.

LOOKING FOR
A FEW GOOD MEN
CHARACTERIZATION IN THE M/M NOVEL

There's a good reason I'm starting with character before plot or theme or pacing or any of the other necessary elements of fiction. In my opinion, all storytelling starts with character. If there's one single aspect more important than any other, one make-or-break thing to get right, it's character.

A strong character can carry a weak story. It's our characters readers fall in love with, not plots twists, not world-building, not vivid language, not perfect grammar. Character. If the reader doesn't care about the characters, nothing else matters, because odds are good she won't keep turning the pages. But if the reader loves the characters, she'll cut an author an awful lot of slack about improbable or derivative storylines, even a bit of clumsy writing. I'm not saying readers won't complain about the silliness and the clichés and the expiration dates of series that have outlived their prime, but they're very loyal to the characters they've come to love.

In fact, readers have a hard time saying goodbye to characters they love, so it's up to the writer to know—like the perfect houseguest—when to depart. Part of being able to do that is planning your series out ahead of time. We'll talk more about that later. Right now we're focused on creating characters that readers love so much they *wish* they were series characters—if not their actual neighbors.

Gay men come in all shapes and sizes: everything from big burly bears to campy little queens. And gay fiction—especially gay literary fiction—reflects that.

But M/M fiction differs from regular gay fiction in that most—though not all—main characters are very much a white heterosexual female fantasy. Sure, M/M romance is more diversified than it was seven years ago. We can take pride in the fact that we now have more disabled, multicultural and multiethnic protagonists. We even have our share—as does regular gay fiction—of nerds and doofuses and, hey!, perfectly ordinary boy-next-door gay characters. Even so, let's remember that the gay characters in M/M romance do not really reflect the typical gay man any more than the traditional heterosexual romance hero reflects the average straight guy. *Or straight gal.*

A perfect specimen of an M/M hero is award-winning romance writer Suzanne Brockmann's FBI agent and counterterrorism expert Jules Cassidy. Jules is a wonderful character, don't get me wrong, but he's the basic heterosexual romance hero—gorgeous, smart, brave, funny, successful, sexy, well-balanced. He just happens to be gay. This is an important point for male writers trying to break into M/M fiction. M/M is romance fiction targeted toward a romance-reading audience. When an M/M reader picks up an M/M romance, he is not looking for gritty reality or a literary masterpiece. He can already turn to the shelf marked GLBT Fiction for that. No, he's looking for a few hours of what amounts to a little bit of romantic fantasy.

This is not to say that you can't make one of your protagonists transgendered or transsexual, or transvestite. You can write anything you want. You can write about bears, you can write about femmes. Your typical M/M reader is open-minded and adventurous. Feel free to write about a transsexual Eskimo if that's the story you're dying to tell. Your M/M reader will be interested and sympathetic. But chances are, you won't be tapping into her fantasies. And in order to write successful romance fiction—meaning stories a LOT of romance readers buy and recommend and read—you have to tap into the *reader's* fantasies.

There are plenty of excellent generic writing books to walk you through crafting secondary and supporting characters. I recommend *Fiction* by Michael Seidman, and *Writing the Breakout Novel* by Donald Maass. And a thorough, though outdated one for a variety of romance topics, is *How to Write a Romance and Get it Published* by Kathryn Falk.

I'll say just three things on the topic of supporting cast members, including villains—and this holds true whether you are writing about vampires, cowboys, pirates, space aliens, or the boys next door:

First, avoid clichés and stereotypes. To be interesting, a character must be more than the sum of a bunch of tics, quirks, and mannerisms. Give your supporting characters hearts and minds and dreams. Avoid black and white. Supporting characters look good in gray.

Second, we learn about our main characters through their interactions and relationships with supporting characters. Take full advantage of the opportunity these characters offer for insight and perspective on our two protagonists.

And, third, supporting characters are often the source of subplots or main plots for future novels. If your supporting characters are interesting enough, you may decide to spin them off into their own stories. That said, remember not to let them overwhelm a story in which they are not starring.

So listen up, guys and dolls. You can include realistic, unorthodox characters from the rainbow spectrum of gay life, but your best choice is to relegate them to supporting cast. The starring roles must, in key ways, fulfill certain genre expectations of the romantic hero archetype.

While we're on the topic of supporting cast, here are some painful clichés I could happily go the rest of my reading life without seeing again: the adorable inherited baby, the sassy black friend, characters named Aiden, the genius kid brother, the Evil Other Woman (I thought we lost her when we turned left after heterosexual romance, but nope, she's still there)— Actually, let's stop here, for a sec, and talk about female characters in M/M romance.

Luckily the genre expectation in M/M fiction is much looser and broader—and a heck of a lot more fun—than in heterosexual romance. Adrien English is a case in point. A slim, quiet bookseller with a heart condition? You don't find a lot of those in Harlequin romances—unless it's the Harlequin heroine of many decades ago.

Margaret Riley, Changeling Press: Pardon me while I climb on my soapbox for a moment. When you write M/M, make sure both of your men—or all three, or whatever the count—make sure they're all MEN. Actually this is a favorite pet peeve of mine with books with het couples as well. One thing that turns me off fast is a hero who was written to act like a woman. I don't know a single gay guy who isn't first and foremost a guy. (Unless he's a transsexual, and that's another theme—one I've written.) You can't just take a family classic, change the heroine to a gay man, and expect readers to "buy" it. Men think different from women—they speak differently, they talk about different things. They think and talk less and do more. A woman will spend 20 minutes picking out an outfit for the perfect date. Don't let your guy do that just because he's gay.

At the same time, don't go overboard in the other direction. Don't fall into the trap of thinking that there's some universal scratch-and-sniff male behavior that you can tap into. Keep your characters in historical and cultural context. Keep them real. Without meaning to be unkind, it's pretty clear to me that many of the women writing M/M fiction are coming up with their notions of gay male behavior based on reading each other's books. It's, at best, a limited perspective.

Case in point. What do Robbie Rogers, Montgomery Clift, Walt Whitman, Adam Lambert, Noel Coward, and Dumbledore have in common? Here's a clue. It's not their keen fashion sense. But being gay is about all they *do* have in common. Don't make the tiresome mistake of believing that masculinity has something to do with using the F-word a lot, or having a military background, or craving sex all the time, or liking sports or beer or barbecue, or being afraid to ask for directions or say *I love you*. Because I know plenty of guys for whom none of that is true. Okay, maybe not the craving sex all the time. That's pretty much the one universal trait you can safely latch on to.

Write *people*, not stereotypes.

Granted, it helps if you like men—or at least know a few.

Alanna, reader: It's not necessarily about M/F or M/M entirely, although you know, M/M is insanely hot (shallow, shallow, shallow, haha). The appeal of books is in characterization. I have to like the main character to read the book. In most of the M/F books I've read, albeit this was when I was way younger and into romance, the female characters just weren't strong enough for me. They didn't have substance, and I couldn't understand why the male characters were falling for them. Which meant, naturally, in my head, just take out the uninteresting character and replace it with a more interesting one—the beginning of fanfic interests if you will. For TV shows, anime series, and movies, the best friend or even villain is more appealing than the targeted love interest usually.If you can't sell me on the characters, you can't sell me on their relationships; you can't get me to care about what's happening with them. The authors that I like (Patricia Briggs, Tanya Huff, Diana Gabaldon, Laurie Marks) really sell that point, especially in M/M, sci-fi, and fantasy. The focus isn't on their relationships or sexuality even, it's about them and whatever story they have to tell.

Now, *you* may get your protagonists served to you on the shell by Zephyrs, but I build mine from the ground up. I usually start with a vague idea and a name. I've no idea why, but until the name feels right, I can't seem to get a handle on the character. If you don't own one of those name-your-kid books, get one. I use *20,001 Names for Baby* by Carol McD. Wallace.

Not to get all mystical on you, but I think there's power in names. At the very least names carry cultural and societal connotations, so I think it's important to get the name right. Male authors tend to go with manly basics: Tom, Jack, Robert, Will. Female authors tend to be more creative: Luc, Darien, Raphael, Brandon. Here's my advice: pick a name that suits the character as much as you understand the character at this point—and don't name him anything that would get him beat up at school.

Don't be afraid to change the character's name as the book progresses. Sometimes an Akihiko turns out to be a Kaemon. Who knows why?

Okay, now for a demonstration of on-the-spot improvisation. At the time I was working on the first edition of *Man, Oh Man*, I was one of three contributors to the 2008 *Hostage!* anthology from MLR Press. The only thing I knew then about my characters in *Dangerous Ground* was they were named

Taylor and Will, and they were some kind of special law enforcement officers. Originally I planned for Taylor to be my POV protagonist, but as I considered whether I would write him from the first or third person, I realized this was one of those times when having an alternating POV would best serve the story, which I pictured sort of like an episode of a favorite buddy-cop show. So a tight and alternating third POV.

I eventually settled on Will and Taylor working for the Department of Justice, specifically the Bureau of Diplomatic Security. Taylor...MacAllister, I decided. It sounded spiky and sharp. Will...Brandt. I anticipated that Will would be a couple of years older than Taylor, but though Taylor is thirty-one when the series starts, I never made a note of Will's age, and in fact I now suspect Taylor is slightly older. But either way, they're both in their mid-thirties, both seasoned professionals.

Oh—while I'm thinking of it: certain guys, especially guys in manly-man professions (and teenagers) refer to each other by their last names, so choose those as carefully as you do the first name. Also be careful with nicknames. Names like "Scooter" or "Chip" might sound cute and boyish, or they might sound like a case of arrested development. Of course you might be trying to make a point by having another character call your protag by a childhood name or even an inappropriate or offensive nickname.

So I named my characters. Then I started narrowing in on how the characters looked. There are only so many options, so this shouldn't take a lot of time. Some writers like to leave the physical details up to the reader, but I'm not a fan of that—as a reader or a writer. I want to know what the characters look like. I want to know the basics: dark hair or light? Tall or short? Willowy or built like The Rock? And then I try to figure out a couple of distinguishing features. A scar, really long eyelashes, a broken nose, a tattoo, or any assorted piercings are all perennially popular in M/M fiction. Big ears, a bad perm, and a unibrow would be more original, but this is romantic fiction, so there are limits to how free you should let your imagination run. Meaning, big ears could be kind of cute, but don't belabor them and don't refer constantly to the character's Dumbo ears.

Remember, the steps for character development are the same whether you're writing about Regency bucks, contemporary firemen, 23rd-century astronauts, or shape-shifting prehistoric shark men.

For some reason I had a visual on Will before Taylor. I saw Will as strong and square, square-jawed, broad-shouldered, stubborn, possibly a little set in his ways. Brown hair and blue eyes and tanned. An unexpectedly boyish grin, but from the start, Will was a pretty serious guy. Quiet. Steady. He reminded me of the old-fashioned lawmen of the mythological west.

Taylor, in contrast, would be sharper. Edgy, I mean. Same height or nearly as Will, but wiry, slim, angular. He'd be fast on his feet, a fast thinker. He'd be more emotional, more reckless. A smart-ass. Was he a player? Did he perhaps have trouble making emotional commitment? Maybe he was the child of an ugly divorce? Yeah. Liked to play around. Liked sex. A lot. Green eyes, dark hair—maybe a new streak of silver in his hair be-cause...because he was still recovering from a nearly fatal shooting a few months earlier.

Oh yeah! I liked that.

But to balance all that, when it came to the job, Taylor would ultimately be the tougher and more ruthless partner. And the one time he wasn't, got him shot.

You've probably noticed that Taylor and Will developed in my imagination as a pair—as romantic foils for each other. That's usually how it works for me. The protags come in tandem, and that's very useful because, again, these stories are all about the relationship.

If you're having problems visualizing your characters, try flipping through *GQ* or *Men's Health* or another men's magazine. Pick an attractive guy at random and try describing him in a paragraph or two. While the guy in the magazine might not be what you want, the guy you've described on paper probably will be.

This is a good time to start putting together a character sketch or bio. It'll make your life easier if you chart your character's age, eye color, height, etc. Because once you mention any of these details in the manuscript, sure as hell you'll never be able to find that paragraph again, and halfway through the book Taylor will have blue eyes and Will will have gray. Or maybe you'll forget to ever give Will a birthdate. Poor Will! No birthday parties. Put down everything you can think of about the character. You might never use his appendix scar or the fact that he graduated from Kent State, but the more you know about him, the easier he'll be to write. And if you go on to write a series, this will be the beginning of your character bible.

Regardless of what your character looks like, he'll eventually be irresistible to his male counterpart, and, ideally, the reader. But that won't be due to his looks; it'll be because of the personality you give him.

While I don't look for Odd Couple opposites, I do try to come up with personality types who will have natural and realistic conflicts—but who also have a lot in common. Complementary opposites are good. And, yes, I really do try to ground my characters with a bit of real-life psychology. If I do this well, there will be plenty of believable obstacles to my two protags's happy ever after (HEA)—but there will be equal grounds for a satisfying and convincing resolution to their differences.

The fact that Will is quiet and steady, that he likes to deliberate before he acts, that he wants to hedge his bets, will naturally and realistically clash with Taylor, who's a little more highly strung. Taylor is, in Will's opinion, too quick off the mark, even impulsive. Will believes Taylor needs to think before he shoots his mouth off. Taylor gets impatient with Will—and he's sharp and snappish when he's annoyed. Oddly, he also takes Will's criticism more seriously than Will takes his. But they've been partners for a few years, and they've learned how to work well together. Taylor is technically the senior partner of the team, but they don't operate like that. Neither of them thinks in terms of rank and seniority. They like each other—a lot—and respect each other, and depend on each other. That would be the job, of course: the fact that they would be agents of the then- undetermined federal law enforcement department, and thus spent their days watching each other's back—and maybe backside. Once I started writing the story, I knew that they were closer than that, that they had grown closer than that, that they were actually best friends. And that closeness would further complicate matters. Yeah, because these guys have something to lose.

If your two main characters aren't convincingly drawn, if at least part of the tension between them doesn't evolve from their strong, contrasting person-alities, then you'll find yourself relying on artificial bickering, miscommu-nication, or—the worst—strained contrivances to keep them apart: what I call, *But, Darling, He's My Brother!* syndrome.

Believable characters are motivated, not manipulated.

So let's talk about developing characters that read like real people—only better.

In mainstream fiction, we don't need to like a protagonist. We merely need to find him believable and interesting enough to follow for three hundred and twenty pages. In heterosexual romance fiction, the female protagonist is often just a placeholder for the reader. But in M/M romantic fiction, we not only need to believe in and care about the main character, we need to fall in love with him. Chances are *you're* already in love with your protagonist. Unfortunately, you love everyone you create, so you're no judge.

You need to think objectively about why readers would want to spend time with your brainchild instead of someone else's. What is it about your main character that will engage a potential reader's heart and mind?

Traditional—cynical—wisdom is that men look for beauty and women look for earning potential. I don't think that's true. I think humans, being human, are equally attracted to success and equally susceptible to good looks—and both of those things are pretty much *de rigueur* in romance novels. Your characters must be attractive (at least to each other) and they must be successful in a way recognized by readers (even if not by themselves). But hopefully it goes without saying that your main characters need to be more than their physical descriptions and their carefully researched professions.

Speaking of which, the demands of the plot may well determine that your protagonist be a mage or a cop or a fur trapper or an artist or a prostitute or a CEO or a nurse or a geologist. But if you haven't figured out what he does for a living, think long and hard. In fiction, at least, people are what they do. Give your character something interesting to do, something that tells us about him, something that gives the potential for subplots. Give your character ambition. Give him hopes, dreams, aspirations. Think about it. Are *you* satisfied with every single thing in your life right now? You're sitting there reading this book, so chances are you have ambition of the writerly kind, correct? Your characters probably want to try new things too.

Anyway, Taylor and Will are going to go camping in the High Sierras to try and rebuild the trust in their partnership damaged after Taylor's nearly fatal shooting. Their job and their partnership factors heavily into the story, even though the story is not about Will and Taylor on the job.

In fact, the real question is this: do Will and Taylor have anything in common outside of work? Think about how your protagonist's profession plays against the man in his life. Does his job bring them into conflict? Is his job the catalyst that brings them together? Is it just a job, or a career? Is it something he does to pay the bills, or is it his vocation?

Add his work experience to that character bio. Don't be afraid to get detailed. Even though you won't use a lot of those details, they'll add to your understanding of the character—they'll help you refine him. What does he like to wear? His clothes should say something about his personality. What does he like to eat? Does he have to think about his weight? What music does he listen to? Are his parents alive? Is he allergic to dogs? Does he have his tonsils? Does he sleep in the nude? (No, all guys do not sleep in the nude.) Does he believe in God? Does he have any hobbies? Any particular skills? Ah, that reminds me: Will has won sharp-shooting contests; that might come in handy later on.

I should probably admit here that I'm not one for writing tools. I'm not even terribly good at keeping character bibles, as we've seen. But if you do like writing exercises, one useful tool is the character interview. There are a lot of versions of this floating around. I think it's best to make up your own questions, focusing on the stuff that's of most interest to you, and then answer the questions in your character's voice. Start with the obvious stuff like where he was born and keep digging until you feel like you know this guy inside out.

A typical character interview question is: *what do you fear most in the world?*

It's good to know what your characters fear most, because they should be coming face to face with it in your story.

Laura Baumbach, MLR Press: I've read a number of well-written M/M characters that were great creations set in terrific stories that despite amazingly good writing, I didn't like at all. Why? Because the author didn't make me care for them or about them. Great guys, terrific love scenes, intriguing plot and I didn't give a damn. I couldn't care enough about the characters to give a hoot if they saved the day or ended up with each other. This is erotic romance. I have to fall in love with these characters, be rooting for them all the way, happy when they are happy and sad when they are. No connection to the characters and I might as well be reading a textbook. A great story isn't enough. I have to fall in love with the men.

A well-written character—no matter how handsome—is not necessarily the same thing as a lovable character. Remember that.

Now, what do *you* find lovable? We're talking personality and character now, so put down that copy of *Men's Health* and focus for a minute. Think about the qualities you prize in a lover. Not *that*! We're talking about disposition, individuality. What would you look for in a mate? What are the traits you value most highly in friends? What do you think your own strengths are as a person? Are you loyal? Conscientious? Are you imaginative? Good at duck calls? We all know that traditional romance novel protagonists are supposed to be brave and über-competent, but M/M fiction allows us more versatility. Take advantage of that. Pick three qualities you really admire or look for in a lover and gift them, good fairy-like, on your still-damp protagonist. Let these be his defining characteristics.

Taylor is clever, resourceful, and confident.

Will is cool under pressure, loyal, and relentless.

Beware the test-tube baby—the perfect protagonist. You know him; he's cloned from the traditional heterosexual romance hero. Handsome, brave, generous, successful, charming, honest, self-controlled... He's got it *all*. Even his faults are society-approved: he's too take-charge, too masterful, too brave, too driven to succeed, too...whatever. Okay, *maybe* he has a secret tragedy in his distant past, but that just makes him more interesting and attractive. He laughs at danger, he scoffs at vicissitude, he's *really* annoying.

Sure, you want your protagonist to fulfill the role of hero, but these paragons aren't fantasy so much as chimera. Maybe they're attractive. They have many attractive qualities, but they're not real. They don't even vaguely resemble real men, and, as such, they aren't *lovable*. Readers don't love perfection. They don't identify with it. They know instinctively it would be unpleasant to live with.

Readers love characters they can identify with, and in order for readers to identify with a character, the character must be multidimensional, fully realized, human—and, therefore, flawed.

Yes, flawed. To go along with all those virtues there's got to be a chink in the armor, an Achilles' heel, a weak spot. You don't have to make him a miser or a kleptomaniac, but a few moments of insecurity, of jealousy, of failure, will make your protag *more* appealing, not less.

The difficulty is our egos are often tied up in our fictional creations; it can be difficult to permit imperfection and ugliness in the embodiment of our romantic ideals. Even if you manage to come up with a few minor flaws—jealousy or possessiveness being the most popular—they don't add any depth to the characterization. Remember, growth of characters usually comes via their *flaws*.

By the way, illness and addiction are not exactly flaws. They are vulnerabilities, yes, and they might give any sensible character pause before getting involved with your protagonist, but they are also outside the control of the protagonist. If the illness or addiction is overwhelming, they can serve as flaws, but mostly their role is to add dramatic interest. What you want is a character who is more than the sum of his illness or addiction.

Back to Taylor and Will. As I studied them, I could see that Taylor was a little arrogant, occasionally reckless, short-tempered...nothing too serious there. But there was this: Taylor was shot because he was overconfident. Or maybe he hesitated. Either way, Taylor made a nearly fatal mistake—and Will is still angry with him and not admitting it, not even to himself. Something else...Taylor is in love with Will. He has been for years. He loves Will more than anyone or anything—and Will doesn't feel the same.

That's a pretty big failing on Will's end. Because if we like and identify with Taylor, we're going to be increasingly mad at Will for hurting Taylor by not loving him back.

You see how that all shaped up? There's an easy and natural synchronicity to character development when you're on the right track. The Dangerous Ground series is now up to four novellas with a fifth planned for this year. Will and Taylor have resolved their early issues, but new issues have taken their place. The guys have grown, matured, but relationships take a lot of work.

Remember to let the reader discover truths about the main characters through the observations and comments of the secondary and supporting characters. Of course, the most important insight into the character will come through his exchanges with his romantic foil.

Here's an example.

> Mitch simmered over that for a time. "I just wondered if being gay made your job harder. That's all."
>
> "It doesn't make it any easier, but then again I don't sashay around in tights and eye makeup." Web pulled neatly up in front of the rental car office.
>
> "Whatever," Mitch muttered, unsnapping his seat belt.
>
> Web sounded brisk. "What are you gettin' riled up about now, Mitch?"
>
> "Gee, I don't know, Davy Crockett." Mitch opened the car door. "Thanks for the ride."
>
> The hand that landed on his shoulder startled him. Even more startling was the way that casual touch shot down through every nerve in his body and centered in his groin.
>
> "That wasn't aimed at you."
>
> "Yeah, right."
>
> Web drew a breath. He said in painstaking tones, "I said that about tights and eye makeup because of what Mamie was talkin' about at breakfast."
>
> "I know why you said it."
>
> Web's blue gaze held Mitch's. "I've never known a touchier bastard than you. You're worse-tempered than a stripper in a cactus patch. What I'm tryin' to say is, it's okay for your job. It wouldn't be okay for mine."
>
> "Maybe that's part of what you're saying, but I don't think that's all of it. It doesn't matter because I stopped caring what you think a long time ago."
>
> "Then I guess I won't waste any more breath apologizin'."
>
> "Fine by me."

"Okay. Glad we got that settled. See you tonight?"

Web's blue eyes smiled teasingly into Mitch's, and to Mitch's exasperation, his bad temper faded beneath that double dose of deliberate charm.

Well, that was how it had always been between them. Mitch, moody and oversensitive, taking offense at some dumb thing, and Web, easygoing and low-key, joking him right out of it.

Lone Star by Josh Lanyon (Carina Press, 2011)

In this exchange between Mitchell Evans and Web Eisley, we learn something about Web, about Mitch, and about their past relationship—as well as their current relationship. We see that Mitch is defensive and ready to be hurt again, and that his reaction is to become hostile and strike first. We see that Web reads Mitch accurately, with the ease of long practice. He's calm and patient with Mitch's flashpoint temper—and Mitch can't help responding to that "double dose of deliberate charm." We see that Web is not afraid to reach out—literally—and apologize. In fact, we learn as much about Web's feelings for Mitch in this simple scene as we do in any scene of lovemaking between them.

Remember that all this information and data that you're collecting on your two main characters are for your own reference. You're not going to do anything clumsy like dump it, exposition-style, into backstory or narrative descriptions. You're not going to have the character reflect at length on his own background.

Anne Brooke: I always start off a novel with not a clue as to character or plot (though I do have one, and usually only one, strong idea of what my main character is like). All I have is one scene in my head, and I take it from there. For me it's always a journey of discovery, and I wing it mostly until I'm about 2/3rds through. It's almost as if writing becomes an act of faith, in a weird sort of way. I learn about my characters as I go on.

When I'm 2/3rds through, I pause and do in-depth character studies for each of my people, and then I'll go on (and, later, back) from those. I've tried doing detailed synopses, character studies

before I start, etc., etc., but the thing just dies in the water and I can't go on. It's got to be organic and off the top of my head (at least initially) or I just can't write it.
Author of *A Dangerous Man, The Hit List*, **etc.**

Fair enough. There's no *wrong* way to write a book, but making it up as you go along will inevitably lead to lots of tentative initial dialogue and scenes that have no true purpose while the writer works through who the characters are and what their story is really about. This isn't a problem so long as you're ruthless when it comes to your rewrite—something we'll talk more about later.

Meantime, here's an easy trick for fleshing out psychologically realized characters—regardless of when in the creative process you decide to do that. This is especially good if you're writing a lot and you're starting to feel like all your characters are turning into clones.

Figure out your protagonist's birth date. Seriously. Pick the month and day you believe he was born. Believe me, even if it's subconscious, something will influence your choice. Once you've given him a birthday, go look up his horoscope. There are all kinds of books and Internet sites. I recommend *Linda Goodman's Sun Signs* by Linda Goodman.

Taylor was born in May. May...25th. That makes him a Gemini. The consensus of the stars is that Geminis are quick-witted, communicative, energetic, contradictory, curious, adaptable, quick-silver—yep, this all sounds like Taylor. This will work well. On the other hand, Geminis can be nervous, restless, unpredictable, insecure, cunning. That all sounds like Taylor as well. Worse, they can be inconsistent, self-centered and promiscuous—but we don't need to take it that far. Taylor doesn't need to be a monster, he just needs a few believable flaws. Of course, Will might have seen a few things that lead him to believe that Taylor is inconsistent, self-centered, and promiscuous, and that might explain why he's reluctant to let himself care for Taylor romantically. Something to think about.

The handy thing about using astrology and horoscopes is that you get the mirror image of any given personality type. It's a quick and easy way to study the day and night within your character's soul. And it's a useful prompt for ideas that wouldn't necessarily occur on their own. For example, Geminis physical vulnerabilities include hands, lungs, thymus gland—and now I know that Taylor took a bullet in the lung.

For the record, I don't believe the stars rule our lives, but I do believe there's more than a smattering of genuine psychology behind astrology. Besides, it's fun playing with all the possibilities.

So we've got Taylor. What about Will?

I think Will is an autumn baby...maybe October. How about Libra?

Libras are strong-willed but believe in partnership and team. They have a powerful sense of justice and fair play. That's all good for a cop. Libras don't like confrontation. Hmmm. Maybe Will avoids confrontation in his personal life, although he doesn't duck from it on the job? Idealistic, able to stand back and judge impartially, unexpectedly sensitive. Is Will more sensitive than he seems? Not sure. On the other hand, Libras can be too conventional—yes, I think that's Will. They love creature comforts, they're easygoing to a fault, and they resist change—no dramatic revelations, but this is all workable stuff.

And by weighing and discarding possible personality traits, I end up giving a lot of consideration to Will and Taylor as individuals *and as a couple.* Remember, in romantic fiction, the story is about how the characters fall in love, not about their personal growth—although sometimes (in the best romances) both are achieved.

By the way, don't forget the intriguing possibilities of creating an antihero protagonist. An antihero is a central character who lacks the usual heroic qualities of a protagonist—perhaps he's a coward—or a killer. Perhaps he's a thief or just a little on the amoral side. Think the Flashman novels or the conflicted heroes of Laura Kinsale's romances. Many of the greatest heroes of classical literature are, in fact, antiheroes. Men of action and adventure who have to be larger than life to survive. Arrogance, cynicism, moral...flexibility are all the characteristics of an antihero. From Odysseus to Heathcliff, the antihero offers wonderful possibilities for romantic fiction. There's nothing like the love of a good man to redeem a bad man.

Laura Baumbach: My favorite character types are consistent throughout my writing. I like big, brawny, confident, powerful men with gentle, understanding hearts coupled with physically smaller, slight men who like a man who doesn't treat them as breakable. Smaller men who enjoy being manhandled in the bedroom but are still treated as an equal in all other aspects of their relationship. I like the sensitivity and vulnerability it lets me write between them. A lot of readers have commented they see one of my characters as seeing himself as "unlovable" as a consistent characteristic, and I guess that is true. I like providing that perfect half to give them what they need to feel loved. I also like exploring why some relationships that look impossible on the surface work well for the characters once you know their private needs and desires.

Author of *Mexican Heat, Out There in the Night,* **etc.**

J.M. Snyder: In my opinion, M/M fiction is much more feminine than gay fiction. M/M fiction is written to appeal specifically to women readers. I don't write with that sort of reader in mind, to be perfectly honest. I think of my stories as gay first, appealing to gay men, and only classify them as M/M to attract potential readers online. It's true that the majority of readers are women. However, I don't write my stories with them in mind, and maybe that shows a bit in my sales. I prefer to write for character first, story second, and sex a distant third (or fourth). Also, I try to keep my characters true to life, and from ALL walks of life, as well.

I like to think that realism is one of the strengths of my writing.

The stereotypical dynamics in gay relationships, as translated into M/M fiction, generally turn my stomach. Too often you have the frail bottom needing protecting from a domineering top. I like to turn that on its side, have a physically strong character who is dominant in all aspects of the relationship but prefers to bottom during sex. Or the emotionally weak character who tops his much larger partner. Or emphasize their differences through race instead of physique. The strong silent type who is noisy in bed, the self-confident jock who worries he isn't good enough to satisfy his partner, the burly biker with the heart of gold. **Author of *Crushed, Power Play*, etc.**

Both Laura and J.M. are talking about the romantic or relationship dynamic between your protagonist and his other—or better—half. You need to take the dynamic into account as you're creating the characters.

Certain dynamics are more popular than others in M/M fiction. One of the most popular is the younger/smaller/weaker bottom paired off with an older/larger/stronger top. That mirrors the traditional heterosexual romance dynamic, although it's just as likely based on the theory that opposites attract. If that's your kink, that's okay, but try to show a little imagination in how you handle this, *especially* if your plot is going to mirror a traditional heterosexual exemplification like the ones we discussed in YOU GOT A BETTER IDEA.

As we said earlier, your POV character can't be a placeholder. He needs to be strong and vivid and lovable all in his own right.

When I wrote the first edition of *Man, Oh Man*, everyone was discussing protagonists in terms of the two traditional romantic hero types: the alpha and the beta.

The alpha is the traditional romantic hero. He's powerful, successful, dominant—a leader in every way. The modern alpha is a lot more interesting than the stereotypical alpha of yesteryear. Now days he's allowed a softer side, a few vulnerabilities, a few flaws, a few losses. Jake Riordan is an alpha. Daniel Moran in *The Dark Horse* is an alpha. Max Prescott in *Come Unto These Yellow Sands* is an alpha. Valentine Strange in *Strange Fortune* is an alpha. I envisioned both Will and Taylor as alphas, but interestingly, a number of readers view Taylor as a beta. And I can certainly see Will being a beta depending on the romantic pairing. Yet if either Will or Taylor were paired with any of my beta characters, I believe they'd each be the unquestioned alpha of the relationship.

Confused much?

Traditionally the beta was the really nice, sensitive, boy-next-door type who inevitably lost the heroine to the alpha. A lot of times he was a perfectly good catch and the heroine often got herself engaged to him while she was struggling to get over her disastrous feelings for the alpha-dog hero. Even heterosexual romance has loosened up enough to permit beta heroes a few wins these days. Betas are not weak; they just appeared weak in contrast to the omnipotent alpha of yesteryear. Hell, Superman appeared weak compared to some of those guys. Superman is an alpha, by the way. Clark Kent is a beta. Adrien English is a beta. Sean Fairchild in *The Dark Horse*, SS Swift in *Come Unto These Yellow Sands*, and Alastair Grimshaw in *Strange Fortune* are also betas.

In M/M fiction there are true alphas but there are mostly betas. There is also something called an omega. The omega is the antithesis of the alpha. He's passive, submissive, emotional, and generally pretty helpless. I don't think you ever find a true omega playing hero in a heterosexual romance, but they turn up in M/M romance on a regular basis. I've never created a genuine omega character. At initial glance Perry Foster in *The Ghost Wore Yellow Socks* comes close, but basically he's just young and a little naive. The omegas are out there, though, in droves. They're the feminized partners so often castigated in reviews, especially reviews written by male readers. If they were female characters, no woman reader would put up with them for two minutes, but apparently a clinging vine with a cock is more palatable.

I want to make it clear that you should *not* be drawing characters based on the broad strokes of alpha, beta, and omega. These terms are useful shorthand for discussing character types and conflict, but these are general classifications. I find it all but impossible to categorize the majority of my characters because they're a blend of traits and behaviors. That's as it should be. If you construct characters based on these profile terms, you'll be creating clichés and stereotypes, not characters—not people.

True alpha/alpha pairings are rare. Even rarer are omega/omega pairings. There are a number of beta/beta pairings, but the most obvious pairing (and, don't get me wrong, it makes sense psychologically) is the alpha/beta. I don't have a problem with that. My problem is with romantic fiction that matches an alpha with an infantilized alpha or beta.

We'll discuss this further when we get to "Rescue Me," the chapter on hurt/comfort, but for starters, your characters should not be looking for parental replacements in a lover. Even the most sensitive and artistic omega should be an autonomous adult.

Now if you've got a seriously damaged POV character, that's okay. Bad things happen to good characters. But even a character recovering from rape or breakdown or incest or serious illness—even if it's all of these at the same time—shouldn't be a helpless, quivering blob 24/7. Not even if that really turns you on, because, believe me, it's not going to turn on the majority of editors, reviewers, or readers—male or female.

Give the guy a sense of humor, or incredible success in his professional life, or a reckless disregard for his own safety—*something* to balance the nightmares, and crying jags, the whimpering, and throwing up, and fainting, and...ugh.

Weak is not attractive. Helpless is not attractive. Dumb is not attractive. It's not any more attractive in a man, no matter how blue his eyes or bubble his butt, than it was in those old heterosexual romance novels you hated as a girl. Okay? Have I made myself clear on this? The more powerful the alpha in your story, the more you have to work to keep the beta capable and interesting in his own right.

For me, the challenge is to create equally strong but different partners. For example, because of a childhood bout of rheumatic fever, bookstore owner Adrien English is physically vulnerable. But Adrien is smart and capable and successful in every other aspect of his life. He's far more emotionally balanced and mentally healthy than his sometimes lover, closeted LAPD homicide detective, Jake Riordan. If classic alpha male Jake has a soft spot, it's Adrien. And Adrien's physical vulnerability allows us to occasionally glimpse a tender, protective side of Jake that we wouldn't see if Adrien was another alpha with whom Jake had to compete.

> When we reached the ranch, Jake called my grisly discovery in while I poured us each a drink. When he got off the phone, I said, "How long before we have to start back for the cave?"
> He took his glass. Knocked back a mouthful of whisky. "You don't need to go. I'll handle it."
> "Stop treating me like—"

He interrupted, "Look, you don't have to keep proving yourself to me, okay? I think you're plenty tough in the ways that count."
I didn't know what to say to that. It was hard to hold his gaze. Suddenly he seemed to see way too much.
"From here on out this has to be handled by professionals. Understand?"
"I guess so."
We drank in a silence that was unexpectedly companionable.

A Dangerous Thing by Josh Lanyon (JustJoshin Publishing, 2012)

Interesting and not overused variations on the alpha/beta dynamic include the exploration of the age dynamic, the disability dynamic, the civilian versus military/law enforcement dynamic. Play around, have some fun with these dynamics.

Create hard-boiled characters and give them a soft side. Create vulnerable characters and give them spines of steel.

Here's your homework. Put down the *The Gay Kama Sutra* and read one of the following: *Masculinity: Bodies, Movies, Culture* by Peter Lehman, *We Boys Together: Teenagers in Love Before Girl-Craziness* by Jeffrey P. Dennis, or *The Male Couple's Guide* by Eric Marcus.

A Man's Man—Exploring Masculinity

It's kind of funny to me how much some women writers worry about whether they're getting the man-on-man sex scenes right in every anatomical detail, while rarely worrying about whether they've nailed the masculine psyche. It's like a point of pride that they can describe anal penetration to the last twitch of sphincter muscle, but a matter of complete indifference that they're writing male clichés.

And there are *a lot* of clichés out there.

Unfortunately far too many women writers seem to believe that frequent use of the F-word, an inability to articulate feelings (or sometimes even thoughts), and a love of smoked meat, beer, and football is the same thing as creating a fully realized, believable male character.

It's not.

Raven McKnight, Loose Id: Don't rely on stereotypes—not every gay/bi character must be either macho or the antithesis; not every gay/bi character or relationship separates into the oft-mentioned top/bottom designations. When you create a character, create someone who's blond, brown-eyed, Irish and Polish, acrophobic, gay, well educated, and a little annoyed with his sister; create someone who's bald, gray-eyed, half Nigerian and half mystery, a pretty decent mechanic, gay, saving for college, and happy to finally have his own house. We'd much rather read about them than about characters who are defined by one aspect of their overall selves. In other words, create real, whole people.

Guys are as diverse and complicated as women. You *know* this. Some guys like to garden, some guys like to read, some guys work with inner city kids, or are connoisseurs of fine wine, old books, ballet, opera, and vintage film—and they're straight! So can we all please try to mix and match our stereotypes in more interesting and fresh ways?

Granted you're writing genre fiction for romance readers, which means you're trying to create male characterizations that play into our western civilization concepts (or maybe wish fulfillment) of who and what men are.

CHEAT SHEETS FOR CHICKS
WHAT IT SOUNDS LIKE

Some general thoughts—also called gross generalizations—about writing 21st century western civilization male characters.

- Men like sex for its own sake.
- Men are logical (except when they are thinking with their dick).
- Men don't talk about their feelings so much.
- Men don't analyze their feelings so much.
- Men have feelings too.
- Men feel responsible.
- *Men* and *adrenaline* rhyme. And there's a reason for that.
- All men are not created equal—but your protagonists must be.
- Men worry about their careers.
- Men channel their emotions—especially when they worry about their careers.
- Men *love* sex for its own sake.
- Men usually know basic guy stuff: how to change a tire, how to tie a tie, how to read a map (or compass), how to drive a manual transmission, how to grill a steak, how to use a torque wrench, how to say "I'm sorry."
- Men cry.
- Men don't like to cry—it's not society-approved and it makes them feel weird and weak.
- Men don't like you to cry either. It makes them feel weird and weak.

- Men do not admit to feeling weak. Helpless is not in the male vocabulary.
- Neither is "taupe," "tiny," "terrified," or "tender."
- Men can be very tender—but please don't comment on it.
- The male ego is not a myth.
- Men *like* to compete.
- The desire to chase things is inbred.
- Men do not multitask well.
- Men are goal oriented—they like to think of it as focused on The Target.
- Men are problem solvers.
- Men like maps, strategies, business plans, game plans, star charts, and manuals to things they no longer—and possibly never did—own.
- Little boys start thinking like big men early on—like the minute the cord gets snipped.
- Men think about sex approximately every sixty seconds.
- Men have a lower pain threshold than women.
- Men don't spend a lot of thought on a room's décor or what people are wearing.
- Did I mention sex?

And then there are the physical facts. Males are typically left-brain dominant. (Females are more evenly balanced between the two hemispheres of the brain.) Left-brain thinking is logical, literal, verbal, analytical, practical, detail-inclined, methodical. Left brain is the part of the brain we use for science, math, spatial perception, and speech. This doesn't mean your characters have to be left-brain dominant, it simply means that most men are. However, a number of studies indicate that brain hemisphere dominance may well be an indication of sexual orientation, and that gay men are more likely to be right-brain dominant and lesbian women are more likely to be left-brain dominant. Ha! But don't think it all ends there. Even if your protagonist is right-brain dominant, society places pressure on him to behave in acceptably male fashion, which means he'll have probably spent a huge part of his life developing left-brain behaviors.

You see where I'm going with this?

Yeah. Neither do I. But it's still interesting, right?

The Romentics: I have not read female writers thoroughly in the genre, but I have had female editors and readers respond to our novels. One comment that jumped out at me was when a female editor commented that a character entered into a sex scene too quickly since he was supposedly closeted and didn't want to allow himself to be seduced. There were several comments like this that seemed to completely miss the sexual-psychological interplay that men experience. Even when it was explained in text, some females didn't grasp the incredible shift that occurs when a man enters into a sexual situation (or how he feels when it's suddenly over). It is the classic "Which head are you thinking with?" joke. But it can be very true, and a man can switch from one logical head to another very illogical one in a moment. A man may have sex when he has promised himself he won't. He may have sex with someone he thought he hated. He may do things during sex he said he never would.

So it is not the mechanics of sex that female writers may get wrong. But it could be the unique emotional experience men have with sex. Perhaps they are writing M/M sex correct physically but portraying it emotionally the way a female would feel. That said, many, many women readers love the intensely male sexual experiences we portray without the slow, logical, flowery descriptions of straight romance.

Authors of *Hot Sauce, Razor Burn*, **etc.**

Some (tongue-firmly-in-cheek) tips for making your male characters *seem* **more male.**

(Remember, this is all about creating the *illusion* of masculinity.)

Limit male internal monologue and introspection to terse, simple sentences—but, honest to God, complete sentences, please!

Wrong: *Try as I might, I couldn't comprehend the strange circumstances which brought me to this place at this particular time.*

Equally wrong: *But, I mean…fuck!*

Right: *Nothing made sense anymore.*

Use simple, direct language for your guy dialogue—unless he's a writer or something equally arcane.

Wrong: *"I desire that mauve cardigan."*

Right: *"I want that pink sweater."*

More right: *"I want that BLUE sweater."*

Use positive, active language for male POV. Male verbs, manly nouns.

Wrong: *I caressed his velvety rod.*

Right: *I pumped his dick.*

WAY more right: *He pumped MY dick...*

Yeah, baby! Oh. Where was I? Right. If you're already writing an ex-air force, bourbon-swilling, poker-playing, basketball-obsessed, 7,000 words-a-day-limit kind of guy, you need to think about rounding him out with a love of thriller novels or comic books or tropical fish—move him away from caricature and into the realm of character. Give him a cat and a mom.

Some generally useless information about guys you might not know.

- Shoes, not clothes, maketh the man.
- Briefs are better than boxers for long plane flights.
- A man wears nothing under his kilt.
- Not too many men carry handkerchiefs anymore.
- Shaving is usually done in the shower or right afterwards (I'm talking faces).
- Leather. Accept no substitutes.
- You can't go by which ear is pierced.
- Or by wedding rings.
- Bathrobes are not obsolete.
- All men look good in black.
- Jockstraps—or, depending, cups—for athletics.
- Straight guys use shoetrees too.

- Got O.J.?
- Acceptable small talk with strangers: the weather, sports, current events.
- Profanity is best used judiciously—and with flair.
- Sunscreen is not for sissies.
- The best tattoos are small, discreet, and for the right reasons.
- It's hard to look tough sucking on a straw.

Show your characters discovering what they have in common—show them laughing together.

Mel Keegan: The other side to the question is, Why can't most male or female writers of gay romance make their work equally acceptable to both sides of the table? I can only guess that there's some aspect of the characterization or plotting which simply doesn't strike the chord.

A male writer might get inside the head of the gay male character better than the female writer…but will he express the character in terms women readers will find appealing? A woman writer might easily get inside the head of a gay male character–zeroing in on common ground–but will she describe the character, and his world, in terms which strike a chord with gay men?

The female writer's challenge would be to not only understand where the gay male character is coming from, but to imagine scenes and dialogue that ring true to guys. If it doesn't have that true-ring nature, the book will still be enjoyed by a lot of women, but many gay men will leave it alone.

The broadly accepted book must have that sense of truth and find the common ground we all share. That said, good writers can always craft a book for a specific readership. It's part of the job. The question is, are the romance writers of either gender interested enough in attracting readers from both sides of the table to evolve a different style? And that's a whole 'nother question. Ultimately, all writers do what we do for our own entertainment.

If other people want to share the fantasy, we're flattered and gratified.

And if we get paid, we're even happier!

Author of *Fortunes of War, Death's Head, Nocturne,* **etc.**

NOTHING NEW
UNDER THE SON
PLOT, CONFLICT, GOALS, AND MOTIVATION

Okay, you've got your characters. It's time to think about how you're going to tell their story. Story = Plot.

I wish I had a dollar for every time someone comes up to me and tells me they've got a great idea for a book—or a fascinating life story—and we should become partners. They'll tell me their great idea, and I'll write the book. We'll make a fortune!

Uh-huh.

As I said way back in YOU GOT A BETTER IDEA, coming up with ideas isn't the hard part. Writing the damn book is the hard part. And one of the hardest parts is coming up with a good solid plot that has enough action and conflict to carry the reader all the way to the end of the story. Too much plot will overwhelm a short story. Not enough plot will lead to saggy, limp novels. God forbid.

But when you start talking about conflict and goals and motivation—the building blocks of plot—a lot of writers get that glazed look on their faces. They want to go back to browsing *Men's Health* magazine. Or *The Gay Kama Sutra*. So listen up. Next to character, the single most important element of your book is the plot.

You have to give the plot of your story some thought. You can't just start writing. Well, you *can*, but you'll work a lot harder for noticeably weaker results. The time has come when throwing two hunky guys together in sex scene after sex scene will not be enough to hold readers' attention; there will be far too many scorching and sexy M/M novels *with actual plots* to choose from. And, let's face it, there are only so many ways to describe the act. Which is why some writers are getting kinkier and kinkier to try and keep it fresh. That's *not* the answer. The answer lies in building a better story.

Eve, reader: I love reading about gay love/relationships because there are still so many struggles and obstacles attached to it, unlike straight relationships, which I think have reached a point that they only have themselves to blame if the relationship doesn't work out. That's what makes gay relationships so much more interesting (and sometimes heart-wrenching) to read.

We'll keep this simple—if you really know your characters, it *will* be simple. Trust me. Plot is your story. In fact, plot is the carefully planned sequence of events that make up your story.

A story is not made up of random things happening. That's called real life; it doesn't always make for good fiction, let alone happy endings. No, the events or scenes of a story evolve naturally—organically—from earlier events or scenes. They have to make sense, they have to be there for a reason—you're not just filling space between sex scenes. And in order for these events or scenes within your story to make sense, you have to *plan* them. (This is why an outline is such a good idea.)

The way it works is that each event or scene will complicate the situation between your protagonists a little more. The divide between them will seem to grow wider and wider Conflict and problems and frustration will rise right along with sexual tension and attraction. Your characters are falling deeper in love—whether they like it or not—while the obstacles between them mount.

Now, you might be thinking that this is the opposite way it should work. There are plenty of obstacles to any two people building a life together, and you've got two great guys who, in theory, should be perfect for one another. Isn't your job to swiftly move them around the potential roadblocks and get them together? Of course it is, but getting them together is called the ending. Your story is over at that point. So, unlike real life, your job isn't to smooth the course of true love starting on page one. Your job is to create enough problems and obstacles to make up a riveting story about how these two met, fell in love, and finally worked out the differences between them so they could have a Happily Ever After. It's called *telling a story*.

Remember when we were discussing coming up with strong ideas or hooks, we talked about the seven basic literary plots:

- man vs. nature
- man vs. man (protagonist vs. antagonist)
- man vs. society (the law, etc.)
- man vs. machines/technology
- man vs. the supernatural
- man vs. self
- man vs. god/religion

One or more of these seven basic plots will provide the context or framework in which your romance occurs. If you're writing a mystery novel, you're probably going to write a combination of man vs. the environment (society), man vs. man, and possibly man vs. self. If you're writing a western, you're probably going to write about man vs. nature, and man vs. man.

But remember, in M/M fiction, the subgenre functions as a sub*plot* of the romance—the romance or the relationship being the most important element of an M/M novel.

It's a question of degrees. In a gay mystery like *The Hell You Say*, the mystery is as important, or—depending on the reader—more important, than the relationship between Jake and Adrien. Jake and Adrien's romance or relationship is not resolved by the end of...well, let's just say, it's not resolved. But in *The Dark Horse*, the mystery is elementary. The real story is about Dan and Sean learning to trust each other and themselves within their new relationship.

Mel Keegan: I don't even like to draw a box around a certain type of book (such as my own) and say categorically, "This is a gay book," because the definition restricts the novels to being only one specific thing, when the fact is, each of my books is several things at once. For example, gay and romance and historical and thriller. Technically, a "gay book" should deal wholly with gay characters doing and saying gay things. The difficulty with this is very few fully fleshed plot lines can be so single-minded, and if a story did manage to conform, it would rob itself of a body of critically important material. Most of the world wouldn't be classified "gay", but (at least for me!) to make a gay romantic thriller get up and go, people have to interact with the whole spectrum of humanity...get involved with all kinds of people, situations, locations.

I guess I could devise some plots involving only gay guys, and only gay situations and locations. However, I'm fairly sure I'd run out of stories pretty soon—and this project also begs the question, would such a book be equally popular with guys and women? A good number of women would certainly read and enjoy it, but my intuition is (and I stress, this is only my own guess, there's no reader poll or whatever to support the speculation) that women readers would simply get less out of the reading experience.

Author of *Fortunes of War, Death's Head, Nocturne,* **etc.**

If you're writing anything other than a contemporary romance, you'll have to meet the category requirements of both M/M romance and whatever genre framework you choose to set your story in. If you're writing a mystery—M/M or other—there are genre expectations: there will be a crime of some kind; the writer will play fair with the reader when it comes to clues, red herrings, and the cast of suspects; the sleuth will solve the crime by methods beyond intuition or happy coincidence; and there will be a believable solution. If you're writing a western, you will be required to deliver a western setting, lots of action, the "code of the west," etc. These elements must be executed as capably as they would be in a straight genre novel. No shortcuts, no cheats. It's challenging, no doubt about it, but my take is that the more plot you have, the easier the story is to write.

That said, plot is where storytelling gets tricky for a lot of M/M writers. Conflict, in particular, has always been a weak point. Yep, an awful lot of authors of M/M fiction do not understand the difference between genuine conflict and contrived bickering between characters. If you can master this concept, you'll have an edge over your fellow writers.

There is no story without conflict.

That's why the seven basic literary plots are all man versus something. The keyword is *versus.*

Conflict is the clash of your characters' opposing goals and motivations—their hopes, dreams, ambitions, and desires running headlong into someone else's fears, insecurities, plans, and prejudices. So, yeah, your characters may squabble about a variety of things, but the squabbling needs to result from something more dramatic and fundamental than he's a neatnik falling hard for a slob—not that the Odd Couple dynamic can't work; it's the stuff of romantic comedy, but at the heart of those differences should be something profound.

In far too many stories, the only conflict or obstacle to the lovers' happy ending is the external conflict provided by the genre plot: amnesia, competing for the same job, marrying for money (or to hide sexuality), zombie apocalypse or a tidal wave. That's fine as far as it goes—but it doesn't go very far. Obstacles have to be complex enough to believably keep two smart, rational, well-suited men apart from each other—and this distance has to be *emotional* as well as physical.

A competently executed romance plot combines external (situational) *and* internal (personal) conflict.

An example of external conflict would be found in *Fatal Shadows* when Jake Riordan suspects Adrien English of murder. That's an external conflict supplied by the plot. Jake's suspicion is a barrier to his growing awareness of and attraction to Adrien. Another potentially final barrier is that Adrien is being stalked. A HEA is contingent on his survival. Both of these are external (situational) conflicts and complications.

External conflicts are relatively easy to resolve.

The *real* barrier to Adrien and Jake's happiness is Jake's conflicted feelings about his own sexuality. Jake is a closeted cop, and he has no intention of leaving the safety of that closet. That's an enormous obstacle to finding a

HEA with Adrien. It is an internal (personal) conflict driven by Jake's personality and character, and it dogs their relationship throughout the course of the series.

Usually the most intense and dramatic conflicts will be the internal ones. But—please take note here—*you need both internal and external conflicts in order to write a satisfying romance.*

Now, having said this a couple of times, I'll—unwillingly—qualify. There are, particularly in fan fiction, charming little exceptions to this rule. These are the slash varietals of Aga sagas. The term Aga saga is used to describe gentle-humored domestic dramas set in quaint villages—usually in England, although there are American small-town cousins to the genus. Think Angela Thirkell or D.E. Stevenson meets *Queer as Folk*. These can be truly delightful little stories—often vignettes filled with dry wit and understated romance, but it takes a skilled and experienced writer to pull them off. There *are* writers who can make a story about two men choosing curtains or buying border collies fascinating, but they are not in huge supply.

Also, in a short story you can probably get away with just an external conflict or complication. Depending on how demanding the plot is, and how short the story is, there may not be room for much more.

Then again, there might be. On the surface, the novelette "In a Dark Wood," is a First Date from Hell story—Tim and Luke end up tracking down a backwoods serial killer. With their survival at stake, romance is low on their list of priorities, but the *real* obstacle to a happy ending is Tim's guilt and alcoholism. This facet of Tim's character makes it difficult to wrap their story up with a bright bow, but at the same time the events of the story have given us enough insight into Luke's character that we can see he's going to be good for Tim, that he's going to see Tim through the difficult road ahead. He's there for the long haul. It's in his nature.

Like I said, I've read way too many M/M novels where there is absolutely no conflict between the two protagonists that isn't entirely based on external circumstances: He's-hot-but-he's-my-boss / employee / professor / student / patient / doctor / partner / stepbrother / enemy. And once the characters work out that being the boss / employee / professor / student / patient

/ doctor / partner / stepbrother / enemy isn't such a big deal, our heroes generally spend the rest of the story having hot sex and tepid conversation.

Which is fine for the readers who are only interested in the sex scenes, but that's a limited market. The majority of readers are looking for original and passionate storytelling—the kind of storytelling that touches our emotions and makes us think.

I don't mean that in a highfalutin, I-only-watch-PBS way. I mean it in the way that a great movie or a terrific novel stays with us for days afterwards. Our hearts and minds have been engaged—and that's what expert storytelling does.

Kellie W., reader: While there are some exceptions, I find a lot of the M/M stuff out there a bit flat. The falling in love is too easy and any conflict is simple or in some cases silly and easily resolved. The only other backdrop that these stories seem to have is the prejudice faced, which of course is relevant but not enough to really get me excited. Then again I feel perhaps I am being too critical as most M/M stories are standalone and not a series, so things need to be wrapped up by the end of the book. Also these are love stories or romances, and it goes without saying the two people will get together in the end and all fighting will cease.

One detail: remember not to cook up conflict so destructive or insurmountable that you're unable to resolve it believably within your allotted timeframe. The reader will work with you, but you've got to do the heavy lifting. Some of this has to do with pacing. If you throw a gigantic and disastrous point of contention between your characters in the final third of the book, you're unlikely to be able to resolve this without rushing—something readers resent. The successful working out of problems and differences is part of what readers find so emotionally satisfying; if you cheat them on this, they won't believe in your HEA—or even your HFN (Happy For Now).

Okay, so remember our special agent partners Will and Taylor from that then unwritten novella? Since we've worked with their characters, we're in position to examine their story for the potential conflicts between them.

Here's the "Dangerous Ground" blurb:

Taylor and Will are relearning to trust each other—and their partnership—after Taylor's nearly fatal shooting a few months earlier. But their male-bonding camping trip in the High Sierras turns into an exercise of survival when they run afoul of escaping bank robbers and Will is taken hostage.

"Dangerous Ground" from *Armed & Dangerous* (JustJoshin Publishing, 2012)

The external conflicts are pretty clear. Bank robbers and the elements—man vs. nature and man vs. man—and the fact that Will and Taylor are partners—man vs. self and possibly man vs. society (the DSS's non-fraternization policy, for example.) These external conflicts offer plenty of material for action and adventure, and that means we should have no trouble constructing a solid story framework. There's lots of material for a meaty plot right there. But it's not enough.

Why? Because we're writing a romance novel, and a romance is the tale of two people making a journey to an emotional destination. Readers want to follow that journey every step of the way.

We can see from that story blurb that there are already problems simmering beneath the surface: "relearning to trust each other—and their partnership—after Taylor's nearly fatal shooting." Will and Taylor no longer trust each other. Now that's a big stumbling block for any relationship, let alone lovers. But then, they aren't lovers. Yet.

Now, I already know that Taylor was shot because of his own carelessness. So why is Will angry? Because Taylor didn't wait for backup. Taylor didn't wait for Will. Will no longer trusts Taylor not to get himself killed.

What about Taylor? Why doesn't he trust Will? Because…Will doesn't trust him to be able to take care of himself anymore? Or because Will doesn't love him?

Really, why *is* Will so angry? Taylor didn't get Will shot, he got himself shot. He nearly died.

Taylor nearly died, and Will is furious about it. Because…Will cares a lot more for Taylor than he will acknowledge even to himself? We already know that Taylor is in love with Will and has been since the first days of their partnership, and Will doesn't—or doesn't seem—to reciprocate. Why? They're friends, they've got a great working partnership, and we're going to quickly establish that they're both irresistibly attractive.

Maybe Will isn't gay? Or maybe he is, but he doesn't want to lose their friendship and strong working partnership—doesn't want to mess it up? Or maybe he's seen Taylor in action for too many years—he doesn't believe Taylor is good long-term relationship material?

You see how this works? The internal conflicts are tied to personality and psychology; they evolve as you develop the characters. The external conflicts are the twists and turns that come from plot that keeps your lovers from being together. The best external twists affect emotions which then trigger internal conflicts.

Romance is character driven. Romance is all about emotion. So the best conflicts are going to be emotional ones—character-driven ones. Typical issues driving internal conflict include trust, control, self-image, sexuality.

In itself, *Gosh, he's cute but he's a vampire!* is not enough conflict. Not for fiction, anyway. Real life, yeah, that could be complicated. Remember, fiction is not real life. Fiction is bigger—and better—than real life. The best fictional conflicts result in one protagonist fighting himself and his attraction to the other protagonist. So our plot becomes *Gosh, he's cute but he's a vampire—and I've sworn my life to destroying all vampires.* This time it's personal.

It's got to be personal, or else the conflict devolves into nothing more than heated intellectual debate, and your characters spend pages bickering. That gets old fast. We expect mature, intelligent, strong-willed people to disagree, and to work their differences out. Your challenge is to make it difficult for them to work those differences out. Take a subject like the outing of public figures. A lot of gay men disagree on whether it's right to forcibly out public figures; that's an intellectual disagreement. But suppose one of your protags is a reclusive, closeted actor, and the other is a crusading reporter for a gay magazine. *Now* they both have something to lose. *Now* it's personal—and painful.

And the main reason it's painful is because of a little something called sexual tension. Sexual tension is the physical desire characters feel for each other but are prevented from acting on because of all that external and internal conflict. The main ingredients are physical awareness—sexual attraction—and conflict.

You write sexual tension by showing your characters reacting to each other in visceral and sensorial ways. Even when the characters aren't in the same room!

> On his walk back to the Administration offices, Elliot phoned Tucker.
>
> "Lance," Tucker answered crisply following the second ring.
>
> Like that, it was as though he stood in front of Elliot, all aggressive masculinity, and Elliot's heart started to pound hard in that fight-or-flight reflex. It irritated the hell out of him, but there was no denying his physical response to Tucker.
>
> "It's Elliot."
>
> A pause. "Elliot." Tucker's tone was neutral. "What do you want?"
>
> "The Lyle kid has been missing four days. According to his aunt, that's not typical. And, as we both know, Terry Baker has yet to turn up after three weeks."
>
> "That's it? That's your connection? Two boys from the same college campus don't show up to class for a few days?"
>
> Elliot lowered his voice to avoid the attention of students sitting nearby on the grass, engrossed in their laptops. "Are you telling me you won't even consider a connection?"
>
> "Let me clarify a point here," Tucker said almost pleasantly. "I don't want you involved in my—"
>
> "And I don't give a flying fuck what you want." That time Elliot hadn't bothered to lower his voice.
>
> The silence that followed was sharp enough to cut an ear on.
>
> Unexpectedly, Tucker laughed. "Okay. Well, I'm glad we've got that cleared up."
>
> Elliot realized he was gripping his cell phone so hard his knuckles were white. Nothing like a little internalized stress. He said

with an effort at evenness, "Montgomery's expectation is that the exchange of information will be a two-way street. You know that as well as I do, Tucker. Why do you have to be such a prick about this?"

Elliot heard the echo of his words with something akin to astonishment. They weren't really going to have this conversation, were they? That was unbelievable enough—let alone that he would be the one to initiate it.

Tucker said cheerfully, "I guess you bring out the worst in me, Elliot."

It was Elliot's turn to laugh, though there wasn't a lot of humor in it.

"Great. Well, maybe we can put aside our differences long enough to get through this case."

There was a pause and then Tucker said, "Tell you what. You want to talk to the Lyle kid's auntie, you go ahead. I have my doubts this is a viable lead, but hey. I've been wrong before. The university is making the connection, so maybe it exists. Let me know what you turn up."

It was a race to see who could disconnect faster.

Fair Game by Josh Lanyon (Carina Press, 2011)

I want to note here that sexual tension is not just about sex. Or rather, it's not just about the act of intercourse. Sure, a large part of it is sexual frustration, but it's also about the longing, the yearning for emotional intimacy your characters feel for each other. So if your characters have sex—and they frequently do in an M/M romance—you can keep the sexual tension alive between them by denying them the emotional satisfaction they (and the reader) crave.

Once you resolve the problems between them, once you let them reach emotional union, once they say "I love you," the story is over. And if you don't want it to be over, you're going to have to work like hell to split them up again—which usually irritates readers because it generally means falling back on external conflict like…pirate attacks or white slavers or the good old *But, darling, he's my brother!* trope.

The course of true love cannot run smooth. Granted, it can't be a non-stop ticket to raging waters, either, or the reader will never believe these two guys could find true happiness together. You have to allow them some tender moments, shared laughter, great sex. But the tiny wins must be followed by seemingly greater losses—and yet, progress has to be made or the happy ending will not be believable. It sounds contradictory, I know. Each resolution brings your characters closer together, and each new complication drives another wedge between them. They're falling harder and deeper, and it's looking more hopeless by the minute. *That's* romance.

An abbreviated outline would look something like this:

The meeting
1st obstacle—External
Partial resolution
2nd obstacle—Internal
Partial resolution
3rd obstacle—External
The climax
The resolution

If you're writing a genre novel like an M/M mystery, you're going to alternate the plot and romance beats. As the mystery or adventure peaks, the romance lulls—meaning, in the middle of a shoot-out, your protagonist doesn't start thinking about what a great ass his love interest has, and in the middle of making love, you don't have the bad guys break down the door—unless one of your guys was about to use the "L" word.

The rise and fall of contrasting storylines will keep your reader riveted. It's all about structure and pacing. Very simply, something interesting has to be happening all the time. We'll explore that amazing concept when we get to the next chapter, which is on pacing.

Some things to remember: While you want to keep emotional distance between your characters, you want to write a story that throws them together as much as possible. You want readers turning pages fast, but not because they can't wait to get to the good parts.

If you're writing a genre M/M novel, wind up the genre plot before the romance.

Again, don't mistake conflict for arguing. I've heard aspiring writers try to justify ceaselessly quarreling protagonists with statements like "There should be conflict in every scene." While characters in conflict may well argue, contrived differences and bickering isn't satisfying storytelling. Mostly it's just annoying. Conflict has to be genuine and believable. It has to be *motivated*.

So let's talk about motivation. Characters are motivated to achieve goals. Every action, every choice your characters make, must be motivated. Motivations, like conflict, must be genuine and believable.

Motivation is the trigger that pushes your protagonists into action. Motivation is based on backstory, the character's recent past, or their history—which is why you have to know your characters thoroughly.

When you create a character, you must decide what he wants. Everybody wants something. The character's wanting = Motive. *What* the character wants = Goal.

It goes without saying that in a romance novel, your characters want to be loved. You have to dig deeper than that.

What is this character's quest? What stands in his way? Different characters have different experiences and perspectives—and that creates a natural conflict. Realistic motives make for real characters. Realistic characters are easy to motivate into action.

The major decisions your characters make should be motivated by emotion, even though men are, for the most part, rational beings.

Will and Taylor are going camping to try to repair their working relationship. They're both motivated by concern and the desire to preserve a previously successful partnership—and friendship. It seems like a logical decision, and on the surface it is. On the surface, they share a mutual goal, but individually they also have goals. Taylor is working past his fear of being shot again, and he's trying to wriggle his way back into Will's good graces. Will is trying to come to terms with his feelings for Taylor—his fear that Taylor means too much to him, that his feelings for Taylor will cripple him on the job, and his fear that Taylor might be killed the next time things go south.

But as the plot progresses, Taylor's and Will's goals will change, and so will their motivations. Falling in love and fighting to stay alive will do that to you.

DO THE MATH
PACING

I mentioned in the previous chapter that you have to alternate the beats of your romance plot line with the beats of your genre storyline. But even if you're writing a straightforward contemporary M/M romance, you have to pay attention to the rhythm of your story—this is called pacing.

Pacing means moving the story forward at a speed appropriate to genre and story requirement. A historical romance won't necessarily be served well by the breakneck speed of a contemporary thriller. That said, most contemporary readers aren't going to enjoy something structured along the lines of *Vanity Fair*.

Here's the rule: *something interesting has to be happening all the time.*

If you're finding yourself writing quickly to get past the boring bits, you need to get rid of the boring bits. Keep the exposition and info dumps to a minimum. Believe me; you need a lot less of that stuff than you think you do.

I'm assuming you know what exposition is, but maybe I shouldn't. Exposition happens when the writer strong-arms his way into the story to explain something necessary to the reader. A certain amount of exposition is required, sure—even useful. The main thing you want to keep in mind about exposition is that it amounts to telling the story instead of letting the reader live it with the characters. I know you've all heard the advice, "Show, don't tell." The best writers don't tell you, and quite frankly they don't just show you—they make you feel it, live it, taste it, touch it. Storytelling is about being in the moment with the characters.

That said, you don't need to live every moment of your protag's shower or breakfast or drive to the office. There are times when exposition is the best way to cover a lot of dull ground fast.

Exposition is generally the enabler of the info-dumping author.

Judith David, Loose Id: At a guess, I'd say that the top three problems that editors see in submissions are indistinct characters, info dumps/exposition, and poor mechanics. It seems to me that the first two are often related. If the characters are denied the opportunity to participate in the story, if the author takes over the telling, takes over driving the action, then the characters never have the voice that can speak to their individuality and motivations. The characters can never actually be a presence in their own story. It's always obvious when the author has written the story and just dropped the characters in. The characters move through the story doing everything that's expected of them to advance the plot, without believable motivation, without really influencing the story, without really having anything at stake. The action just washes over them without any real effect. Exposition is the opposite of dialogue. You can't have character without dialogue.

The term "info dump" should be self-explanatory. It's the literary equivalent of *Oi, too much information!* Basically the author empties a dossier worth of intelligence on the hapless reader's head. Often this is in the form of the extensive and painstaking research the writer did. We all hate to waste those hours we spent in the library or on the Net boning up on forensics or dog shows or automatic weapons. But info dumping can also be the filling in of backstory through a character's thoughts or dialogue—or even straightforward author narration. You often find it in the speech the villain (or master detective) gives at the end of a mystery or crime novel: the part where all is explained in one fell and long-winded swoop. Instead of working all this information piecemeal into the story to be digested unconsciously by the reader, the author plops it all in a lump right there on the page like a bad waitress in a cheap diner.

There is a rise and fall—a rhythm—to storytelling. Timing is everything. One action scene following on the heels of another, whether it's a car chase, a murder, or a sexual encounter, is just as boring as pages of bickering, or description, or backstory.

This is yet another place where outlining can be a big help to an inexperienced writer. As you map out the flow of your story, you can see if you're piling too much into a chapter, or not enough. You want a smooth flow, big action scenes followed by brief scenes of reflection.

A story is made up of scenes or events. There has to be a point or a purpose to every scene. Otherwise we're back to random happenings that mirror real life but not good fiction. Each scene must move your story forward.

In M/M fiction, no matter how beautifully written or clever a scene is, if it doesn't advance the plot, you need to cut it. Character development is not, in itself, enough of a justification for a scene—although we should be learning more about the characters and their motivations, goals, and conflicts in each scene.

Scenes are built upon action. Action is everything your characters do. There are large actions, like a chase scene or having sex, and there are small actions, like opening a can of tuna or meeting someone's eyes. Small actions build toward larger actions or *re*actions.

It's called cause and effect, and it's a one-two punch: action triggers reaction that then triggers another reaction. Think of it as the dialogue of motion.

> He finished unbuttoning my shirt, and I half-raised to shrug out of it; he pulled his T-shirt up over his head and tossed it away. His hands went to the button fly of my jeans, and I thrust up at him, already so hard the stiff denim was torture. My hands fastened on his belt and I worked it like I had seconds to disarm a bomb—which is what it was starting to feel like. Sweat broke out on my forehead, my breath came fast. I felt wild, out of control with wanting him. Wanting him now.
> He had me free of the constriction of briefs and jeans, yanking them down where they hung up on my tennis shoes, and I didn't give a damn because by then I had got him free as well, and his dick, hard and thick, was giving the high five to my own.
> "Oh, God," I groaned.

Ghost of a Chance by Josh Lanyon (JustJoshin Publishing, 2012)

You'll notice that I don't just follow one character's action with the other character's reaction, followed by the first character's reaction, followed by the second character's reaction. It's not ping-pong. You want to alter the rhythm for dramatic effect, and you've got to allow for some emotional response as well.

Use reactions, quantity and quality, to emphasize the importance of the initial action. Sometimes a low-key response underscores more effectively than a big reaction. Sometimes a whisper grabs attention more effectively than a shout, right? In real life we look for the tiny clues that tell us what someone else is thinking or feeling. Make your reader pay close attention.

> "He sounds a lot like you. No wonder you identify."
> I laughed nervously. "Oh, right!"
> Dan's brows drew together, and to keep him from drawing any more ridiculous comparisons, I said quickly, "I guess it's his or-dinariness that appeals to me—appeals to most guys who read the book. I don't know if he's afraid to face the reality of who he is—what he is. Maybe he's just afraid to lose himself by loving someone completely."
> Dan's expression was odd.

The Dark Horse by Josh Lanyon, (JustJoshin Publishing, 2012)

Use the rhythm of action and reaction to build tension and suspense, and increase conflict.

> "You're not that stupid," he said. "Then again, maybe you are. I go to the trouble of lying—of falsifying police reports—to keep you out of this shit, and you turn right around and walk back into it."
> My heart slipped into heavy, slow punches against my rib cage. "Give me a break," I said. "You didn't lie to protect me, you lied to protect yourself. You never asked me what I wanted. And I

sure as hell never made you any promises about what I would or wouldn't do."

His finger jabbed the air, punctuating his words. "Stay. Out. Of. It. Or this time, bad heart or not, I will throw your ass in jail."

"No you won't," I said. "You wouldn't want to risk anyone discovering the connection between us."

His face changed, grew ugly, dangerous. "Are you threatening me?"

I hadn't been, but like an ember in dry grass, a self-destructive impulse flicked to life in my mind.

"My existence threatens you."

He shoved me back hard. I crashed into the hall table, knocking it over, smashing the jar of old marbles I had collected. Glass balls skipped and bounced along the corridor. I landed on my back, my head banging down on the hardwood floor.

I lay there for a second, blinking up at the lighting fixture, taking in the years of dust and dead moths gathered in the etched glass globe. The silence that followed was more startling then the collision of me and the table and the floor. I heard Jake's harsh breathing and a marble rolling away down the hall—which seemed pretty damned appropriate since I'd apparently lost all of mine.

The Hell You Say by Josh Lanyon (JustJoshin Publishing, 2012)

Action and reaction sequences make for scenes that are strong, active, and fully realized, but avoid empty stage business, actions that are there simply to fill a page. Pointless busyness is the trademark of the inexperienced writer. If your characters meet each other's gaze, it should be to underline an important moment. If your protagonist slides open a drawer, let it be in contrast to the fact that he's closing himself off in a conversation.

Real life is full of rambling discussions and pointless gestures. We don't have that luxury in fiction. There must be point and purpose to all dialogue and action—and to every scene.

It might help to picture your scenes as if you were filming them. Keep them visually interesting, and aim for a dramatic arc. Just as your story has a beginning, middle, and end, so should each scene.

Start at an interesting point in the scene and write through to the natural ending—ideally breaking at a point which leaves the reader wanting to find out what will happen next.

For more information on plotting and pacing romance in general, try *Writing a Romance Novel For Dummies* by Leslie Wainger, and *The Complete Idiot's Guide to Writing Erotic Romance* by Alison Kent.

Also, don't overlook some structural sleight of hand. Brief paragraphs broken up with dialogue, and short punchy chapters will give an illusion of a faster-paced story. The current theory in publishing is that modern readers don't have time or the necessary attention span for reading; lots of white space, that's the ideal.

If plot and pacing remain a struggle for you, take a look at one of your favorite romance novels and analyze it chapter by chapter.

Or, turn once again to the Old Masters—er—Mistresses. Find a Harlequin romance with a plot line that sounds like something you could work with, break it down scene by scene, and outline it. Use that outline to construct your own original, tightly paced M/M novel.

But please don't name anyone Raoul Germon.

G.I. JOE, U.S. ARMY, REPORTING FOR DUTY!
WRITING ACTION SCENES

Because most of M/M fiction is crossover genre fiction, action—both large and small scale—is an integral element. For the purpose of this chapter, we're concentrating on large action. The typical M/M novel could conceivably contain everything from a battle scene to a scene of seduction. Gunfights, rapes, beatings, car chases, forest fires, sword fights, football games, physical therapy, shapeshifting—if you can picture it, you can probably find it in an M/M novel.

This means that a lot of writers are going to be writing about things of which they know *nada*.

That's not a bad thing. One of the most misunderstood pieces of advice new writers absorb is the bit about Writing What You Know. If we all stuck to writing strictly what we knew, not many people would be writing mysteries—let alone science fiction and fantasy. I guess a few elderly scribes might still be turning out westerns or noir thrillers, but I guaran-damn-tee you no one would be writing paranormals.

Of course, if you want to write a story about a twenty-something West Hollywood film editor falling in love with his doctor—and you just happen to be a twenty-something West Hollywood film editor in love with your doctor, you have a natural advantage. In fact, you have what's known in the biz as a *platform*. Same holds true if you're a gay ex-cop and you'd like to write a police procedural about a gay cop.

But suppose you want to write a novel about a twenty-something film editor in West Hollywood who solves his doctor's murder. Do you have to go work as a PI for six months or join the police academy? Do you have to murder your doctor? Of course not. That's what research and imagination and (this one is key) empathy are for. Editors and agents and marketing departments love platform, but good writing trumps platform almost every day of the week. And twice on Sunday. And good writing is largely about research, imagination, and empathy.

If you don't have natural empathy for people, it's a drawback in writing—especially when it comes to characterization—but you can make up for it by being extra diligent with the research. If you don't have much imagination, *I* can't imagine why you would want to be a writer, so you're excused from class.

Writing what you know is especially useful when it comes to the little telling details that add veracity to any story. And of course the more observant you are, the more you know, and the more you have to draw from.

You know how it feels to be cold, right? Maybe you've never been on the point of freezing to death, but you take the details of what you know (being cold) and add them to your research on freezing to death, and with the help of your imagination, you should be able to write a pretty good scene showing your hero struggling to avoid falling asleep in the snow after a car crash. Even if you've never been in a car crash.

You're still essentially writing what you know, but you're also using your imagination and research. The scene will be better if you can recapture the sting of snow melting against your face, breath freezing in your lungs, the sodden, heavy feeling of just wanting to lie down for one little minute…

It's very interesting to me how often new and weak writers fail to capture…reality. Too many characters in books and films are merely stick figures drawn to people the storyline. They fail to behave like real live people. Keep characters real by having them react in believable ways. Keep the little details accurate, and you'll find readers are far more likely to suspend disbelief. When you ask them to swallow the greater lie, like a sexy pirate ghost or an amorous space alien, they'll willingly—even happily—go along.

We all have a lifetime of experience to draw on for our writing. Use that experience to make your action scenes more real. Maybe you've never driven a race car or a tank, but you've probably been behind the wheel of some vehicle. Use what you know and fill in the rest with your research and imagination.

Also, don't tell or summarize the action scene. Remember our discussion of exposition? Put your characters right into it; make your reader live each moment with your characters. This is where skillful use of point of view comes in. POV is the filter that allows your reader to experience the action with your protagonist, instead of simply visualizing the hero within the scene. Key to that is relating your POV character's reactions.

There are a few basic techniques for keeping the action fast-paced and intense.

Stay focused

Stay with your POV character. Now is not the time to head hop. Concentrate on what your POV character is doing and feeling—his actions and reactions. But keep the focus narrow. Your protag should not be noticing how handsome his lover looks in those khaki shorts, or what beautiful weather they're having when he's running for his life or being shot at. Unless your character is in shock, he—and you—should stay focused on the action.

Don't interrupt the action to explain it. If explaining is necessary, get it over with before the shooting starts.

Details matter

Use all five senses to put the reader right into the scene with the characters. Let the reader smell the sharp coppery scent of blood; feel the itch of tears or the prickle of sweat; taste the salty pre-cum; feel the brush of a hand on sensitized skin. Sensory details bring a scene alive. They create immediacy and a sense of urgency. And, while we're on the subject, all the adjectives and the adverbs in the world can't replace a little genuine biofeedback, know what I mean?

In a large action scene the conflict is external. There isn't time to brood over internal conflicts when someone's coming at you with a saber.

Style is not for sissies

Write crisp, clean sentences. Be terse. Aim for a rat-a-tat-tat effect.

Or use connectors to give the feeling of a breathless, headlong rush. Keep going, don't stop, don't look back.

Either way, don't spend valuable time on descriptive passages or internal reflection.

Stay in character

Most importantly, keep your characters *in* character.

Yes, real live people do occasionally behave out of character, but good fiction, unlike real life, has to make sense, and characters must abide by the rules of good fiction. So, if your character is suddenly going to demonstrate abilities making it possible for him to outwit killers, outmaneuver pirates, or outrun werewolves, you'll need to establish early the foundation for that skillset.

And if your protag *does* do something completely out of character, you'll need to have every other character comment on it—*and* have already foreshadowed this peculiar behavior. There are no shortcuts in good writing.

Sometimes it's easier to demonstrate rather than explain. The following is an example of a very bad action sequence—title and author name withheld as the intention here is not to embarrass anyone—with my own explanation of what works and what doesn't. Mostly what doesn't.

> Joe's seventh sense, the one that along with his Logan-sense kept him alive, clicked in. He was off-balance, right hand gripping a tree above him, legs splayed with little or no purchase on the slippery ground as he heard it. The faint, but distinctive sound of a gun being cocked—the same sound as he had heard just under twenty-four hours ago when he had been bathing and Huntley had pulled a gun on him.

As far as I know, there is no "seventh sense." In fact, there are plenty of folks who will argue over whether there's even a sixth sense. Joe apparently has eight senses because in addition to his seventh sense, he has something called a "Logan-sense" which works with his seventh sense (which actually sounds like his sixth sense) to keep him alive.

Confused yet? And that's just the first sentence.

Equally confusing is the phrase "legs splayed with little or no purchase on the slippery ground as he heard it." As he heard what? The ground?

Part of the problem—though only a small part—is punctuation. A colon at the end of the second sentence would lead us naturally into "the faint, but distinctive sound of a gun being cocked."

By the way, instead of describing "the sound of a gun being cocked," why not tell us what that sound is? Is it a click? Is it a tick or a tock or a metallic slide? Is it a ka-chunk? Soft or loud?

> Now, like then, he reacted. Without letting go of the branch, he whisked Logan's Magnum from his belt, removing the safety and aiming in one smooth, panther-like move and fired three rounds, just as a bullet zipped past his head hitting the tree against which he had been resting.

I'm thinking maybe the gun control advocates are right if it's reached the point that panthers are armed and shooting at citizens.

"Now, like then, he reacted" is Joe reflecting on an earlier incident. It's slowing the action, isn't it? You could simply write, "He reacted," but that's self-evident. Better to cut that first line.

Detailing each of the actions in the second sentence slows the pacing—and it's awkward as hell. Much faster would be: "Without letting go of the branch, he whipped Logan's Magnum from his belt and fired off three rounds." You can also cut the "just as a…" and start the next sentence with "A bullet zipped past his head, hitting the tree against which he had been resting."

But strengthen those verbs. "A bullet *burned* past his cheek and *plowed* into the tree…" sounds a lot more deadly than "zipping" and "hitting."

> The quadruple shot shattered the air and cozy peace, sent birds screeching into the sky and squirrels quivering across the ground. The tang of cordite hung almost visible in the air, settling around him in the familiar pattern.

The "quadruple shot" causes the reader to pause. "Shots shattered the air" is plenty. "Cozy peace" is just plain silly—especially since Joe was searching for his missing partner and should not have been experiencing "cozy peace" in these woods.

Cordite and gun smoke are frequently confused with each other. They aren't the same. What Joe smells is going to depend on the weapon and the era of your story—and if smoke is hanging in the air, it's not cordite, which is a smokeless propellant.

A tang can be a taste or a scent, but it isn't going to be visible in the air and it wouldn't have a familiar pattern.

Does it seem like I'm nitpicking? Get used to it. Editors nitpick, and copyeditors are worse—and you only get the privilege of being nitpicked if you're good enough to get past the nitpicky gatekeeper.

> In another swift seamless move, he let go of the tree towards which he had been aiming to move, regained his balance and whipped out his own Lugar and settled it in his right hand. Then moving carefully and steadily, eyes, ears, nose and seventh sense all in play, he began to half walk and half scramble in the direction of the single shot. Glancing around as he went, his gaze skimming over the ground and through branches and leaves, every pore, sinew, bone and organ on red alert. From the boom of the shot, he gauged the distance to where the shooter must have stood and came to a halt, caution now over-riding all other thoughts.

Swift and seamless. That's something to aim for, certainly. So in the previous paragraph Joe was still hanging on to the tree branch and holding Logan's Magnum. I'm not sure why he hasn't jumped behind the tree since someone just opened fire on him? Instead, he lets go of the tree and pulls out his own Lugar—why? He already had a gun in his hand. What did he do with it?

"…moving carefully and steadily." Carefully and steadily are just about interchangeable, and in this case they add nothing to our understanding of Joe's movements.

"Eyes, ears, nose, and seventh sense all in play." Uh-huh. Well, I hope they're having a good time. I'm picturing Mr. Potato Head pieces being moved around a gameboard.

"He began to half walk and half scramble." Really? I want to see someone try that. My seventh sense tells me the writer didn't take time to picture this scene.

"Glancing around as he went, his gaze skimming over the ground and through branches and leaves, every pore—" STOP! Let me catch my breath. And while we're taking a breather, let me recommend *Eats, Shoots & Leaves* by Lynne Truss.

Okay, Joe's apparently having some kind of fit. "Every pore, sinew, bone and organ" is on red alert. Now, unlike Joe, I don't have a state-of-the-art internal security system, so I guess I shouldn't comment on his alarmed status.

"…came to a halt, caution now over-riding all other thoughts." And we can tell that how?

What happened to the shooter? He shot once and disappeared?

> He came out into a clearing and gasped as he came face to face with the perfect cylinder that rose above him disappearing into the sun as he squinted up at it. It was constructed of brown-gray bricks and stood tall and firm, guarding the hillock and staring down on all that it surveyed.

Is that like a phallic symbol or what?

So did Joe get the shooter or not? What happened to the guy? He was close enough that Joe could hear his gun cock, but he apparently vanished without a trace. And whatever happened to Logan's gun?

And how come Joe didn't notice that towering cylinder reaching to the clouds until he's standing with his nose pressed up against it?

> Something kicked his ankle and he whirled gun in hand, catch back and pointed the Lugar straight at his partner, who sprawled on the ground with his hands tied behind him, his ankles bound and mouth taped.

Not very observant, is Joe? For all that red-alert glancing and skimming, someone is close enough to kick him, and he doesn't notice? Oh, and where's that famous Logan-sense?

The commas in this scene are running amok. I have no idea what a catch back is—I guess it's a catch, and it's back, but is it Joe's or the gun's?

> Above the taping two brilliant sapphires sparkled and gazed at Joe with utter and complete love.

NOT THE BRILLIANT SAPPHIRE EYES!!!!

> Never before, not even in the few minutes at HQ the day before, had Logan been so open.

Since the writer just told us "never before," the additional "not even in the few minutes at Central the day before" is redundant. And it weakens the impact of the revelation of Logan's powerful feelings for Joe.

(Which, by the way, seem inappropriate and just plain goofy given their current plight.)

> Joe gulped, ignored the prickling that filled his eyes, and the tickling at the back of his nose and sank to the ground, unsteady hands reaching out towards the ropes. "Logan," he whispered and sniffed hard, before burrowing in Logan's pocket for the knife his partner always carried.

Joe seems awfully shaken for a tough guy. Really, for any guy. He's gulping, prickling, tickling and sniffing—and this is all relief that his partner is okay. I hate to think what would have happened if Logan was not in one piece.

Secondly, a lot of guys carry pocketknives. Joe, who appears to be some kind of a spy or law enforcement agent, certainly would carry a pocketknife or some kind of sharp and useful tool—particularly in this kind of situation. Especially since Logan carries a knife "always." It's almost as though the writer were deliberately complicating the scene.

Speaking of complications, this paragraph too is a mess.

A smoother read would be, "Ignoring the prickling behind his eyes, the tickling in his nose, Joe gulped and sank to the ground, unsteady hands reaching for the bindings."

Much better would be, "Joe knelt, hands not quite steady as he cut the ropes that bound his partner."

That way we see that Joe is moved to find his partner okay, but we don't make heavy weather of it, and we get a sense of the speed at which Joe is acting by condensing all that sinking, reaching, and burrowing to "cut the ropes."

> He freed his partner, hands first, then feet and finally mouth—having no idea as to why he chose to do it that way.

Much like the writer?

Personally, I think you would probably rip the gag off first so that your partner could fill you in on where the bad guy you failed to shoot got to—or whether someone was sneaking up behind you. Not necessarily, though. People aren't always logical under pressure, so you might simply tackle what presented itself first. One thing for sure, you'd be moving fast. Asides like "having no idea as to why he chose to do it that way," slow the sense of speed and dilute the tension of the scene. Short, punchy sentences and clean simple directions are what you want.

"Hello, babe. Wondered when you'd get here. Don't suppose you brought anything to eat, did you?" Logan's voice, so normal, after one or two minor false starts, raced into his ears and settled in his body, making him feel whole. He reached out a still shaking hand and touched the distinguished face.

This is beyond confusing. We get Logan's dialogue *before* we find out that he had "one or two minor false starts" at speaking. Huh? We learn that his voice is "so normal," but the fact is it wouldn't be so normal after his having been gagged for a couple of hours; it would probably be raspy or hoarse. Again, we're getting stage business that doesn't make sense, doesn't read true, and adds nothing to the scene.

Also, let's take a look at what Logan says. I understand that the writer is trying for that sort of insouciant, wise-cracking-guy thing that we all expect from our action heroes under pressure, but this just rings false. "Hello, babe" is too breezy. It dispels any and all sense of danger or suspense. "Wondered when you'd get here" equals "What took you so long," and it is *absolutely forbidden in all its variations*. I can't think of a single worse cliché in action-scene dialogue. "Don't suppose you brought anything to eat, did you?" is worst of all. I mean, maybe if Logan has an eating disorder or has been tied up for days he might ask about food in the middle of a major action scene, but it shouldn't be among the first words out of his mouth. Even if there's a running joke about Logan's eating habits, the timing is off. No, what's happening here is the writer—God help her—is trying to be funny.

For the love of God, DON'T DO IT!

Then we have "raced into his ears and settled in his body, making him feel whole."

Can someone explain to me what just happened?

Logan's voice apparently raced into whose ears? How does a voice race into someone's ears?

…"and settled in his body"

The voice did? Ouch!

…"making him feel whole." Who? Joe? Hearing Logan's voice made Joe feel whole? Wow. Usually we require sex for that.

This is an example of a writer not taking time to find the exact and correct phrase she wants. Part of the problem is she hasn't defined what she really wants to say, which I'm guessing is that Joe feels weak with relief at hearing Logan's voice.

"He reached out a still shaking hand and touched the distinguished face."

WHO did? If it's Joe, we've already heard enough about his shaking, sniffing, prickling, tickling, and gulping. The more it's mentioned, the less impact it has. At this point he just sounds like a wuss.

And, by the way, "distinguished face" feels wrong there. Logan's face might be "beloved" or "drawn" or "grimy" or "weary" but "distinguished" conveys the wrong image for this scene, in my opinion. As does the stagy touching-face bit.

My advice with this kind of scene is to stick to crisp dialogue and understated action to cue the reader into the subtext of the scene rather than spelling it all out:

"Wondered when you'd turn up," Logan rasped. He worked his jaw, winced.

Joe was grinning like a fool. "Yeah, well the birds must have eaten your bread crumbs." He offered Logan a hand, pulling the other man to his feet.

And if it's an action scene, pick up the pace. Don't detail every move, every expression, every moment. Speed it up.

The bonus is you'll have less chance of making obvious mistakes if you don't spell out every single action, especially when you're not sure of what you're doing.

RESCUE ME
Hurt/Comfort and Angst

I'd never heard the term "Hurt/Comfort" or "H/C" until I discovered fan fiction. Basically it's where one character is ill, injured, or traumatized, thus requiring the loving care and attention of another character. The scenario isn't unique to fan fiction, of course. It's similar to the classic heterosexual romance dynamic where the powerful hero becomes weak and injured, requiring the nurturing attention of the spunky heroine, thereby resulting in a temporary shift of the power dynamic, and allowing the heroine insight into some aspect of the hero's character previously unknown to her.

When that setup is moved to original M/M fiction, there are key differences from heterosexual romance. The main difference is one of intensity. Characters (in fan fiction especially) are generally *very* ill, *very* injured, and/or *very* traumatized. Addiction is not unheard of. Rape is not unusual—nor is being forced to confront long-buried memories of childhood abuse. Lives and, not infrequently, sanity are at stake.

Jill P., reader: I think that H/C is so popular because, if it's well written, it's how we ALL would like our partners to treat us if something bad happened…or maybe because so many of us have HAD something bad happen, and had to deal with it alone/with an unsupportive partner.

The other interesting thing is that, often as not, it isn't the alpha male brought to his knees by illness, injury, or trauma, it's the beta male. So no particular shift in power dynamics takes place unless it's seeing the tough alpha male having to assume the caretaker role. And perhaps that *is* part of the attraction. An alpha having to comfort and cuddle his vulnerable male companion is, in theory, an alpha showing a side not often seen.

Liz, reader: I'm not sure, but for me it shows me the men taking care of each other's needs… In my family the men don't comfort one another. They fight and hurt a lot. So, I like reading the dynamics and the range of emotions between two men in an H/C story. I think when I cry or laugh while reading, then the author did a damn fine job.

The male psyche being what it is, the situation must be pretty damn unusual and the level of damage inflicted has to be extreme for one male to passively accept being coddled by another—or for the other male to feel comfortable taking on the role of nurturer. In short, we're seeing characters behaving out of character but in believable circumstances.

For this to be effective, the writer has to make sure that both charac-ters have been portrayed as strong, independent, and healthy (emotion-ally, mentally, and physically) previous to the illness, injury, or trauma. It's the contrast between their usual tough and resilient selves and their new—temporary—roles as hurting and comforting that appeal to most readers.

Keep in mind, though, that strength isn't about muscles or even a hard-man attitude. There's also a certain appeal in a sensitive, smart character suddenly shoved into treacherous water, and struggling to stay on his feet.

> We moved over to the sofa. He left me for a moment or two. I scrubbed my face, wiping away tears I didn't remember crying. I rested my head in my hands and tried to think. Nothing made sense. The postcards had stopped, but Hammond had escalated to violence. It had been all threats up until this point. What had changed?
> Dan sat down beside me. Set a glass of water on the table. He held a small brown vial that I recognized from my bathroom cabinet. I had news for him; those pills were well past their expiration date—like me apparently. I watched him shake two tablets into his palm.

"I don't want those."

"I know. But you need them."

I gave him a hostile look. Anything I said now would be put down to my irrational state of mind. I held out my hand. He dropped the pills in my palm, I popped them in to my mouth, took the glass of water he handed over. I washed the pills down, handed him back the glass, stretched out on the sofa, and closed my eyes.

Dan brushed my hair from my forehead. I kept my eyes closed, rejecting that light, tender touch.

"Just relax."

Yeah. Right.

"Everything will be okay, I promise you." I swallowed. Didn't answer. Kept my eyes closed. He said that a lot: "I promise you." But what did that mean? He couldn't promise me anything. Not when he didn't even believe me—when his main concern was to shut me up.

He kept stroking my hair. I didn't want him to. I didn't want to be comforted by him. I didn't like the fact that his touch seemed to find a way through my defenses, that he seemed to be able to converse with me through his fingertips and my nerve endings. I tried to shut out my response, but my scalp seemed to tingle beneath the deft fingers threading my hair. The tears stopped leaking beneath my lashes. The torpidity lurking at the edge of my consciousness eddied around and sucked me down.

The Dark Horse by Josh Lanyon (JustJoshin Publishing, 2011)

In my opinion, the dependency of the hurt character needs to be restricted to a specific time frame—even if the character is left permanently disabled. Helplessness isn't very attractive.

By the way, being hostile, bad-tempered, and throwing tantrums isn't the same thing as showing strength. That's all an expression of fear, and fear is just a different face of weakness.

In fact, hurt/comfort offers the opportunity to show the character rising above adversity. Injured, he still manages to escape from the burning building or crawl out of the car wreck. Recovering from his deadly tropical fever, he confronts his fears of mortality and realizes what's important to him. Facing life in a wheelchair, he has the courage to offer his lover his freedom rather than...you get the idea. Character growth. It's a good thing.

And on the opposite side of the padded cell, we have the brusque, authoritative, sexy-as-hell partner ready to do whatever it takes to get his lover back on his feet: putting his own needs a distant second, showing a tenderness and attentiveness *he* didn't even know he was capable of. He doesn't give up searching for his missing partner, he sits at his bedside reading aloud no matter how long the coma lasts, he jumps in front of the bullet. Whatever it takes. Nothing is too good for the man he just discovered he loves.

And, yes, that's another of the most useful aspects of hurt/comfort: it often serves as catalyst to one character's recognition of his true feelings for the other. There's nothing like a near brush with death—yours or a loved one's—to put everything into focus.

Even if the characters were previously attracted or in love, they will bond still more deeply through hurt/comfort.

Jill P., reader: When it comes to H/C, I like mainly physical. And YES—I hate when the comforter turns into a 12-year-old girl… I love my H/C to be a strong man who shows his emotions (even if he is normally uncomfortable with doing so…), who is realistic about the whole situation—as in, "THIS SUCKS. We know it sucks, let's deal with it and get on with things."

It's difficult to say who really has the starring role in the hurt/comfort scenario. Is it the one hurting or the one comforting? It probably depends on the individual reader's kink, as does preference about which partner is damaged. One thing's for sure; switching roles midway through is guaranteed to annoy most readers, although I've seen writers do this in the interests of preserving some kind of power balance.

Caretakers who are overwhelmed by caretaking, or by how ill, injured, traumatized their beloved is, are pretty much a turn-off. A few tears, a moment of panic, a little stress is only to be expected—readers like strong men to be vulnerable—but you can't have both characters competing for Wimp of the Year Award, okey-dokey?

My personal take is that you get more mileage if you keep the hurt/comfort stuff understated and minimal—without cheating the reader. Don't hospitalize your protag and then send his boyfriend out of town—unless his love interest is going to be one of his doctors. There's no point in injuring a character and leaving him to suffer on his own or in the hands of strangers. *It's the caretaking element readers are interested in.*

Try to devise a sequence that leaves the characters no option but to care and take it: getting lost or snowed in together, waiting for the ambulance/helicopter/boat to arrive, long convalescences. Give the characters quality time alone together to show one in pain, and one concerned and caring. That's basically what it's all about.

Chris Owen: I think one of the primary joys of hurt/comfort fiction is the idea that someone can come in and perhaps not save the day but at the very least be supportive and caring and helpful. People often feel alone in their real lives, and as reading a story can, in some cases, be a type of escape, it adds to the fantasy to give the primary romantic pairing a full and loving emotional support system or have them earn such a relationship.
Author of *Bareback, An Agreement Among Gentlemen*, **etc.**

Through it all, the characters must stay in character. The reader is seeing a side to your characters that wouldn't ordinarily show, but this facet of personality still has to be psychologically possible for both characters. There are degrees of trauma, and pain can be nuanced. Everybody doesn't react the same to every trauma—some guys are tougher and more resilient than others, which is how they got to be who they are in the first place. So don't change them into something else merely for the sake of the story.

A large part of hurt/comfort has nothing to do with character arcs, but if the character *should* learn something from his illness or adversity, if he *should* demonstrate growth and maturity through his suffering—or his caretaking—then that needs to be demonstrated. Your injured protag can't stay curled up in a fetal position forever. Likewise, once his lover realizes how much he cares, he can't plausibly return to complete and chilly indifference. I don't care how many incriminating snapshots he finds searching through his lover's sock drawer.

Furthermore, if a normally strong, sensible man is reduced to a quivering wreck, the circumstances need to be suitably dramatic. Like…rape.

Which leads us to sex.

While hurt/comfort doesn't necessarily wind up with the characters realizing their love and having sex…*a lot* of the time it does.

Yes, cue the Marvin Gaye. Part of the recovery process often involves long and lovely sexual healing. You'll have to follow your own instincts here, but I personally think that characters need to be pretty much convalescent before they're fucking like minks. And—seriously—hot sex is not a cure-all for rape or childhood abuse.

Beyond that, there's no doubt that physical and emotional intimacy are generally beneficial. Who doesn't want to be held after something horrific happens? Who doesn't long to be reassured that they're still lovable, desirable following an emasculating experience (which major illness and trauma generally are).

Just keep it real. I've read way too many stories about half-dead characters having sex in hospital beds under the very noses of medical staff. Granted, if your protag's love interest is a physician, nurse, or therapist, this scenario probably ties into a few variations on the theme—which is nice for the fetishists in the room.

I hate to tell you, but risky sex, uniforms, and the potential for bondage aside, critically ill guys are often—temporarily—unable to get it up. Trauma, whether physical, mental, or emotional, generally does *not* act as an aphrodisiac.

Close calls, on the other hand, often *do*. There's nothing like not getting one head blown off to make you want to use the other.

When it comes to hurt/comfort, male writers tend to be sketchy on details. They set up great scenarios, but they tend to shy away from really…getting into it. Don't be shy. Use all the senses when describing these scenes.

Just keep it plausible, and keep your characters *in* character.

I tried to lift my head. Really bad idea. I bit back a curse and managed, "How long have I been here? Where am I exactly?"
"Almost forty-eight hours. You're in Calavares County Hospital running up a sizable bill even as we speak. I hope you've got health insurance."
I hoped I had enough. I've known solvent, gainfully employed people bankrupted by a hospital stay.
"Next question. When can I leave?"
Jake looked vague. "A day or two. They want to keep an eye on you."
I knew what that meant.
"Going by my missing clothes, they've had a plenty good look already." I hate hospitals. When I die, I don't want it to be in some hospital. I started feeling around the IV needle, raised my head and checked out the technology on my bare chest. Instant Panic: just add water. "I want to talk to the doctor," I jerked out. "I want to go home."
Jake planted his hand on my shoulder. It was like having a brick dropped on my chest. My head dropped back on the spongy pillow, pain thudding in dizzy time with my pulse beat.
"Simmer down, baby." He traced my collarbone with his thumb. I couldn't have moved if I had wanted to; I was too surprised to try. "Just relax."
The feel of his calloused thumb on my sensitized skin was weirdly hypnotic. I blinked up at him like I had been shot by a tranquilizer dart.
"When they brought you in, your heartbeat was a little funky. It's been fine for twenty-four hours so they're going to release you pretty soon. Okay?"
I assented weakly.
Jake made a fist and hooked a playful right to the angle of my jaw.

A Dangerous Thing by Josh Lanyon (JustJoshin Publishing, 2012)

Closely aligned to—and often resulting in or from hurt/comfort—is angst.

If your protag is critically injured and languishing in hospital, and his boyfriend is out of town on a secret mission, the hurt/comfort quotient drops, but the angst quotient skyrockets. See how that works?

Like hurt/comfort, angst is a staple of fan fiction. As you can imagine, all those serious illnesses, critical injuries, nervous breakdowns, rapes, betrayals, addictions, kidnappings, stalkings, deaths in the family, broken dreams, shattered hopes, and really *really* REALLY bad days lead to a certain amount of tension. Even anxiety.

Angst is actually a Germanic word meaning "anxiety." The Danish philosopher and theologian Kierkegaard used the term angst to express his belief that the human condition was riddled with despair. He wrote a philosophical novel called *Fear and Trembling*. What does that tell you?

Typically we associate angst with adolescence. Few people are better at suffering loudly and noticeably than teenagers. It's an art form with them, and you have to respect that.

Acne and existential quandaries aside, angst is also a very important ingredient in M/M fiction. Well, not all M/M fiction. Romantic comedy and action/adventure are mercifully angst-free for the most part, but any time your characters are suffering over their conflicted feelings—generally for each other—they are usually angsting.

Please note: if they're just depressed and insecure, that's not angst. Angst requires *serious* suffering. Breaking up with your boyfriend is sad. Your boyfriend dying is tragic. Finding out after your boyfriend dies that he was seeing someone else—now *that's* angst.

Death, disease, disaster—this is all angstilicious stuff. High drama is what separates true angst from the anxiety normal to the human condition.

Historical M/M lends itself particularly well to angst. It's the whole, love-that-dare-not-speak-its-name thing. *Yaoi* is also angstful: all those giant cartoon eyes veritably *brim* with grief at the human condition—mostly their own.

Wondering if the object of your affections feels the same is not technically angst—unless you're under 18. Having a closeted lover, however, *is* generally grounds for angst.

Because I have a weird sense of humor, the more angstful the story, the more likely I am to find it funny. I guess someone left a banana peel on my pain threshold. Anyway, my advice is that you use angst sparingly. Less is more. Heaping coals on your hapless character's head in chapter after chapter just reminds me of those sappy Victorian novels where the noble and long-suffering hero (or heroine) endures tragedy after tragedy only to die with a brave smile and an angelic sentiment upon his rosebud lips after saving a child from the wheels of a train.

In my opinion the more angsty the journey, the more life-affirming and reassuring the happy ending should be—but that's just me. I'm in favor of happy endings from a purely philosophical standpoint.

Sometimes angst is its own reward—some protagonists do suffer beauti-fully—but generally it requires comforting. Ideally from the other protag-onist. You can see what a vicious cycle this could turn into. It's enough to make a grown man cry.

WHAT'S IT ALL ABOUT, ALFIE?
THEME

One of the least understood elements of writing is theme. The very word makes some writers break out in hives as they flash back to high school compositions on *Moby Dick* and *The Scarlet Letter*.

Very simply, theme is the moral of our story. It's your message, it's the point you're trying to get across—the point of your story, in fact.

Did you realize that even sexy little man-on-man romances were supposed to have a point?

The themes you choose to write about reveal your personal philosophy about life and love. It sounds intimidating, doesn't it? But when you write about two people in love, whether those people are male, female, vampires, space aliens, or all of the above, you reveal your own feelings and beliefs about relationships and society and sex and all kinds of things you may not have consciously been thinking about.

Our plan here is to get you to consciously think about those things. To strengthen thematic elements within your writing so that your philosophy becomes an integral part of the story you're trying to tell.

Why? Because these are the stories that stick with readers. These are the stories that resonate. These are the stories that touch our hearts and our minds. Every classic work of literature has a clear and easily recognized point to it.

Calm down. I'm not going to force you to dissect *To Kill a Mockingbird* or even *Green Eggs and Ham*. Just think about a book that meant a lot to you when you were young. Young*er*. What was that story about?

I don't mean, what happened during the story. Plot is what happens in a story; theme is what the story is *about*.

For example, Mary Renault's oft-cited *The Charioteer* is about a young man coming to terms with his sexuality—and his identity. That's what the story is about. What happens in the story is Laurie Odell is wounded after Dunkirk and falls hopelessly in love with a young conscientious objector—only to run into the boyhood idol of his prep school days—the man who, coincidentally, rescued him at Dunkirk.

Now if you're just in this for the money and you're cranking out blazing-hot novellas by the six-pack to cash in on a lucrative corner of the erotic market, you're excused from class today. Go write an M/F/M story about a voluptuous psychic cop, her studly wererat partner, and the dashing—but angst-filled—ghost pirate they both adore.

The rest of you, listen up. The genre that we're working in is rich in thematic material. In our culture, sad to say, to write about men loving each other openly is, in itself, a thematic statement. In fact, some people would view your literary efforts as subversive.

(And here you thought you were just writing about what turns you on!)

However, since the boom of the M/M market, man-love stories are no longer rare, so simply writing about two guys in love isn't quite enough for our purposes.

COMMON THEMES IN M/M STORIES:

- Coming out
- Self-hate/self-acceptance
- Isolation/alienation
- Illness/disability
- Family
- Superficial values/material world
- Facing prejudice
- Addiction
- Monogamy

- Obsession
- Death
- The power dynamic
- The closet

Obviously there are others. Almost any generic theme is appropriate for M/M fiction as well. In fact, one of the conscious themes in my own work is the illustration of normal, ordinary gay men fully integrated into contemporary society. This is assuming that you can accept that a normal, ordinary guy would keep getting involved in murder.

Your theme doesn't have to be some big lofty PRINCIPLE. In fact, it's generally better if you don't put your message in flashing neon lights. Even readers who agree with you philosophically and morally don't like having an agenda rammed down their throats. You don't want to be heavy-handed or blatant.

Maybe you just want to say something about the healing power of love. Or maybe you just want to comment on the importance of equality in relationships between men. Maybe you're digging a little deeper, trying to say something about how different people find different closets to hide in—and how ultimately destructive hiding in the dark can be. *Whatever is important to you is a theme worth writing about.*

Ideally theme is not something that can be lifted out of one story and plugged into another. It should be integral to this particular story and these particular characters. Theme is, in fact, closely linked to character. Theme often develops through the conflict of your two main characters. Each man brings his own experiences, expectations, attitudes, beliefs, and dreams to a relationship. When those different personalities collide it creates conflict, and through conflict we explore our themes about love and belonging and compromise and whatever else we think important in human relationships.

Murphy C., reader: Now days het romance doesn't really have a lot of barriers to loving somebody. Religion, financial circumstances, etc. aren't big issues like they were in the past. But men choosing to love men, that takes a lot of courage and soul-searching because it is still a taboo in most religions, most families. You have to have a real passion for that person to risk so much family and societal rejection. It hit me that is why the M/M books appeal to women. We all want to be desired—but so desired that a person is willing to risk everything for you!

Let your characters argue out two sides of an issue that's important to you. Allow your characters to be wrong once in a while. Allow them to learn from each other. Allow them to genuinely disagree. When they disagree on important issues—issues important to you *and* them—you have the genuine and believable conflict we discussed earlier.

Through the course of the story your characters will discover what is important to them, and *that* is the exploration and development of theme. That's what you want. You want the characters *and the reader* to explore your themes together.

But keep this in mind: when you're writing these themes, your own lack of experience and knowledge can turn something well-intentioned into something pretentious or just plain silly. Be sensitive to that.

Neil Plakcy: Here is an example of something I read recently, by a woman, writing about a young man's first gay experience. I think that it's easier for a woman to make the change from straight to gay than a man, so I think this woman underestimated the emotional impact of the change:

"He knew, as he lay sprawled under the quilt next to X's warm, hard body, that his life had changed irrevocably. X had done something to him that went beyond a simple broadening of his sexual horizon. Now all Y had to do was figure out what to do with that change."

It was that easy for him—just an OK, I'm gay now. I just don't think that's realistic in a twenty-something guy. You can't be that self-unaware not to realize that male bodies turn you on, for example. It's been said that women fall in love with a person, while men fall in love with a person of the gender that attracts them. I think that idea is one that women stumble over sometime. **Author of *Mahu, Mahu Surfer*, etc.**

The balance of power in relationships has always been of interest to me. When is strength a weakness, and when is weakness strength?

When I set out to write the Adrien English series, I saddled my protagonist with a heart condition. Partly I did it because heart problems run rampant in my family, so that was always in the back of my mind. But partly I did it because I knew that readers would instinctively realize there was little risk of Adrien, a series character, not surviving any given adventure, but his physical vulnerability upped the ante a little. And it created an interesting dynamic with his extremely aggressive alpha male romantic interest. Exploring that particular dynamic between Jake and Adrien worked so well that it's become a common motif in my stories. A number of my characters have some weakness or disability that allows me to explore concepts of strength, masculinity, and power within the context of a romantic relationship.

As you outline your next story—or read over the current one—ask yourself: *What am I trying to say?*

If you're not sure, or if that message doesn't come through clearly in the story, then you need to rework a few scenes so that the premise of your story, the point driving it, becomes clear.

Every scene should underline and illustrate your theme.

I can feel your resistance to this idea right through my laptop screen. But this concept ties back to my assertion that every scene must be there for a reason, and the reason should be twofold: to move the plot along and to illustrate your theme. These two things work in tandem because the story you tell should illustrate the themes that matter to you. Granted, sometimes you don't really know what you're trying to say until you've said it—and reworked it a few times.

It's okay if you haven't decided on a theme before you start writing. Theme often develops organically through the creative process. Sometimes the most powerful themes gradually reveal themselves through the course of the story, through the journey the characters take.

Almost always you'll have to go back and refine or define theme in a few scenes. You grow comfortable with your characters through the course of the story. Sometimes your characters will surprise you; sometimes the theme turns out to be something different than you imagined it would be.

Sometimes—often, in fact—there is more than one theme to a story. That's okay. Like I said, often the very best way is to let theme develop naturally out of the characters' journey and the events of the story.

Now. Very important. *You must not preach.* Despite the richness and wealth of thematic material in our chosen genre, you must restrain yourself from jumping on the nearest soapbox.

There's a fine line between subtly and skillfully getting your point across, and preaching from the pulpit. Readers of M/M fiction look to us for entertainment and escape. You must avoid the temptation of whanging them over the head with your 24kt message. Readers are not a captive audience. Irritate them and they will not buy your next book.

Your opinions are always better coming from the mouths of your characters. Use your characters beliefs, actions, dialogue to say what you want to say.

> Steve said, "Yeah. But there's a problem. Lenny Norman is directing and he doesn't want you."
> I sat up, dislodging Dan's hand. "You're kidding!"
> "Nope."
> "I've never even worked with him. Why doesn't he want me?"
> "For one thing he thinks you're too good looking for the part of Laurie."
> I glanced across at the reflection of myself in the mirror hanging over the bureau dresser: tall, lanky, brown eyes, brown hair. "I'm not that good looking," I protested.
> "I agree. I don't think you're so good looking. In fact, I think you're butt ugly. This is his opinion."
> I gnawed my lip, ignoring these witticisms. "That's it? He doesn't want me because of my looks?"
> Steve said, a little more serious now, "That, and he thinks you're not gay enough."
> "What? What the hell does that mean?"
> "Hey, I'm just telling you what was said."
> "But what does that even mean? I'm gay. I'm out. What more does he want?" Dan's hand closed around the nape of my neck, his fingers knowledgeably prodding the muscles knotting up. I

felt a spark of annoyance; I could practically hear him telling me to take a deep breath, relax. I didn't feel like relaxing. This was business. This was my career.

"It's not like we had an in-depth discussion. I think it's a political thing with him. He feels like you're walking a line with straight audiences, that you're not openly gay. 'You play it too straight,' that's what he said."

"Well, so does Laurie! So does Ralph. I mean, it's historical drama. It's World War Two. Nobody was out. What's this idiot planning to do, portray them as a couple of flaming queens?"

"Chill, dude. Don't kill the messenger. I'm just letting you know what you're up against. He went ahead and FedExed me a copy of the script, so you're not totally out of the running."

The Dark Horse by Josh Lanyon (JustJoshin Publishing, 2012)

Several things are happening in that scene, two of them related to theme. Dan's attempt to protect Sean, even when Sean doesn't want to be protected, is an ongoing theme directly related to the plot. The other has to do with my own views on the idea of a public sexual identity, a theme that shows up a lot in my work.

Please avoid clichés. Realistically, not *everyone* is going to be okay with your protag's sexuality. Even your protag may not be totally comfortable all of the time. Likewise, avoid populating your world with crazed fundamentalists and hate-filled bigots. People are complex. The world is full of contradictions. Black-and-white photography requires the ability to work with light and shadows—if you're not good with the sharps and angles, stick to color, and keep the camera moving.

Don't take yourself too seriously. But don't underestimate your audience, either.

And remember: *having to make a difficult moral choice is one of the best dramatic means of showing conflict and demonstrating theme.*

Probably the most powerful theme in the Adrien English series is Jake Riordan's struggle to come to terms with his sexuality. At the end of *The Hell*

You Say he makes a difficult choice that will have lasting ramifications for himself and Adrien.

As you try to find ways of strengthening theme in your work, look to using thematic recurrent symbols, physical objects, weather, colors, songs, etc. For example, Adrien English's heart condition is a thematic symbol of his quest for love. Setting will often tie into theme. Look to the supporting characters and the subplots—although my feeling is theme is more potent when it personally affects your protagonists.

Not to make heavy weather of it, because we're writing romance here, but there are social and moral implications in writing M/M or GLBT fiction.

Like a physician, your duty, your responsibility, is *first, do no harm*.

Italian bookseller Elisa Rolle has been reviewing M/M and gay fiction on her blog for several years. Elisa is a major fan and supporter of M/M and gay fiction—not an easy thing in her native country. I asked her what it's like for gay writers in Italy: How difficult is it for them. Is there stigma attached to writing gay literature?

Absolutely yes. In Italy, gay writers can be only intellectual writers. If a gay writes fiction, it can't be mainstream; he has to use underground channels or very small publishers. It seems like gay writers have to justify themselves being cultured people: Look I'm gay but I'm also an "intellectual" so being gay is not so important, is it? But really, Italian gay writers are very few. Rather, Italian "openly" gay writers are very few: in Italy coming out is still a taboo, something that brings you to face the public judgment, and that can destroy your career. In a country of over 60 million inhabitants, we have maybe two gay politicians, one writer, two or three entertainers... We have had a great artist, writer, journalist, poet, director: Pier Paolo Pasolini. But he was beaten to death thirty years ago—"officially" by a hustler. After thirty years, most people know him as the "murdered gay writer" and not as the "murdered writer."

Yes, we're writing sexy little stories of love, adventure, fantasy, and mystery, but these stories should not be meaningless. Commercial fiction can still inform and teach us about life. Have some respect for yourself as a writer. Use the stories you tell as a vehicle to share your beliefs and values.

A MAN OF FEW WORDS
DIALOGUE

"Now. Need you."
"Need?"
"Want you. Now."
"Want…"
"So sexy. God, aching for you, lover."
"You? Always. And I'm gonna eat you up."
"Oh… Ohhhhh, that feels… Yeah."
"Yeah, my sugar. So sensual."
"Tell me again. Tell me I'm yours."
"You know. M-mine. All mine."
"Oh shit. Gabe. You… You tease. *Fuuuuuuuuuck…*"
"Need. Fuck! Love you!"
"Uhn. Oh. Oh. God. Oh. Love you. Gonna suck you off before you leave. And tonight? Tonight need you to fuck me sooooo hard."
"Sugar. Surgarbaby, please…"
"Fuck!"
"Yeah!"

Now that's romance, eh?

What've you just read, assuming you could get through it, was my painstaking recreation of some typical M/M pillow talk minus the physical action. No, I'm *not* exaggerating.

You might be thinking to yourself, that's cheating. What's the point of this dialogue without the physical action? It doesn't even make sense.

You got it. My point exactly.

This is not dialogue any more than the moans and salacious comments on a prefix 900 call are conversation. This vocal-orgasm paddleball is simply there to help the reader get off. You could take it out or exchange it with another Ooooooh-Ooooooh-Baby sequence, and virtually nothing in the scene or the story would change.

And that is not a good thing. Really.

Dialogue serves several purposes, but each purpose is designed to one end: to advance the story.

(Actually, I guess there is an additional purpose, if you want to count "getting the reader off," although that one isn't listed in most of those *other* writing books.)

Personally, the sample dialogue above didn't do it for me. But then, as my significant other tells me, I'm a tough audience. I prefer my pillow talk to offer insight into the characters and their complicated relationship—to be meaningful *and* sexy. Of course that would take a few minutes to figure out, and might slow the assembly-line production of books from certain writers and publishers.

When human beings have sex with someone they love, they're vulnerable. Which means it's a great time to insert romantic and heartfelt dialogue. Every sex scene should have a point—beyond the obvious one. It should signal some change, some development in the romantic relationship between our two protags.

If the sex scenes are coming (behave!) so fast and furiously they don't signal anything beyond cranking up the word count, then we've got a problem. Or rather, you have, because I don't do that.

Every sex scene I write is there for a purpose. I want these episodes to resonate with the reader. I want them to impact the characters and the story. I want them to be memorable. And dialogue is one of the key ways to keep sex scenes distinct and significant.

Yeah, yeah, I know there are readers who are totally happy with the moans-and-groans school of pillow talk, but even four years ago, before we were operating in a glutted market, readers were complaining about derivative sex scenes and cornball dialogue. You can bet they aren't getting *less* picky as more and more books are pumped out into a flooded market. Sure, it's easy to get published merely because you're writing M/M, but it's not so easy to get *read*. And as the competition grows stiffer (yes, I know, *focus*) you're going to have to get better at what you do. You're going to need an edge, and believe or not, getting raunchier and rougher between the sheets isn't going to do it for most of the M/M readers out there—not once the novelty wears off.

Some of you may recall a few decades back when the market for bodice rippers or sexy historicals went, ahem, bust. My dear old mum read a lot of those things, and being a tyke with an inquiring mind, I read a few too. There was a certain tiresome sameness to them, and eventually my mother and a million other readers grew bored and moved on to something else. The sexy historical market still exists, but a lot fewer writers earn a living in it, and those who do are the cream of the crop.

Hear me now and believe me later: *skill* is the best insurance policy for a writing career.

Anyway, your characters will—should—say things when they're in bed together that they wouldn't say anywhere else. They'll reveal things about themselves through dialogue and action in those particular scenes that could only happen in those particular scenes.

Bedroom dialogue isn't interchangeable with other dialogue. It *is* sexier—sensual and emotional and naked—but it still needs to be coherent. And your story shouldn't make sense if you remove that dialogue because very often that dialogue is going to be a turning point. At the very least it should be an emotional turning point.

And my personal preference is that even if you took all the physical action out, the dialogue would still make sense. Mostly.

Weirdly enough a lot of M/M authors either resort to a version of the example above or they have almost no dialogue at all—mostly the latter. I'm not sure if it's because so many women writers are focused on getting the mechanics right to the exclusion of all else. In fairness a number of male writers make the same mistake, although that's a little more understandable, the big lugs. Any way you look at it, it's a lost opportunity.

Okay. Read the scene below while paying close attention to the dialogue. True, there isn't a lot of it, but you don't need a lot. Like anything else in your writing, it's about the quality, not the quantity. Pay special mind to the internal versus external dialogue.

"This is enough for you? Just...this?"

"Enough...?" I gasped, humping against his hand. He had wonderful hands, long strong fingers and a delicate touch despite the calluses. "I'm not saying I wouldn't like...oh, God that's nice..." I closed my eyes, savoring the sustained caress, then opened them as his words sank in. "Is it not enough for you?" I wasn't sure what we were talking about. The sex itself or the fact that for him sex was all it was? Did he want to put a cock ring on me or did he fear I wanted to put a wedding ring on him?

"I didn't say that." Then, strangely, he said, "I heard you with Green that night."

It took effort to concentrate on his words rather than his touch. I didn't understand what he meant at first, and then I did. I blinked up at him, not quite knowing what to say. The night he referred to, the night I had discovered who had killed two of my closest friends—and why—was something I still couldn't bring myself to think about. At first I'd been too shocked and sickened. And now...it felt safer not to look back.

"He hurt you."

"I don't remember. Maybe."

"You let it happen."

Again I didn't have an answer. It weirded me out to think of Jake listening to Bruce fuck me, but that was hardly the weirdest part of that particular evening.

And that evening was hardly the weirdest part of my relationship with Bruce.

"You let it happen, but you didn't enjoy it."

"Well, no." I asked carefully, "Did you enjoy it? Hearing us, I mean."

"No." All at once his face looked older: tight, bleak. "You were afraid. And I was afraid. I thought you were going to die."

I had thought I was going to die that night too. It was strange looking back from the safety of Jake's arms. Bruce, who said he loved me, had fucked me over in every possible sense. And Jake, who only spoke of fucking, never caring, had already proved to be an unselfish lover.

I said—and I thought I was kidding, but somehow it didn't come out like that, "I knew you'd save me."

The pain in his face closed down my throat. He seemed about to add something, but changed his mind. Instead his mouth found mine with sudden hunger.

My turn to stroke and soothe.

A Dangerous Thing by Josh Lanyon (JustJoshin Publishing, 2012)

Does the dialogue still make sense (for the most part) without the physical action: meaning, are these two characters actually *communicating* with each other? Even without knowing the backstory or the characters, is this dialogue interchangeable? Can you see that we're watching a turning point in this relationship—learning something about the characters and their feelings for each other? It couldn't happen at another time in the story; this dialogue has to happen at this point.

Dialogue in your sex scenes: yes, you do need it, and yes, you need to take as much time and trouble with it as you do with the rest of your dialogue.

How Important Is Dialogue To You?

Elisa Rolle, reviewer and bookstore owner: Very important. A mix of dialogue and description. Both of them of right length. My attention is easily lost if I have no dialogue for too long, but at the same time, without description I can imagine the story in my mind. Not knowing all the words I read, I try to build the story in my mind and replace the unknown words with my intuition. I don't use a dictionary. I skip the word and try to understand it in the context of the phrase. No hiding here. I read romance, and now M/M romance, because I like a love story, and I read erotica because I like to read sex scenes. But if a book is only an unending sex scene, it loses my attention.

Ladymol, Squashduck Reviews: Dialogue makes a story for me. As a writer it's where I begin to form the plot—I let the characters speak for themselves and the rest follows. False dialogue, stilted or unrealistic, grates so much on me I usually stop reading. But clever dialogue can say so much without saying anything at all.

Poicale, reader: I think to me dialogue is so important because it makes me feel like the characters are real, like they could be people out in the world. As much as I would love to have access to the internal monologue of other people...well, only if I could turn it off and on at will...I don't. And the challenge of being human is trying to figure out people's motives and feelings based on just what they say.

Dialogue in a story does that. That feeling of...ooh, Character A just said Y but did he really mean it that way? Or was he just saying that so that Character B would think Z?

There is internal dialogue and external dialogue. Internal dialogue is your character's private thoughts and reflections. External dialogue is what your characters say aloud. They are equally important. Both rely rather heavily on the author's voice. We'll go into that a little later.

There is also nonverbal and verbal dialogue or communication. Nonverbal communication is the gestures, expressions, body language, and other unspoken cues we give our readers to tell them what's *really* going on in a scene.

I mentioned earlier that dialogue—all dialogue—serves several purposes. Let's review those purposes.

Dialogue establishes character.

You've put time and thought into making sure each of your characters is unique and fully rounded. Obviously you don't want to spoil that by having your characters all sound alike.

"Hey, y'all, it's Frank!"

"Bloody hell! Frank, you here, mate?"

"Whoa, dude. They'll let anybody in this place."

Use the rhythms and cadence of speech to differentiate between characters.

Kellie W., reader: `Apparently X has a huge following, but I cannot` `get into her stuff at all. I read her big bestseller, and I cannot` `tell you what it is about except that one character speaks very` `bad slang English that grates since it is obviously coming from` `an American writer.`

Be sparing with dialect, accents, obscenity, foreign words, speech impediments, slang—a little bit of that goes a long way. Mostly you're just trying to give a feel or a flavor. You don't want to sound like Huck and Jim floating down the Mississippi. Or worse, Huck and Jim floating down the Thames.

Details matter.

The challenge is a little different if you're writing historical romance. The dialogue of Regency or other period characters is going to require a fair bit of research on your part. Be careful to get it right. Words and their usage change as time goes by. Avoid anachronisms. Read fiction from the period you plan to write about.

Just so you know, nonverbal dialogue is especially good for establishing character.

Dialogue reveals background, values, and beliefs.

You can cover a lot of ground with dialogue, and it makes for more interesting reading than long sections of narrative, or pages of a character thinking about his life story.

Still, you want to avoid those painful exchanges of exposition that plainly exist only to fill the reader in on information she needs to know.

"Ever since your younger brother Frank, who hates homosexuals, married Jo Beth, the mayor's daughter, and moved to Silverbrook, a neighboring town still within driving distance, things have been a lot more peaceful around here!"

Editor and author K.M. Frontain: If I have a complaint about women writing M/M fiction, it's that they make their male characters think way too much in some stories. Pages of thinking is horrible to read. Most aspiring M/M writers need to find the balance between thinking and action. They really overbalance on thinking. Some stories seem to be entirely thinking, some sex, more thinking, and a very minimal plot to back up the thinking. The world is often very vague because, well, the entire story is told through the filter of some fictional man's head, and the thinking sometimes doesn't come off very male. So I'd tell female M/M writers to pay more attention to how men think, not how they work their plumbing.

Pages of thinking, especially of what passes for masculine thinking in the imagination of some women, *is* pretty horrible to read. The success of a character's internal reflections is going to largely depend on the "voice" the writer gives him—which largely depends on the writer's own "voice."

Dialogue foreshadows coming events.

Your characters can unconsciously reveal clues to the unknown future through spoken and unspoken dialogue.

"Ever since your younger brother Frank, who hates homosexuals, married Jo Beth, the mayor's daughter, and moved to Silverbrook, a neighboring town still within driving distance, things have been a lot more peaceful around here!"

Is anyone in any doubt that young Frank will soon be making an unscheduled visit?

You see foreshadowing through dialogue and gesture used a lot in films and television. A character rubs his forehead. The second character asks if he has a headache. The first characters says, nah, it's just the heat—and in the next scene he's having a stroke.

Foreshadowing is a great tool, but you have to be subtle with it.

Dialogue breaks up all that print so there's plenty of white space.

You just *think* I'm kidding about that one.

Dialogue describes setting and characters.

Ideally, dialogue serves more than one purpose at a time.

> "They ordered burgers, cokes, and fries—onion rings for Tug—and talked casually about food and the music they liked and the movies they'd seen, and their work. It was so normal, it felt surreal. It was as though the accident had never happened at all. As though it were an ordinary day and they were two guys having a nice lunch and getting to know each other.
> "What kind of greeting cards do you design?" Tug picked up an onion ring. Ridge smiled inwardly at the thought of Tug having to pull double duty with the mouth spray. He wondered how Tug's mouth tasted after onion rings and how it tasted after Binaca.
> "What do you mean?"
> The dimples appeared briefly, vanished in a wry smile. "Are they the funny, sarcastic kind?"
> "No," Ridge admitted. "They're not."
> For some reason that seemed to relieve Tug. He smiled. "And they sell well?"
> "They used to. I haven't worked much…lately."
> "Sure." Tug seemed to recollect himself. "Did you want an onion ring?"
> Ridge shook his head. "Is your first name really Thomas?"
> "Yeah, it is." Tug's expression changed. "That was weird, wasn't it? Chance knew my name."

Petit Morts 14: Just Desserts by Josh Lanyon (JCP Books, 2011)

Through just a few lines of out-of-context dialogue we see that the plot has advanced; the mysterious "Chance" knows something about Tug he couldn't possibly know. But we also learn that Tug is a little afraid of that sharp, sarcastic, mean side of Ridge—but also that maybe Ridge isn't as sharp, sarcastic, or mean as Tug fears.

Dialogue is useful for propelling the plot forward and for making quick, seamless transitions.

In fact, starting chapters and even occasionally the novel or story itself with dialogue can be an excellent way of immediately involving the reader, dumping him right into the thick of the action. But you have to be careful that the dialogue is sufficiently interesting and not too confusing.

A few general comments about male dialogue in the M/M novel.

What you have to remember is that while all guys are not the same, and there are plenty of articulate, well-spoken men out there—as well as arch and campy queens, and Neanderthals who rely on grunts to communicate—what you're trying to create with your M/M characters is, in many ways, a *composite*. And this is because most of the time in M/M fiction, the main characters are presented as normal or average (though reeeeally, reeeeally gooooood-looking, as Zoolander would say) Joes.

With the exception of sex scenes, most M/M protagonists talk way too much—and about the wrong stuff. I don't mean that there's too much dialogue, per se, but these guys talk *way* too much about their feelings. And not just their feelings, *everybody's* feelings! I've never known men so interested in who's dating who, and who's having a baby, and who's getting divorced. And they remember all the details, and everybody's names, and who said what to whom...

And they don't only talk to each other about how they feel, they talk to their mothers, fathers, sisters, brothers, friends, employees, bosses—oh, and not merely their own, but their *lover's* mother, father, sisters, brothers, friends, employees, boss, therapist, neighbor, cook, dog—you name it.

I'm not saying you can't have a chatty protagonist, but go easy. All your male protags cannot be Chatty Cathys. Okay?

Now, I know part of the charm of these books is getting to see a side of men not often glimpsed in real life, but again, it's the *quality* and not the quantity of emotional openness you're going for. If your protags are constantly prattling about how much they care about each other, you dilute the impact and importance of these revelations.

Also, admitting that you love someone is a big moment in a romance novel—any romance novel. When both characters finally admit that they love each other, it's generally the end of the book. Big screen kiss and fade to black.

Actually, your protagonist admitting even to *himself* that he's in love should be a big moment in your story. Don't just brush past it like it's a common, everyday occurrence, because it's not.

And admitting to his significant other that this is it, this is the real thing, should be dramatic, important, emotional. Don't spoil the moment with…premature ejaculation…if you know what I mean.

Word To The Wise

Book dialogue is not supposed to mirror real conversation. Real conversation is frequently pointless, repetitive, and dull. It may be realistic to have your characters ramble for pages with "uh, er, oh, hmm," but your readers will tire quickly. Fictional dialogue is supposed to be better than the real thing. In addition to serving one of the several purposes we covered previously, it should be pleasurable to read. But be honest with yourself. If you're not funny, steer clear of banter and witty repartee. Nothing falls flatter when it's done badly. Develop a clean, crisp, straightforward voice.

Don't hamper dialogue with verbiage. Just say what you're trying to say. Get to the point. Stick to the point.

Don't slow dialogue down with a bunch of attributions, tags, and meaningless gestures and expressions. If you've properly developed your characters, they should have distinct voices, and those voices should make it reasonably easy to follow who's saying what in a given scene.

Don't pull a muscle trying to avoid repeating taglines. "He said" is pretty much invisible. At the same time, you don't have to be afraid to vary the lineup—sometimes people do sneer or murmur or whisper or chuckle the things they say. Don't let the MFA grads intimidate you; there are fashions in writing like everything else. The English language is full of marvelous, precise, and nuanced words, and "he said" doesn't begin to cover it. Choose your words carefully.

Break dialogue up with action when possible. However, avoid cluttering a scene with empty gestures and pointless motions. Busyness won't add anything; in fact, it will simply distract from what your characters are saying.

Use masculine—or gender neutral—analogies and metaphors. Think sports, math, war, nature, science—yes, I'm being sexist, but I really can't take one more guy thinking in terms of some feminine point of reference like baking or paper dolls.

Unless your protag has newly emigrated, use contractions where you can. Otherwise your protag's formal speech is going to make him sound like English is his second language. Of course, if English *is* his second language, then a more stilted style of speaking will serve him and you well.

Ease up on the profanity, little lady. Although the F-word is dearly beloved by M/M writers everywhere as definitive proof of masculinity, not every guy uses it in place of all other adverbs and adjectives. There are other swear words. As a matter of fact all guys don't express deep emotion by swearing. Since when did *male* become synonymous with *simple*?

Here's a good test as to whether you're overusing the all purpose F-word. Use search and replace to substitute "fuck" for an innocuous word like…"blue." If the use of blue becomes ridiculous and conspicuous, you know it's time to pull out the thesaurus and find a new crutch to prop your prose on.

In short, make *less is more* your motto, and the added payoff will be that your dialogue will sound and read more masculine.

VENI, VIDI, VICI
I CAME, I SAW, I CONQUERED—WRITING SEX SCENES

You might be wondering why I've waited so late in this writing guide to get to what some readers refer to as "the good part."

Well, it's for a couple of reasons. The first reason is I personally think the sex scenes will have more emotional impact if the reader has gotten to know the characters a bit before they're tangled in the sheets with them. All things being equal, sex with the people we love is better than sex with strangers.

Granted, not everyone—writers or readers or even publishers—agree with this theory, but I think slowly building the sexual tension, teasing and tantalizing the reader—and exploring the other possibilities for sexual and emotional gratification—make for a richer story *and* more satisfying erotic scenes.

Kellie W., reader: I like a good sex scene. I like to know how characters relate to one another, how they make each other feel, how they long for each other, but I do sometimes find that when the sex scenes happen too quickly after each other and go on for page after page that I do lose interest. Also I am not interested in the exact description of what a penis looks like, even the one belonging to the main character. I can work that out for myself. Less mechanical description and more feelings for me is the key.

This leads me to my second peeve. Sex scenes that carry most of the book or are too interested in the mechanics rather than what the men are feeling or experiencing. Obviously some description is necessary so you know what they are in fact doing, but often it feels like "and this went here and it felt good…" It could be sex between any two people.

The second reason I've waited to talk dirty to you is that, believe it or not, M/M fiction is not synonymous with erotica, despite the fact that a (happily shrinking) percentage of publishers, readers, and even reviewers still try to argue that it is. M/M is about a romantic relationship between two men, and yes, in all likelihood, sex will be a big part of that relationship, but technically an M/M novel need not contain graphic and explicit sex scenes.

While consummation of the relationship will certainly take place, there are a number of well-known mainstream M/M novels that brush over the act with literary flourish: *The Charioteer* by Mary Renault (as well as her historical novels), *The God in Flight* by Laura Argiri, *Kirith Kirin* by Jim Grimsley, and *Gaywyck* by Vincent Virga to name just a few. It's even possible that by closing the door you'll up your odds of finding a mainstream publisher.

So far Suzanne Brockmann's Troubleshooter novels have not contained explicit sex scenes between FBI agent Jules Cassidy and actor Robin Chadwick, but this is clearly Brockmann hoping to gently acclimatize her readers to the idea of M/M romance—and still not offend anyone too much. Reader expectation for J.R. Ward's *Lover at Last,* featuring the same-sex relationship between vampires Qhuinn and Blay, was that Ward would deliver the same explicit erotic content as in the rest of the series, and by most accounts, deliver she did.

Is Sex A Requirement In M/M Fiction?

Angela James, Carina Press: Absolutely not.

Deborah Nemeth, Carina Press: No, in fact one of my recent M/M releases for Carina Press contains no sex: Promises Made Under Fire by Charlie Cochrane.

Irene Williams, Loose Id: Sex in some form seems to be a part of slash. And it definitely is for Loose Id, though interestingly, of all our releases lately, it's our M/M stories that often are more "romantic" than sexual. Many of our M/M stories are traditional romances.

Sasha Knight, Samhain Publishing: Not at all. We have titles all across the board, from sweet to uber-erotic. As our motto states, it's all about the story. And not all stories require sex. Readers are looking for M/M stories to fit every mood, and books don't have to have sex to garner reader interest.

Aleksandr Voinov, Riptide Publishing: I think hot stories sell better, on average, but that is the same as in heterosexual romance. Erotic romance is performing more strongly than less hot romance, whether it's hetero or gay. However, I think the real secret is sexual tension. If an author can build amazing tension, maintain it, and then deliver on the promise with a scorching sex scene, that's brilliant, and often seems to satisfy readers more than plenty of sex scenes strung together without a sexual arch/sexual tension actually building anticipation. Personally, I no longer read for the sex scenes, but having written so many, I might just get a little jaded, and I think there's enough sales potential in stories that are less hot to make it worthwhile. It's just a different segment of the overall readership that is getting targeted.

Trace Edward Zaber, Amber Quill Press: From our experience, hotter stories are always better sellers (when it comes to customer satisfaction), however, we will be releasing our first non-erotic M/M story in the next few weeks, so it's anyone's guess how the customers will receive it. Obviously, we hope the interest in M/M fiction extends beyond the bounds of erotic romance, and we would love to explore the possibilities.

Margaret Riley, Changeling Press: Absolutely. We publish ONLY erotica. Specifically over-the-top-hot erotica.

Tina Burns, Liquid Silver Books: For us yes, we are publishing erotic romance, so that does require sex. There is a possibility in the future of opening up our parent publisher, Atlantic Bridge, for mainstream fiction.

Nicole Kimberling, Blind Eye Books: Yes, because it proves the characters are actually gay. But the sex does not have to be terrifically explicit. One or two sentences is adequate for me.

Is M/M fiction synonymous with erotica? No. Is sex a requirement for your story? It all depends on who you're trying to sell to. The majority of M/M readers seem to prefer erotic scenes. Sexy M/M novels, in general, sell better than non-sexy M/M novels (with the exception of those published through mainstream publishers, which have larger print runs to begin with).

Sex sells. No argument there.

Porn is big business for a reason. Which reminds me. I guess we should discuss the difference between erotica and porn.

I've read a lot of different arguments—debates?—on the topic:
Erotica is healthy, legal, and has artistic merit, while porn doesn't
Porn is for men, erotica is for women
Erotica is for the mind, porn is for the body
There is no difference

I guess there's a measure of truth in all of that. What you need to keep in mind is that *you* are writing romantic fiction, and your approach to everything—including the sex scenes—needs to stay focused on that fact.

K.A. Mitchell: My opinionated definitions (and I value all of these forms and believe they can all be examples of good writing):

Porn: Uses explicit description to arouse a reader; focuses completely on the actions between the participants; any emotion or growth displayed is purely incidental to the story

Erotica: Uses explicit description to arouse a reader; focuses on the sexual growth and experiences of one or more characters, building to a conclusion that shows that growth and change

Erotic romance: Uses explicit description; the scenes of intimacy are integral to the growth and development of both the romance and the characters' arcs; has a satisfactory romantic conclusion

Sensual romance: Describes intimate scenes; scenes may help develop character arc and romantic growth; intimate scenes show or confirm emotional shifts in the characters; has a satisfactory romantic conclusion

Author of *Regularly Scheduled Life, Collision Course*, etc.

That works for me. Traditionally, porn doesn't spend a lot of time on plot or characterization or style. It's all about the act of intercourse. Everything is aimed at bringing the reader/viewer off as quickly—and frequently—as possible. Erotica is most definitely about style. It's about the choice of words, the use of language, the appeal to all the senses—and to the emotions. It might also be about plot and characterization; I can't say for sure. But what I *can* say for sure is that you're writing M/M romance, and *you* most definitely need to be concerned with plot and characterization in order to get the most bang for your erotic buck.

The Romentics: For us, sex is integral to the telling of a romance. It is not just erotica. It shows how the heroes relate to each other and how their relationship develops throughout the novel. It is a unique and very effective method of showing their emotional journey. I am sure it is possible to write a love story without sex. But it would have to be for a good reason that is essential to the plot. We don't see the need to tackle that challenge right now.
Authors of *Hot Sauce, Razor Burn*, etc.

Basically it boils down to this: Write what you enjoy reading—like I do. The odds are good that if you write well, you'll find a market for whatever you like to write. My personal favorite motivational quote: *If you write it, they will come.*

Ladymol, Squashduck Reviews: Yes, I do think sex is pretty critical for M/M fiction. Including it reminds everyone that these are MEN we're writing about—or should be. It helps overcome the temptation to make the characters women by any other name. However, I do like stories where the sex is rare but powerful, where simmering passions are more important than the sex. I'd quote As Meat Loves Salt by Maria McCann as a great example of this style of writing. It's the not being able to have sex that makes her story so incredibly powerful.

When I began writing the Adrien English series, my work was classified as gay fiction or gay mystery. My then-publisher was Gay Men's Press, and they published a lot of gay porn as well as gay literary novels. I tried to hit a happy medium with my work by including brief—quite brief—erotic scenes. By the time I wrote the third book, *The Hell You Say*, I was targeting a mainstream mystery audience, and I cut the erotic scenes down to nothing.

I suppose part of that was the fear that I wouldn't be taken seriously as a writer if I included sex scenes. But the truth is the true literary snob doesn't take *anyone* writing genre fiction seriously, so an erotic scene here and there isn't going to make a hell of a lot of difference—even if I really, truly cared what some unknown parvenu thinks.

Ironically this was just at the point that M/M fiction was beginning to break out, and I began to hear from a number of female readers, one message in particular coming through loud and clear: they didn't like the fact that I "closed the bedroom door" on Jake and Adrien.

And because they argued so convincingly for what those scenes meant to the developing intimacy of the characters, the insight it offered into a side of the characters we would not otherwise see, I began to reconsider my...uh...position.

Bella, TwoLips Reviews: Sex is incredibly important. 100% important.

So not only did I begin writing erotic M/M novellas, I re-edited my original work to include scenes of explicit lovemaking—taking my own pleasure in making each one unique and significant to the characters and their developing relationship.

Even so, I'm pretty tame by most M/M standards, and I thought I'd get some help from my friend and colleague—a writer known for her blazing hot and intensely emotional scenes of lovemaking—K.A. Mitchell. (Who, buy the way, probably sells more books than all of us put together. Although that's gotta be a coincidence, right?)

K.A. Mitchell: The first thing that's key to writing any intimate scene is to forget all of the critical voices, especially those telling you that Grandma's going to read this. Listening to those critics will take you, your characters, and eventually your readers out of the mood. Keep in mind that it's unlikely anyone reading it arrived here by immaculate conception.

Okay, I don't know how K.A. knew about my grandma, but it turns out EVERYONE in my family was conceived by immaculate conception.

K.A. Mitchell: Love scenes, like any other scene in your book, need to have a purpose. To me, a romance without a love scene of some kind is like a spy movie without a chase scene or a murder mystery without a body-discovery scene. It doesn't matter how explicit your writing is, every time the characters hold hands, or kiss, or do an elaborate BDSM scene for an audience, the action has to be there for a reason and it has to show a change in the characters.

We interrupt this broadcast for a public service announcement.

I must still be thinking about my grandma, but I think this is a good place to note a couple of things. Most of the reputable M/M publishers are strict about things like pedophilia, necrophilia (vampires and other supernatural beings excepted), bestiality (not including werewolves, shapeshifters, and aliens) rape for titillation's sake, incest (although twincest and sex between consenting adult brothers is apparently mostly okay), scat, golden showers, fetishes in general, and snuff.

Infidelity can be a problem, depending on the individual house—and I cannot stress enough the importance of reading publisher guidelines before you submit your work.

Even unsafe sex generally takes place with condoms and between consenting adults.

All of the above possibly help to define some of the differences between porn and erotica.

K.A. Mitchell: I usually think of two main purposes in a love scene:

There is a major change or conflict or hook.

For example, the character's inner conflict might go something like this: "I don't like you but you turn me on. The sex was good, damn it. Maybe you're not so bad. Argh, now I really hate you because you were all smug afterward. I will never do it with you again even though it's all I can think about." Simplistic and clichéd, but it changes the character and creates further conflict.

If everything is great after the sex, you risk a reader putting down the book and never picking it up again. Until the end there always has to be a but following the sex scene. (Yes, I am conscious of the pun. Go ahead and giggle.)

Examples:

The sex is good, but...(you ruined my life, I don't do repeats, I'm leaving for Antarctica in the morning.)

The sex is earth-shattering, but...(tomorrow I must kill your brother in a duel.)

The sex is bad, but...(you're so cute you deserve another chance.)

The sex is good, but...(I hate you, I don't do repeats, I must leave forever for Australia.)

The sex is good and we're almost there, but we have to stop because (I'm not who you think I am, there's a knock at the door, is that a dead body?)

Whatever the hook is, it has to come from who the characters are and what's happening in the story or a reader will feel manipulated. **Author of *Regularly Scheduled Life, Collision Course*, etc.**

This relates directly to what we were discussing in the chapters on plotting and pacing. Once your protagonists have declared their love for each other—or really even privately admitted to feeling love—your story is done UNLESS you can throw some powerful and believable obstacles in their way.

The same is true with sex. If your protags are going to have coitus, then it damn well better be of the interruptus variety, emotionally speaking. There is no plot without conflict.

K.A. Mitchell: The other main purpose of a love scene is to show how the characters' feelings have changed. This scene shows the new way they interact and what's different about their contact with each other. These scenes are typically shorter and less detailed. It's more of an impressionist painting than a diagram for assembling furniture. Again, remember that there should be a hook, a reason for the reader to keep turning pages.

The main way to make your love scenes different is in the selection of details. You don't have to escalate the actions through the course of your story, but you should escalate the feelings provoked by the actions. Describing every hip thrust isn't necessary if there isn't an accompanying shift in feelings and emotions. Think about what details best show the feeling, the emotion you're trying to show. What can you show about why these characters are together? What can you show about why this scene is necessary? What can you show about the characters' level of risk or vulnerability?

Choosing details:

What will be left for marriage?

This is what makes the scenes different. You don't have to get more elaborate. You don't have to escalate. Never need every hip thrust. Something about this scene is really important. What is that?

Take the scene: what made that character give into wanting sex in the first place, what can you show about that? Why have sex with someone you hate/compete with? What feeling drives that? How can you make that feeling part of the scene? How can you show risk/fear/vulnerability/anger? Why does this scene matter? What emotional blind spots will be hit during this scene?

Author of *Regularly Scheduled Life, Collision Course,* **etc.**

Here's something to be aware of. There are only so many ways to describe the act of intercourse. Pretty much everyone in M/M is using the same terminology and phrases, and generally the same sequence of erotic milestones in any given work. The way you make your scenes different is through dialogue—internal and external—sensory details and emotional subtext. Fresh language and original metaphors are wonderful if you can think of them, but step cautiously. It's alarmingly easy to skid from the sublime into the ridiculous when you're writing about sex.

I'm not a big fan of euphemisms. "Twin orbs" and "velvet rods" sound like something an interior decorator should be concerned with. I like simple, effective writing. Use evocative, sensual language, *focus on the emotions*, and remember to have your characters talk to each other.

Playful is good, but "dueling purple-helmed love gods"…not so much.

Explicit language is not only okay, it's encouraged—just keep it in historical and cultural context. Straightforward and sensuous—never clinical and never cold. You can be tasteful—I encourage tasteful—but don't be coy.

Go easy on the adjectives and adverbs—some of these scenes read like the rape of a thesaurus. Your erotic tableaux should be written in the same style, the same voice you've used throughout the novel.

In addition to reading gay men's porn, analyze how sex scenes are handled in literary fiction and heterosexual romance novels for a slightly fresh perspective. With all of us reading each other's work there's a danger of M/M fiction developing into a literary circle jerk.

K.A. Mitchell: One of the topics that creates much discussion among readers is word choice. Nothing pulls a reader out of a story faster than words that don't seem natural to the character. Think about your character's background and education, his experiences. They will give him a unique way of describing things. Don't worry about finding too many synonyms. This is a time when most people's language gets pretty basic. I can remember that the worst description I ever read in an M/M romance had to do with trying to blend both a poetic description with a vulgar term in the same sentence. It had me backing away swiftly, hands up in surrender. I would have been fine with either, but the juxtaposition threw me right out of the story. Also, consider what word a character might say out loud vs. what he would say in his internal narration. I think readers will accept any style of descriptive language as long as it feels right for that character at that moment.

If you're still struggling with word choice, look at where you want to sell. Look at the books that sell well and see what those authors are using. Look at your target publisher's books and see what works there.

Come closer. I'm going to gift you with a big secret. There is a certain, if you'll pardon the expression, rhythm to these scenes, that works in lots of kinds of actions. Like anything else, if you use it too much, it becomes distracting due to repetition, but here you go.

For everything that goes on in your love scene, here's the basic way you can make it impact the reader and keep the pages turning.

Action/Reaction/Emotion

Action: a touch

Reaction/sensation: what that touch does to a character

Emotion: how the character feels about the action and reaction

This will lead to a character acting and you're rolling along.

Action: a brush of lips

Sensation: a rush of warmth

Emotion: unwilling attraction

Marco breathed the words against Will's skin. Marco might only have been trying to whisper, might have been only whispering, but the rush of air teased and tingled behind Will's ear, sending an unwanted rush of blood to his cock.

Author of *Regularly Scheduled Life, Collision Course*, etc.

While I'm thinking of it (because, yeah, I am totally thinking of bookshelves right now) a couple of books for your writing library are: *The Romance Writers' Phrase Book* by Jean Kent and Candace Shelton, *The Joy of Writing Sex* by Elizabeth Benedict, *The Emotion Thesaurus* by Angela Ackerman and Becca Puglisi, and *Elements of Arousal* by Lars Eighner.

First and foremost: take as much care with these scenes as you would with any other.

Part of how you keep the sex scenes vivid and intense is that you make them true to the characters. We've all got our little quirks and preferences when it comes to the bedroom, and characterization in your sex scenes has to hold true with the rest of the story.

Don't be afraid to give your protagonists preferences. I know one school of thought is that it's important to show the male lovers meticulously taking turns with topping each other, but the fact is, that's generic and boring. One size does not fit all. Not in the bedroom. Tell us something about the characters by showing what they like and don't like between the sheets—or on the kitchen table. Give them opinions, predilections, desires—give them fantasies—give them insecurities and hang ups. Make their sex as unique and individual as they are.

For example, Adrien English is totally at ease with his sexuality; he's intuitive, slightly conservative, and emotionally generous. He has no problem taking the role of bottom to Jake Riordan. Jake is into the S/M scene. He's a Master, and there's no way in hell he's going to be penetrated by Adrien or anyone else—at least, not that we ever saw in the series. With another partner, Adrien might have other preferences, take another role. It would hinge on the personality of that other character. Jake? Well, Jake's a whole 'nother story.

In the historical novella *Snowball in Hell*, Nathan Doyle is the experienced sexual partner. He craves physical and emotional intimacy through physical union, and his need to submit, to be dominated sexually, drives the sexual dynamic with Mathew Spain. So while Nathan is very much the bottom in that relationship—in all his relationships—he's still the one controlling the shots.

Now, in *The Dark Horse*, Sean Fairchild panics at the idea of anal intercourse, period. Still struggling on an unrecognized level with his sexual orientation, Sean can't quite deal with the invasiveness, the emotional nakedness—and when his lover, Daniel Moran, who is about as sexually healthy and integrated as they come, offers Sean the option of doing *him*, Sean recoils. Sean's got a few hang-ups; Dan recognizes this, and he's patient and gentle with Sean. Who these men are doesn't change based on which room of their house they're standing in.

And then there are Will and Taylor of the *Dangerous Ground* series. There is a lot more sex in those stories, and the two characters meticulously—consciously—take turns topping each other because their testosterone-drenched partnership pivots delicately on their total equality, the complementary balance of strengths and skills.

Use depictions of intimacy to show us something about the characters we wouldn't—couldn't—otherwise see. Give us insight into their characters and their relationship.

Strip your protagonists naked during sex—emotionally, spiritually, mentally naked. All right, they can keep their shoes and socks on.

Irene Williams, Loose Id: In terms of M/M, I have problems with stories that have the same kind of sex over and over in the story without a lot of emotion—the emotion needn't be expressed girlie-style, but it should be there. Oh, and stories that are about males but written too much from a female POV. I know much of our audience is female and have fantasies of what men really are like when they're away from females (apparently they're romantic and loving and tender when we aren't looking) but men express that differently than women do.

So let's talk about the rhythm method. Pacing is just as critical for writing sex scenes as it is for the rest of the work—both in the number of scenes and the length of the scenes.

When it comes to the number of scenes within a given work, think quality over quantity. I've read way too many novels and novellas where the plot merely existed to string together a numbing sequence of non-distinct humping, grinding, and thrusting.

That was fine in the early days of the M/M renaissance, but the competition is too…well, too stiff now. Not only do you have gay writers dropped from their indie publishers scrambling for a new home, you've got mainstream writers caught in the crunch. A lot of writers are turning to e-publishing, and one of the most lucrative areas of e-publishing right now is M/M fiction.

Judith David, Loose Id: The market is moving fast. Writers need to be aware that publishers are trying to keep up with it, whether it's to cut back the pornography or ramp up the eroticism. Guidelines are hybrids, an amalgam of the publishers' tolerances and the customers' preferences as revealed by their buying habits. Both those elements change over time. It's inevitable that the guidelines will follow suit. In practice, yes, the stakes are getting higher. Regardless, whatever the guidelines might seek in the way of erotic content, every erotic moment must advance the emotional stakes in some way. The consistent element in romance is, ta-da, the romance. Emotion is the key.

The biggest taboos are pretty consistent publisher to publisher: rape as titillation, underage sex, bestiality. Hardly the stuff of romance.

Too many sex scenes dilute the impact and importance of what should be a big moment within the story. Don't spoil the romantic tension by satisfying your lovers—let alone your reader—too quickly. Tease, tantalize. Make everybody work for it.

Eve, reader: As to what works and what doesn't work for me. I've tried a couple of very raunchy M/M novels, where the sex/plot ratio is about 70:30, I was bored by the 3rd sex scene.

It's always good to have an engaging storyline, well-drawn characters (such as Adrien & Jake, who I am totally obsessed with) and good sex scenes that are plot-related or tell you something about the characters. Because sex is never just sex, right?

When it comes to the individual scenes of erotic intimacy, don't be afraid to slow the pace. In these sections it's okay to let the characters reflect and remember as they respond to each other. Within reason. You don't want anyone falling asleep before…well, before.

During *these* action scenes your readers do want details and attention to the little things.

Details, details.

When the action is between the sheets (or up against a brick wall) it's okay to talk about the moonlight, the flicker of candles and the shadow of leaves, the feel of wool blankets—or silk pajamas—on bare skin. Let the reader feel the warmth of firelight, the taste of whisky—or semen—in a lover's mouth. Let her hear the pants or groans or whimpers; let her smell the soap, so to speak.

And describing the setting is not only okay, it's preferable. The reader wants to be in the moment with the characters. Don't belabor, but be specific. Where are the characters? Who is doing what to whom?

And please make sure that whatever anyone is doing, it's within the realm of physical possibility.

> Fingers digging into Rick's skin, Peter began to rotate in a see-sawing figure-eight which he knew from experience brought a barreling, pulsating orgasm every time.

Like, what just happened there? The last thing you want is to yank the reader out of the story while she tries to picture the logistics of your characters' sexual acrobatics. You want her engaged, you want her—yes—*aroused*. If you're having trouble figuring spatial relations, you might try a trick Laura Baumbach mentioned using once: she takes two male action figure dolls and tries out different positions with them. Uh, I mean, Laura positions the dolls with each *other*. But you could go a different route; anything that helps you visualize the scene is good.

Here's the thing, though: you don't need to give a blow-by-blow description of every move, every position. It's more important to let the reader know how everything feels, tastes, smells than to give the exact coordinates of hands and feet.

Pan and scan.

Even if you're writing from first-person POV, make sure you include the reactions of your POV character's lover. This isn't masturbation (unless it is, of course).

It's more satisfying for the reader if you go big picture with scenes of intimacy. I'm not saying start head-hopping, but allow your reader to observe what both characters are feeling through the senses of the POV character.

The observations your POV character makes about his partner and lover give your reader necessary insight into a brain and emotions she doesn't otherwise have access to. So pay attention to the revealing details: a change in breathing, a bitten-off comment, a smothered laugh.

Show and tell.

Aim for simple, elegant language. Yes, adjectives and adverbs are okay—even expected here, but use some restraint.

You can structure your sentences for flow and movement rather than speed and urgency—although speed and urgency will be good at some point. Fever pitch will be good at some point.

The main thing is take your time with these scenes. Don't rush through them, and don't cheat the reader. Even if you're tired of writing about the horizontal bounce, you can't let your ennui show. Not in mixed company. And it will. If it's routine for you, it will read as mechanical and rote. That's not sexy, and it's not good writing.

William Maltese: For guys, sex usually comes first, relationships, if at all, after; for women, it's just the opposite. Which may sound stereotypical, but it has been my personal observation that that's just the way life goes. So if a woman writes about two men having a nice sweet and lengthy courtship, then sex, then a loving relationship—when, more realistically, they should be quickly down and dirty, doing it on the bathroom floor of some gay bar, before they likely even know each other's names, then going their separate ways—I suspect it's the former that's more likely to appeal the most to heterosexual women readers. So, why should any female author change anything in her M/M writing, just to make it more realistic? Hell, most of literature is make-believe, which is why a good part of it is called fiction. You don't have to write "real" to sell books, so why should you, especially if your readers are more enthralled and caught up in the fantasy? **Author** *of Love Hurts, Diary of a Hustler,* **etc.**

Don't miss the opportunity to build sexual tension and satisfaction by including erotic scenes that don't end with fucking. Showers, baths, hot tubs, moonlight swims, feeding each other, undressing each other, dancing, cuddling, massage—full body and otherwise—not to mention good old-fashioned kissing can all feel—er—*read* wonderfully well.

Use these to build up the sexual tension between the characters.

K.A. Mitchell: To make a love scene readable and unique, it has to be about the characters. About where they are at the beginning and the new place they are at the end. It's particularly vulnerable to be skin to skin, to let another into your body, to put your favorite part inside someone else. But even if sex is old hat to the characters, why is this scene so important that you're detailing it for the reader? What happens here? What are they afraid of? Why him? The scariest thing about love is that it really is worth the risks. Bring your characters and readers to that edge where everything changes and you'll have them hooked. **Author of** *Regularly Scheduled Life, Collision Course,* **etc.**

Don't be afraid to experiment.

Don't be afraid to have fun with these scenes. If your characters have a sense of humor or a playful streak, let that side of them show in the bedroom.

The important thing to remember in M/M fiction is that the sex is not simply about sex. It's about *love.*

Kink 101 by Kari Gregg

Kiren, TwoLips Reviews: I love angst and I enjoy BDSM—I can't think of anything hotter than two strong men in a relationship involving trust, control, and bondage. Since I'm not a gay male, I don't claim to understand the dynamics of bottoms and tops but love the switch because, as a reader, the sex scenes become more creative and unpredictable.

After *50 Shades of Grey*'s popularity exploded, the demand for kinky stories skyrocketed in romance genre fiction. Readers want more. Publishers want more, too. Writers who have no knowledge base or experience with kink decided to give it a shot, some quite disastrously, but that doesn't need to be you. BDSM (Bondage and discipline, Dominance and submission, Sadism, Masochism), be it straightforward BDSM or kink fantasy, can be incredibly fun to write as well as lucrative. But where to start?

If you don't know about or have experience with BDSM, learn.

Fortunately, there is a wealth of information on the Internet. Although familiarizing yourself with the market by reading BDSM novels is a good idea, don't rely on other authors for research. Copying what you've seen in other writers' works risks repeating their mistakes, which adds to misinformation and truly bad stories. Don't guess about BDSM practices, jargon, and appeal. Know. Talk to people. Visit a dungeon or an adult store near you, if possible. Ask questions. Cruise amateur video websites to see BDSM play, or scenes, in action. You don't need to be flogged to write about it, but you should understand how a flogger is used, what it looks like, and find out how flogging feels on both a physical and emotional level.

Always keep the central tenet of BDSM in mind—SSC, Safe, Sane, and Consensual.

Preparing for responsible play means discussing and agreeing on what will take place. Dangers are assessed as well as precautions to mitigate those risks. BDSM heroes know what safe words are and use safe words properly: to halt a scene that, for whatever reason, is going wrong.

If, after picking a guy up at a bar, your hero allows that complete stranger to handcuff him and dangle him from the rafters to be whipped, he isn't being safe. Or especially sane, in my opinion. He's taking extremely dangerous chances and, frankly, that character doesn't seem especially bright to me. You aren't doing your hero or your story any favors. Is it safe or sane for someone who has never used a single-tail to have his first try on you? Or should that person practice to develop knowledge and skill with a single-tail before playing with a partner? Safe isn't just a matter of knowing and preparing for the dangers of a particular toy or gaining the expertise to wield it well. In your novels, safety should also include common sense coupled with a dose of caution as well as a healthy instinct for self-preservation. If you wouldn't leave a bar with a complete stranger to allow that stranger to handcuff you—and I hope you're too smart for that—your hero wouldn't gamble his life and safety doing it, either. Whether in fiction or in real life, BDSM is a trust relationship. Do not mock that trust by rushing it and showing your character doing spectacularly stupid things.

Don't hyper-focus on toys and props.

Yes, toys are important. Paddles, floggers, rope, slings, sounds, and cuffs for both ankles and wrists are only a few, and readers will expect to see toys in your stories. Many household items can be repurposed for play, too. You should know what the toy looks like and how it is used in a BDSM context. Some require more precision and skill than others, and you should research special precautions that should be taken. Your book shouldn't be a catalog of kinky products, however. Toys can take over your story and overshadow your characters' journeys. Limit toys and attention on them. The physical and emotional responses stirred in both the person wielding a toy and the person it is used on is a great deal more significant. Concentrate on the emotional development of your heroes.

Understanding the emotional journey is key.

The Dom, or Top, is the one in control of the scene. The sub, or bottom, is the one who is tied, spanked, whipped, submits to, and serves the Dom, etc., but the sub should never, ever be presumed to be weak. Nothing could be farther from the truth. Submission is a deliberate choice, not a weakness or character fault. Subs are every bit as strong as Doms. In many ways, I would argue subs are more so. Surrendering control to someone else, even those we love and trust, takes a yard of guts. Doms carefully monitor subs to assess how subs are responding to play and ask how they are doing. A

Dom pays close attention to cues from the sub for safety purposes, but also to enrich their mutual satisfaction. Doms take pleasure in being in control. Subs enjoy giving up that control, but through an attentive Dom's scrutiny, the sub is actually the one driving a scene. The sub's responses are what guide the Dom's actions.

Though BDSM can certainly be arousing, play isn't about sex. Doms and subs may never become sexually involved, just as some never do S/M. BDSM is about power, not sex. Of course, we are writing romance, so our heroes should become aroused during a scene, even when pain is involved. When we are hurt, our body releases endorphins that can deliver a natural high. Subs enter into a pleasurable frame of mind called subspace, which feels like floating or flying. Sex during or after a scene can certainly enhance those feelings, but sex isn't necessary for fostering subspace.

BDSM scenes should end in aftercare, which eases the transition from that intense emotional and physical experience. Aftercare acknowledges the end of play. Doms should be supportive, reassuring, and comforting to subs. They should check and tend to any soreness, which could include first aid and rehydrating the sub. A Dom may talk about what happened with his sub, offering his praise and gratitude, or vice versa. Both heroes can also be very affectionate, their intimacy growing from what has just taken place between them. Some Doms even call subs days later to check on them. Aftercare is vital in revealing how the relationship has evolved. Has their trust grown stronger? Show that. After an intense scene, readers may like experiencing this soothing aftercare, too. Remember above all else that this is a romance. Focus on the emotions.

With the basics now covered, what are some of the common pitfalls to avoid?

Doms are often written as socially powerful and wealthy men, who know everything and never make any significant mistakes.

They are like you and me, though. Some have careers that put them in the top income brackets and at the height of the social ladder, but many don't. They work middle class or blue collar jobs, with mortgages to pay. Doms don't spring from the womb knowing exactly what to do in every circumstance like an eternally wise Yoda of Kink, either. Doms and subs both must grow to deliver a rich, fulfilling story. Doms can misread subs' needs and limits. As their bond deepens, a Dom better understands his sub and becomes more adept at assessing physical and emotional cues, too. Don't be afraid to show that character arc.

Unfortunately, subs are sometimes presented as inferior.

Subs in these stories have jobs as unskilled labor, if they have a job at all. They're portrayed as emotionally needy, clingy, and weak, as though they require someone to tell them what to do because they are incapable of making decisions—or worse, because they consistently make the wrong ones. Subs are people like you and me, too, though. They have jobs that don't demand a visor or a nametag and they don't need every aspect of their lives micromanaged. Some choose a full-time D/s relationship and decide to give submission on a 24/7 basis, but that isn't based on need, weakness, or any failure in the sub. That is founded on choice and pleasure. Please show respect for subs by creating characters who are functional and capable men.

Know the difference between kink fantasy and BDSM.

Kink fantasy breaks the rules of SSC, usually in the realm of consent. Slave fiction, also known as noncon (nonconsensual or rape fantasy), falls under this umbrella, as does my personal favorite—dubcon, or dubious consent. Who remembers the old bodice ripper romances? In M/M, those stories are called breeches rippers. Hero1 wants his Hero2, but for whatever reason, Hero2 resists. He is courted and seduced—rather forcefully. An example of dubious consent could involve a character in the grips of changing from human to vampire (or shifter), with hormones ping ponging so badly he may be unable to give his clear and genuine consent. Leaving the answer to that question in the hands of each individual reader can be very sexy, and it's a theme to which I'm continually drawn.

If kink fantasy sounds right up your alley, be aware of which rules you are breaking. Calling your book kink fantasy instead of BDSM is no excuse for shoddy research. Kink fantasy writers are obligated to act as their own advocate for appropriate labeling with publishers in order to ensure content warnings are appropriate and readers as well as reviewers are signaled that the book is kink fantasy with BDSM elements instead of straightforward BDSM. Honestly, even when your novel is properly labeled and tagged, some will complain about elements that remove it from a traditional BDSM category, anyway. No, there isn't anything you can do about it. Protesting a review based on your novel not showing clear consent, when your story is properly labeled as "dubious consent," won't win you points. Them's the breaks. Resolve yourself now to taking occasional whacks from the rare few who didn't pay attention to your content warnings and tags. Or simply don't write kink fantasy.

Writing kink can be extremely satisfying, be the book BDSM or kink fantasy. If BDSM intrigues you, give it a shot. Many fans and writers of this niche within a niche are friendly and happy to talk about what is so appealing about these stories. Don't be afraid to ask questions. Relax. Have fun. You may be surprised to discover how much you enjoy exploring kinky plots and characters, too.

IT'S DIFFERENT FOR GIRLS
SEX SCENE BEFORE AND AFTER

Laura Baumbach, Publisher MLR Press: Your Adrien books are a terrific example of a great story re-grabbing the reader's attention when you humanized it even more by letting them see the romance and intimacy of the core relationship in the series. It is a perfect example of the genre. You show it's not just sex, it's love. Two intelligent, successful, professional, could-be-your-coworker guys in love.

Probably the simplest way to demonstrate the difference a detailed and explicit sex scene can make to your story is to offer an example of "before and after."

The excerpt below is the original version of the first time Adrien English and Jake Riordan have sex. Readers waited until book two for this moment:

"So," he said casually. "You want to fuck?"

"Sure," I said.

But I was less sure when we walked into my bedroom and undressed. For one thing, I knew sex wasn't going to solve anything, but it might change things. For the worse.

Secondly, as I watched Jake unbuckle his belt in a businesslike fashion, I remembered that this was a guy who liked to do it with whips and chains—and strangers.

If we could have fallen to the kitchen floor, swept away on a tide of passion…but the lag time of walking to the bedroom, stripping, lying down on the bed…it gave time to think. To reflect.

To pause.

Jake knelt on the bed and slipped his condom on with a little snap like a detective donning latex gloves to examine a crime scene. Not a romantic noise.

I'd had enough to drink that I should have been incapable of rational thought, but for some damn reason, I was still thinking. I felt a little detached, a little distant as Jake bent over me.

The muscles on his arms stood out like ropes, his big hands denting the mattress on either side of me as he balanced himself. His cock looked like a warhead; I felt my eyes going wide. I had waited a long time for this moment though this wasn't exactly the moment I had waited for. Suddenly there seemed to be knees and elbows everywhere.

"Ouch," Jake said.

"Sorry."

He bent forward at the same moment I raised my head, and we banged noses.

"What the hell?" Jake's voice came out muffledly behind his hand.

"Sorry."

"You've done this before, right?"

I don't know why that hit me as funny, but I started to laugh, and Jake pushed back and said exasperatedly, "What the hell is so funny?"

I shook my head.

"You sure know how to break the mood." However he didn't appear to be giving up. His mouth found mine and he kissed me.

Whoopee ty yi yea!

Suddenly it was going to be okay. Better than okay.

I kissed Jake back, tasting the licorice-bite of the whisky on his tongue. He licked my mouth, which was different, sort of playful. My lips parted, anticipating, but he softly bit the side of my neck—and then a little harder. There was a lot of strength and heat in the body poised over mine. He smelled good, like my almond soap, and he tasted good, and he felt very good, his hand between my thighs doing things other men had done, but in his own way.

We realigned ourselves, the mattress squeaking noisily, and I raised my legs over Jake's shoulders. I wasn't expecting much in the way of foreplay, and I didn't get it. Jake pressed into me and I gritted my jaw as my muscles submitted.

"You with me?"

I grunted acknowledgment. Oh yeah, I was with him.

He began to rock against me, and I hung on for the ride of my life: a day at the rodeo and the Fourth of July all rolled into one. Yeeha!

A Dangerous Thing by Josh Lanyon (Gay Men's Press, 2002)

It's not bad, exactly. It's clear that they're having sex, who takes what role; there's a bit of humor and a little sensual detail. As far as it goes, it's all right—and I kept most of it for the rewrite.

Here's the revised version:

"So," he said casually. "You want to fuck?"

"Sure," I said.

But I was less sure when we walked into my bedroom and undressed. For one thing, I knew sex wasn't going to solve anything, but it might change things. For the worse.

As I watched Jake unbuckle his belt in a businesslike fashion, I remembered that this was a guy who liked to do it with whips and chains—and strangers.

If we could have fallen on the kitchen table, swept away on a tide of passion...but the lag time of walking to the bedroom, stripping, lying down on the bed...it gave time to think. To reflect. To pause.

To remember the last time I'd had sex with a guy I didn't know that well. Not exactly a joyride.

It was cold in the room. The light seemed too bright. I crawled onto the bed and wondered what the hell to do next. Had he ever done this without tying someone to the bed? Assuming he even did it in bed. My knowledge of the BDSM scene was sketchy at best—which was kind of the way I wanted to keep it. Jake knelt on the mattress and slipped his condom on with a snap like a detective donning latex gloves to examine a crime scene. Not a romantic noise.

"Have you got lube?" he asked.

"Uh…no. I wasn't planning…"

He glanced up and smiled. The smile disarmed me. He looked a little self-conscious. There was a flush across his cheekbones and his eyes were very bright.

I smiled back, and he leaned forward and kissed me. The kiss reassured. His mouth was warm and already tasted familiar.

"I like kissing you," he said softly. "I didn't think I would. But I do."

"Good," I said. "I like kissing you too."

We kissed again. I tasted the licorice-bite of the whisky on his tongue.

He kissed harder and said against my mouth, "I want to fuck you so bad."

I nodded.

"Lie back."

I stretched out. I wasn't exactly sexually active these days, but I wasn't a virgin either. I knew what to expect, and whatever Jake's range of experience, I figured it would be okay. Probably not great for him, without all his little toys and costumes, and maybe not great for me either since he probably was not much into giving pleasure that didn't involve the release of some serious endorphins. I'd do my best to make sure he enjoyed himself; I wanted him to see that it could be good without the improper use of kitchen utensils.

He touched my face. "Okay?"

"Yeah. Of course." Maybe a little puzzled that he seemed unsure about it.

I ran a light hand over the hard planes of his chest. Flicked one flat brown nipple with my thumbnail. He swallowed hard, and I smiled. Teased the other nipple into a hard point.

He sucked in a breath, let it out slowly.

I'd had enough to drink that I should have been incapable of rational thought, but for some damn reason, the wheels were still turning. Way too fast. Spinning, in fact. I felt detached, a little distant as he bent over me, big hands denting the mattress, the muscles on his arms standing out like ropes. His cock looked like a warhead.

I remembered the last time—and flinched at the sudden stark vision of all that strength and frustration slamming into me. I stared up into his hard face. He was watching me closely. My stomach knotted with anxiety.

But that other time hadn't been Jake. That didn't have anything to do with…us. I wanted Jake. I did want him. And if I let myself think about that other time, I was giving the memory power. And I'd been waiting for this moment for way too long.

He said, "What if I—"

"Maybe if I —"

Suddenly there seemed to be knees and elbows everywhere.

"Ouch," Jake said.

"Sorry."

He bent forward at the same moment I raised my head, and we banged noses.

"What the hell?" His voice came out muffled behind his hand.

"Sorry."

"You've done this before, right?"

I don't know why that hit me as funny, but I started to laugh, and Jake pushed back and said exasperatedly, "What the hell is so funny?"

I shook my head.

"You sure know how to break the mood." However he didn't appear to be giving up. His mouth found mine and he kissed me again, insistently. I felt myself quieting, giving into the unexpected tenderness.

He drew back, licked my mouth, which was different, sort of playful. My lips parted, anticipating, but he softly bit the side of my neck—then harder.

I bit back a yelp.

"Going to behave?" His eyes were amused.

I said in my best hypnotic-subject voice, "Yeees…Maaaster."

He nuzzled the bite mark, and I shivered.

There was a lot of strength and heat in the body poised over mine. He smelled good, like my almond soap, and he tasted good, and he felt very good, his hand slowly stroking my belly. I said huskily, "I'm having trouble believing this is you."

He reached across to the nightstand with his free hand and picked up my sunscreen. "Nah," he said. "You knew this was going to happen. Like I did. You called it right. I came after you. Every step of the way."

He squirted a glop of sunscreen on his fingers and warmed it. I bent my knees, opening wide for him. Focused on relaxing my muscles. Jake's fingers slipped along my crack, slick and silky. I'd wondered what those long sensitive fingers would feel like and now one of them was pressing against my hole.

I bit my lip, trying to keep it quiet, trying not to scare him away. He pushed in. Just a fingertip. "You're so tight," he murmured. He pulled out. Dipped in, dipped out. Pushed further in. That friction felt so good. I moaned. I couldn't help it.

"Yeah," he said with slow satisfaction. "You need it bad. Worse than I do."

I gasped, "Is it a competition? What do I win?"

"Shhh. Turn off for a few seconds, Adrien."

"A few seconds? Is that all it's—" I caught my breath as his finger moved knowledgeably, unerringly.

"There's the off button," he murmured.

I pushed back hard on his hand. Not like I'd never felt this before, and yet somehow I'd never felt it quite so intensely. It was like he was reaching right into me, stretching me open, finding every little secret place, stroking, smoothing, soothing the naked underbelly of need. I wanted to talk myself away from feeling too much, too keenly, but all that came out was a something unnervingly like a whimper.

So much for my theory on his lack of expertise. It was going to be okay. I was going to be more than okay.

"Baby, that little sound you made…" He stroked with two fingers. "What about this? Is this good too?"

Where had I got the idea he might not be experienced at this?

He was in total control, perfectly gauging my responses and expertly bringing me to the edge with each electric—and deliberate—stroke across the gland.

No way was that beginner's luck.

The pressure built unbearably. My eyes flew open. "I-I think I'm going to come."

"You think?" His eyes were crinkled at the corner, like he was laughing inside.

"But..." *It's way too soon.* I let the half-formed protest go. Too hard to form thoughts, let alone words. I strained against his hand, aching for more, trying to capture that maddening touch, draw it deeper into my body, ease that screaming tension.

"Yeah, that's right. I've got you. Just let go..."

The wildness welled up inside me and began to pump hard, spilling through my body, sizzling along nerve endings, shooting out in creamy plumes. A half-sob of relief tore out of my throat.

"Whoa," Jake murmured eons later. He traced some design in the sticky wet splash on my abdomen. I opened my eyes, blinked at him. He was smiling, looking as relaxed as I felt.

I managed a grin. He leaned over me, kissed me again, said quietly, "Yeah, I like that."

I ran a hand over the top of his head, feeling the crisp texture of his cropped hair. It was the first time in our friendship I felt free to look my fill: the hard line of his cheek and jaw at odds with the sensual fullness of his mouth, the knowing gleam of his hazel eyes. My breathing had slowed back down, my heart raced happily along like the start of summer vacation. "You'll like the next bit even more."

He was still smiling. "There's no rush."

"Speak for yourself," I said. I was tired, but it was a good tired. Loose and light. I sat up, but he pushed me back gently.

"On your back. I want to watch your face." He met my eyes. "And you'll like the...stimulation."

We realigned ourselves, the mattress squeaking noisily, and I raised my legs over Jake's shoulders, leaving myself exposed and vulnerable, but I wasn't worried now. His warm hands slid over my ass, spreading me wider. His cock rested against my wet, slick hole. Holding my gaze, he pushed in. "Christ, that's sweet."

I gritted my jaw, forced my muscles to submit.

He paused. Even stretched and prepped, my body needed a chance to adjust; he was a big man.

"Say my name," he urged.

"Jake," I said huskily.

Something lit in his eyes. He shoved the rest of the way in. I gasped, sphincter muscle spasming around his stiffness.

"Christ, you feel good. Like a glove." He thrust against me, just once like he couldn't help himself.

I panted, writhed a little, still trying to accommodate him. Making room for him in my head and in my body.

His hands covered my chest, tugging the nipples. I've never particularly got off on having my breast touched, but this felt weirdly good. I rubbed against his palm. He lowered himself, kissed me, hotly, hungrily, pushing his tongue in. I moaned into his mouth, wanting more, needing more.

His mouth ground down on mine, his fingers pinched my nipples. So much sensation distracting me from the massive cock crammed in my ass.

"What are you feeling?" Jake's breath was warm against my face, my bruised lips tingled. "Tell me what it feels like with me inside you." His hips thrust against me again.

What did it feel like? My legs felt weak and trembly, my belly soft and liquid; my channel felt scraped and burned with satisfying friction. It felt like invasion—the invasion that comes with a liberating army. I felt my face quiver with that mix of pain and pleasure, lifted my lashes. He was staring into my eyes.

Something snapped inside me, relented, freed itself. I began to move, contracting my muscles around him, trying to arch up against him. My fierce response triggered him. He made some exclamation, began to move, hips pounding against my ass, impaling me with each thrust. The relief was that I could be rough back; I could let go and take what I needed too.

The mattress springs squeaked, the wooden frame creaked. Jake's hands closed on my hips. He redirected his efforts, thrust harder, deeper, and hit the spot that sent exquisite sensation crackling through me. I cried out. Jake was grunting fiercely in time to the bang of the headboard against the wall. I gripped hard and felt him stiffen.

"Oh, baby," he groaned. His body went rigid, his face twisting in distressed delight. I felt him come hard, hot seed shooting into me.

Startled, I realized that I was coming too. Twice in one evening. It had been a long time since that happened.

"Adrien…" His voice shook. His arms slid under me, gathering me against him. I wrapped my arms around him, and we rocked together while our bodies played out, cocooned in warm and sticky closeness.

A Dangerous Thing by Josh Lanyon (JustJoshin Publishing, 2012)

The obvious difference, besides about 1500 words, is the fact that the reedited scene is rich in sensual details and emotional subtext. We're getting a lot more backstory, a lot more of Adrien's thoughts and Jake's reactions. There is no change as far as plot or theme go, but the revised scene makes a world of difference to our understanding of the characters—in particular the difficult and complex character of Jake.

Even I have to admit that the revised scene was more satisfying to write.

IT'S A MAN'S, MAN'S, MAN'S WORLD
SETTING

One element frequently glossed over or ignored in M/M fiction is setting. Setting—where and when your stories take place—is one of those subtle components that can take a story from good to great.

Setting includes everything from the country where you've staged your story, to the sofa your characters tumble off the first time they make love. Setting is the weather, the time of day, the temperature, the wallpaper, the terrain. It's important for a lot of reasons, not least because setting directly determines the mood and atmosphere of your story.

To be effective, setting has to *feel* realistic, regardless of whether the story takes place in a Denny's on Topanga Canyon Blvd., a goth club in New York, or an ice cavern on some distant planet in the year 3001.

And the way you achieve realism is by tapping into the five senses—which is simply another way of writing what you know.

No, you've never been on an ice cavern on a distant planet (and thank God for that because sure as hell, no matter how carefully you researched it you'd have some reader from outer space contacting you to tell you the cavern was torn down in '66 to make way for a Bank of America), but chances are you *have* been in a cave or in the snow. And you can use what you know about the way caves smell and the way snow feels for your alien setting.

Too often setting consists of a catalog of meaningless detail. The moon was shining brightly, the lawn was a manicured square of green, the room was large and sunny with flowered wallpaper, the wind was gusting leaves, blah, blah, blah.

Not that there's anything wrong with all that, but your descriptions have to be more than a recitation of the facts as you see them. And that's the key thing right there. Most setting revolves around visual cues of what the author is allowing the POV character to *see*.

There's nothing wrong with that. Humans—male humans in particular—are visual creatures.

But don't describe everything, and limit what you do describe to a few *telling* details.

> Sitting on the tree-shaded patio of the Coral Beach Cantina, I ordered a micro brew and nachos. The jukebox was playing "Boys of Summer" by Don Henley, and I was counting the disproportionate number of blonds, both male and female, filling the seats around me, when Steve dropped into the chair across the table.
>
> *The Dark Horse* by Josh Lanyon (JustJoshin Publishing, 2012)

Stay in character as you describe the scene. What would your character be most likely to notice? *The description you give us is actually your POV character's commentary on the scene.* So what would be important or significant to the character?

Use all five senses to describe your scenes—but (as always) think quality not quantity. Stick with the essentials. Readers don't need to know what the POV characters sees, smells, hears, tastes, and touches in every scene. Decide what's most important for a particular scene, and give us that. For contemporary fiction, usually a sentence or two will be sufficient.

Setting grounds your stories—quite literally. A vivid, well-drawn setting pulls your reader right into the moment with your characters.

The night smelled of rain and lemon and wood smoke as we made our way back across the arched bridge. The moon's red reflection in the still water of the lake was absurdly magnified, the tall reeds appeared gilded, the face in the clock tower shining benignly.

The Dickens with Love by Josh Lanyon (Samhain Publishing, 2010)

Below we get exposition without sensory detail, but the choices of what we see through Nathan Doyle's point of view put us in historical context—and I think contribute to the mood of the story as well as establishing setting.

He expected to be followed, and although he could see no sign of a tail, he took it for granted that he was shadowed. It didn't present an immediate problem. Stopping for breakfast at a diner, he treated himself to eggs and bacon, not because he was hungry but because he knew he had to keep his energy up. He paid with cash and his red stamp coupons—practically the first he'd used since getting back—and then had a cup of real coffee, watching through the Christmas-painted windows as a phalanx of P-38 Lightnings headed out toward the ocean.

Snowball in Hell by Josh Lanyon (Carina Press, 2011)

If you're a control freak like me, it's tempting to describe everything down to the knobs on the kitchen cupboards and the hooks on the bathroom door. Resist. Readers actually enjoy filling in some of the blanks. That's part of the pleasure of reading, being allowed to use one's own imagination.

Give the reader enough precise detail to put her in the moment—then let her do the rest.

It helps to visualize the scene. Not just the real estate, but the mapping out of your characters movements within the framework of the scene.

Ask yourself some basic questions:

Where exactly does this scene take place?
Where are the characters standing in relation to each other?
When and why do the characters move? (Take note of body language.)
Is anything happening in the background?

Keep track of the stage props. If your character picks up a glass or pulls a gun, keep track of what he does with it. In the scene below there are two props. A cigarette and chocolates.

> Bat slept in the château that night. He fully expected Cowboy to come to him—and braced himself to repel all boarders—and Cowboy did come, but he sat on the foot of Bat's bed and shared the contents of a package from home, apparently content to smoke and chat and divvy up small, silver-wrapped chocolates. The red tip of Cowboy's cigarette wagged in the darkness as he said, "Henderson says the prevailing theory is some French pilot might have killed Orton."
> "Henderson?" Bat asked around the bite of milk chocolate.
> "One of the mechanics assigned to my bus." Cowboy studied Bat through the veil of cigarette smoke. "Turns out Orton was something of a ladies' man."
> "You're joking."
> Cowboy shook his head. "Nope. Furthermore, it seems our Sidney was no respecter of the sacred vows of marriage."
> Bat unpeeled another chocolate thoughtfully.

> *Out of the Blue* by Josh Lanyon (JustJoshin Publishing, 2012)

You can also use setting to establish and affirm character. There's some truth to that old saying about a man's home being his castle. Just as the clothes your character wears should say something about him, so should his domicile.

> Jacob shut the door and looked around himself. I imagined his place was probably as spic and span as an operating room. I pictured something modern and utilitarian. Steel frames and glass tops.

My living space, on the other hand, was a clutter of books, clothes, papers. The computer sat on the dining room table, screensaver rolling an endless view of outer space. The stereo was on but silent. Trash bins overflowed, the sink was full of dishes, there were books everywhere. The dining room walls were paneled in bookshelves—which was ultimately going to cost me the cost of my deposit. There were books stacked on the floors, the counters, the tabletops, every conceivable flat surface including the top of the fridge.

Jacob's brows rose. All he said was, "I like it. Early Dewey Decimal, isn't it?"

Heart Trouble by Josh Lanyon (JustJoshin Publishing, 2012)

Remember, ideally we learn something about the POV character through what he chooses to notice—whether the POV is first person or third—and we learn something about the character who belongs to the place or setting being described. In the scene below, we're seeing the setting through the third-person POV of the romantic interest, Matt.

Doyle lived in an apartment in one of the old original Victorian houses on Olive Street.

Matt and Jonesy identified themselves, and the apartment manager led them upstairs into a chilly room with large bay windows overlooking what must have once been a lovely garden. There was an unmade pull-down bed and a table with a typewriter—a half-full bottle of Teacher's blended Scotch whisky beside it.

There were no pictures and no religious icons. There was a tall bookshelf, mostly empty except for a couple of Christmas cards, a parcel wrapped in reindeer paper, and several volumes on travel and history and archeology. There was a copy of the dialogs of Plato, and a couple of books about Thomas Aquinas.

You could tell a lot about a man by what he chose to read, in Matt's opinion. He liked a good western himself, but it was a long time since he'd read any.

There were more books stacked on the table, a couple of medical books, and books on psychology. A book lying next to the bed bore the title *The Homosexual Neurosis*.

Snowball in Hell by Josh Lanyon (Carina Press, 2011)

And so should the domicile of every other character tell us about that character. Whether your secondary and supporting cast lives on a horse ranch in the outback or a castle in Transylvania, let the scene and setting tell us about more than square footage and collectibles.

Laura Baumbach: If the story is well told, I'll read any plot again and again. That said, I do get tired of vampire themes where the vampires have this huge society set up like the mafia. I can't see that. Living and working among us in secret I can deal with, but a huge population of them all killing each other and taking humans over the world undetected, I can't believe in this day and age. If I can't believe the setup, I can't believe the story. Of course, I'm a vampire fan.
Author of *Mexican Heat*, *Out There in the Night*, etc.

Remember that your setting takes place within a larger setting or context—a world.

Chances are, unless you really are writing what you know and only what you know, you're going to have to do a certain amount of research. Maybe your story takes place within the world of horseracing or organized crime or the occult. Unless you're a jockey or a mob boss or a witch, you're likely going to need to do a bit of research.

The fact is, if you can get the little things right, the reader will be a lot more likely to swallow the big things—like a love story between the son of a Yakuza mob boss and the boss's first lieutenant, or an underground vampire subculture, or a ghostly romance.

Chris Owen: The amount of research I do is directly related to how important a role the subject plays in the story—which is a very confusing way of saying "not much and almost entirely online". I did do a great deal of research with Jodi Payne for the Deviations series. I read a lot, I asked questions of people I met who were in the scene, and I spent hours with Jodi online following links and sharing information. BDSM and D/s were something that we clearly had to know a lot about for our story to work at all.

However, I know nothing about ranches, I have never ridden a horse without being led, and the cows I've met have all been dairy cows and not beef cattle. If I don't know something, I ask people who do know these things, and I'm lucky enough to know people who understand the way a ranch works. It really helps to have people who are not scared to point out mistakes read over my work—and it really helps to go looking for that kind of a beta reader.

Also, I've never been on a spaceship of any kind. Yet.
Author of *Bareback, An Agreement Among Gentlemen*, **etc.**

By their very nature, certain genre stories require more research than others. A contemporary crime story may require you to learn something about forensics, police procedure and…maybe archeology, or Broadway theater, or wine fraud, whereas historical fiction is going to require study on everything from period costume to the slang of the era. The research involved in historicals is extensive and intensive. Odds are good that you won't get through a single page without having to double-check some fact. Don't kid yourself that because you're writing sexy romance novels you don't have to get it right. You do.

The novella *Snowball in Hell* is set in 1943 Los Angeles. The story takes place during World War II. One of my protags is a newspaper reporter just back from the European Theater; the other is a LAPD detective. While I was able to do a little Internet research on the war and Los Angeles in the '40s, I needed to get more in-depth info on attitudes and treatment of gays, as well as police procedure and Los Angeles back then. I ordered a couple of books actually published in the '40s from the Advanced Book Exchange (www.abebooks.com/) including *Turn Off the Sunshine* by Timothy G. Turner, *The Homosexual Neurosis* by Dr. William Stekel, *Going Places In and Near Los Angeles* by Margaret Gilbert Mackey, and *Homicide Investigation* by LeMoyne Snyder. I referred to *Gay L.A.* by Lillian Faderman and Stuart Timmons. I read a bunch of pulp fiction from the 1940s including Raymond Chandler and Dashiell Hammett, and I watched many hours of film noir. I bought several old copies of *Esquire* from the 1940s.

Having spent time and money researching this period, I knew I would almost certainly set other stories within the same world. To my unexpected pleasure, by the time I finished the novella I knew I wanted to do many more stories with these particular characters.

For contemporary settings there are lots of good resources including travel brochures, magazines (old and new), and catalogs. Films and documentaries can be useful.

Fantasy, science fiction, and paranormal stories require world-building, and world-building requires hitting the books and pounding the cyber streets. Studying other cultures and histories is going to provide a prime resource for these kinds of stories.

What Kind Of Research Do You Do For The Setting Or Location For Your Stories?

Harper Fox: I'll go there if I can. Having said that, I won't let distance put me off. I've lived in Newcastle upon Tyne all my life and never once visited the Roman Campagna, but I found I was able to draw as detailed a background for my Italy-set story All Roads Lead To You as I was for my chilly English Half Moon Chambers. Location is a wonderful tool for me. I'm in the habit of peopling every environment I visit with future protagonists, and when I'm running short on inspiration, a new beach, a strange city, a day in the misty Lake District will usually set me off. It's a kind of lifelong reflex to interiorise my external world by writing stories about it, and I'm very grateful that the impulse persists and is as strong as ever, even thirteen books into my writing career. So a lot of my research is sensory, instinctive reactions to places—colours, lights, scents. And a lot of it is brass-tacks basics! I've never sailed in my life, for example, but I wanted Mitch and Owen to have a convincingly scary time during the storm scene of In Search of Saints, and so I spent long hours reading about rudders and tillers and rigid-inflatable boats. Another great trick is to find passionate, dedicated bloggers on any given subject I want to write about. For Kestrel's Chance, I tracked down a truly impassioned solo mountain climber who detailed online all the joys and terrors of his days on the slopes, got in touch

with him, and asked if he minded being my inspiration and jargon-buster. He was very happy to help, though he asked me not to give his name when I told him my genre! Anyway, for me, the upshot is a balance of emotional and technical attention to detail, and a determination to get location right, to deliver authenticity and respect for the locations and actions I'm describing.
Author of *Life After Joe, Scrap Metal,* **etc.**

The wind had dropped. The morning was clear, a peach-gold sunrise painting the flanks of Wester Fleet. The traverse between Red Peak and White, nothing but a thin snake of basalt under snow, didn't allow for conversation. The climbers picked their way across in taut-nerved silence, rescue-leader Kestrel Shaw on point.

Kestrel's Chance, Harper Fox (FoxTales, 2013)

Sarah Black: I do quite a bit, mostly to get me in the mood for the story, and so when I'm ready to start writing, I don't have to stop and look things up. I usually spend about a week reading and researching the setting. I have an idea to start what the setting will be, including place, the year, the season—I'm thinking about a story set in Vietnam right now, and I'm looking at maps on the Internet, photos, so I know what it looks like, and am reading several memoirs by people who served in Vietnam during 1968, the year the story will be set. I've found memoirs to be the best research, especially by non-writers, some of whom are so crystal clear and honest about how things felt. The Internet has such wonderful resources in all media. When I was writing the murder mystery called Death of a Blues Angel, I listened to blues music on YouTube, watched the musicians play, and then checked out more of their music from the library. I really have a thing for food, too, and I rarely write anything that doesn't have food in it—so I will cook whatever the characters are cooking or eating, so the house smells the same. I've been eating mole all week, because I was playing with mole recipes for a story. For me, the music and the food go a long way to putting me in the setting, so when

I start writing, I'm already there, with the characters. I think the sensory details really make the setting come alive—weather, smells, colors, music, but I use them to put myself in the setting, so the writing really flows—it's like hearing a character's voice, when you get the setting that way.

I also like it when the setting suggests conflict. A story set in Mississippi in 1966 is a setting that will suggest racial conflict, rural poverty, and…the blues! A story set in Vietnam in 1968—the Tet offensive, POWs—our pilots in prison in Hanoi, being tortured, Robert Kennedy and Martin Luther King, war protests, Chicago and Kent State, moon landing, and the music—Buffalo Springfield, The Stones, the Animals, Janis Joplin, Blood Sweat and Tears. This setting is so rich with conflict I'm going to have a hard time figuring out which ones to use!

Author of *Fearless, Border Roads*, **etc.**

> He should never have come back here. Clayton had walked out-side his mother's tiny, two-bedroom house, the cinder blocks the same yellow-tan as the sand, stared at the trash blowing down the empty street. Dust swirled in the hot air, coating everything with a yellow haze. The houses had been built by the BIA back in the sixties, concrete block houses built close together so they could share utilities. When the old aluminum-clad windows fell out, they were replaced with plywood or plastic or miscella-neous pieces of window glass shimmed up to fit. The roofs were dotted with tires. The tires helped hold the shingles on when the wind was strong.

Border Roads by Sarah Black (Loose Id, 2007)

What Elements Do You Consider Essential For Setting Up A Scene?

Sarah Black: For me, I need to know the mood and feel of a scene first, because that will dictate the language. If the scene is going to be sorrowful, for example, or something is going to go badly wrong, I can use language to put some of that mood across, even before the action or dialogue that suggests something going wrong. And going into the scene you need to know the conflict that is going to be worked on—not to forget, when the conflict is over, the story is over. So when the scene ends, you need to have the conflict pointing to the next scene.

Author of *Fearless, Border Roads*, **etc.**

He leaned in the doorway to the dining room, drying his hands on the linen towel tucked in the waistband of his cords. Jacob was sitting in the corner, his cello between his knees, bare feet, and he was playing with his head bent over the instrument. His lashes were dark against his cheeks. Peter felt his heart do a slow stumble in his chest, at the beauty of the morning, the beauty of the music, happiness moving like a gentle wind through his hotel.

Murder at the Heartbreak Hotel by Sarah Black (MLR Press, 2007)

Harper Fox: Interesting question! I've never really tried to analyse this one before. I tend to just head to where I'm going, but even that's part of an answer, I guess—to decide where this scene falls within the arc of a story, what its function is, how far it advances the plot or contributes to character development. So I need to know those abstract things, and I also need my "reality", my own belief in the background, the place, weather, time of day. I might not describe all those things for each scene—in fact it would be fairly painful if I did—but I need to know and feel them myself. And I need to get inside the skin of my protagonists and know what's going on in there, so I can turn their experience outward into my writing. So I need a "goal" for the scene, a three-dimensional stage, and strong empathy for my players. If I've got those essentials, I often find the scene will gallop off on its own quite happily, and having that framework in place allows me a lot of spontaneity with details and dialogue.

Author of *Life After Joe, Scrap Metal*, **etc.**

The northern lights were shimmering like windblown curtains over the MRT base. For once Rory didn't spare them a glance. He was aware of them as a kind of silent music, a symphony his mind was tuning out in favour of immediate concerns. The car park was just as he had left it. The same vehicles watched him from blank, frosted headlights, including the Rover with the tarped-up back seat. The squat cement-poured block that housed the control and operations room, gym and shabby little pub—just the same, sharply reminding him that inner worlds could fall apart without making the smallest impact on sky, stars or stone.

Kestrel's Chance, Harper Fox (FoxTales, 2013)

How Much Sensory Detail—And Of What Kind—Do You Think Necessary For Creating Believable Settings/Locations? Do Some Scenes Require More Detail Than Others?

Harper Fox: Well, you can set up store like Dickens and tell it from the outside, a wondrous description of smoky, foggy London and crowded streets before you even get to the protags and the plot, but as an M/M writer I find I need to jump in a bit more directly, intertwining scene-sets with character building. (Not that Dickens doesn't do that too, and sublimely.) That's where sensory detail comes in as such a beautifully useful tool. I love to describe freezing city streets, but it's so much more fun to get inside the head of a wealthy, impressionable young man like Laurie in A Midwinter Prince and have his skin stinging in the bitter air, the contrasts between that and the oppressive warmth of the waiting family limo, and suck it all in through his eyes and ears. Or to have that old roué of a cop, James McBride in Nine Lights Over Edinburgh, stumbling off about illicit business through the wynds, his feet slipping on the ice, his nose twitching with the smells from the pubs and the restaurants. If you can hit a balance of not laying it on too thick, of having your protag observe and experience as you would, you can introduce whole worlds quite unobtrusively, bring your readers to join you on the

street before they know what's happening to them! To answer the second part of the question, yes—these initial scenes where I'm world-building through the sensory experiences of a protag—they do require considerable detail, carefully balanced against action. But I tend to run a fair amount of sensory reaction through the whole of a story as a good way of keeping the environment real, my characters strongly attached to it, ramping up the detail—of course—for sex scenes, physical fights, injury, any point of the story when the body and its responses are the main focus.
Author of *Life After Joe, Scrap Metal*, etc.

> The cabin was a glorified shed, one big room with a bed at one end and a sink and calor-gas hob at the other. Condensation was running down the walls. A smell of damp timber pervaded everything. Depression hit me like a bag of wet sand, and I dropped the cases I was holding and sat down on a rickety chair. Owen looked me over, but offered no comment. I put my face into my hands. I heard soft thuds and the rip of velcro straps, and a towel dropped onto my head. For a second I thought he'd dry me off—he'd rendered me more intimate services than that, the night I'd tried to drown my sorrows in Jim Beam—but he left me alone, and I did it myself, listening without much interest to the back-and-forth creak of his tread on the boards.

Saints and Sinners, Harper Fox (FoxTails, 2012)

Sarah Black: The scenes that have a lot of fast-paced action or brilliant dialogue may not need as much sensory detail, but I love feeling in the story, feeling like I'm right there, so I tend to use a lot—smells and music, especially, feel, but vision, not so much—I'm trying to do more of this. I think character's voice is critical, and setting also has a voice that you can't break. If your landscape, for instance, is threatening and dangerous and slightly sinister, it needs to retain a bit of that even when the sun is shining and your character is thinking everything is okay.
Author of *Fearless, Border Roads*, etc.

JOSH LANYON

What Are Your Thoughts On Creating Mood Or Atmosphere Within A Story? How Necessary Is Mood Or Atmosphere In Your Opinion?

Sarah Black: I like mood, because we can really play around with the language, use our best word play. My primary interest is character, to tell you the truth, and I just think of the setting as another character, but mood is fun. I depend on weather too much for mood, though. Probably like everything, the fresher images and the more carefully thought-out ideas will have the strongest impact. A strong contrast between the character's mood and the weather, for example, makes each stand out more strongly. It would be more interesting to have a sad character looking out to brilliant sunshine and laughing children, rather than having a character who is feeling sad staring out at a rain-streaked window and a gray sky.
Author of *Fearless, Border Roads*, **etc.**

Harper Fox: I find I can't work without it. I'm now thinking of my favourite joke—why can't you have a bar on the Moon? No atmosphere! Awful, but it does illustrate a point. When I say "atmosphere", I'm not necessarily thinking about windswept coasts or moors wreathed in mist.   And by "mood", not necessarily a desolate young hero gazing upon his lover's grave. I'm thinking about the atmospheres and moods that pervade all our daily lives. I need to know, when I'm setting about a story, how it feels to be in Vince's police-headquarters building in Half Moon Chambers—the neon lights, the carpet tiles, the desks, the potted plants. These are ordinary things, but I want to process and evolve them through the eyes of an extraordinary man, or a unique one at any rate, and so these prosaic details of atmosphere also become unique. Having said all that, I do love a lonely young windswept hero gazing at the mist-wreathed grave of his… Well. You get my drift. You can have grand set-piece scenes and they're wonderful, but you also need a lively grasp of how it feels to be a unique, ordinary soul in an ordinary, unique world, and the ability to convey all that to a reader.
Author of *Life After Joe, Scrap Metal*, **etc.**

Any Thoughts About Creating A Masculine Environment?

Sarah Black: Hmmm. I never considered a masculine environment, to tell you the truth, but I'm fairly nonconformist, so I don't know. I think what women should remember about men is that each character is individual and very different, but testosterone is a powerful hormone! I suspect some men have thoughts of punching other guys in the face on a fairly regular basis. I suspect all men crave attention. I suspect many men have the urge to protect people and take care of the people they are responsible for. But how gender specific are these qualities?

The thing is, though, writers are going to write about the kind of men who are interesting to them. Not saying they want to take them home and keep them, but I write about guys I would probably like, even when I feel exasperated with them, and who have some of my interests. I wouldn't write a character, for instance, who was deeply into fashion, or who cared a lot about shoes. I've known guys who were really into those things, but I just don't share their interests, so it would be hard for me to sustain an empathetic interest in the character. But I never thought of environments as being masculine or feminine.
Author of *Fearless, Border Roads*, **etc.**

Harper Fox: Masculine environments are sexy. Perhaps they oughtn't to be, and I do end up scratching my anti-war, pro-gun-control, pacifist's little head as I send poor Vince off into a blazing gun battle with a bunch of drug dealers, or settle down rubbing my palms with joy to create a damn good military helicopter. And I ask myself why certain types of environment—battlefields, barracks, dockyards fraught with crossfire—are quintessentially masculine, but the answers to that, even if I had them all, would take up a book in themselves. Rightly or wrongly, battlefields and hostile environments breed the kind of camaraderie that fuels a lot of my work. I love the idea of a guy being strong enough to tough it out in a gunfight and tender enough to fall in love with a fellow soldier. That contrast, right there, that reconciled conflict, is the essence of sexy M/M writing for me. But, fortunately, you can carry that tough/tender alchemy into domestic situations too. I can have my mafia chef Lauro in All Roads Lead to You tie on an apron and cook lunch for his skinny, hungry model boy Sam, and keep Lauro just as quietly fierce and dignified as any officer facing his duties, just as tender in his relenting to Sam's charms.

Slowly, as if hypnotised, Sam padded back through the living room. A short flight of steps led out of it on the far side. At the top of these, an arched doorway opened up into a bright, enormous kitchen. There was nothing stark or modern-deco here. Everything was perfect, up to date, but this was a workspace, a place that got used. Copper pots hung in burnished rows from beams across the ceiling. The central space was occupied by a massive table whose polished surface was scored and rubbed by generations of daily routine. A subtle scent was in the air—not quite garlic, not quite onions. It made Sam's nose prickle. His empty belly gave a sudden yowl.

Lauro turned round from the superb Aga range. He had put on a chef's apron and, unlike his visitor, was otherwise still fully dressed. He took Sam in, feet to scalp, one dark eyebrow on the rise. "What are you staring at?" he asked softly. "I watched you on your catwalk often enough. Now you can sit down and see what I do best." He adjusted a dial on the hob, pulled out a chair. "Besides, you look as if you haven't had a decent meal in months." A tiny smile touched one corner of his mouth. "Er—don't you think you should put that robe on?"

All Roads Lead to You by Harper Fox (FoxTales, 2012)

It's just a sexy equation no matter where or how often you set out to solve it—and apparently inexhaustible, which is great news for me as a writer!

Author of *Life After Joe, Scrap Metal*, **etc.**

BONUS GENRE WRITING SECTION

THIRTY-ONE FLAVORS

Writing genre-specific stories

While a lot of M/M fiction is strictly contemporary romance, more and more of it falls into specific subgenres: M/M mystery, M/M fantasy or science fiction or paranormal, M/M historical. As we discussed earlier, if you're writing an M/M genre novel, you have to meet the requirements of both the M/M romance and the genre fiction.

This bonus section includes essays and roundtable discussions on the three major subgenres—mystery, historical, and speculative fiction.

MYSTERY/SUSPENSE/THRILLER

Kiss, Kiss. Kill, Kill by Josh Lanyon

One of the hottest genres to come out of the ebook revolution is that of male-male fiction, and one of the noticeably bestselling subgenres of M/M fiction is that of the M/M mystery. "Mystery" is something of a misnomer since every conceivable subset of crime fiction including thriller, romantic-suspense, action-adventure, and mystery are all lumped under the same umbrella.

A common misconception is that a gay or male/male mystery is merely a mystery featuring a gay protagonist. Yes, the protagonist of a gay mystery must himself be gay. Drewey Wayne Gunn, author of the definitive *The Gay Male Sleuth in Print and Film*, writes, "A gay mystery must feature a gay protagonist: one who is out at least to himself, perhaps to his friends and others, and absolutely to readers."

It's helpful to remember that in early gay mystery, the protagonist was himself an outlaw—a sexual outlaw—and an outsider. To some extent, that outsider POV continues to this day. It's a distinctly different mindset than that of a mainstream sleuth.

Sexuality is never incidental in the gay mystery. The same exact story could not be told just as easily from the viewpoint of a heterosexual character. Through the course of solving the case at hand, the gay protagonist will explore and come to a greater understanding of his own sexuality—and thus his identity as a gay man. His investigation is as much one of self-actualization as it is crime-solving. Through his new understanding, his awakening, the gay protagonist comes to unlock the secrets of his own heart.

But perhaps romance is not so much a subplot in gay mystery as it is a theme. To paraphrase Gunn (because I agree with him), unlike his straight counterpart who often swings from promiscuity to celibacy, the romantic quest in a gay mystery novel is both more romantic (in the classic sense) and idealistic than we typically see in mainstream mystery. The gay sleuth is not merely seeking sex, but love and mutual commitment.

It's important to note here that this quest does not always end successfully. This is the crux of the difference between gay mystery and M/M mystery. All M/M fiction is romantic fiction, and there is a genre expectation for romantic fiction, which frequently involves a level of eroticism frowned on in mainstream and traditional gay mystery both. In M/M mystery, the romance plot will share equal page time with the mystery plot. In the gay mystery, the romantic quest is perhaps a theme, perhaps a subplot, but either way that quest may just as easily be ongoing—or even end badly.

The challenge with M/M mystery, as with the other main subgenres of M/M fiction, is how to balance the demands of romance with the demands of the mystery genre. Let's briefly consider the essential building blocks of the M/M mystery.

Characterization:

Think about how their work or hobbies mesh with developing the skills and personality traits that will allow your protagonists to believably survive their involvement in this particular and unique crime or mystery.

Note: Romantic relationships with cops or other law enforcement is a staple in mystery and crime fiction, but try and give your protagonist some useful skills and abilities in his own right.

Remember that if your protagonist will need some special knowledge or talent to solve the crime or save himself, you need to establish that talent or background early on. For example, if your character needs to speak Russian to decipher a mysterious message, at the very least hang a print by Karl Bryullov on the wall of his apartment.

Plot:

If it's true that a plot is a logical sequence of events (and it is), every action your character takes (or doesn't take) brings about a result which requires reaction which will bring about another result which will require reaction…and all this action and reaction keeps the ball moving forward.

In a mystery or crime novel, that logical sequence of events is the investigation of the crime (usually, but not always, murder). It is because the plot is an investigation that logic is required. Your sleuth—and this includes sleuths with psychic powers, by the way—cannot solve the crime through intuition, coincidence, acts of God, or visions from beyond the grave. Or at least not solely—primarily—through such happy strokes of fate. All sleuths must investigate. They may have their own wacky method of investigation, but investigate they must.

By the way, this remains true even if you are writing an inverted mystery or a thriller where the criminal's identity is already known to the investigator.

Now, before you start to sweat, let me make your life a lot easier. Regardless of whether you are writing a cozy mystery or a police procedural, all investigations amount to the same thing: a series of "interviews" or interesting conversations with your other well-drawn characters. That's pretty simple, right?

In the course of those conversations your sleuth will uncover one bit of information that leads him closer to solving the mystery (even if he doesn't recognize it at the time) and several pieces of information that will lead him in the wrong direction.

Got it? All the rest of the stuff that fills your book—lab reports, DNA results, the inquest, attempts on your hero's life…that's all it basically is: filler. Filler and subplots. Which is not to say that it isn't excellent stuff—sometimes a subplot (often your main character's romance) is even the primary reason readers keep coming back to your books. And here you were thinking it was your locked-door puzzles!

The second thing to remember is that there is no plot without conflict.

Now…by conflict, I don't mean your main character spends 230 pages bickering with the guy he's romantically interested in. The primary conflict in a mystery or crime novel is that while your protagonist is trying to solve a crime, his antagonist is trying to get away with murder. Usually literally.

In other words, your protagonist and his antagonist want two separate things—which puts them in conflict with each other. While your protagonist is trying to unravel the mystery, the antagonist is trying to make sure there are no loose ends.

As you plot your mystery, focus on the two things that any investigator would focus on: motive and opportunity. Make sure that you have a couple of characters with both motive and opportunity. And make sure that nearly every character has good solid motive—even if it is not immediately apparent to your sleuth. Crazy is not a good, solid motive, for the record. And while serial killers remain a fixture on crime fiction lists, the bar is pretty high on creating truly chilling and memorable ones.

You must have enough suspects to keep both the reader and the protagonist busy. Not so many that your reader can't keep track of them, but enough so that she has fun wondering if her initial guess could be right.

You must play fair with the reader—and we'll talk more about that when we get to clues and red herrings.

Finally, do not make the mistake of confusing literary crime fiction with real-life criminal investigations. In real life, most crime is not that interesting and a lot of it goes unsolved. You don't have that luxury. All your crimes must be interesting—as must all your criminal investigations—and your sleuth will always figure out who dunnit. Usually either a little before or a little after but generally around the same time the reader figures it all out.

Setting:

Setting often determines what type of mystery you're writing—certainly readers are quick to make assumptions as to what subgenre goes with what setting: isolated country house means traditional mystery, small New England town means cozy, multiple international metropolises mean thriller, grungy urban settings mean hardboiled. And setting also determines what life experiences and challenges your gay protagonist can expect to confront. The only son of a Baptist minister who grows up in a conservative Midwestern town is going to be a very different character than the youngest son of a famous Hollywood starlet.

This is not to say that you can't shake things up, write against type, and set a spy thriller in a small New England town or make your son of a Baptist minister out and an open advocate for gay rights in his conservative community, but either way you're working with or against reader expectation.

There are geographic trends in mystery writing—Scandinavian crime fiction is very hot right now, and part of the allure is that Sweden, Norway,

Denmark all feel rather exotic to jaded readers who've burnt out on England, New York, Los Angeles, Florida, and New Orleans. Ireland is trendy as is Scotland. Midwestern noir is way hotter than urban noir.

Sex:

The traditional mystery reader is generally not a fan of mixing sex and clues. In fact, even mixing romance and mystery can be tricky, although the sub-sub genre of romantic suspense is alive and well. Maybe this general distaste for sexy sleuthing is because of the cerebral nature of mystery fiction. Maybe it's because of a little built-in genre snobbery, but whatever the basis for this bias, it holds true for the traditional gay mystery reader as well. Graphic sex scenes do not win Edgars, Agathas, Shamuses, Lefties, or Lambdas.

But M/M is a subgenre of romance and, as such, the M/M mystery is more closely aligned to romantic suspense than traditional mystery. In an M/M mystery, romance is always going to be half the story, and while it is true that M/M romance is not, by definition, erotic romance, the majority of M/M does contain some erotic content.

Which is A-OK as far as the majority of fans of M/M mystery are concerned.

Sex sells. We all know that. But boosted sales are not the primary reason for including sex scenes in your M/M mystery or thriller. The two main reasons for including sex scenes in your M/M mystery are to show the developing intimacy—the changing relationship—of the characters, and to offer insight into a side of the characters we would not otherwise see.

However, because you're also writing a mystery, you do have to balance the romantic aspects with the crime solving. If you short-change either the romance or the mystery, readers are going to be disappointed. That means no stopping for sex while running from a serial killer. It also means the discussion will have to occasionally revolve around personal and relationship matters as well as clues and leads on the case.

Pacing is just as critical for writing sex scenes as it is for the rest of the work—both in the number of scenes and the length of the scenes. Again, the heat of a gun battle is not the time to be thinking about someone's cute freckles or tight ass.

The important thing to remember in all M/M fiction is that the sex is not simply about sex. It's about love. The important thing to remember in M/M mystery is that as important as the love story is, it cannot be given more importance than the mystery plot.

Clues and Red Herrings:

In *Mystery Fiction Theory and Technique*, Rodell writes:

> Clues are the traces of guilt which the murderer leaves behind him. Whether they are tangible, material things, like a button torn off at the scene of the crime; or personal traces like footprints or fingerprints; or whether they are intangible habit patterns or character traits, they are the signposts leading detective—and reader—in the right—or sometimes wrong—direction.

A single clue does not, in itself, prove guilt. Rather, these are the breadcrumbs the sleuth gathers up along the way that then allow him to follow the trail to the correct solution. Some clues mislead the sleuth, and those are called Red Herrings.

The best clues appear to initially lead in the wrong direction, but in fact ultimately form part of the final deduction.

In the Golden Age of mystery writing, and particularly the screwball comedies of the '30s and '40s, tangible clues were often puzzling, even crazy, minor mysteries within the greater mystery: footprints on the ceiling or a blue rose or whistling from a sealed crypt. The sleuth would have to figure out how the footprints got on the ceiling or how a rose could turn blue or how a corpse could whistle—and that solution would eventually, against the odds, lead to the identity of the murderer.

In real life, clues are more typically known as evidence. There are four types of evidence: Statistical, Testimonial, Anecdotal, and Analogical. But mystery fiction is not real life, and therefore our clues are not typically DNA samples, ballistic reports, or witness testimony. Although these are all part of building a case and solving a crime. Therefore a partial fingerprint is not really a clue UNLESS it is the fingerprint of an innocent person, in which case it is a red herring.

Classic mystery fiction clues are personal rather than scientific. Thus we have an abundance of overheard bits of conversation, lost cellphones, threatening letters pasted from bits of magazines, and smashed wristwatch dials. These are fine, as far as they go. But ideally the importance of the tangible clue is not in the clue itself, so much as what the clue reveals: a smudge of lipstick in a color few women can wear; a strange whiff of smoke that turns out to be, not incense, but clove cigarettes; a haunting melody that is revealed to be a fragment of an old folk song.

Alternatively, the clue might not be significant in itself, but yet triggers some train of thought or memory for the sleuth that helps him connect the dots that form the murderer's portrait. This kind of clue is ideal when you're writing a series because it helps flesh out your protagonist as well as help solve the crime.

The challenge is to describe the clue fairly without putting undo emphasis on it. Or to put huge emphasis on it, thereby fooling the astute mystery reader into thinking the clue is not important. The experienced reader now knows that any character who seems a little too suspicious or obviously guilty is almost always a red herring. Equally, they know that the least likely suspect is generally the one whodunit. So the real least likely suspect is the genuinely least likely suspect, which in fact is the MOST likely suspect.

And if that didn't confuse you, nothing will!

A favorite tangible clue is the clue that is not immediately recognizable. The puzzling shard of glass or sliver of wood that, once placed, provide a key to the solution. Again, you have to play fair with the reader and make sure the reader has access to whatever the betraying item is.

"The dog did nothing in the night-time." Then again, sometimes it is the absence of the tangible clue that is most revealing.

Tangible clues, though fun, are increasingly outdated by the advancement of science. This brings us to intangible clues. Intangible clues are closely linked to psychological profiling. They are clues to character traits or behavioral patterns.

Clues to character traits are generally linked to motive. Behavioral patterns are linked to identity.

There are three basic methods for concealing clues:

1. Distraction. Immediately after the introduction of the clue, something exciting and dramatic should happen to distract the reader from fully noting the significance of the new discovery. It's a bit of literary sleight of hand.

2. Disguise. Bury the clue in a list of other similarly innocuous items. Better yet, include a hard-to-ignore item in that innocuous inventory. A drawer contains a bunch of junk including keys and a gun. One of the keys is to a safe deposit box, but it's likely that the reader will notice the gun and not pay special attention to all those loose keys.

3. Delay. Present the clue in a straightforward manner but delay revealing its possible application for a good fifty or so pages. Hopefully the reader will have forgotten about the original item by the time the significance of the second bit of information is clear.

Clues supply much of the fun of mystery writing, both for the reader and the writer. The main thing to remember is that you must play fair with the reader, even though the modern mystery reader has already seen and read every possible trick in the, er, book.

All clues must be logical and have a believable and reasonable function within the story. They cannot exist merely because you know a mystery story should have clues.

Crime and Mystery Fiction Roundtable featuring P.A. Brown, L.B. Gregg, Josh Lanyon, Elliott Mackle, AM Riley, Abigail Roux, Marshall Thornton, Haley Walsh.

Why mystery or crime fiction?

Abigail Roux (*According to Hoyle*) - There are so many reasons! Crime and mystery fiction puts characters into positions they would rarely find themselves facing from other genres. There's the added spice of life-threatening situations, nefarious unknowns, and being forced to arm yourself with odd implements. There are so many quirky things that can happen and avenues to be explored with these sorts of plots. Whether it's a gritty mystery or a lighter action romp, they're endlessly entertaining.

Elliott Mackle (*Only Make Believe*) - First of all, keep in mind I'm a trained historian and the novels I write are historicals. Call them mysteries, crime fiction, romances, thrillers, or military adventure novels, only one is set later than 1970.

Probably my first exposure to mysteries was the Hardy Boys series at age thirteen; we read them at summer camp; I found them pretty tame stuff. A high school buddy pushed Mickey Spillane hard, but the writing was so over the top we read them more as camp than lit.

Finally, two very different collisions. My partner and I were big Masterpiece Theater fans. The tolling of bells in the 1974 British miniseries based on Dorothy L. Sayers's *The Nine Tailors* hit me as hard as anything had since discovering *Moby-Dick* in high school. I eventually read most of Sayers's elegant mystery fiction. A bit later, we went on a transAtlantic cruise and part of the entertainment was a seminar in crime and caper fiction led by master novelists John D. MacDonald and Donald Westlake. On the first full day of the voyage, they set up a shipboard mystery that was supposed to take three days to solve. It took me a couple of hours. They swiftly added me to their team. "I can do this," I thought at the time. I spent twenty years as a working journalist after several in P.R., but eventually returned to writing fiction on the side (I'd written a lot of lame short stories in college, none publishable) and came up with Dan Ewing, Bud Wright, and the Caloosa Hotel.

P.A. Brown (*L.A. Boneyard*) - I've always had an unhealthy fascination with the darker side of humanity. What makes some people do things that are totally abhorrent to nearly everyone else?

L.B. Gregg (*Trust Me if You Dare*) - I like to use elements from other genres, specifically mystery and comedy, to construct fun, fast-paced love stories. An external goal—Who did it? Where is it? Help me find the thing. Don't let him find the thing before I do. Don't let him find me. Find him—moves these heroes from point to point while they overcome the internal conflict keeping them from the real goal: the HEA.

Solving mysteries also puts my guys in atypical and stressful situations where they can have inappropriate, unbridled sex. I am in favor of characters making love in new, exciting, sometimes dangerous, often crowded places.

Marshall Thornton (*Boystown 5: Murder Book*) - I've always been a mystery fan. One of the best rules I've heard about writing is that you should write the kind of book that you want to read. Still, it took me a long time to get around to writing a detective series. I think the key for me was setting it in a period that I was very familiar with. I had to research the police/detective bits, of course, but the rest I felt very comfortable with.

One of my favorite things about mystery writing is that you have a great deal of freedom to investigate a subject that might not necessarily stand on its own. My latest book, *Boystown 5: Murder Book*, is very much about grief. If you went out and said to readers "Hey, you wanna read a book about grief?" most of them would be like "no". But, wrap it in a mystery and it becomes much more intriguing.

Haley Walsh (*Skyler Foxe Mysteries: Out-Foxed*) - A couple of reasons. It allows for another layer of the story, something else to sink one's teeth into. And it also allows for me to keep writing about the characters in a continual series. Readers who might not pick up a book with a gay theme might choose it for the mystery. And people enjoy mysteries, they like the puzzles, like to see their favorite characters in jeopardy and watch how they get out of it.

AM Riley (*Son of a Gun*) - I've always preferred reading mysteries. They are like crossword puzzles in a way. And when they are well-written, the ending feels as satisfying as solving a puzzle. So, of course, when I began writing, I wanted to write mysteries.

Josh Lanyon (*Somebody Killed His Editor*) - A lot of reasons. Certainly one thing that appeals to me is that there is justice—or at least logic—in a properly written mystery or crime novel. Whereas real life is often short of both those things. But it's more than that. In a mystery, the unthinkable—murder—is explained, the important questions are all resolved, even if justice is *not* meted out. I think that's why mysteries satisfy, because not understanding, the lack of answers, is something we humans really suffer over. Even more so than lack of justice.

Drewey Wayne Gunn wrote in *The Gay Male Sleuth in Print and Film*, "The gay sleuth symbolically confronts the ultimate mystery every gay man must face at some point in his life: his difference from his family and the general society into which he has been born." Can you expound on this as it relates to your own work?

EM - That's true as far as it goes. To some extent, all literary sleuths are outsiders. The best know how to work—and work within—the system, be it family, social class, or general society. Two of my favorite sleuths—not necessarily models—are examples. Dorothy L. Sayers's nominally heterosexual, unmarried Lord Peter Wimsey employs a chauffeur-assistant and solves crimes in country houses and private clubs frequented by the nobility of post-World War I England. He uses his privileged position as well as his wits and intelligence to gain information and solve mysteries. His peers value his services but some laugh behind his back. Joseph Hansen's gay insurance-claims investigator, Dave Brandstetter, is a battle-hardened veteran of Korea, out to his employer-father, and resourceful in following cold trails and hot hunches. But he has few close friends, is clinically depressed, has bad luck keeping his (usually) younger lovers around, or even alive, and is routinely assigned to cases involving gays, young males or bent, misbehaving Hollywood figures.

I give my sleuths and heroes an even break. Only recently did I realize that most of them are orphans and singletons of some sort, either raised by loving uncles and grannies or adopted out, with no siblings. Whether gay or bisexual, however, my male heroes and narrators learn early on that they live, love, and work in an overwhelmingly heterosexual world and that, to put bread and booze on the table, they must accept themselves for who and what they are and do whatever it takes to survive. If that means being closeted, at least to some people, family included, so be it.

PB - My gay characters struggle with that, some handling it better than others. In my L.A. series, Christopher Bellamere has accepted his differences and for the most part deals with them well. When he feels threatened or challenged, he responds with snarky sarcasm. On the other hand David has spent most of his life trying to pretend he isn't different. He is out to his family, but not many other people. Because of this, he is not very social. This has made him very successful in his job, but very lonely in private. Socially, he's awkward. He has to listen to the homophobia among the other cops and on the street and has to keep from responding in any way. Generally he's very careful about what he says, this makes him look like a man of few words.

LG - Can I say this? I avoid gender politics/gay specific questions because given the shifting tides of gender identity in our country and the increasingly antagonistic attitude toward the straight women who write gay romantic fiction, no matter what I say, it becomes arguable.

From my heart, I tell you this: I don't purposely intend for my stories to reflect the ultimate gay mystery. My hope is to illuminate the innate human desire inside all people to love and be loved, regardless of orientation, and to feel like they belong.

MT - The character of sleuth always seems to work better if the sleuth is something of an outsider. An old lady (Miss Marple), a Belgian in the English countryside (Hercule Poirot), a woman (Kinsey Millhone and many, many others), a black man (Easy Rawlins)... Though our society is changing, gay men are still natural outsiders. Part of the reason I set the Boystown series in the early '80s was to heighten this sense of the outsider—though it still works well in a contemporary. As an outsider, a gay sleuth is allowed, even encouraged, to see things that others cannot. And there lies the value of outsiders to society: they're mirrors.

HW - It's definitely an undercurrent for the first three books in the series, and even as the series goes on it can hardly be avoided. Skyler Foxe is out to his friends and plays the field at the local gay bar, bringing home numerous tricks, some of whom have become his close friends, what they affectionately call the "Skyler Fuck Club" or S.F.C. But he isn't out at the high school where he teaches or to his mother. In fact, I like exploring this aspect of his personality, how very different he is to each of his associations: He's professional and "Mr. Foxe" to his students, the dutiful son to his mom, out and proud to his friends and tricks—he has to wear many faces. And when he does get outed, he feels that his world crumbles—which of course it doesn't because this is a humorous mystery and though there are sensitive moments it is tempered with absurdity. I think that there are so many gay-themed books or books with gay characters that get awfully heavy. There's enough angst in the world, so my goal has been to lighten it up.

AMR - This doesn't relate to my work, really. I write gay and lesbian characters because those are the people I know, the people in my real world. I do personally believe, though, that for a white male in America, who was born entitled in many ways, the discovery of his homosexuality is perhaps his one opportunity to find redemption. And for a white female, to discover she is lesbian, is to find herself immediately a feminist. Out of necessity if nothing else. A private investigator, or homicide detective, is naturally outside the situation that created the crime. As a gay person this outsiderness is enhanced. I find that interesting as a writer.

JL - To be honest, while I agree with Gunn regarding gay mystery, I don't know how true that statement is of M/M. Here in M/M we have so many stories apparently about a fictional society where being gay is unremarkable and almost universally accepted. I don't know if it's wishful thinking or lack of research, but I think M/M mysteries are possibly more about integration and assimilation rather than an emphasis on difference and separation. However, in M/M *romance*, I think we see that struggle to explore and define identity within the context of trying to learn to share another person's life.

AR - Obviously who we are and the experiences we take with us form the way we look at the world, and a fictional character should be no different. Those are the pieces that make us whole, and for a reader to connect, the character must be whole as well. If the sleuth in question is a gay man, then of course that's going to impact the way he approaches his mysteries, his colleagues, his lovers. In my own work, the characters have often faced those questions already, even if they haven't necessarily been answered.

Perhaps more than any other genre, the mystery genre is defined by rules of fair play and procedure. Are there any mystery/crime writing rules you consider inviolable?

<u>PB</u> - Since most of my novels are police procedurals, I try to keep my cops inside the rules. They can't torture people, they can't murder the villains or beat them up. Other rules that can never be broken are never harm children or animals, at least not in a scene.

<u>LG</u> - If you're going to break the rules, you'd better have a damn good book. So yes, and no.

<u>MT</u> - None really. If you can convince the reader something is just, then it's just. There's a wide swath of vigilante behavior in the mystery genre. Depending on the rules of particular series, sleuths can break and enter, beat up the wrong guy, or even kill the right one. Readers will accept behavior that they'd never accept in life if it's well drawn out and supported. For example, in fiction you know with absolute certainty that the killer is the killer, so if the sleuth impatiently carries out a death sentence, it doesn't often bother the reader—even a reader with grave doubts about capital punishment—because there's a clarity that we seldom have in life. Real-life vigilantes are frightening because we don't know them and can't be sure they're doing good; but we do know our sleuths and we know that what they're doing is right and just.

<u>HW</u> - I do like to play fair with the clues as much as I can. They are always mentioned somewhere. Obscurely, but they are mentioned. And the main protagonist must solve the crime. But it's always tough writing an amateur sleuth because you start with the premise that an ordinary person would bother to solve a crime when the police department is so much better equipped and trained to do it. And then you don't want to fall into the Jessica Fletcher Syndrome. That's from the TV show *Murder She Wrote*. Jessica Fletcher was the fictional mystery writer who solved crimes in her little mythical town of Cabot Cove. Everywhere she looked in her small town people were getting murdered. Soon there'd be no one left! (And believe me, mystery writers would be terrible at solving crimes. We look clever because of the twists in our stories but we make up all the clues…and the crime!) So it's an added frustration forcing the protagonist to even want to solve the crime and give him the means in which to do it without

benefit of forensics or other scientific assistance. There's a certain amount of suspension of disbelief.

AMR - The guilty party must appear as early as possible in the novel. The reasons for the homicide should appear clear in retrospect and a few decent clues should have been dropped along the way. I also believe the criminal should have at least a little humanity in him/her. There is nothing more annoying to me than a purely evil bad guy.

JL - Fiction has to make sense in a way that real life does not. I think motives have to be plausible, which gets down to writing believable characters. Sleuths must sleuth. The mystery cannot be solved by coincidence, intuition, or acts of God, although these things may figure into the sleuth's ratiocination. The villain cannot come out of left field in the final chapter nor burst into confession because that's the quickest way of winding everything up. All essential loose ends must be tied up or it must be acknowledged that they cannot be tied up but a best guess is offered. That's pretty much it, in my opinion.

AR - I don't think any rules are inviolable. Sometimes it makes for the best twists if you break one or two of those rules, if you do so in moderation. Go ahead and have your bad guy get away once. Let your MC lose an eye in a fight. Have dumb luck play a part in the plot once in a blue moon. Procedure and rules of the game are important. But so is giving the reader a bit of a ride.

EM - If the sleuth is going to fire a pistol or rifle late in the novel, it must be established early on that he knows how to use it. Same-same for knives, bayonets, and explosives. A body must be found or reported or a crime discovered in chapter one. The sleuth is allowed no more than one coincidence that helps solve the puzzle. Whether or not the sleuth and his sidekick are lovers, there must be sexual and competitive tension between them. Do not introduce a major character, especially one central to solving the puzzle, late in the narrative. Never kill off a house pet.

What are some of your favorite themes to explore through the lens of mystery fiction?

LG - Family, friendship, community, good vs. evil, vanity, secrets and lies, and truth or consequences.

MT - Betrayal. Obsession. Lust. You know, things the average American deals with before breakfast.

HW - How one person can touch so many others. Can love triumph under adversity? How do family relationships shape a person? What's it like being a gay man today (and all the shades of what that means).

AMR - As I said above, being an outsider. Also, redemption, retribution, hope. Justice should always be done in fiction if not in real life.

JL - Identity, redemption, the power dynamics within any relationship, the shades of gray in ethics and morality, faith. My books are basically about smart, civilized grownups trying to figure out how to build a life with a person, who at least initially seems like a terrible match.

AR - I adore loyalty and betrayal. Those are my favorite things to explore through any lens, but they can be especially intriguing in the mystery realm, where being betrayed could mean your life, and loyalty means being willing to take a bullet for your friend. What better place to examine the gears of a character who puts loyalty and keeping their word above their own life? You pit them against the type of person who would let you whisper secrets into his ear merely for the chance to use them against you. It's beautiful.

EM - Successful M/M partnerships require significant differences in order to make up for the human differentness in M/F roles and socialization. Class, the level and type of education, religion, upbringing, sexual tastes—all or some of these can be varied and blended to create characters that work and play well together. Captain Joe Harding is resolutely middle-class and sexually outgoing. His fellow sleuth in the first two novels is a married air policeman with a taste for hired discipline and *Playboy* centerfolds. The love of Joe's life is an aristocratic, upper-class teenager. His other partners include an older, working-class prizefighter/administrator, an older enlisted medic, and a younger, married, bisexual pilot.

"Getting away with it," whatever that may be—surviving the military closet, drinking on Sunday in a bible-belt town, paying officials to look the other way—all of these find a ready audience among fans of gay and romantic mystery fiction. Too many readers seem to lead lives of either quiet desperation or dull-normal routine. Our job is to take them out of themselves and show them an entertaining, exotic, sometimes dangerous world that they may enter without risk. It's another form of travel writing.

And, obviously, my literary calling card is military life before Don't Ask, Don't Tell. Getting drafted, joining the air force and serving four years as an officer, in California and overseas, changed my own life. I went in a spoiled brat and frat rat. I came out with some idea of how a decent adult should conduct his affairs. War and violent death shape the lives of the main characters in four of my five novels. Their experiences, reactions, and changed world views are not all the same, of course. Lieutenant Dan Ewing loses everything during the last month of World War II: His ship, his lover, and all of his men. Thereafter, he feels and acts as if he has nothing more to lose. Marine Sergeant Bud Wright, on the other hand, kills Japanese soldiers as if they were spiders and easily shakes off the loss of a beloved commanding officer who dies in his arms. Back home, nothing is more natural for this conventional-minded man than dating a waitress, joining the local police force, and packing a pistol, "licensed to kill."

PB - The darkness inside all of us. On being different and facing intolerance and even hate and still functioning within society.

M/M mystery differs most widely from traditional mystery in its emphasis of romantic subplot. How do you balance the demands of mystery with the demands of satisfying romance?

MT - This one's a toughie for me… Though many people use the term M/M to be synonymous with gay, I don't. The M/M romance genre comes from a distinctly different place than traditional gay fiction and, while there is crossover in both genre rules and readership, I view the genres as unique. I think of myself as a gay mystery writer, a subgenre of gay fiction; M/M mystery is a subgenre of M/M romance.

Since both of the publishers I've worked with are romance publishers, the amount of sex and romance in my series is probably higher than it might have been otherwise. At the same time, I'm not very good at following the rules of M/M romance, so I can't really call myself that kind of writer. It's rare to find a happy ending in the Boystown series or even a happy-for-now, and I'm much more interested in capturing the way gay men behaved in the '80s than in fulfilling contemporary reader's fantasies—which, of course, is the point of a romance. That said, I find that many fans of M/M romance enjoy my books.

As far as balance is concerned, with this series it's all about what feels real to me.

HW - I think a key to it is to allow the mystery to get in the way of the romance and the romance to get in the way of the mystery. That way they are sure to get intertwined. But I make no apologies for the romance, because I always like my characters to be three-dimensional people. I write biographies for each of them. I know things about them that may never come out in the books, but it's stuff that informs what they say, what they do, and what makes them tick. And most everyone likes a good romance. I like for my readers to root for my characters.

AMR - With a great deal of difficulty.

You are incorrect in saying that the romantic subplot is not part of traditional mystery. Ngaio Marsh, Christie and others all included romance in their mysteries. Marsh's mysteries follow a romance and the couples' subsequent lives as a definite subtext. There are strong romantic elements (if a little misogynistic) in the classic crime fiction of Raymond Chandler. There are romantic subplots in Michael Connelly and Robert Crais. I can look up more if you want. I LOVE romantic subplot in my murder mysteries. I believe it invests the characters more deeply in the outcome.

JL - Regardless of the subgenre, M/M is marketed and promoted first and foremost as romance. So while it is certainly true that a romantic subplot is nothing new in crime and mystery fiction, the focus, the *emphasis* on applying the rules of romance—in particular a Happy Ever After—can be a real challenge in crafting a truly baffling mystery.

So while it is perfectly possible to write a brilliant mystery and completely fool readers by having the love interest turn out to be the villain (a la *The Maltese Falcon)*, you will have failed in your mission to write a satisfying romance.

And there is a price to be paid for breaking that unwritten contract with the reader. But keeping the bargain automatically limits the possibilities of the mysteries we write.

AR - I'm not sure I do balance them. The M/M genre demands a happy couple walking into the sunset, and it can be a terrifying prospect to rock that boat if it doesn't fit with the culmination of your plot. It's a scary high wire to walk, and I think mystery writers especially are trying to ride a unicycle across it. Sometimes the main character can't solve the crime and get the guy. Mostly, I bypassed that by making both MCs the law!

EM - I disagree with the premise. Take John D. MacDonald's hugely successful Travis McGee series. In many cases, an attractive woman in trouble applies to Travis for help in dealing with an errant husband, missing money, a deal gone bad or some similar situation. In the course of solving the crime or fixing the problem, Travis and the woman become intimately or otherwise involved. Toward the end, the woman and several colorful bad guys die painful, piteous deaths. Travis returns to his boat at Bahia Mar, pensive but satisfied, having deposited the reward money in his safe deposit box or given it to his sidekick Meyer to invest. A HEA of a sort. Or take another of my (heterosexual) models, *L.A. Confidential*, by James Ellroy. Murders, mysteries, gunplay, and sleazy corruption abound, but there's also love, lust, romance, heroics, extremely kinky sex, and a HEA fadeout. Neither author's collection of incidents and acts would work or be so entertaining without the other components.

Steve Berman, my publisher at Lethe Press, referred to my novels as "interstitial," part mystery, part romance, part thriller, and not classifiable as one particular M/M genre. InsightOut Book Club catalogs the Harding books as gay literary fiction and gay popular fiction but not as mystery & suspense. Conversely, customers in TLA's Gaybies Awards voted Captain Harding's *Six-Day War* the Best Romance of 2011. I think of them as simply novels, literally something new, not formula, a surprise in every chapter rather than a collection of tropes and familiar situations. To do that, I try to keep my sleuths and heroes always on edge and threatened. To quote the back-jacket copy for my recent *Captain Harding and His Men*, "When a kidnapping goes terribly wrong, Joe must fight for everything he holds dear: duty, honor, country, and love."

PB - The romantic side comes out of the character interactions. In most cases it weaves through the crime story, but I prefer it not to supersede the police investigation. Sometimes the two are linked, sometimes the link is minimal. In *L.A. Boneyard*, LAPD homicide detective David Eric Laine investigates a series of murders that his lover, Christopher Bellamere, has no part in. The only link there is the triangle created by Chris, David, and David's new partner, Jairo, who is trying to seduce David. One thing I did do that was different than most other M/M crime novels was not to make the crimes committed by gays or against gays. They were simply terrible crimes—human trafficking, cyberterrorism, drug wars, and child abuse.

LG - I manage the balancing act better in some books than in others. In the Romano and Albright series, I'm developing a larger story arc for Dan and Ce. Their love story is slow and the mysteries/capers are highlighted. It's so much fun, and the stories are often so big, they're often difficult to contain. In all my other books, the romance takes the spotlight.

True fact: I believe in the classical Aristotelian Unities, which sounds ludicrous given some of my convoluted plots and limitless characters, but the thought is to keep at least one element of a story (somewhat) restricted: location, time, or action. In doing so, I'm able to keep the story centered on the romance.

This works particularly well when writing in shorter formats.

What, in your opinion, are the most overused tropes in mystery and crime fiction?

HW - This usually happens in police procedurals, not amateur sleuth stories, but the police captain telling the detective to hurry up because he's got to tell the press something (of course, later I've discovered from real homicide detectives that this is true! Go figure) but also asking for the overzealous cop's badge and gun, which almost never happens. In amateur sleuth stories, getting the sleuth into outlandish and unrealistic jeopardy; making the crime itself overly freakish and eccentric.

AMR - The bitchy older woman a la Morgan Fairchild. Enough already. The femme fatale is used so much but I never get tired of it. Honestly, I LIKE my tropes. They are like archetypes. There is always a new way to use them.

JL - The omnipotent and fiendishly brilliant serial killer, prologues from the POV of the omnipotent and fiendishly brilliant serial killer. The detective battling his demons and addictions who is handpicked by the omnipotent and fiendishly brilliant serial killer to match wits in a game to the death. (By the way, what's wrong with a smart and professional sleuth who can handle his booze?)

But the single most overused trope in M/M Mystery is simply The Cop. The cop in love with his suspect, the cop in love with his partner, the cop in love with the omnipotent and fiendishly bril—okay, not that one. But I am really sick of cops. I never thought the day would come. I think too often cops are used as a shortcut to save authors from actually having to go through the steps of logical investigation and sleuthing.

That said, a good writer can make anything fresh and entertaining.

AR - At this point in the timeline of mystery writing, you could make an argument for saying everything is overused. I dislike learning the ex was the bad guy because it's been done, but if it's done well, then I don't care. Red herrings are tossed around so often to throw the reader off the scent, but if it increases the adventure, the mystery, then do it! The brooding, rebel cop with a drinking problem and odd oral fixation? If you can make me like him, you've got a winner regardless of the seven other MCs that look kind of like him in other releases that week. If a writer can have the butler do it and still make me enjoy the ride there, I'm a happy reader. As writers we're often aiming for the same destination, and that's why tropes are there. Use them. Abuse them. Make fun of them.

EM - In M/M mysteries? The male whore with a heart of gold. The lesbian or other best female friend who contributes nothing to the action but serves simply as a sounding board for the male sleuth and his creator. Clichés such as "Gay as a goose." The depressed sleuth. AIDS as metaphor. Partner-sleuths who once were lovers.

PB - The alcoholic cop or PI fighting his demons. The man who becomes a cop because his partner or husband is murdered and the killer has never been found. The cop who falls for the suspect and risks his life or his job to prove the wrongly accused is innocent. (Yes, I've used this in at least 3 novels, so I know it's overused.)

LG - Shootouts. I'm sick of guns. Seriously.

I like smart comic capers featuring wiry, witty sleuths and the big-boned detectives who pull their hair out trying to protect… That might be an overused trope as well, but done right, that's as good as it gets.

<u>MT</u> - Personally, I'm a bit tired of sex workers turned detective and have never been too excited about psychic detectives. A psychic escort turned sleuth would probably not interest me. That said, I'm often surprised by what good writing can put over. I've begun books in a very dubious state (oh, not this again) and been pleasantly surprised. So, any overused trope can work if it's handled right.

How heavily do you depend on traditional elements such as red herrings, MacGuffins, and non-forensic or evidential clues?

<u>AMR</u> - I use red herrings quite a bit since I believe in presenting valid clues as early and often as possible. I have to distract the reader with red herrings. Also, accidentally misspoken statements by the bad dude are helpful. AH-HAH moments that occur hopefully just before the reader has the same moment.

JL - As dearly as I love those Golden Age mysteries, I rely mostly on psychology, misdirection, and physical evidence.

<u>AR</u> - I love them like cheesecake. I've only written one pure mystery story, one that wasn't hindered by a lot of gunfire and explosions, so it's hard to analyze my propensity for using such devices, but when I've been able to, I have immensely enjoyed putting them into practice. I think a favorite tactic of mine is presenting something as red herring, showing it to the reader and saying, "This is your red herring, enjoy," but then pulling it back in the end as the actual key to the case. A reverse red herring, I suppose.

<u>EM</u> - I had to look up MacGuffin so, obviously, that's not a trope or device I depend on. At least I don't think so. Red herrings and false clues, yes, of course, unless one is writing the kind of artsy-fartsy novel that describes and explains the crime in chapter one and then goes on to reveal and deconstruct the existential details and deeper meaning of the backstory in another three hundred pages. I prefer to let my readers identify with my sleuths and become participants in figuring out the mystery and nailing the villains. Non-forensic and evidential clues? Yes, again. I let my characters talk. My

sleuths listen, though not always carefully the first time around. They're easily distracted—usually by lust, ambition, alcohol, or the pre-Stonewall fear of exposure as men who prefer the company of men. They're also perfectly willing to go outside the chain of command, whatever that may be.

PB - I like to have things point to someone else, but that doesn't always work. I'm actually not very good at thinking of complex plots with lots of clues and red herrings. I prefer to drop my characters into the middle of trouble and watch them try to get out.

LG - Those are all integral elements in the game of story building, so I depend on them. If your characters don't have a mutual goal or conflicting interests or a reason to move from place to place, you don't have a book worth a damn. You just have a sex story, and rumor has it you can find those for free online.

My books aren't about who did it, or where the cake is, or why the money is missing—my goal is for readers to have fun while they fall in love with my characters. The real romance happens between the reader and the characters. The rest is all trappings.

MT - Two things impact the Boystown series. As a private investigator, Nick Nowak does not have access to any forensics so most of his work is interviewing people. Also, since the series is set in the early '80s the available forensics is limited anyway. Beyond that, real-world police work—regardless of what happens on television shows—is primarily about talking to suspects and getting confessions. (One of the reasons *The Closer* is my favorite cop show.) I do use red herrings a lot—though they usually take the form of Nick making mistakes. He's far from being Sherlock Holmes. In fact, his most useful investigative quality is sheer stubbornness.

HW - All of the above. A red herring is simply something or someone that looks like a plausible suspect but turns out to be leading the detective down the wrong path. A MacGuffin is something that the plot turns on. It never matters what it is because ultimately it isn't important, but it sets the plot moving. (I mostly used MacGuffins in my other mystery series). And because Skyler Foxe is an English teacher he has no access to scientific methods of detection, though his best friend Sidney is a police detective, and she can tell him what's right and what isn't since her people have already gone over the evidence. Skyler has to be extra clever.

What are three of your favorite research resources?

JL - For historical mystery I like the music, films, and/or popular literature of the time. I want to immerse myself as much as possible in that world. Of course I use the Internet, but I also love magazines, old and new. And I still buy lots and lots of books for research. I love to read in preparation for writing. Some of the best ideas for the plot arise from the research.

AR - My favorite resource is experience. Either my own or that of family and friends, I would rather research something by seeing it with my own eyes or hearing it from someone who has. I travel to the destination I write about. I have been known to have someone tie me up to see if it's possible to get out of a situation in the way I'm wanting to. It's the best part of being a writer. My second favorite resource is the Internet. You can find all kinds of things on the Internet, and I have a death pact with a writer friend to wipe my browser history when I die to protect my good name. The other resource I will hit is books and even television. You learn such odd things watching the Discovery or History Channel at 2 a.m.

EM - Boots on the ground, first of all. I know what it feels like to eat, sleep, and work aboard a World War II ship of the U.S. Navy, ride an air force transport, and be seriously ill in a military hospital. My favorite form of travel for a long while was visiting battlefields and military cemeteries. I think it would be difficult to write convincing fiction about the Pacific war on the ground without visiting important sites such as Guadalcanal, Guam, Peleliu, and the Solomon Islands. There's a resort island in Florida I need to revisit sometime in 2013 before picking up the pieces of a third Dan-and-Bud.

Second, writers of police procedurals routinely milk their friends in uniform. Without the advice and good memories of my ex-military buddies, as well as my own experience as an air force officer, I doubt that you or our readers would give me the time of day.

Third, of course, the Web. It's changed the way many of us conduct research. I can pull up blogs containing the reminiscences of Vietnam-era fighter pilots, street maps of Fort Myers, Florida, government reports, charts, diagrams, illustrated uniform and insignia catalogs, the lot. The favorites list of tabs on my homepage includes Books, Travel, Air Force Slang, Vietnam War Timelines, and so on. To be sure, as a historian and journalist, I take little of cyber-reality as proven fact. In many cases, however, the Web has made cobbling together ideas, adventures, and personalities much, much easier than, say, reading microfilm.

PB - The Internet is very important. Online research often produces serendipitous discoveries, sometimes so good it will take the story in a whole new direction. This is one of the reasons I don't write outlines since I find them stifling. I also own a number of books on police procedure, many specific to the LAPD. One of the best things I did for research was attend the Writer's Police Academy, a 3-day marathon of classes and hands-on experience at a real police academy. Nothing comes closer than real hands-on experience.

LG - Media (TV, film, Internet, magazines), extensive travel because if you can—do, and asking experts a lot of dumb questions.

MT - For the Boystown series there are some very specific sources I love. Chicago Gay History (www.chicagogayhistory.com) is a terrific website that features video interviews with community members covering the last forty years of LGBT life in Chicago. *And the Band Played On* by Randy Shilts. And Google Maps.

HW - The library, the Internet, and networking. I'm led to the library more often than not for deeper research, especially with my other series. The Internet can answer quick questions, give you maps of areas where you just need a street name, lets you listen to songs your character might be listening to on his iPod or in a dance club (YouTube or Pandora), gets you started with research that is better off done in a library where it is more reliable. Networking with other mystery authors on the quirks of the business is invaluable, and then talking with people who have more experience in the situations I need to write about helps me get into the heart of my characters. Since I'm a straight woman it's helpful to talk with my gay male friends on issues that affect them. But while we're on this subject, I don't think it matters what gender, orientation, religion, or whatever the writer is. If the writer has done his/her job, the characters should be wholly believable to the reader.

AMR - Police procedurals. Actual interviews with police and other persons involved in the occupations I write about. I Google excessively, but in the end I try to spend a lot of time in the location and with the people. Nothing beats actual experience.

How important is the puzzle element in the contemporary mystery?

AR - I think it's vital. My books lean toward adventures, so rarely have I been able to implement a true puzzle. But a reader who picks up a mystery book wants a puzzle to work through, they want to be given enough clues to solve the crime. We should be able to go back to the beginning after reading a mystery and read a line we thought nothing of the first time and see where the light bulb could have gone off. That's half the fun.

EM - Depends upon the subgenre, I'd say. In an M/M cozy, with little or no physical action, blood spatters or graphic sex, solving the puzzle is essentially the point. In gay mystery lite, sexy clothes, toned bodies, exotic locations, and close friendships with at least one lesbian are typically as important as the puzzle. In an adventure-romance, mystery-thriller or noir, not so much. For my purposes, narrative drive and mounting tension (lust, danger, nasty surprises, and unexpected betrayals) trump the mere puzzle. But it depends on the story. In my two recent novels, solving the puzzle (i.e. identifying and capturing the killer) is paramount in the noir *Only Make Believe* whereas in the more satirical, action-packed *Captain Harding and His Men* the reader becomes aware of the identities of the bad guys well before the climax of the novel; the payoff is in discovering in the last few pages who's left standing.

PB - For me, not terribly important. I'm more interested in the dynamics between people. Not just the criminals and the cops, but even more between the "good" guys.

LG - I don't come from a crime or mystery background. But I love farce. I love physical comedy. I love scenes where people run in and out of doors and the hero has no idea what's going to happen next. I love to set up long jokes, and the punch line isn't always clear to the other characters, but it's available to the reader. So, the puzzle element is essential in my stories to keep the reader as engaged in the action as the hero.

MT - The more mysteries there are out there, the harder it is to fool the astute reader. One of the things I've noticed in my own reading is that if the writing is good enough, I don't really mind if I figure out what's going on fairly quickly. I think about that a lot as I'm writing. I try to keep every element of my stories compelling for those readers who figure out what's happening quickly.

HW - It's always been important. Now granted, because I emphasize the relationships, romance, and erotic elements in my Skyler stories, the mystery sometimes takes a backseat and might be a bit lighter, but everyone likes to solve a puzzle or two. But if the puzzle is light fare, then I like to keep the characters interesting and their problems and situations meaty.

AMR - Absolutely essential.

JL - I think mystery readers like a solid whodunnit, but I don't think the puzzle—in a locked-room sense—is as crucial as it was in the Golden Age of mystery writing. In fact, I think puzzles for the sake of puzzles generally feel contrived. For me the single most interesting element is motive, and that gets back to character. But I do expect a genuine mystery. I don't want to pinpoint the killer the instant he walks in wearing ascot and cufflinks.

I also think it's increasingly difficult to fool the modern mystery reader. They've seen every possible variation on TV and at the movies. And it's especially hard to fool them if they consistently read your work. They quickly learn all your tricks.

Have you ever had to scrap a story? What was the final deciding factor?

EM - Unfortunately yes. Early on, I wrote a Dan-and-Bud mystery based in part on a group of well-meaning, idealistic people whose lives I had investigated and written about as an academic historian. At the center of the narrative, however, I wove in a borrowed, sexually sensational series of incidents that would have been abhorrent to the people on whom I'd partially based my fictional characters. Decades later, my name is still associated with documenting the actual lives of these good people. Rereading the manuscript I realized that I would embarrass myself and disturb their descendants by publishing the work. It's in a drawer and will remain there.

PB - Yes. About 2 years ago I started a police procedural I gave the working title of *In Death We Trust*. It was about an elite robbery homicide detective investigating a bizarre celebrity's murder. I'd written about 3,000 words then it fizzled out. This question made me pull it out and take another look and it's not too bad. I may have to finish it some day. Not sure why it went belly-up. It was different than any of my other crime books. The main character was an older, very cynical cop who'd been in 3 failed marriages and was looking for number 4.

LG - I scrapped a story that had grown too wildly complicated to rein in. It broke my heart to kill it. I later raided those files and used sections in three other novellas.

The deciding factor? The bucket filled with tears.

MT - Yes and no. I have stories that I've put on a back burner and keep telling myself I'll get back to. Maybe I'm just in denial and won't admit to myself that I've scraped them. Or maybe I'll one day pick them up again. Only time will tell.

HW - I've scrapped stories, only later to pick them up again. It simply wasn't the right time to write that story. It wasn't coming to me. What helps prevent that is to outline the entire book. That also helps prevent writer's block because you know in any given chapter what needs to happen. My outlines aren't etched in stone, however, and if I veer off course—an inevitability—I rework the outline so I can keep going.

AMR - I've scrapped almost everything I've written at some point. I get stuck. I hate the characters, whatever. Sooner or later though I come back to it. I don't like to leave things unfinished.

JL - No. Not since I began writing professionally. I've postponed projects. That may turn out to be indefinitely, I guess. Maybe there are projects I *should* have scrapped...

AR - I've scrapped plenty of stories. Some just weren't working, and I cannibalized their parts for other stories. Some I got bored with, and if

I'm bored writing it, it's surely going to bore a reader. I never truly toss anything, but I have a handful of stories that will never see the light of day. If I don't think of it as I'm trying to sleep, if it doesn't spark something in me, I don't want to put my name to it. It's easier to make those calls now than it was at the beginning of my career.

HISTORICALS

Writing historical M/M fiction by Aleksandr Voinov

Let's get the bad news out of the way: writing historical fiction is hard. And being a trained historian doesn't make it easier, either. Historians might have a head start over lay people as they know how much they don't know, but that's pretty much it. History is so vast, especially if we step outside the Western world, that nobody can know everything. So much of it isn't covered even at university. You may learn about the witch craze, but your professor might not have covered the Church's stance on sodomy. And you'd need to know about that if you were going to write about, say, a pair of "sodomites" falling in love during the late Middle Ages.

What is a historical?

The gay historical fiction review blog Speak Its Name (www.speakitsname.com) defines historicals as stories set pre-Stonewall riots, or the beginning of the gay liberation movement in 1969. Obviously, the attempt to emancipate the gay community has much older roots, with academics and intellectuals working on decriminalising gay activities before that date. This definition also doesn't really work outside the western world, where gay rights may be at very different stages, but it's workable for the moment for our purposes.

Historical fiction, AU, and punk genres

Not all historical fiction is created equally. For this little overview, let me quickly discuss three different kinds of "historicals". Some stories set in the past make every effort to reflect their period, using an appropriate writing style and staying true to events that actually happened and people who actually lived. I'd call those "true historicals". Ideally, they'd stand up to academic scrutiny. Your knights won't eat potatoes and your gay Renaissance lovers won't get married by the Pope in Rome.

If that is too restrictive, you can always mesh things up. Say, you want all the shinies that the Middle Ages have to offer, but you want gay rights and gay marriage, or the Templars are colonizing America. You could also rearrange the timeline, or important events didn't or did happen (Alexander the Great/Jesus Christ didn't die in his thirties, Nero never turned evil,

Leonardo da Vinci invented cold fusion). In these cases, we're dealing with an AU ("alternative universe"). These are fun "what if" exercises, and the possibilities are endless. Space aliens invaded during the Thirty Years' War. The use of magick made the Industrial Revolution moot. Slavery was never abolished. Hitler died in the First World War. You're still using a historical setting, but it's radically different in some aspects. Do bear in mind, however, that it will still require research to pull off convincingly.

While I'm not an expert on the "-punk genres" (Steampunk, Dieselpunk, and the others), I believe these belong here. A Steampunk author will still research the Victorian age before she starts twisting and changing it up. Certainly, all deviation from recorded history and inventions are deliberate, and the author will have thought long and hard about how airships, for example, will change international trade or traffic. Readers can tell the difference between "creative license" and "I can't be bothered to do the groundwork". The most important thing to bear in mind is: All changes to the actual historical setting are there for a reason, which must be integral to the story. The same goes, obviously, if you add paranormal elements like vampires or werewolves; these will have an impact on your overall world and story—otherwise, why bother with them?

Wallpaper historicals/mistorical

The ugly stepchild in historical fiction is often called "wallpaper historical" or "mistorical". A wallpaper historical is a historical almost only in name. Dead giveaways for a wallpaper historical are: inappropriate language, research is minimal or nonexistent (or might as well have been, since it's all wrong); modern people and modern plots were just dropped into a historical period/place on a whim. Essentially, the story could happen anywhere and the characters have a decided modern feel and hold modern attitudes.

Often it comes down to "modern people fucking in historical costumes", and I can't even make an effort to like those, but I am a purist. I like people to reflect their times, I like to get an idea that the author has done their homework beyond watching *Braveheart* or *Spartacus* and cracked open a book. Or a pile of them. I also struggle to see the purpose of them, especially in M/M or gay fiction. It's so interesting to see the characters react to their surroundings and the attitudes of their time, and experience the impact of the choices they are forced to make. Why would anybody not use the setting to its full potential?

Historical fiction can be a time-travel portal. As a reader, I want to get sucked in and not come back until the last page spits me back out. And an author's laziness and disregard for readers' intelligence and education destroys that time-travel experience. I still remember a discussion I've had with an author who complained that she'd received a bad review for a "historical romance". I mentioned to her that the reviewer had read it as a historical story, and the research problems were evident just from reading the review. The author was much put-upon at me siding with a reviewer. Her response was: "It's romance, for God's sake. It's not like it's a proper book."

For the record: There's nothing wrong with writing one over the other. The main problem is that publishers market all of those, from "proper historical" to "mistorical" as "historical fiction"—with predictable results. Those readers who put down their cash for a "proper historical" throw the book across the room when it isn't, and reviewers will make their displeasure public. Once the story is labelled appropriately, it helps people to find what they are looking for.

Personally, I really enjoy AU and Steampunk and "proper historicals," but if I've been mis-sold a slapdash fake historical as the real thing, I will not pick up any further historical efforts from the author and will be extremely leery picking up historicals from that publisher, since their editorial policy seems to not draw the line between historical fiction and the fiction that isn't historical.

This, by the way, is an attitude shared by many bloggers (yes, I asked them), and these are people whom authors cross at their own peril. That said, all of them can tell the difference between a loving homage and authorial incompetence. As an example, many fans of historicals prefer the movie *A Knight's Tale* over *Braveheart*. The former was ridiculous and goofy and wildly inaccurate, but it worked because the makers clearly love history and had the confidence to poke fun at it without being smarmy or disrespectful. (Also, you can bet if "We Will Rock You" from Queen had been around at that time, it would have been played at a joust.) *Braveheart*, on the other hand, has the same people foaming at the mouth.

Writing historicals is hard

Between these subgroups, it's really the research that makes all the difference. In our genre, the pressure to publish a lot, and quickly, can lead to authors cutting corners out of a sense of "I don't have time to research whether a Duke is addressed with 'your Highness' or 'your Lordship'". And then there are some authors (and editors, agents, and publishers…) who seem to believe that readers are stupid and/or uneducated and won't notice the difference. It's "just romance". Not like what we're doing is "real" or even, gods forbid, "art".

That was sarcasm.

The thing is, historicals have their readership. It's not that different from SF/F readers—a SF/F reader will feel short-changed if they are being sold a book as a sci-fi/fantasy story that isn't. Historical readers are very much the same. There are lots and lots of highly educated readers who are hungry for good historical fiction, but they have all been burned by bad writing and bad research. And yes, while everybody makes mistakes (I certainly do), make too many of them and you lose the trust of the reader. It's hard to pull off, but the authors who manage find readers for life, who will, over time, turn into a devoted readership that buys everything they put out and recommend it to all their friends. So, while historicals take extra effort, I think it's worth it just for the loyal following that'll help to sell your books.

Research, research, research

Why is research such a crucial part of writing historical fiction? In short, it's the blood feeding the whole story. It informs the characters, the plot, and the tone/feel of the piece. It's also a vital part of the world-building, and that takes more than a scattered "thou hast" or "'twas" taken from Shakespeare. If it doesn't inform every element of the story, it's either done wrong, or represents a huge wasted potential.

Often, only research will uncover interesting facts that will enrich your story. In my case, research is my start and end point of any historical I'm writing. A sentence on the exorbitant price of spices in the Middle Ages might trigger a book on a spice trader and his bodyguard. A note on how tournaments were banned for forty years in England might lead my English knight to travel to France to win honour and glory, turning my book into a medieval road movie. A book on shady art deals done during the Occupation in France might add a layer to a German soldier in my current story and turn him from a villain to a tragic character who needs art to stay sane after having been traumatised in the trenches in WWI.

To write historicals, I'd suggest you read as widely as possible about the period and location(s) you're setting your story in. Every detail you discover has the potential to not only trigger a story idea, but make your story richer and deeper. Make plenty of notes of such interesting factoids—you'll never know what they are good for. I call those bits of research "gold dust"—they are that precious. Make sure you have a pocketful of those as starters to get you going. One of the factoids I'm currently carrying around in my head is the reputation of Viking raiders as enthusiastic rapists of English/Irish monks. Now, there's an M/M story in there somewhere—quite possibly a dark one.

Making research more painless

If you don't enjoy research, you might want to stay away from historicals. But if you do enjoy getting your hands dirty in a library, here are a few cheats I'm using to make thing easier:

1) Wikipedia

While my professor would disagree, Wikipedia is a good start; just don't trust it. Usually, Wikipedia articles are curated by people with a specialist interest in a given subject. They might be very good, like the German article on gladiators. However, always cross-check all information you take from Wikipedia against some other source. Two independent sources usually give you a good footing. If you use contemporary sources (that is, written in the period), check them against modern books from reputable publishers (university presses tend to be decent, and historians working/teaching in the field can often be relied on). Mistrust everything else: A book written in the 1950s claiming Richard Lionheart may have had gay tendencies is not enough of a basis for you to depict King Richard as a sadistic Dom with a ménage kink and a travelling canvas sex dungeon and still claim this is historical.

2) Other M/M writers active in the same period

Thankfully, whatever period you're interested in, you're likely not the first or only one. Get in touch with other writers of historicals for some mutual sanity-checking. Somebody who's researched the Age of Sail can likely catch issues in your Age of Sail story—or at least point you to books she found useful. Make sure, once you're an expert yourself, to return the favour. Also, offer something in compensation—proofing or beta-reading is likely welcome. Most authors are tremendously generous with their time, but make sure you do your homework first and don't expect them to do your research for you. You find these authors on Goodreads or mailing lists or via Speak Its Name.

3) Experts

Once you have a decent footing in your chosen time period, you might be able to draw upon the generosity of people who "do" history professionally. I've had very interesting discussions with curators or guides working in museums. If you're really hardcore, you may get in touch with a reenactment society. These people know a huge amount and can be absolutely vicious about the nitty-gritty details, but they might know things few academic historians would have considered. Ideally, approach them with a specific question, and listen. Keep them talking—these people have the gold dust. Make notes.

Once you're done, thank them for their time, and if they are interested, you can offer to send them the manuscript for a historical check. By all means, thank them in the book itself—give credit where it's due, and people love helping writers, as long as they are happy to learn and do their part of the work. Whatever you do, do not lecture an expert on their field or bring your strong opinions; I've once spent several minutes cringing while a self-appointed wannabe lectured a professor of Ancient History on how Augustus was exactly like Adolf Hitler.

To meet experts, go to museums that cover your period or a subject that you're dealing with in your book. If at all possible, attend lectures; many local museums will have guests of honor giving talks on their subjects. I've once had a fantastic ten-minute discussion with a medical historian (also a retired military surgeon) on what kind of emergency care a German officer would have received in 1942—research that could have taken me days to uncover by traditional means.

4) Your library

Libraries are wonderful things (and free, or cheap), so use them. Librarians are tremendously helpful uncovering books you didn't know existed, and they can point you at magazines (which they can likely get you, too) that cover your period. While I have one of the best resources in the world within reachable distance (the British Library), as a working writer, I don't have that much time to actually go there. I buy a lot of books and tend to build a book collection for every book I write. I scour used bookshops, normal bookshops, public libraries, the reference library of museums, specialist bookshops, ebay, Amazon Marketplace, and Google Books. There's a phase in my research where I just accumulate material. Not all of it makes it into the story, but many of the books I buy will not only go into one of my books, but several. These are also great to procrastinate, so use this with caution.

5) Mainstream historical writers

I absolutely recommend reading mainstream historical novels. It can be incredibly helpful to read a mainstream historical novel covering the same time period. It'll show you how a colleague tackled the period, and how they present all that information they've researched. It's an enjoyable way to learn about the period you're writing in, though, again, do not trust their research. Even mainstream historicals are full of mistakes, so cross-check everything.

The 5-Minute Rule & the Secret of the Square Bracket

I'm a stickler for details. Just recently, I was in full swing writing about a WWII soldier, when I mentioned one of his decorations. And my writing flow hit a brick wall. The Iron Cross First Class—is that the one worn on the breast pocket? Or as a ribbon on the second button on the tunic? Is it fastened with a needle? A ribbon? What's the colour of the ribbon? This stuff has me in a frantic mess with no effort. My inner movie rips apart and I freak out and scour the Internet for a page that covers this detail, and my writing session ends abruptly and my productivity goes to hell.

These days, I'm employing two rules: The 5-Minute Rule says that if I hit a wall like that, I set a timer on my phone and have five minutes during which I try to find the information on Wikipedia or specialist sites. If the problem is more complex, I might give it 10 or 15 minutes. If that time passes without a solution, I bring the heavy guns: The Square Bracket. The sentence then reads:

He reached for the Iron Cross on [research exact location of Iron Cross First Class], felt its weight and sharp edges.

I use square brackets exclusively for research holes, so I can find the bits that need fact-checking or extra research after I've finished the first draft. I'm also using comment bubbles on facts I'm not sure about or that need a second check. I have a comment on my current WWII book where one character tells another that the Germans have just invaded Russia—obviously, that happened on a specific day, and I have to make sure that the timeline of historical events meshes with the timeline in my novel. I comment on anything I'm not sure about and then do the fact check once I have the first draft completed, or, in some cases, when I'm stuck. Even if I'm not adding pages, at least I'm making progress by cleaning up the research.

Exterminate with extreme prejudice: The info dump

I think we've all read books where the author just shows off how clever she is and how much research she's done. Say, we're in the middle of a battle scene, and suddenly our main character starts talking about the metallurgy of his age, how his sword was made and how much it cost and how many weeks' wages he paid for it, or what else he could have bought for the amount of money. He might give us an overview on why the Swedish troops are invading Poland and who else is politically involved, and what will happen if the battle goes a certain way. At that point, most Kindles/Nooks/iPads are getting tested for their aeronautical qualities.

This research might be necessary (certainly the author should know this), but under no circumstances should it be allowed to interfere with the story. If readers wanted just the facts of the Northern Wars, they'd get a book by a historian.

Any research that made it onto the page and that ends up detracting from the story itself needs to go. Anything the reader can imply from what's been said and done before can be cut. When it comes to the info dump,

I strongly suggest cutting more rather than less, even if it's cool and interesting stuff and you worked so hard to research it. The research is mostly for you rather than the reader. If the characters have no way of knowing and don't care in that situation, then the information needs to go. A soldier on a battlefield won't think about the politics. He'll think about immediate matters of survival. Don't put it in to show off how great your research was, don't put it in to boost your word count. What facts you do absolutely need, weave them into the story, making them almost feel invisible, like a spice in a dish that's everywhere and heightens the taste and experience, but if the dish is just spices, it's inedible and will be rejected. Again, check how good mainstream authors work in facts and period detail without bogging down their books.

Oh, by the way—Author's Notes

Sometimes, you might end up tweaking the facts. Sometimes, it might be impossible to get your hands on a piece of information that's vital for the story. In those cases, I like to add an Author's Note to explain this—I write about why I made the choices I made, or where I'm assuming things because it's impossible to verify. In these, it's important to not lecture. Don't show off, don't ramble through the minutiae of why you don't mention the number of buttons on a peasant's shirt on page 5 because you couldn't find a good source.

Imagine instead you're sharing some cool research bits ("I found out the Scottish did not wear kilts in the Middle Ages, fancy that!") with a friend over coffee. I also always include that all research mistakes are my fault. Essentially, they are, and I own it. Despite my best effort, I will have mistakes in the text, so that's where I plead for forgiveness.

Last but not least: Good luck. It's a difficult genre full of challenges, but so, so worth it.

Historical Fiction Roundtable featuring Tamara Allen, Alex Beecroft, Charlie Cochet, Charlie Cochrane, Ava March, Aleksandr Voinov.

What historical period do you write in? Why this period? Do you also write contemporary fiction?

Alex Beecroft (*False Colors*) - I mostly write 18th Century Age of Sail, though I have also written a Saxon novel (currently in my agent's hands, not yet published.) I love the many contrasts of the Age of Sail—the world is opening up, Western man is discovering strange new worlds and new civilizations where no Western man has gone before. The vulgar vivacity of the common man contrasts with the elegant deadliness of the aristocracy, and both contrast with the emerging ideas of equality and the Rights of Man. And that's without the glamour and peril of the sea.

I have written one plain contemporary novel and a contemporary fantasy. I enjoyed the fantasy, but don't think I will write plain contemporary again.

Charlie Cochet (*The Auspicious Troubles of Chance*) - I write early twentieth century, specifically the 1920s and 1930s. I've always had a passion for these periods thanks to a certain Mr. Cary Grant who swept me up into the glamorous world of classic Hollywood all those years ago, and it hasn't let go of me since. I'm absolutely fascinated by everything about these periods, by the history, fashion, art, music, movies, architecture, and more. When I started reading M/M Romance, I sought out all the stories I could which took place during these periods and had pretty soon exhausted my list. I knew what sort of stories I wanted to read and figured if they weren't out there, maybe I should write them.

Until very recently I've mainly been concentrating on historical, but I had known when I started writing that I didn't want to limit myself to one genre. I wanted the freedom to explore my imagination and run with whatever story took my fancy. Though no matter what genre I get into, historical will always be there because I love it too much to give it up.

Ava March (*Brook Street: Thief*) - I write Regency-set historical romances, typically around 1820. Trousers became more socially acceptable around 1820, and since I can't type the word pantaloons without snickering, I set my books so my characters can wear trousers without being frowned upon.

Overall, I love the Regency era, the adherence to proper decorum coupled with the element of indulgence/excess. And no, I don't also write contemporary fiction.

Tamara Allen (*Whistling in the Dark*) - I've written post-WWI, Depression era, and late Victorian. I chose these time periods because events within them fit the story I wanted to tell. Most of my story ideas blossom from historical incidents that intrigue me, no matter the time period.

I've written contemporary scenes within a time-travel novel (two novels now, though one is still a work-in-progress.) I've never written a novel set entirely in the present.

Aleksandr Voinov (*Skybound*) - I'm largely a Middle Ages (especially 12-14th century) and WWII kind of guy. And thinking about why those, I think what I like exploring is the change and shift in societies (and people) by war and conflict, fuelled by ideology. But my interests range far wider than that—once I'm done wrapping my head around the Crusades and the Second World War, I'd be interested to look into Antiquity.

I do write contemporary fiction; my Muse burns out of any genre or period after a couple books, so I'm jumping around quite frantically between contemporary genres, fantasy, straight-laced historicals, and science fiction, only to begin the circle anew a couple years later.

Charlie Cochrane (*Lessons in Trust*) - I write primarily in the early twentieth century. I have tried my hand at Regency and WWII, but my heart lies within the thirty or so years either side of 1900. Why? Because ever since childhood, I've read authors from that era. Conan Doyle, Jerome K. Jerome, Wilkie Collins, E.M. Forster and the like. I can almost see and hear that time, and writing the right cadence for the dialogue comes naturally. Add to that a passion for WWI poetry and living in an Edwardian house, and choosing that era almost seems inevitable.

If you write contemporary fiction, can you draw sales comparisons?

CCochet - At the moment, my only non-historical piece is a Christmas story about elves at the North Pole, which seems to have sold very well, but then again it was during the holiday season, so I can't draw a real comparison with historical as of yet. Though from my understanding, the sales figures for contemporary are usually consistently higher than for historical, but I'm pretty certain that can be said of most genres that aren't contemporary.

AM - Does not write contemporary fiction.

TA - No, but interestingly enough, my time-travel novel sells far better than any of my other work, probably because of the modern-day main character.

AV - *The Lion of Kent*, co-written with Kate Cotoner and published with Carina, did reasonably well, all told, considering the state of my career I was at and the fact that Carina has marketing muscle. *Skybound*, my WWII story about a German fighter ace and a mechanic, has three strikes against it, sales-wise: It's short, literary, and low on sex. First-person present tense puts some people off, too. Sales-wise, nothing beats funny, light, sexy contemporaries, which I write very rarely. *Skybound* has sold a fraction of any contemporary I've done, and sells roughly equal to my science fiction. Still, both genres have devotees, and many of my readers are happy to follow me across genres, but that's my "core" audience and not the "mass market" by any stretch of the imagination.

CC - Not a lot of difference, to be honest. The most striking contrast is between ebook sales and paperback, the former dwarfing the latter. I've heard some readers say that one of the biggest influences on sales (i.e. their buying more books from an author or in the genre) is quality of product. A bad experience with a poorly written M/M book can put people off for life!

AB - My contemporary novel has outsold all my historicals. If I was writing for the money rather than for the love, I would concentrate on contemporaries.

Can you share your top three resources for historical research?

AM - 1818 Map of London from the UCLA Department of Epidemiology (available online), *The Regency Underworld* by Donald A. Low, *British Titles of Nobility* by Laura A. Wallace (available online).

TA - Google Books (though they've made research more difficult by removing the buttons that allowed a specific time period search,) *New York Times* newspaper archives, and my own growing library of 19th and 20th century diaries and history books.

AV -I'm a book hoarder, so my top resource tends to be my own library. Any project starts with a weekend raid of all available bookshops. If it has a military bend, Osprey Publishing tends to get a good chunk of my money. That said, there's excellent stuff on the Internet.

I use the etymological dictionary at www.etymonline.com to try to catch the worst in terms of modern usage.

A site I've recently used when I did a historical check on a historical published by Riptide was www.roman-empire.net, which has a very good gallery. For ancient sites, I often check Flickr, too.

YouTube is surprisingly useful for research. For Skybound, I watched footage from airshows where WWII planes are filmed in action, as it were. Nothing beats actually hearing the engine sound of a plane you're describing. Similarly, WWII footage on YouTube is plentiful, and just recently I found a video very helpful of a re-enactor putting on a German WWII uniform (the things people film!). It answered questions about dressing and, uhm, undressing in a crucial scene.

CC - For me, the best resources are ones contemporary to the time. Books or plays written in the same decade, newspapers from the era, nonfiction books which draw on the experiences of people alive then (like Max Arthur's wonderful series of "voices" from various wars). If you read a history textbook, you always get the story told with the writer's bias and a touch of whichever axe they're trying to grind. Take some of that away and you build up a truer picture—and the better a picture you can build up in your head of ordinary life, the more convincing your portrayal will be. And I'd also recommend Oxford English Dictionary online, to check if words and phrases are appropriate for the time. Some words go back a lot further than you'd think and some ("blizzard" for example) are surprisingly modern.

AB - If you're interested in the same period as me, then *The Wooden World* by N.A.M. Rodger and *Seamanship in the Age of Sail* by John H. Harland are indispensable, but if you mean in general, then I always default to books. Go to your library and take out all the books you can find on your subject. Then check out their bibliographies and hunt down those books too. The Internet just doesn't compare.

CCochet - I use a never-ending list of books and websites for research, depending on when and where the story takes place, as well as what it's about, though I always try to make certain I double-check my facts. The history side of things can be found easily, it's the facts regarding real gay men living during these times that's a little harder to find, but I try to use resources that can back up their research with evidence, such as one of my favorite books: George Chauncey's *Gay New York: Gender, Urban Culture, and the Making of the Gay Male World, 1890-1940*. The Jazz Age Club (www.jazzageclub.com) is a great website put together by Gary Chapman containing everything from fashion to the gay-subculture. Third is Paper Dragon (www.paper-dragon.com/1939/) This site is intended to be a sourcebook for RPG games, including pulp or noir games, but I found it has accumulated a fantastic collection of everything you need to get started writing in the 1930s, from slang to the Great Depression. It's a little dramatic, but great fun and a good place to start.

What's your opinion on using dialect, archaic language, accents, or foreign words?

TA - I like a little of it for verisimilitude, but dialect in every line of dialogue always throws me out of the story. I won't buy a book that's dialect-heavy, no matter how well reviewed.

Foreign words, accents, and archaic language are all fine, as long as the author uses them for a good reason and not just for show.

AV - If thou dost use methinks and 'twas, please be a historical linguist or have a historical linguist friend reading your manuscript. Ripping off two words from Shakespeare and scattering them in your modern porn dialogue won't make it a historical.

There are authors who do an amazing job using the cadences of then-contemporary speech (Maria McCann set the bar extremely high with *As Meat Loves Salt*) and I absolutely suggest reading mainstream peers to see how they handle it, but unless you're an artist at McCann's level, I'd suggest using period language sparingly and mostly for flavour. More important, however, is avoiding modern concepts. You cannot have a Roman gladiator ponder whether his lanista has an Oedipus complex (Freud wasn't born), for example. Similarly, before corpses were opened for study, most people had only a very, very rough idea of where organs were in the body, what they were and how everything worked (I read a fascinating Roman, I think, text, about how the heart heats the air in the chest). Even medical professionals of the day had no clue. Metaphors and similes that are absolutely modern throw readers out of the headspace at that particular time. I'd be cross about an Ancient Egyptian pondering democracy, too.

That said, I like foreign words in text (again, for flavour, or when any translation simply wouldn't work or add the same thing), and I think most readers are okay with that. In that case, I believe in glossaries—some readers don't want to feel "left behind". Not everybody had Latin at school. So while the meaning of the foreign word/sentence should be very clear from the context, it can't hurt to have a glossary—if nothing else but for courtesy and to sneak in some more cool stuff (I'm guilty of that).

CC - I think it's a minefield. Like those awful films where you have people in France, clearly talking in French, but they're just speaking English with a French accent. Any aspiring historical author should read Mary Renault's Alexander Trilogy. Nobody speaks cod-Greek or cod-Persian. It's the cadence of the language and the sprinkling of specialist terms (like names for items of clothing) which depict the setting and the era. I don't mind using—or reading—some dialect terms, especially if the story is set in a part of Britain where the local argot is distinctive. Geordies don't use the same words as cockneys and a reasonable amount of local words helps to flavour the story. But if you use so many your readers can't understand what's going on (or if you need to provide an index to explain the words) then you've gone too far. Don't let the detail get in the way of telling the story; everything in moderation.

AB - Your goal is to achieve verisimilitude, not mimicry. Use enough of all of the above to enable your reader to feel that they are really hearing from an ancient Pictish warrior, or an Aztec priest, or whatever. Ancient and foreign people did not sound exactly like modern Americans, so don't write them that way. But don't make them so inaccessible that a modern reader can't understand or sympathise with them. It's a balancing act and an art. Too modern and they are false to their time, not modern enough and the reader balks—figure out your own happy medium.

CCochet - In my opinion they should be used sparingly. The devil is in the details, as they say. For me, these tiny details can make all the difference in achieving believability, but only if you're not constantly bludgeoning your readers over the head with them. If you have a character with a heavy accent, there's no need to phonetically spell out every word he or she says. That could get annoying really quickly. Listen to someone with that accent speak. Break it down. Do they speak fluent English and simply have a prominent accent, or do they speak little English? Research it, even if it's for a small part. Use a real person for reference, not a caricature of one, unless that's what you're aiming for. If you use foreign words—unless it's meant to be a mystery, let the reader know what the words mean fairly soon. You don't want a reader stopping three paragraphs later after their need to know what was said is so great they have to go Google a translation.

AM - With dialect and accents, I only use enough to give the flavor/feel to the character's speech. Too much, and it becomes hard and/or annoying to read. Above all, a book needs to be enjoyable to read. My goal is to capture the speech patterns of the time period without forcing a reader to turn to a dictionary. For example, foreign or archaic words used in context so a reader can deduce the meaning.

How do you balance the genre expectations of writing romance with the historical reality of the bias and oppression gay men and gay relationships have faced during different time periods?

AV - Research. We can safely assume that gay people always found a way to stay under the radar, as it were. Close friendships weren't necessarily suspect, either, and there's a lot of male-male affection/interaction on display that would look alien and suspicious to our modern eyes (I mean, what's up with Richard Lionheart sleeping in the same bed with the French king?), so real gay couples could get away with quite a few things. For example, in *Lion of Kent*, William sleeps in his lord's bedchamber, ostensibly to guard him. (Spoiler: guarding isn't all that happens.) In war, comradeship is an intense and intimate bond, that can easily cross the line, but in a men-only context, "these things" happen. Any military commander knows that, and will he waste good men to uphold morality if there's a battle to fight (especially if he has the choice to ignore it or warn the guys in question to at least keep it in their pants while under orders)?

It also depends on the power and status of a man. You may whisper about the king of England, but gods help you if you don't have some solid power to back you up.

There's also the matter of how characters deal with their homosexuality. In my WWII books, there's a whole range of behaviours. Wolfgang, an SS officer, twists his repressed homosexuality into a sadistic urge to punish and break people. Richard, another soldier, decides that, yes, homosexuality is wrong, but as long as he's celibate and a productive member of society, it's not amoral or harmful. Yves, a singer in Paris in 1942, grows up in the hugely queer subculture of the Montmartre entertainment/red light district. Every one of those men has a different sexual history, tackles his issues in different ways, and will hide away from society once they've paired up (apart from Wolfgang—he dies). Yves takes his lover as a secretary. Richard, always a "confirmed bachelor" (which is code for: not interested in women) will live a quiet, secluded life in the countryside with a "close friend".

CC - With a delicate hand and a lot of pragmatism! There always have been gay men and some of them have managed to stay under the radar (or the equivalent to radar of the time!) Using discretion, employing marriages of convenience, hiding in plain sight (for example within traditionally all-male institutions), gay men have found ways to survive, deflect suspicion, and find a sort of happy ever after, or at least a happy for now.

Clearly one can't have the big white wedding or other typical romance genre ending, but you can find imaginative ways for your heroes to stay together. And actually, that's a great challenge and stimulus for a writer, creating that believable happy ending.

The advantage we have, of course, is that we don't have to conjure some threat or danger to a relationship. Having to keep the emotions hidden to the world supplies that ongoing tension—and creates plenty of space for UST (Unresolved Sexual Tension).

AB - Romance has always consisted of two characters facing desperate risks to be with one another, so I don't see why there is a problem. Gay men suffered terribly in the historical past, but in a romance you can be sure that your characters will win through that risk and that oppression and come to a happy ending. The greater the peril, the happier the reader can be at the eventual triumph of the characters. And after all, there must have been some men who lived happily even then, it's just that by virtue of them slipping under the radar of society, we can't know about it. (My *Blessed Isle* is imagined as the story of one such couple, sealed away in a bank vault until it could safely be told, centuries later.)

CCochet - Obviously when writing romance, the romance part is very important. Whichever way an author tackles said romance is up to them, but if it isn't there, your readers will understandably be disappointed. A big part of it has to do with the type of story you want to tell. My stories tend to have a combination of humor, drama, and action mixed in, but at heart, it is most certainly a romance. I also accepted a long time ago that I write to entertain, so although I won't ignore the oppression and hardship these men went through, it's not always the main focus of my stories, but it is, however, a part of them, of what defines them, and it shows in the way they interact with the people around them as well as how they react to whatever situations I throw them in. They are always aware of their surroundings and what it means to be a gay man in that world.

Whether my story is about a detective, prohibition agent, or chorus boy, I try my best to make certain my characters are always a product of their time. I want them to be as true to the men of these periods as possible, even if I may not agree with the way they think. I have several characters who have come to terms with their sexuality—some more easily than others, but they are always aware of what it means, of the pain, suffering, and confusion they experienced to get there, as well as the dangers they face should they be exposed. It's engrained in their minds and reflects in their actions.

Where and when my story takes place also has a great impact on the characters and who they are. If I want my characters to have a little more freedom with their way of thinking and their relationships, then I have to place them in cities which would have allowed them that. Places like Chicago, L.A., New York, or Paris where gay-subculture not only existed but thrived would be more appropriate than rural Kansas. Happily ever after is important to me, but I have no intention of ignoring what these men faced during these periods.

AM - That balance is one of the key elements of a historical gay romance, and I handle it different ways based on the characters. The historical reality is always there—gay relationships had to be kept hidden from the law, the church, and society. Yet each character is his own person. Some may feel those constraints more than others, some may be more accepting of themselves than others. I've found if I write from the character's head and keep the focus on the romance, then I can find the balance that best fits each book.

TA - After reading George Chauncey's book on gay culture in turn-of-the-century New York, I incorporated in my first M/M the more tolerant attitude a minority of gay men were fortunate to find in the time period. While there was documented truth in what I wrote, some reviewers took issue with it, and I learned that it was probably wiser (and I think now, fairer) to tell the tale of the majority, as far as imitation of life goes. As I tend to write soft rather than gritty stories, I don't go into the details of the brutality as much as other authors do. I've read some of the early twentieth century diaries of gay men to get a feel for their mindsets and how they coped with a prejudiced world, and I do my best to write characters who live their lives as optimistically as those men did, keeping in mind the special care they had to take just to find each other. A happily ever after is more difficult to come by, but people can be amazingly resilient in their pursuit of it.

What are your thoughts on historical romances that are more costume drama than realistic and accurate portrayals of historical reality? Is there a place for these stories in the broader genre of gay romance?

CC - My thoughts? Mixed. I like a historical romp as much as the next person (fond memories of black-and-white films on the telly on a wet afternoon) but there's a point at which even I go "Ow!" Like someone in Regency times listening to Big Ben chime, or Robin Hood saying he'll travel from Kent to Nottingham in a day. Real howlers bring the genre into disrepute—as does bad writing of any sort—although people aren't really likely to want the gruesome details from an era. Do we want to know about bad breath or body odour or dirty linen or bad teeth? So I guess writing historicals is about employing a light touch; don't say somebody's teeth are gleaming when they're likely to have been pretty ghastly. Just don't mention them. Just say your hero has a charming smile.

AB - Each to their own. I like historicals because the past was not like the present. For me the appeal of a historical is the appeal of visiting a strange, exotic country—I like as much difference and oddity as I can get. But I know there are people who want the clothes and the titles without the OMG bizarre worldview and risk of syphilis. If that's what they want, more power to them. There's room for both sorts in the world.

CCochet - Absolutely! I think as long as the reader is aware of what they're getting, there's something for everyone. Like plenty of folks, I didn't go to see *Pirates of the Caribbean* for an accurate portrayal of the time period. It was just smashing good fun. There's nothing wrong with fun, and I personally enjoy costume dramas, but like with anything else, I expect to know what I'm getting into. There has to be a good reason behind someone writing a costume drama where the author takes creative liberties other than the fact they can't be bothered to do the research or want their fellas kissing out in the open. If you're going to do it, do it well, and don't try to pass it off as something it's not.

AM - If readers want to read historical romances that are more costume dramas, then there is definitely a place for them within gay romance. Romance is within the broader fiction genre, after all. But if a book jumps outside historical reality to a point where, for example, gay relationships are socially acceptable during a time period when they were in fact illegal, then such a book should be in the historical-fantasy subgenre of gay romance versus historical gay romance.

TA - I read historical romance to be immersed in the period and to live it through the eyes of period characters, so I don't read the costume dramas, but I know there are readers who are very happy with them, so yes, I think there's a place for them in the genre. I do often wonder about the authors. If you have enough fascination with a time period to set a novel in it, why not be as accurate as you can in your details? I think I just hate to see such potential unfulfilled.

AV - As long as these wallpaper historicals are clearly labelled so I can avoid them, I'm just fine with them. I do think they have a readership, but I'm really not one of them. But I'm a historian by training, so my demands are pretty high. For me, the whole point of a historical is to delve into the issues and mindsets of the day (though much of that is conjecture, but that's fine, as long as it's done with respect for the period and the reader).

What's your best tip for avoiding the dreaded historical info dump?

<u>AB</u> - Just don't do it. Think of historical facts as being like pepper. Shake a light scattering over the whole dish, don't dig pits in the mashed potato and fill them full of it. Remember that, to your characters, the era they live in is the modern world. Do you feel the need to explain modern politics and medicine and customs to yourself and your friends? Neither would they. You as the author should know it all, but your characters only need to know enough to decide what to do next.

<u>CCochet</u> - The history is obviously important, but to me it should be so well integrated into the story that you feel as though you've been transported back into that time period rather than receiving a history lesson. It should be there in the background, seep through your characters' voices, their wardrobe, their manner, their conversations, their very being. It should be in the relevant little details of what they drink or what they drive, what they read or listen to. Whatever facts you use should be relevant to the story.

I give enough details to set up the scene, but there's no need for me to tell readers the name of every single knickknack in the room with my character. If he's reading a dime novel, unless it's important to what's going on, you don't need to know exactly what title he's reading. I don't need to describe in detail the car my character is driving. If you know the story takes place in 1930s, black four-door sedan, Buick, or roadster should suffice. I don't need to go into how many cylinders, or the exact make and model, unless it's pertinent to the story. If my character is a mechanic, of course he'll know it's a 1931 Deluxe Phaeton with chrome steel top frame and natural-finish wood bows. If my character's a detective, he probably wouldn't care, and if he's driving it, he shouldn't be—it's well out his price range. Whatever my character is doing, I make certain it makes sense for the period, the story, and there's enough detail to paint you a picture without making it sound like you're reading a page out of a Sears & Roebuck catalogue.

<u>AM</u> - Write from within your characters' heads, from their point of view of the time period.

<u>TA</u> - Nurture your fear of boring the reader. Too much description and your reader stops visualizing the setting and starts to yawn and skim. As for backstory, I find it's much easier to catch the irrelevant stuff after I've

finished a first draft. With the first draft, I'm telling myself the story, so I info dump freely. I need it on the page if I'm going to trim it into an enlightening bit of information or slip parts of it somewhere else in the story where it will work to better advantage. Info dumping freely in first draft has helped me learn to edit.

<u>AV</u> - Ultimately: Have a very good editor who'll cut it ruthlessly. Will a peasant carrying a pike into battle really spend pages and pages discussing the political setup of the early seventeenth century and explain who the warring parties are and what they want? No. He'll be scared, maybe excited, he might hope to get a new pair of shoes (or any shoes at all) from the battlefield. He might think about things that are important to him at that point in time. Will he worry about family? Hate the enemy because they torched his crop? Be on the lookout for water because it's a hot day and he's been marching for hours now? Keeping a very tight focus on the characters help. Readers can usually fill in the blanks with a few carefully placed hints and details.

<u>CC</u> - Um. Just don't do it? Seriously, if you feel tempted to show off your knowledge, restrain yourself. Or edit it out. And never explain—if something needs explanation or a glossary, find another way to say it. To give an example, if you're writing about some upper-class lads in the Edwardian era, you could have them raising their hats as they pass a lady in the street, or have a scene where they change for dinner (with perhaps a valet at hand to help them). You don't need to explain why they're doing any of these things. It's just part of their lives.

And please (personal plea to historical writers) could you restrain yourselves from the sort of "Oh, I see the Titanic's sunk!" type of conversations? If you can't find another way of telling us your story's set in 1912 London, put the date and location as a chapter heading. By all means have people discussing contemporary events, but make the dialogue believable. Rant over.

Share your thoughts on the challenge of writing characters who are true to the beliefs and historical attitudes of their time and yet remain sympathetic and relatable to the contemporary reader. What is more important to you: political sensitivity or historical accuracy?

<u>CCochet</u> - It's very difficult, because you're depending a lot on the reader to understand these were different times. I'm not saying the behavior is

excusable, but you have to respect the fact that society has evolved. Our way of thinking has evolved. You can't write a historically accurate story with characters who think like we do, and you can't judge the way these characters talk and think based on our modern mentality. I'm not talking about bigots, because you'll find them everywhere. I'm talking about your protagonists, and holding them up to a standard they couldn't hope to live up to in current climates. One of my favorite detectives is Raymond Chandler's Philip Marlowe, who is very much a man of his time. Am I going to hold him up to today's standard? No. These books were written in the 1930s, '40s, and well into the '50s by an author who was also very much a man of his time. Am I going to frown every time I come across Marlowe being politically incorrect? No. Should I judge any other character set in these periods any differently simply because it was written by a modern-day author? Definitely not. I certainly have no intention of compromising authenticity in my own writing. Why bother writing historical to begin with if we're going to ignore the history?

As for remaining sympathetic and relatable to the contemporary reader, it's up to me as an author to make my characters sympathetic despite their flaws, to make the reader understand why he is the way he is. Something about them has to resonate within the reader. The level of political sensitivity will depend on the type of characters you have, what circumstances bring those beliefs and attitudes to the forefront, and how significant it is to the story. When my protagonist refers to another gay man as a fairy, my character development should be strong enough to draw about the appropriate reaction from a reader, and it should be different from the reaction drawn about when the term is used by a bigoted, spiteful character, because believe me, there will be a difference, and everything I write, everything I set up should lead the reader to understand these differences. If a reader can't separate the mindset of a historical character to a modern day one, then perhaps the historical genre is not for them. It's perfectly understandable.

AM - There's a balance there, but it's all in how the author crafts a character and where the author puts the reader's focus in the book.

TA - I prefer historical accuracy over political sensitivity. It's not a story truly set in the past if you allow your characters to react with modern mindsets. I say this, but I've yet to write about any really controversial issues.

Some reviewers think my work tends toward a rosy, almost fairytale view of the past, and they're right. But as I gain more confidence as a writer, I hope to reach a point where I can tackle the challenge of creating characters who reflect the prejudices of the times without being off-putting to the reader.

AV - Hoh boy. So far, I've avoided the worst of that. My WWII main characters tend to be middle to upper class and educated, so they step into their world with a fairly wide mental horizon from the start. (I'm not saying lower-class or less-educated people can't have/be that—but free access to education certainly helps.) Richard, while a typical Eastern Prussian noble and hence from a very conservative and nationalistic background, is not a fanatic. He actually remembers that Jews used to be front-line fighters in WWI, and he simply doesn't get the anti-Semitism of the Nazis. In fact, he resents the Nazis as petite bourgeoisie playing at world-domination games and believing in nonsense like horoscopes and expects them to plunge Germany into chaos. His tragedy is that he is increasingly isolated and under threat and has to go into "inner emigration", a kind of emotional deadening and detachment that helps him get through the war. He focuses on his horses instead.

The villain in that story, however, is a "true believer"—the archetypical Nazi, young, brash, with all that entails. As a bad guy, I can go to town with him, and writing the things he says is emotionally exhausting, let alone really offensive to my own sensibilities. Still, he can't just "be a Nazi"—that's a lazy shortcut. We do learn how he became a believer, what drives him (essentially, ambition, which is a positive trait), and he gets punished, so the reader's sense of poetic justice is served.

I have another main character who's SS, and it's clear he's young and idealistic and was very much instrumentalised by the regime. He's not much interested in racial theory (in fact, studying Aryan skull shapes is "boring and useless" for what he's really interested in—defending his homeland). Once he acknowledges his homosexuality, he realises he'd get exterminated just like the Jews and "gypsies", and that destroys his faith in the system. He has a huge amount of good qualities, and he comes out of the POW camp in America as a "good democrat" and in love with an American, so I'm hoping readers will forgive him for mistakes he made as a youth.

I think what's important is to show why these beliefs were held and also show characters open-minded and questioning themselves. A crusader may arrive in Jerusalem cursing the "filthy heathens", but realities of coexistence can easily soften him up, and what happens if he encounters that hot Saracen warrior who teaches him a trick or two? Culture clash and prejudice provide a huge amount of conflict and potential for growth, so I wouldn't soften it all into a Disney version of itself. But by all means feel free to add an Author's Note at the end to explain the choices you made.

Also, what's really, really important to bear in mind is attitude versus setup of the book or conscious choices you make as the author. For example, it's okay, in my mind, to show a character being a racist. For example, he believes—as many did—that French colonial soldiers were all out to rape white German women, that's the propaganda of the day and absolutely a period attitude, distasteful as it is now. However, if you make the choice to have a French colonial soldier show up and actually rape a white woman, that's a totally different matter, and yep, racist (made worse if he's the only one committing rape in the story and that's all he does—you get the idea).

CC - Accuracy, all the time. It's completely unfair on your reader to fill your characters' dialogue and thoughts with modern opinions or make their actions anachronistic just to make everyone feel comfortable. A simple trick is just to avoid them discussing slavery or the role of women or whatever it is that's relevant to the situation. Or if they do discuss it, you can take a philosophical approach, perhaps having them debate the pros and cons of getting rid of deportation for those convicted of robbery or anything else which seems barbaric to our modern eyes, but don't feel obliged that they have to see the barbarity of it. If you can't do that, avoid the topic altogether.

One of the ways I handle it is just to have people act as they would most likely act/think and just get on with the story. I don't need to explain why they change for dinner, so do I need to explain their seemingly old-fashioned attitudes?

AB - Trick question, yes? Both are important. Again, it's a balancing act between your characters' authenticity and your reader's sensitivity. Yes, it's highly unlikely that your characters will share a modern American's viewpoint on things like slavery, sexism, classism, racism, etc. They do not share the centuries of development of thought that allow a modern reader to frame their opinions the way they do. That doesn't mean they have to be disgusting bigots, however. In all ages there have been people who thought for themselves. If your character has a good heart and a decent amount of empathy, this will express itself no matter what the beliefs of his society. In short, try to satisfy both.

What, in your opinion, is the single greatest mistake writers new to the genre make?

AM - Not understanding how to transfer the essence of research into a historical romance book. For an author new to historical romance, the majority of research will be about getting the feel of the time period—taking everything they've researched and using it to put their characters in the time period. Research shouldn't be shoved in a reader's face. It should feel seamless, effortless, so the reader feels immersed in the time period without the book coming across as a history lesson.

TA - This is a tougher question to answer, because what I consider a mistake is something that seems to mostly benefit those writers in terms of sales and popularity among readers. When sex scenes dominate a book to the extent that it feels as though the characters are defined solely by their sexuality, that book is a DNF for me. I don't feel invested in characters who seem to have nothing else going on in their lives. They never become real. I think a lot of writers are doing themselves a disservice by limiting the scope of their work that way, but I don't believe they'll ever see it as a mistake as long as it sells.

AV - Treat historicals as contemporaries in sexy clothes. Research is vital, readers will spot whatever shortcut you've taken from a mile, and they will call you out on it. If you do write wallpaper historicals, make sure it's clear from the marketing/promo material that it's taking liberties with fact and accuracy. Essentially, don't dress up industrially produced turkey as hand-reared capon. Readers can tell the difference.

CC - Trying to show off all their lovely, newly acquired knowledge of the era. Or trying too hard to emulate *Pride and Prejudice* or *Downton Abbey* or whatever's flavour of the month. Or trying to make the dialogue sound historical.

At the other end of the scale, they don't always check what seems obvious, or what they've assumed must be so because they've seen it in a TV drama.

Hence the frequent Big Ben mistake—it hasn't been chiming in London since time immemorial, but only since 1859.

AB - They either add too much research or too little. As I say, it's a balancing act, and it can take a while to hit that balance.

CCochet - I know a lot of folks will say research, but for me it's the characters. I'm very character driven, and if I don't like the characters, no matter how well researched the story is, I'm going to have trouble getting into it. If your characters think and talk like modern-day men and women, that's going to disappoint me. I want the characters to transport me back in time, to capture my heart, squeeze it, and hold on tight as I read about them struggling to attain or keep their love. You're telling me this character grew up in the 1800s, 1900s? Make me believe it.

How is historical fiction relevant in a genre often dismissed as porn or fluff?

TA - About a year ago, a gentleman by the name of Ulysses Dietz wrote to tell me he thought my stories were a sort of speculative fiction. He said they read as if they could have been written in the era they were set, which led him to imagine a past where M/M romance stood on the bookshelves alongside m/f. It was a "what if" that made him happy to think about. To this day, I remember his email as the one that opened my eyes to just how relevant historical fiction is to the genre. Authors who take the time and care to write historicals with respect for both history and the lives of men who endured in the face of ignorance and prejudice are creating a body of work that will make it increasingly difficult for anyone to dismiss it.

AV - How is historical writing relevant in the mainstream? I think gay historical fiction entertains and teaches, just as straight historical fiction. Gay historical romance occupies a similar niche to straight historical romance—entertain, revel in the love of history, tell a damn good story that takes the reader somewhere else and delights them, gives them an emotional release of some sort, even turns them on.

I'm quite sex-positive there, I do like writing a good sex scene that has the reader panting or squirming. Getting to somebody on that visceral level is a huge power trip for me. Words I put on the page turn a total stranger on. How brilliant is that? And fluff—well, it's not been long that all fiction was considered fluff. Literary authors wrote romances for educated women readers that they, or the literary establishment of their time, didn't really respect themselves. But guess which books survived? The romances, now re-labelled as high literature or even classics. So I don't really give two hoots about anybody dismissing my stuff as porn or fluff, even if they are lighter or sexier reads (which I do occasionally write).

I know I'm using every bit of sweat and energy I have to tell the best story I can, and my readers are all who matter on that count. And as anybody who's been in a bookshop lately and browsed the writing of the titles so prominently on display—they don't actually write better than we do. They just had the luck of the draw that they ended up writing about straight couples and what big publishing thought would sell a lot of copies. I'm quite positive that the genre will be harder and harder to ignore or belittle as time progresses. In the meantime, I'm doing all I can to tell the best stories I can and be just as painstaking in my research and self-editing as any self-respecting and ambitious author in any other genre would be.

CC - How long have we got? Sad to say, some historical fiction is simply porn/fluff with added ruffles, poorly researched, poorly written. Fine if you want plenty of sex and no plot but not if you want a solid storyline. So a well-written, well-researched story transcends the accusations of this not being serious writing. (And I'd like to see anyone dismiss *The Persian Boy* or the *Regeneration* trilogy as fluff.)

AB - The genre ought not to be dismissed as porn or fluff. Obviously, there are books out there which are one or the other (or both at once), but there are also writers in all the subgenres of M/M romance trying their hardest to write works of decent literature. I really object to the idea that it's not possible to write M/M romances which are also good books. Good historicals, just as much as good contemporaries, good fantasies, good mysteries, etc. are absolutely vital to the quest to make people stop dismissing the genre as simply porn or fluff. M/M romance can be literature too. I certainly prefer it to be.

CCochet - Just as many dismiss the genre as fluff or porn, I think within the genre, historical fiction is often misjudged. It's seen as a chore to read by some or that it's going to be all doom and gloom. The moment they read "historical", you can hear their heavy sigh. As if you were about to tape their eyelids open and force them to watch a four-hour documentary on the various compositions of mud in war throughout history. Granted, there may be some historical fiction where you need nothing short of a PhD to get through it, but you can't dismiss the whole genre as being the same. Of course every reader has their favorite genres. I don't read a lot of horror fiction, and I certainly don't go out of my way to read it, but if someone recommends a good title or I'm looking for something a little different, I'm certainly not against giving the book a go.

When I set out to write historical, I did so with the intention that anyone who reads one of my books could enjoy it regardless of whether they were a fan of historical or not. Like I mentioned, for me, it's first and foremost about the characters and the romance. The history is there to create a believable and accurate world, to draw the reader in and add to the characters, not detract from it. I've had plenty of folks tell me they don't normally read historical but they love my books, which to me means I'm doing what I set out to do, and most importantly, enjoying every minute of it. There's room in the genre for all types of stories, drama, comedy, dark, fluff, as long as you love what you do and do it to the best of your abilities. Your passion will show through in your work, and isn't that part of being in love? Passion?

AM - Historical romances are above all romances, stories about people finding lasting love. That path to love usually has challenges contemporary people don't face. And it's those challenges that can give a reader a different appreciation for life in the 21st century, and for how strong love must have been to triumph against the historical odds.

JOSH LANYON

SPECULATIVE FICTION

Welcome to Fantasy Island by Nicole Kimberling

In a genre so huge and diverse as romance, there are bound to be subcategories. One of the most prominent at the moment is the crossover between romance and speculative fiction.

So what is speculative fiction? It is what we could loosely describe as the literature of the fantastic, such as science-fiction, alternative history, and urban fantasy, as well as horror, magical realism, slipstream or the big, epic classics such as *Lord of the Rings*. Speculative fiction often starts with the question, "What if?" As in, "What if some humans had psychic powers?" or "What if there was a human colony established on Ganymede?"

Within romance, speculative fiction has three big subgenres: futuristic, time-travel, and paranormal.

Futuristic romance is, as one might imagine, set in the future. It can be on a spaceship, a distant world, or an accelerated version of our own. Time-travel is self-explanatory. Paranormal romance deals with vampires, werewolves, witches, or demon-hunters.

Arguably there is a fourth category, simply called fantasy romance. This can include stories of angels coming down to Earth or historicals containing a magical element, such as an Irish lad who has the power to heal with song. Or fantasy romances can be set on whole new worlds that are completely unrelated to our own.

Writing any fantastical romance is similar to writing historical in that the author must create a satisfying romance plot while building a credible world.

However, unlike the historical author, who may simply research her chosen time period, the fantastical author bears the burden of inventing not only the characters, but the entire world they inhabit.

I suggest that the key to building a believable, unique fantasy setting lies in wild extrapolation combined with rigorous adherence to rules.

Sounds contradictory, huh? But it's not—not really.

Extrapolation is how an author gets her "What if?" idea from a germ of thought to practical, plot-advancing scenes written down on paper. But before any extrapolation can begin, the author must establish some rules.

If, for example, some humans have psychic powers, then what are the parameters of these powers? Can characters start fires using their minds? Can they tell the future? If the characters do have powers of precognition, what are the limits of those powers? Can the character see only three days in advance? Must he be touching another person to foresee his or her fate?

Establishing rules is crucial to maintaining dramatic tension in a story, because it is only possible to feel fear for a character who has some chance of failing.

The good news is that as the author, you make the rules. The corresponding bad news is that once these rules are established, you may not break them without losing the reader. If your vampire is barred from stepping on consecrated ground, then you best not have him strolling around inside some mega-church, drinking coffee and noshing on stale butter cookies.

On the other hand, if what you want is to write a scene where a vampire does this very thing, just don't make the rule that he can't. Have his ability restrained and his actions curtailed in some other fashion.

So the first step in stepping away from reality is, perversely, making some new rules. What then is extrapolation? It's the process by which an author pushes the rules that she's made to their logical end, thereby creating unique situations for her fantastical characters while maintaining a sense of reality.

Let's say that you've established that your character can start fires using the power of his mind. First, is he also somehow immune to fire? Let's say that he is. If he has a nightmare where he is engulfed in flames, will he make that a reality and set his own house on fire? And if he keeps setting his house on fire in his sleep, how does he keep from committing sleep-arson?

Here is where a speculative author comes to a crossroads. Faced with the sleep-arson problem, she can choose to go several different directions. She can go back and decide that he's not immune to fire and also that he must start fires consciously.

But I wouldn't advise that, because it solves the problem too easily and is therefore boring.

More interesting would be for the author to go research some real sleep disorders and apply the details of them to her story. Research does have a place in fantastical fiction. It can serve as an armature for wacky ideas to climb up. Realistic details are what make a piece of fantastical fiction believable as opposed to laughable.

Let's go back to our sleep-arsonist. Consider his life as if it were real—as if it were your own.

If I were a sleep-arsonist, I would have so many fire alarms. Maybe if I were rich enough, I'd have a whole fire-suppression system. That fire-suppression system would be constantly triggered, which would bring me under the close scrutiny of the local fire department. Adding that kind of detail—the ceiling being polka-dotted with fire alarms, or the impromptu visit from one very suspicious fire chief—to a story does more for the believability than pages and pages of explanation about how pyrokinetics might work on a molecular level.

Why? Because these details, generated via extrapolation, show cause and effect. The reader can see that being a sleep-arsonist has real-life ramifications for the character. The gap between fantasy and reality is bridged via these details. The line between them blurs and suddenly that a character should be a sleep-arsonist or superhero or hobbit does not seem so farfetched.

With all this extrapolation going on, the fantastic writer must become a master of exposition. The world-building aspect of fantastical fiction requires an author to explain and describe far beyond the requirement of other kinds of contemporary fiction.

Therefore the fantastic fiction writer must become a ninja of information delivery. She must find ways to hide information about her world in every part of the prose rather than just using the narrative summary. Using descriptions of setting, side characters, or stories told in dialogue, an author can get huge amounts of information to the reader without resorting to the dreadful, story-stopping, info dump.

Ginn Hale is a fantasy author who is excellent at making prose do double duty. I've excerpted a couple of passages from her novel *Wicked Gentlemen*, to show how it can be done. The first is a description of the story's love interest, William Harper:

> The Inquisition captain caught my attention at once. Just his uniform sent a skittering rush of panic through my languid muscles. A deep desire to slam the door and bolt it shut swept through me. But even when I was drugged to a stupor, my contrary nature arose. I looked the captain over as if he were a mere curiosity. He was a lean man. His black uniform made him seem even more compressed and hard. He wore gloves, as if he did not wish to leave even a fingerprint to attest to where he might have been. His hair was hidden under his cap.

Wicked Gentlemen by Ginn Hale (Blind Eye Books, 2007)

Outwardly this is just a description of the protagonist Belimai Sykes opening up a door, seeing a guy standing outside it and reacting to what he sees. But notice how much information Hale gets into the scene indirectly. We now know that Sykes reflexively fears the Inquisition and that although he is a drug user and afraid of the law he is also naturally defiant.

During the actual description of Harper, Hale uses language to characterize Harper by describing his clothes. We know he is compressed, hard, and hidden.

Here's another excerpt from the same novel that demonstrates how worldbuilding can be threaded into a story. This is a description of a mosaic on the wall of a staircase heading down to an underworld ghetto, which happens to be Belimai's hometown.

> Some optimistic bishop had christened the place Hopetown. Anyone who had ever gone there called it Hells Below. That summed it up well enough.
> It might have been beautiful three hundred years ago when the Covenant of Redemption had brought my fallen ancestors up

from Damnation. They abandoned their great kingdom of endless darkness in exchange for the promise of Salvation for themselves and their descendants.

The walls of the staircase were adorned with mosaics of the Great Conversion. Ashmedai, Sariel, Satanel. The pride and glory of hell had come in their robes of fire, in their chariots of beaten gold. Some were adorned with jewels, while others wore the polished bones of the angels that had fallen beneath their blades. They had each bowed down before the Silver Cross and submitted to baptism at the hands of the Inquisition.

The brilliant glazes were darkened with lamp smoke and factory grease now, but the images were still discernable. Somewhere among the glittering host of demons, one of my own ancestors stood. They all looked fierce and beautiful. I found it difficult to imagine that I could have descended from such creatures. The blood had certainly thinned.

Wicked Gentlemen by Ginn Hale (Blind Eye Books, 2007)

Here Hale gives us a basic history of the world—pretty much all the history that readers get—disguised as a one hundred and ninety-six-word description of a wall. But Hale goes farther, letting us know Belimai's opinion of himself in comparison to his ancestors. That's a lot of different kinds of information being transmitted simultaneously.

So here's the real irony of fantastical fiction—because it's less real the author must be more premeditated and methodical than almost any other sort of writer. But the trade off is that the fantastical writer gets to make her own rules and own world as she would like it to be. She can make the king a gay centaur in love with an elf and have nobody in the kingdom care about that because they're all much more worried about the economy. For a brief time she can share her egalitarian vision with others.

And that's what I love about speculative fiction. In the words of William Arthur Ward, "If you can imagine it you can achieve it; if you can dream it you can become it."

I'm pretty sure he was talking about gay centaurs when he said that, but he could have also been talking about the enormous potential present in allowing people to spend a few minutes entertaining an apparently meaningless fantasy.

I'm with him either way.

Speculative Fiction Roundtable featuring Astrid Amara, Lynn Flewelling, Ginn Hale, Nicole Kimberling, Jordan Castillo Price, KZ Snow, Andrea Speed.

Why speculative fiction?

Ginn Hale (*Wicked Gentlemen*) - Speculative fiction makes the most allowances for anything the author wants to write about. For me that means that I can play with the laws of time and space and create strange new worlds to share with other people. At the same time there's this huge challenge to make the fantastic seem somehow believable, even normal—like how do you convince a reader that everyone in this world is okay with giant spiders working in their daycares. How do you as an author rethink your assumptions and biases and then lure your readers into doing the same?

It's often really, really difficult but also great fun.

KZ Snow (*Mongrel*) - The answer lies in the word speculative. In many ways it's a genre unbound, free of many of the get-it-right constraints that govern contemporaries, mysteries, hardcore sci-fi, and historicals. I'm not sure if spec fic is the realm of lazy writers who are crazy dreamers or ambitious writers who are disciplined dreamers. In either case, speculative fiction is what "Jabberwocky" is to "The Charge of the Light Brigade," or an e. e. cummings poem to a Shakespeare sonnet. There's a high level of craft if it's done right (read China Miéville or Neil Gaiman), but the expression of that craft is...wonkier.

I have a restless imagination anyway, which is why I genre hop. Spec fic allows it to gyre and gimble in the wabe.

Jordan Castillo Price (*Mnevermind 1: Persistence of Memory*) - It makes sense to write what you prefer to read, and I adore reading spec fic. The "what if?" is the nucleus of what interests me most in any story. I also feel that the speculative elements give me a more interesting way to explore characterization than a contemporary slice-of-life story. "What if?" is the pivot point around which everything else revolves.

Astrid Amara (*The Archer's Heart*) - I like the creative aspects of building a world and staying true to the logic and physics of that world; I like the escapist component of fantasy writing, where you can imagine having a greater impact on the world around you; I'm a nerd.

Andrea Speed (*Infected: Shift*) - Why not? I love reading it, so it seems natural to write it.

Nicole Kimberling (*Heir of Starlight*) - Because those are the ideas that occur to me. It's as simple as that. I guess I never outgrew magical thinking—I just learned to confine the magical thoughts to the fictional realm.

Lynn Flewelling (*Casket of Souls*: Book 7 of the Nightrunner Series) - Writing fantasy is a lot of work, given how much background research I do, and the level of detail it demands, but it also gives me lots of elbow room. It allows me to incorporate some of my favorite genres—fantasy, mystery, history, and horror—with some things I want to say about issues such as racism, sexual and gender identity, honor, and love.

Do you also write in other genres? Can you draw sales comparisons?

KS - I do write/have written in other genres. Contemporaries generally sell the best. Then again, spec-fic stories with popular tropes (e.g., BDSM or slavery elements, wolf and big-cat shifters) or by popular authors can easily outsell many contemporaries.

JCP - All of my novels and series are speculative. Since short stories can be carried with something as simple as a cute plot twist, I've written a few non-speculative shorts—and readers have commented that they'd love to see a contemporary novel from me—but I don't have an interest in writing one. In terms of sales, I suspect I'd sell better if I wrote contemporaries, but I'd feel pretty unfulfilled if I wrote a contemporary just for the sake of sales.

AA - I also write contemporary humor. Sales-wise, the contemporary humor does much better, especially my holiday titles. I think there's a broader audience.

AS - It depends on what fits within the boundaries of spec fiction. Is it science fiction, fantasy, horror? I write all of those. Is it crime fiction and humor? Maybe not. I write those as well. No matter what genre I write in, I only write in ones that sell poorly.

NK - I also write contemporary mysteries now. They outsell my spec fic by a lot.

LF - N/A

GH - I stick to fantasy and science fiction. It's where I do my best writing and have the most fun. I can see the beauty in other genres—I like reading them—but speculative fiction is the field where I work.

If I were writing for purely economical reasons, I'd focus on contemporary romance. That strikes me as the most accessible genre with the greatest number of potential readers.

Given the boundless opportunities of speculative fiction, why do you think we see so few minority and multicultural protagonists?

JCP - I'd suspect it has to do with sales figures. In my Turbulence series, a significant percentage of the downloaders each month and across all markets are skipping the installments that feature a black character on the cover, even at the sites where the download is free. So I imagine that unless a writer's entire platform is about multiculturalism, reduced sales would discourage someone who's begun to experiment with writing diverse characters from pursuing that diversity.

AA - Regardless of whether the setting is Planet X207b or Cleveland, the writing is still done by an author who is going to tell a story from their own experiences. I think as writers we often forget to look outside our own world not only for plot or for setting, but for characters as well. And one unfortunate outcome of the lack of minority protagonists is that when we do write multicultural characters into stories, the story gets billed specifically as a multicultural story, or the race of the protagonist becomes an important part of the marketing, regardless of whether or not that was the author's intent.

AS - Lack of imagination? A funny thing to say when it comes to spec fiction, but there's simply no other reason for it. People need to stop pulling from the same cultural well and branch out more. It's a big world, but it's an even more massive universe.

NK - Until recently, I think that science fiction and fantasy have been seen as a genre for white dudes written by other white dudes. Most of the classics have few female characters, let alone persons of color or LGBT characters. So often when minority authors come to spec fic, in order to maximize the reach of their stories they adopt the standard genre protagonist: a straight white dude. James Tiptree, for example, was a woman who wrote science fiction—mainly about white dudes—under a male pen name in order to be taken seriously.

Since the seventies the genre has slowly stretched to include minority characters. I feel that the most recent expansions in character range have come because of the adoption of Japanese manga and anime storylines and tropes by the younger generation. That isn't to say that Japanese stories are more diverse. They're not. But being Japanese, the protagonists are by definition not white. The ethnic diversity of attendees at an anime convention is quite high, as opposed to a mainstream science fiction convention, where most of the visible people of color are members of the con hotel staff. It will be interesting to see what sort of stories the younger generation is going to write. I fully embrace the notion that speculative fiction is for everyone who wants to dream up a new world—not just the mental playground middle-class white people.

LF - That's a good question. I think historically that most fantasy writers have been white, and write from that perspective. That's changed and changing, with wonderful writers like Nalo Hopkinson, Octavia Butler, N.K. Jemisin, and Cindy Pon.

GH - Well, currently the majority of English-language authors writing speculative fiction are straight white men, and most authors write what they know best—themselves. But I also believe that many authors shy away from writing minority characters for fear of insulting or misrepresenting the people they're trying to write about. (I can't say that this doesn't happen. Token characters and painful stereotypes are a real danger when an author focuses only on the minority status of a character to the exclusion of their humanity.)

But I don't think the solution is to just give up. As a genre, speculative fiction can push boundaries and can break norms established by the societies that create it. As authors and readers of the genre, we have the same capacities.

I think readers who take a chance on stories that do represent minority viewpoints can make a huge difference. Think of the joy of discovering and then getting to tell everyone you know about an amazing new author—maybe the next Octavia Butler. That step alone helps to support and inspire the authors, and it sends a message to publishers that there is an audience that wants a broader perspective in their speculative fiction.

As authors, I feel that we should stretch out of our comfort zones from time to time. As long as we write characters as rounded human beings first and foremost—regardless of race, gender, or social background—we can break away from cardboard cutouts and stereotypes informed entirely by sitcoms.

KS - The answer depends on how you define minority and multicultural. In alternate universes (to borrow a phrase from fanfic), "otherness" can be portrayed in countless ways; it isn't necessarily tied to race or religion or ethnic origin—at least not as we know them here and now. Protagonists' physical characteristics and lineages can come in as many varieties as an author's vision allows.

So, if writers of spec fic address issues like marginalization and alienation, prejudice and discrimination, oppression and persecution, or if they want to explore and celebrate diversity, they'll likely do so through characters and sociopolitical structures they've created. It's simply the nature of this genre that familiar people, places, and things are viewed through unique filters.

What are some of your favorite themes to explore through the lens of speculative fiction?

AA - I'm a sucker for end-of-the-world stories, and I'm-going-to-turn-irrevocably-evil stories. I like settings that are big and melodramatic to better test the mettle of the characters, and I like playing with the ideas of what a character is "supposed" to be—either set by fictional culture or our expectations—and what they instead develop into. Speculative fiction allows us to blow up real-life, critical but maybe everyday themes into mega-crises. So instead of the "I'm gay and worried about what my family will think of me" conflict, which is relatable to real life, we take the same theme and go "I'm gay and also I don't want to be dissected and rebuilt as a robot assassin judge like all the sons in my cyber-family have done before me."

AS - Transformation, isolation, triumphing over difficulties, and those on the outside looking in. No matter how optimistically you look at things, there are always going to be people who don't quite fit the mold. Even in a super-advanced society. I mean, look at *Star Trek*. The strange, offbeat characters were usually the most interesting ones.

NK - I especially like writing working-class characters because with the notable exception of characters in the military, they're so often shafted in science fiction and fantasy settings.

I find I'm also fascinated with characters bodies. Every story I write seems to have characters who can change their bodies, move from body to body, become disembodied, split their consciousness into more than one body. Why? I certainly don't know. I suppose once I figure out why I include this aspect, I won't have to write about it anymore.

LF - I'm probably best known for my gay heroes, Alec and Seregil, in the Nightrunner Series. In conceiving those books I set out to see if positively portrayed gay characters could sell in the mainstream market, and they did. When I first created them, back in the early '80s, most of the gay characters I'd seen in books and films were victims or villains, or worse yet, neutered sidekicks. It was important to me that my characters not only have center stage as the heroes, but also that they have fully functional lives—they fall in love, they become lovers, they have a sex life, they have strengths and foibles, in addition to all their adventuring. And neither of them dies.

In the Tamír Triad, I dealt with gender identity, something near and dear to my heart. What does it mean to be male or female? The main character in that series is a girl who's magically changed to a boy as an infant, then has to deal with finding out that she must change back in adolescence. She experiences a sort of gender whiplash, along with the usual adolescent ups and downs. I also touch on racism, with the deplorable treatment of the indigenous Reth'anoi population by the now dominate Skalans. I modeled that on the way we treated/treat Native Americans.

GH - I really enjoy thinking about the way different cultures and classes clash and come to terms. Also I like to build the ecology and history of a place into the story of its people…and of course I loves me some explosions and kick-ass battles!

KS - Pretty much the same themes I explore in other genres, although often within a darker, more threatening framework. Not to put too high-toned a spin on it, but I seem to write about forces that afflict or attack one's quality of life, even one's soul, as well as the struggle required to overcome such forces. Good spec fic, like any good fiction, is more about the characters than their environment. Yet in good spec fic, unlike much other fiction, the environment often becomes a significant *secondary* character.

JCP - Unintended consequences are always fascinating. Maybe that's rooted in our inherent desire for fairness, or the idea that there is no free lunch. Also, maybe it makes readers feel a bit self-satisfied, like they've dodged a bullet. "We may not have rocket cars like the people in this book, but at least we haven't caused all the helium to leak out of the atmosphere." (Note, I actually have no idea what would happen if all the helium was gone, other than balloons being a lot less fun. That's where research comes in.)

How do you world build a universe that is both original and unique—and yet somehow make it accessible and recognizable to readers?

AS - Good question. And the honest answer? I don't know. Usually I start with an idea and a character, and I see where it all takes me. In the best outcome, the character and the idea help build each other.

NK - Honestly, I never try to make a unique universe. Because what interests me is pushing ideas to their logical (if highly unlikely) extremes, I usually end up with settings and concepts readers have not seen before. The challenge for me is to make these wild ideas accessible. I try to temper the weird stuff with very mundane details. For example, if I have a world covered entirely in concrete (really implausible for many reasons), I make sure to talk about drainage problems or flash floods (totally plausible and even boring). In my book *Heir of Starlight*, I have a human character whose soul is implanted in the body of an orangutan. Because in this world placing human souls in the bodies of animals is common, I made sure to mention that the character has a couple of self-help books with titles like *Legal Strategies for the Disembodied*, and *Outlook: What Inhabiting An Animal Can Teach You About Being a Better Person*. The presence of a self-help book—a real object which everybody has at least seen if not read—legitimizes the speculative claim that humans could be transferred into animal bodies at all.

LF - I look to history and our world for inspiration, and do tons of research on everything from medieval cookery to castle building, sewers to fashion, and lots and lots of politics and language. Paying attention to small details without boring the reader with endless exposition is a challenge. I also try to make my characters real people with whom the reader can identify.

GH - I can get crazy with my universes, so I try not to purposely build wildly elaborate worlds, but instead to create settings and histories that tie into the plot and affect the characters. At the same time I try to make sure that the characters seem like they really do come from their worlds.

That's not to say that I wouldn't set something in a floating castle or an underground city, but in each case the setting should be bringing something out in the characters or telling the readers more about the plot—not just taking up pages with descriptions and exposition.

KS - Through the characters. Always through the characters. Seeding them with humanity is the key. They could be sandworms or demons, androids or animate flank steaks; their world could be an asteroid or cesspit or iceberg. But if readers feel for them, can relate to them, the door is open.

JCP - I enjoy changing only a small element, and extrapolating the results of that small change, but otherwise having the storyverse exist as people would expect in a contemporary. A reader recently told me that she didn't like fantasy because it was too much work to re-imagine every single aspect of the story world. That's often true for me as a reader, too. With novels high in world-building, there can be new geography, new technology, new customs, new names...and that really is a lot to take in on the part of the reader. I think by concentrating on the small but significant speculative difference, and especially in anchoring that difference in an otherwise familiar world, an author can direct the reader's attention more precisely to the focal point of the story.

AA - Does it take an entire page to describe your setting? Then it's probably too complicated and will be hard for readers to follow along. I usually try to find a way I can describe my universe in under a sentence, e.g. "It's set on a slave ship but the slaves are humans trapped in the bodies of little bunnies and the ship is in outer space." Yikes, that's an awful premise. I'm already crying for those bunnies! How about, "The world is set during the French Revolution…" (okay, good because I can now create a visual in my head of costume, architecture, culture) "…only the poor underclass are trying to overthrow a leading class that has lasers for eyes and chainsaw fingers." (Original, yes. But WTF?) But that's the idea. I like to play with something we can easily place as readers—a historic or contemporary time or place—and then add in the original "speculative" twist. As far as creativity goes, I have a simple rule: Is my character's magical abilities easily explained with a single word like, say, "vampire"? If so, it isn't creative. But that's my personal pet peeve—I realize I'm alone on a vampireless, zombieless, werewolfless island out here.

Supertext refers to ideas so frequently explored and developed by writers that those ideas become mythos. For example, the trope of vampires having no reflection and suffering sunlight intolerance is now supertext. Can you offer any examples of how you've expanded and evolved on supertext within your own work?

NK - Normally I try to avoid tropes because it's sometimes more work to struggle against an existing trope than to just make up something new. However, in the Irregulars anthology I wrote a story called "Cherries Worth Getting," which did include a vampire. I didn't address the idea of vampires having no reflection in the text, but the reason I came up with for this trope to exist is that in my story the vampires all had illusion spells on them because they were hideously ugly. I also linked stories of spontaneous human combustion to the vampire mythos. Basically I claimed that all the humans who had spontaneously combusted were not humans at all, but vampires. My method when using supertext is to push farther into it to see if I can explain it in some new way.

LF - I don't think I can answer that. You'd have to ask my readers.

GH - Tropes are tricky!

On one hand they limit what readers will accept and expect, but on the other hand they can save you a lot of expository work—because the Prodigals in *Wicked Gentlemen* are the descendants of "Devils", readers quickly accepted their odd physical attributes as well as the premise of the entire book. If I'd said they were descended from some magical beings whom I had just made up, I would have then been burdened with pages and pages of exposition and explanation.

While physically maintaining the supertext of devils I was able to explore their humanity and in that way break from the concepts of pure evil and pure good on which so much devil mythos is built.

I think it's quite important to consider why you're writing about a trope when you decide to take one on. I mean, if you say that a character is a leprechaun, then readers have certain very strong expectations about how that character will appear and behave.

If you break with those expectations—your leprechaun is a black guy who stands nearly seven feet tall—then readers are going to be dismayed and you're going to have to do some quick, clever writing to convince them to go along with you. Now if the point of your story is the explanation and it tells them something new—the leprechaun is a changeling and you want the story to speak to themes of interracial adoption—then readers will often go along with you and even find the alteration fun and refreshing.

It's all in the thoughtfulness of how the subject is handled, I think.

KS - I've had vampires of different breeds, which makes sense to me. I've had one, who happens to be Jewish, pierce with a fingernail rather than teeth; he eventually reverts to mortality (in the Jackson Spey-Adin Swift cycle of stories). I've had one who eats normal food but can't eat lentil soup because it gives him gas. He also takes a drug to make him diurnal (the Utopia-X series). I've had a zombie who's sentient and dresses better than the men around him (*Abercrombie Zombie*), and a post-apocalyptic world that isn't grim and monochromatic but instead composed of diverse city-states governed by flawed angel-demon-human hybrids (*Utopia-X*). I have a magician who's primarily a stage illusionist, and who constructs a penis-shaped automaton that's a profane Aladdin's Lamp (*Mobry's Dick*). I have a dystopian thriller that's like Margaret Atwood's *A Handmaid's Tale* yet unlike it in more ways than I can quickly explain (*Acts of the Saints*). I have a powerful urban wizard who's a middle-aged ex-biker going through manopause and battling insecurity (the Jackson Spey-Adin Swift stories).

But no matter how much I stray, I harbor enormous respect and appreciation for tradition—Stoker's kind of vampire, Romero's kind of zombie,

Lovecraft's kind of monsters, Orwell's and Bradbury's visions of the future—and I believe those classic types can still be successfully interpreted by contemporary writers.

JCP - I tend to avoid tropes wherever I can, or at least twist them, because once something has been written a certain way, I don't see the need to keep repeating the same trope. So for my Channeling Morpheus series, I did have the vampires inactive during the day, because that seems to be one of the main weaknesses vampires have in popular culture, and it nicely balances out all the vampires' advantages. However, I avoided the tropes of the vamps belonging to clans and being fabulously wealthy and owning nightclubs, because those things have already been done…done to death. One of the traditional lore-based vampire weaknesses I expanded on is the inability to cross running water, which I figured would be a more interesting liability to explore. I got a lot of mileage out of what I eventually grew to call the "water willies." It seemed like a fresher take on a pop culture figure that still nodded to tradition.

AA - Supertext is actually something I rebel against for the reason I mention above.

AS – Hmm… I suppose it all relates to the infected virus, in my Infected series. (Has anyone noticed the virus doesn't have an official name? That was a deliberate choice. The virus is so strange, it's just assumed, in this universe, when you say infected, you mean specifically the cat virus.) The virus kills and kills hard. Becoming a werecat is horrible and dooms you to an early death and a poor remaining life. Except in one case. (The most important plot point of them all.)

Speculative fiction is all about the What If? What is your litmus test for deciding whether an idea is strong enough to carry a story?

LF - It has to hold my attention enough to write about it. Writing is a long and often arduous process, and if you're boring yourself, you're sure to bore your reader, too, assuming it ever sees the light of day.

GH - I tend to think that a really good author can find the story in any idea. That said, I am not that skilled of an author, so I tend to look for the conflict in an idea and try to consider how compelling it is and how difficult it would be to resolve. That tells me if there's enough plot in the concept to fuel a story.

KS - Simple. If it's something I'd be interested in reading, it's something I'm willing to try writing.

JCP - I'm pretty intuitive about choosing my story concepts, although it's easier in a series because you're starting with a certain amount of world-building and characterization under your belt, and the challenge there is taking the characters to the next satisfying place in the series arc.

Usually an idea with a lot of strong potential keeps me wondering. It continues to lure my attention and my imagination back to it. I find myself daydreaming about different ways various scenes could pan out.

AA - Does the "what if" premise provide a good setting for a character to emotionally evolve? The "what if" is always a good starting point... What if our protagonist wakes up to find herself completely alone in the world, but nothing else has changed? Okay, so that's a "what if" premise, but now the real test for me is what can a character DO in this setting? Obviously if she is the only person on the whole planet, she might investigate to figure out why, but the plot isn't going to go far until there's conflict. And for me, the best stories involve the evolution of a character, so how does this experience change our protagonist from the person she was at the outset? If it can be a good backdrop for character development, or an interesting plot, then I go for it.

AS - Write it and see. If it peters out a few pages in, it's done. A good idea should keep building.

NK - If I ask, "What if..." and then I answer myself, "So what?" I don't write the story. In other words, if I can't make the "What if..." mean anything beyond the obvious, I know I don't have anything to say about the subject. An example would be, "What if this girl found some big mysterious machine buried underground and then after excavating it she realized it was a terraforming machine and that her planet had been terraformed?" To which, I would mentally reply, "...so what's the point of that?" If I can't take it to the next step, the idea gets shelved until I have something to say about terraforming or childhood discovery or buried machines.

What are three of your favorite research resources?

GH - I LOVE this question because I'm a huge nerd!

For me research resources depend entirely on what kind of information I need. If it's just data that I want, then I like books best—paper or electronic, I don't care. Libraries, Project Gutenberg, freebooks.com and bookstores are like treasure houses to me. You can also find lists of resources to investigate on Wikipedia—but I'm hesitant to rely on Wikipedia alone for any large, or very detailed subject.

But research also involves things that aren't going to be found in books or online. There's a great deal of real-life experience that informs writing—and the most evocative and insightful writing is going to come from personal experience: be it the feel of a kiss or the taste of fried grasshoppers.

For a fantasy author, I'd certainly recommend taking at least a few fencing or martial arts classes. No online video or textbook is going to let you feel how time seems to slow down or how your whole body goes hot and fluid when you're fighting really hard. And even if you could look a description up in a book or watch an interview, that isn't going to give you, as an author, your own personal insight.

I know not everyone can spend years studying Aikido or sail across the Atlantic like a pirate of yore. But as authors we can extrapolate from other experiences, and the more we do, the more personal resources and insights we have to draw upon when writing.

So, maybe you're not going to race from wolves that are hunting you through a forest. You can still take your dog for a run in the park. And you'll certainly come closer to the feeling of wind on your skin, the slip of vegetation beneath your feet, and the feeling of your heart pounding in your chest than you would have if you'd looked it up online.

(I guess I could have just summed all this up by saying "read books but also do things!")

KS - They change with each book, so I have no regular go-to sources.

JCP - Interviews - Although it's a lot of work to set up—and although many of us writers are shy wallflower types—if you can interview an expert, it's huge. I've interviewed a taxidermist, a travel agent, and a pilot, just to name a few. Going into an interview, you may think you know what your questions are. But it's usually something the expert says that's unrelated to your direct questions that gives you a critical insight into how their experience actually feels, and how you might convey that feeling in your story. Personal observations made by a crime scene tech, about how the job makes her think about humanity in general and how her family can never grasp the things she sees, have greatly influenced the way I think about my PsyCop series and the motivations of my main characters.

Message Boards - Some subjects feel too intense or personal or impractical to directly interview an expert about. When I wanted to find more information on chemical castration for my novel *Zero Hour*, I discovered message boards where chemically castrated men were giving one another advice. I go back and forth as to whether it's ethical to utilize a resource like that for the purpose of writing fiction, but in the end I think we do honor to sensitive topics by portraying them in as realistic a light as we can.

Google Maps - Since it's not financially feasible for me to visit every location I'd like to use, the "street view" on Google Maps can at least help me avoid certain blunders, like putting skyscrapers in cities where buildings top out at ten stories, or sticking a Victorian in a neighborhood full of bungalows. Access this feature by searching for a location or address in Google Maps, then grabbing the yellow person-shaped icon and dragging it onto the map. This feature was very useful in allowing me to wander virtually through the Bermuda airport for my Turbulence series.

AA - Uh, yeah. Wikipedia. I know it's lame, but it is ALWAYS a good first source. From there I usually branch into topic-specific books and websites. For example, I'm writing a speculative fiction novel at the moment set during the Crimean War. And while I got most of my details from books, I also use an online Victorian Wars forum for great answers to the questions I had regarding the minutiae of the time (what was the name of the ship that carried so-and-so's regiment, what kind of oil did they use in lanterns, etc).

AS - In specific or in general? In specific, I love the *Science News*. In general, I love both the web (ha-ha! What a cop out...) and my local library. (Yes! I still occasionally do research at my local library. Because it's fun.) But the Internet has opened up research in a way that just wasn't possible to the average writer ten years ago. It's amazing.

NK - My wife is probably my favorite resource. She knows something about almost everything. And what she doesn't know she'll look up and tell you about. After her, I use other real people. I consult experts, interview friends, relatives, and acquaintances. I always favor verbal interviews with real people over printed materials because I get better language. Lots of jargon and slang. And, of course, there's always Google for the subjects for which I lack an interviewee, but I always try to personalize the research.

Like, one time I was researching the experience of gay law enforcement officers. So I picked a specific gay officer whose name came up in a lot of different contexts and on many different pages. I researched only his life rather than doing a broad survey so that I had a person who is a gay law enforcement officer rather than a generalized collage of a gay law enforcement officer with no personality.

LF - I'll give you four! *The Archer's Craft* by Adrian E. Hodgkin (not easy to get these days), *Ancient Inventions* by Peter James & Nick Thorpe, *Rodale's Illustrated Encyclopedia of Herbs* by Claire Kowalchik and William H. Hylton, *The Medieval Cookbook* by Maggie Black.

One of the potential weaknesses in speculative fiction is when world-building and technology overwhelm characterization and relationship. How do you balance that?

KS - So regrettable, yet it happens all the time! In steampunk, for example, I cannot abide stories that belabor their steampunkiness. If I open a book and immediately run into the same old Victorian London setting, continual references to machinery and gadgetry, detailed descriptions of period clothing, repeated mentions of the word *steam*, and similar whacks over the head, I won't get further than a few pages. Invariably, I want to shake the author and scream, "I get it already!" No book, regardless of genre, should make the reader feel s/he is attending a fan convention.

How can a writer avoid this trap? The most effective way is to realize the characters and storyline more fully than you realize the setting. By all means, let the environment come alive in your mind, and vividly conjure it on the page...but not in a ham-handed, info-dumpy, TMI way. Any defining aspects of a world can be woven into the narrative—as it proceeds and when appropriate—without disrupting it.

Two other important things to keep in mind are these: First, trying too strenuously to explain the workings of an object that doesn't exist is an exercise in futility. Unless you're a theoretical engineer (if there even is such a profession), you're not going to know what you're talking about—and neither will your readers. Instead, give the vehicle/contraption/machine/mystical *thing* an evocative name and convey a sense of its appearance and purpose. That should be sufficient. Reading is an interactive experience, after all, and most readers would rather develop their own mental images than be bored to tears by tortuous verbal blueprints.

Second, the inhabitants of an AU take their environment for granted, like we take suburbs and cellphones and satellite TV for granted. So it's unnatural—unrealistic, if you will—to go off on a tangent about something that's commonplace in that world, a *fait accompli*. A new invention or discovery, on the other hand, warrants more text space, because the characters themselves are trying to understand it.

<u>JCP</u> - Remember the old TV commercial that showed a Ginsu knife cutting through a tin can and then slicing right through a tomato? They could have talked about what kind of steel it was made from and how it was forged and to what angle the blade was honed. But would you remember all of that detail thirty years later? Unless you're a knife expert, probably not.

Showing something in action is worth ten times its word count in exposition. The old saw is "show, don't tell", but I find that directive so overused that it's no longer resonant. What it means is that showing a concept in action makes that idea more easily understood by the reader than by simply explaining the concept. You could show the element via scene, or you can tell a little anecdote about it, or you could sneak clues about the concept into your world-building.

Including the Ginsu knife story was actually an example of how to use anecdotes to illustrate a point rather than presenting ideas in an expository way. See how I snuck that in?

<u>AA</u> - It is hard to avoid the info-dump but critical to explain enough to make sure readers aren't confused. The world-building and technology should never get in the way of the story, however, so if I find while re-reading something I wrote that the narrative is paused while I describe the intricate workings of the "shootemgizmometer", then I need to rework that information in elsewhere.

<u>AS</u> - Luckily, the world of Infected is a parallel universe to ours, so the technology is at an equivalent level. But I do have more of a space-opera type sci-fi that I'm writing, and the key there is just not to go overboard. Yes, you can have amazing technology, but just don't go overboard describing it, or you'll get lost in a sea of exposition real fast. Stick to what is good for the reader to know, and move on. The characters should be paramount in the story. The reader is following them, not your nifty new antigravity system, so keep that in mind.

<u>NK</u> - I give as little information as is necessary to understand the plot and then stop. If while writing I discover that I need to add a few more sentences of world-building, I go find some spot in the manuscript where I can slip the information into a description or the character's internal monologue. I try to give the characters opinions about the information so that it seems like characterization, rather than exposition.

An example would be to write a line like, "Howard turned left to avoid having to pass by the Xertaxian War Memorial. Seeing fresh flowers laying against the bronze took him right back to Danver's funeral. Traveling ten years backward in a second—that wasn't the sort of time-trip anyone would want."

Rather than writing something like "The Xertaxian War Memorial stood proud in the center of the town as it had for the past ten years. Built of bronze to honor fallen soldiers, it formed the business district's central land-mark. Mourners still placed fresh flowers there, and most days the base was strewn with bouquets."

In the first example we not only learn that there was something called the Xertaxian War, but that it's now over. But it hasn't been over long enough for people to stop putting out flowers. We also learn that Howard had a friend named Danver who is dead. We infer that he was a soldier because of the war memorial. We also know that Howard still does not want to confront Danver's death for some reason.

In the second example we learn some stuff about a statue, but have no idea of the relatedness of that statue to Howard, our protagonist, so it's hard to remember it or even to care. Getting the character involved with the exposition should always be the first choice.

LF - Characterization and relationships are first and foremost for me, so that's not a big problem. I really have to watch out for big chunks of exposition, though. I find you can give the reader a lot of background and cultural information through dialogue, something else I love writing. Just avoid the "As we both know" pitfall. That's just bad writing.

In first draft I will have a lot of exposition because I am telling myself the story and showing myself the world. In subsequent drafts I pare out a lot, and portion the rest into manageable bits that let the story flow like a stream around stones. Too much exposition becomes a dam that kills the flow. The balance between world-building and characterization differs from writer to writer, but overall it's something I've learned to do by ear, as it were. I just know when it works and when it doesn't.

GH -Yeah, this is something I have to be very careful of in my own writing. It's one of my worst faults because I like details and complexity, which can get easily out of hand.

When I catch myself writing in a bunch of details about a nifty setting that don't effect or drive the characters in any way, then I know I have to cut it. Otherwise I might as well just be designing an elaborate board game with dice instead of characters.

When I'm cutting details I really liked, I just remind myself that the story is the whole point of world-building not the other way around.

Have you ever had to scrap a story? What was the final deciding factor?

JCP - I scrapped a story sequel during the research stage, which was disappointing because I'd done quite a bit of work on it, including interviews and travel. In the first story, I'd established that the love interest was from central Iowa. I'd intended to explore his home and his life in a follow-up book.

But my trip to central Iowa was so miserable—lonely miles and miles and miles of corporate corn—that I lost heart in the project and didn't pursue it. I have so many potentially usable ideas that it seemed like a bad investment of my time to cling to a project I didn't love anymore simply because I'd put in the upfront effort.

AA - I wrote an end-of-the-world novel, but the problem was, by the time it concluded, I had to actually end the world. That was a bummer. I learned a valuable lesson that day. Don't write end-of-the-world stories, because the ending is always a letdown. I wrote another novel about the devil trying to get a vasectomy so he never has a son, so there would never be an antichrist, so there would never be a judgment day, and the devil would never end up shackled and driven back to hell as prophesized. I learned another valuable lesson from that failure—don't have a protagonist be inherently unlikeable like, oh…Satan.

AS - Yes. The deciding factor was it was a chore to write. If it's a chore to write, it's a chore to read. Although, here's a fun fact. The first version of *Infected* I finished, I felt there was something wrong with it that I couldn't put my finger on. It didn't seem right at all. So I shelved it, even though I really liked the idea. Years later, I decided I really wanted to write that story, but I had to figure out what was wrong with the first draft. I deduced the lead character was all wrong, and I wrote it instead with Roan as the lead, and voila—problem solved. If your story doesn't have the right character at the helm, it will never work.

NK - Yes, of course. I round-filed a 90K space opera because the theme and tone were grossly disjointed between the beginning and the end. Nothing short of a complete rewrite would have worked to fix it.

LF - I've scrapped a couple of book ideas and a number of short stories because I didn't have more than the kernel of idea, a seed that wouldn't grow in my imagination. If it can't hold my attention, it's not going to hold anyone else's.

GH - I scrap stories often, even completed ones. I've thrown away at least four entire novels and I don't know how many short stories. For me the reason is simple, but painful; I wasn't a skilled enough author to really bring the stories to life or do the ideas they contained justice. I try to use my failures to recognize just where I need to improve, and in that way use them to ensure that my next story doesn't end up in the recycling bin.

<u>KS</u> - Once, but it wasn't a spec-fic piece. It was a contemporary Christmas story, and I wasn't enjoying writing it. That, for me, is the ultimate test of whether or not to proceed.

A SERIES OF UNFORTUNATE EVENTS

WRITING A SERIES

Readers are very fond of series characters, so the temptation often exists to take appealing characters and turn them into series stars.

The first thing to know about writing a series is you don't begin a series because you love your characters. Loving them is a plus, but not being able to let go of your characters is not really enough. Nor is it enough that readers—or even your publisher—beg for more. Again, that's all great, and those are all factors in the decision to continue writing about a particular set of characters, but the main reason to write a series is you have a story to tell that can't be done justice in one book.

Writing a mystery series is a little different from writing a romance series where often the subsequent books will feature supporting cast members from previous stories (all those Hot Men of Seal Team 8 or Sexy Donahue Brothers or Sassy MacCafferty Sisters type things spring to mind). It's also different from writing fantasy where there's such a huge overarching plot that the hero's personal quest is almost secondary.

In a mystery series, each story—case—is complete in itself, although there may be a greater and overarching mystery to be solved. But just like in romance or in fantasy, the real story has to do with the central protagonist(s) major and ongoing conflict with…well, whatever that conflict might be. The conflict might be internal and personal or it might be with a powerful antagonist. But in all instances, we begin with the protagonist(s). The characters are what keep readers coming back for more, even in series books that seem to have run their course (and we can all name several of those).

An ideal series protagonist is someone readers will be willing to spend a long time with, years with, someone they will watch grow and change—and yet still recognize as an old and familiar friend. What makes readers fall in love with some characters and not others is as great a mystery as any concocted by Agatha Christie, and I don't have any real insight there beyond making your character as real as you can—giving him both strengths and weaknesses, but don't let the strengths be superpowers and don't let the weaknesses be more interesting and dominant than the strengths.

I do have some useful tips, though. **Don't** give your protagonist a lot of quirks and mannerisms. However amusing that stuff is in the first book, by the fifth book, you won't be laughing. **Don't** saddle him with a disability or any kind of health issue unless you're prepared to deal with it realistically and long term. **Don't** make the supporting cast of friends and family too large, too zany, or too psychotic. **Don't** make your main character a cop or any other member of law enforcement unless you're willing to do a LOT of homework.

Do keep extensive notes on supporting cast as well as the main characters. It doesn't seem like it when you're writing the first book, but you will forget the make of your protag's car (let alone the color), what year he graduated from college, and the middle name of his youngest sister. Yet without fail these are the very kinds of trivial details you'll have put down in print in one book or another.

Do consider carefully where your protagonist will live (and how easy it will be for you to research that place) and what he does for a living (same as above). If you're writing a mystery series, consider whether his profession is something conducive to a life of crime. Any category of crime fiction is suitable for a series, but consider *carefully* what you want to write in the long term. Don't write a comical amateur sleuth first book if you don't actually enjoy writing comedy or amateur sleuths. You can't change tone and genre mid-series without some heavy reader attrition.

Do give your protagonist family and friends and a community to live in. Your supporting cast is not only the source of subplots, they will be useful for future main plots. A personal investment on the part of the protagonist always makes for a more intense and interesting story.

It helps to know you're writing a series BEFORE you start writing the series. That allows you to do two very important things: plan the course of your character (and perhaps story) arcs and—most important—avoid tying up all the loose ends at the end of the first book.

That last point is especially important because, while readers will inevitably complain at the end of the first book that you didn't tie up all the loose ends, if you *do* tie up all the loose ends, there is no point to writing the rest of the series. While you don't want to leave readers entirely unsatisfied, you do not want *closure* at the end of any but the final book in a series. "Closure" is succinctly defined by Sara Paretsky in *Writing Mysteries: A Handbook by the Mystery Writers of America*, "…the decisive resolution of conflicts plaguing the protagonist in such a way that a sequel can destroy or intrude on the reader's relief."

MM MM! GOOD!

CHOOSING A PUBLISHER

Before we delve into what to look for in a publishing partner—and what to avoid—I want to point out that this post relates to niche publishing with small and indie presses. Much of what I'm discussing here is a non-issue in mainstream publishing.

With so many mini and micromini presses popping up in the M/M genre, it's important to be clear about what you should be looking for in a publishing partner, including what publishers can offer that you can't easily achieve on your own. We write for ourselves. We publish for others. Thanks to Amazon's Kindle program, more and more authors in our genre are biting the bullet and becoming their own publisher—with varying success.

Enthusiasm, energy, and even experience as an author will only take you so far. Publishing requires its own skill set. The bottom line: we're not all cut out to be publishers. Even our own publisher.

That said, a couple of the very best publishers I work with started out as self-publishers, and every week I seem to notice another author turned publisher. For these entrepreneurs, the old saying still goes. *If you want something done right, do it yourself.*

As one highly successful author/publisher put it:

My overall gripe is that I don't think most e-publishers and their staff are professionals. They're more like enthusiastic amateurs. And they'll try to force weird things on authors like weird editing or horrible covers, and treat authors like they don't know any better. Sometimes we do.

Yep. We do.

On the other hand, there's no question that there's a certain validation that comes from someone not related to you being willing to plunk down their own hard-earned cash to publish your work. So much so, that as I think through this section, I know that a lot of what I'm saying will fall on deaf ears. When your dream is to be a published writer, it's very hard to turn down an offer to make your book a reality, even if you know in your heart you're signing a less than favorable contract. Even when you hear your fellow authors whispering ominous things about a particular publisher.

Guess what? That's okay so long as you go into that contract with your eyes open. The fact is, our needs change throughout our publishing career. When you're starting out, the imperative is simply to get published. Getting into print used to be the next goal; that may be changing. As you move up the publishing food chain, you'll find creative control and creative partnerships become more of an issue.

This might be hard to believe if you're currently still unpublished, but no matter where you are in your publishing career, a publisher is not doing you a favor when he or she signs you. A publisher contracts your work because s/he believes it will appeal to enough readers to make it worth his investment. You contract your work to a publisher because you believe you will be able to reach more readers with the tools the publisher offers than you would be able to do on your own. Within that basic publishing paradigm there are the usual variables. I've signed with publishers because I wanted to work with a certain editor or writer or because I wanted to support a certain political or social cause, but most of the time I sign with publishers because I think I'll make money with them. I'm a professional writer and I support myself with my storytelling. I'm in business, and my business is writing.

The reasons that I *stay* with a publisher are more complex. I've been in the business longer than any of my M/M publishers have been around. Frankly, at this stage in my publishing career, I *do* expect to be treated differently than a first-time writer. I expect to sell stories on proposals rather than completed manuscripts, I expect to have my occasional problems or questions treated respectfully and taken seriously, I expect to be kept up to date on changes regarding my book releases or anything else that specifically concerns me. In short, I expect to be treated like a valued equal. **I expect to be treated like a partner.**

I threw out the question *What do you look for in a publishing partner?* to my fellow writers, and we came up with a wish list. I think it's interesting to note here that nearly all the writers I spoke to were mostly satisfied with their current publishers. When authors aren't happy, they tend to move on. There are a lot of publishers out there. (Of course, there are also a lot of hungry authors, which is why publishers with less than favorable business practices can usually survive for some time.)

Qualities to look for in a potential publisher.

Partnership

This is both philosophy and attitude. The relationship between publisher and author is a symbiotic one. Neither can survive without the other. Yes, there *is* a never-ending supply of cannon-fodder authors desperate to be published, but the best authors have multiple choices in publishers. You can tell a lot about a publishing house by checking out the *current* author roster.

And then contact some of those authors, past and present, and compare what they have to say. *Compare.* That means talk to more than one author. Ask them about such things as communication, transparency, accountability, integrity, and quality.

Communication

The clock starts on this one with your initial submission to the publisher. Come to think of it, it starts before that. It starts with the first time you check out the publisher's website. Is it easy to find your way around their site? Are their submission guidelines clear? Is the submission process easy to follow? Are they easy to contact? Do they respond in a timely fashion? Are they courteous and professional? This is the easy part. If you run into problems at this stage, chances are you're going to have that failure to communicate throughout your publishing relationship.

Ironically, the inability to communicate effectively is one of the number one complaints authors have about their publishers. Things that authors would like to have communicated? Everything from being kept apprised on publishing schedule delays to information on how to market and promote their work.

Publishers that score highly on communication: Carina Press, Ellora's Cave and Samhain. Carina Press, notably, holds periodic and highly informative conference calls with their authors. Color me impressed.

Transparency

To some extent we all have to take our publishers on trust. Which is why you want to ask around before you jump into bed with the first publisher who asks nicely. Yes, we can all call for accounting audits, but I've yet to meet an author who's done so. There is a lot of lump-sum accounting in this segment of the publishing industry. However innocent, it encourages inaccuracy.

A proper royalty statement should, at the absolute minimum, break down sales by vendor and by dollar amount.

When it comes to transparency in accounting, Loose Id does an especially good job. Their monthly royalty statements are probably the most detailed and easiest to read of any publisher I've worked with.

Accountability

Publishing houses are made up of people, and people are fallible. Mistakes happen. Sometimes they're little insignificant mistakes—I hate to break it to the Grammar Nazis, but there's no such thing as perfection in line and copyediting—and sometimes the goofs are big ones—changing a book launch date and forgetting to let the author know. Authors don't get it right all the time either. We miss deadlines, we ask dumb questions, we change our minds.

The goal is not to find a mistake-proof publisher, it's to find a publisher who acts like a grownup when mistakes happen.

Integrity

This is one of those tricky ones. How do you know if a publisher has integrity? Again, ask around. Talk to authors on the publisher's roster.

One clue might be longevity. It's possible to conduct bad business and still stay afloat for a certain period of time, but after a few years the word spreads and the bad business practices catch you up. A press that's been around for a reasonable length of time—say five years or more—is probably doing something right. A publisher who uses author royalties to keep his sinking company afloat...not so much.

Another clue is professionalism. Jess Faraday put it this way:

This is hard to judge until one has actually interacted with a publisher, but things that turned me off during my search included misspellings on the website, a bad website, poor articulation of policies, and lack of transparency in policies. After I did sub to BSB (Bold Stroke Books), I was impressed that they contacted me exactly when they said they would *to the day*, the contract was easy to read and they encouraged me to show it to an agent or lawyer before signing, and my editor and the marketing department contacted me within two weeks of acceptance.

A lot of publishers attend conferences and book fairs. Take the opportunity to observe them in action. See how they conduct themselves. How they treat readers and authors and other publishers. Do they play well with others?

A publisher who backstabs another publisher to you or discloses information about one author to another is a publisher behaving VERY badly. Not just as a publisher, but as a decent human being. You want to partner with professionals. Or, at the very least, grownups.

Quality

This is one where it makes sense to listen to what readers have to say about a particular publishing house. Readers will be frank about things like cover art, copy-editing, ease of ordering in a way authors may not be—may not even be aware of.

A major key to quality has to do with how much a publisher is willing to invest in editorial staff. Editorial staff includes both content editors and copyeditors. Content editors are the editors responsible for acquiring work and developing authors. **Finding the right content editor is one of the most important creative partnerships an author can form.**

In mainstream publishing you rarely have authors serving as editors. There are several reasons for this, but one of the most obvious is that you don't have to be a great writer yourself to understand, appreciate, and teach great writing. There are different skill sets involved and sometimes terrific writers are *not* terrific editors. Or, let me put it this way: the best doctors are usually not also patients. Not at the same time, anyway.

Here in niche publishing, authors often pull double duty. I'll just be frank. My preference is for editors who are not concerned with building their own writing careers and competing with me within a publishing house for promo dollars and shelf space. But I'll allow that there are exceptions to any rule.

Copyeditors are a different thing entirely, but ideally they should have a rudimentary understanding of style and a decent background in literature as well as being trained in the rules of grammar and punctuation. In this genre, finding truly qualified copyeditors seems to be like the quest for the Holy Grail. I suspect that might be because they are often paid in books rather than cold, hard cash. There is a reason that, despite all the cutbacks in mainstream publishing, big publishers still pay for copyediting. *It matters.*

In fact, *you get what you pay for* seems to be pretty much the golden rule of niche publishing. Hideous cover art, nonexistent editing, and house "style" manuals put together by people who apparently learned to write from eHow are all too prevalent here. Again, don't take my word for it, listen to what readers have to say. They're pretty vocal on the subject.

And now a few general thoughts about contracts.

Let me just say here and now, I'm no lawyer and any advice I offer cannot be construed as getting proper legal advice. But at least this may help you figure out what kinds of questions to ask. Anyway, I know this is hard. If you're at the stage of looking over a contract, you want to sign. You *badly* want to sign. I understand and I sympathize. And here's the sort of good news. Sometimes it makes sense to sign a bad contract. Sometimes the benefits of a bad contract will outweigh the negatives, but at least understand the implications of the negatives before you sign.

First and foremost: no matter what it is, get it in writing.

This can be awkward. I once signed with a start-up publisher who I considered to be a good friend. We were both taking a risk, that was a given, but my friend promised several times in writing and verbally that if the day came and I was unhappy, I would be released from the contract. The contract did not reflect this escape clause. I knew I should insist on it, but...we were friends. It seemed rude. It seemed untrusting to make an issue of it. I couldn't imagine the day would come when I would be that unhappy.

I don't need to tell you how the story ends.

Get it in writing.

Look for royalties paid on gross not net. Don't take my word for it. Read the extensive information that's out there. This is probably a losing battle, but each time we fall back on one of these crucial negotiating points, we lose ground that is unlikely to ever be regained.

Don't accept less than 30% royalties on ebooks. Mainstream publishers do not typically pay the high royalty rates we receive here in niche publishing. And our indie publishers don't pay what Amazon, B&N, Smashwords, All Romance Ebooks do. It is not inconceivable that the day will come when one of our niche publishing partners proposes twenty-five percent royalties in exchange for...well, I'll leave it to your imagination. Superior distribution? Greater marketing and promotion? I can hear it now.

It's a slippery slope. Don't take that first false step.

Pay attention to the secondary rights you're handing over. Publishers will routinely ask for every right under the sun, but if they don't plan on selling your foreign rights or putting your work into audio, it makes no sense to give them away. Hang on to your secondary rights.

One of the single most important things to watch for in any contract you sign is a timeline and end dates. Attaching timeframes and dates to the following points are especially important: how long the publisher can hold off on offering a contract—this pertains to having previously assigned the publisher first refusal to your next work or the next work in a series or featuring major characters from a previous work; how long the publisher can hold your contracted work without actually publishing it; and, most important, how long the publisher will hold your copyright to the work.

Mainstream publishers try to hold your print rights (and increasingly your ebook rights) for as long as they possibly can. The tradeoff, the thing that makes it worth your while to hand your rights over for so many years, is that mainstream publishers are offering advances against royalties (yes, those advances are dwindling, but while five thousand dollars might be chickenfeed to Stephen King, it still makes a difference to the rest of us) and doing actual print runs to get your books into brick-and-mortar stores. Even when it comes to ebooks, they have the potential to get your work in the hands of many thousands more readers which can add up to significant revenue.

A publisher using POD technology is not offering you a significant advance, is not doing print runs, and is not getting your books into bookstores in comparable numbers to a traditional mainstream press. You do not want to hand over your copyright for eight years to a small press publisher using POD. This is not to say that POD is not a perfectly valid technology or that publishers using that technology are not serious industry players, but eight years is a very long time in the current publishing environment, and it is not reasonable or fair for a publisher to demand the same rights without being able to offer the same advantages of a mainstream publisher.

If the book does well for you both, you'll happily sign on for another year or three. If both partners are *not* happy, then it's not an equitable arrangement. It is not a true partnership, and we should always be looking for *partners* in our publishing life.

One other thing on that first refusal clause—this is another one I learned the hard way. Exclusive options and first refusals are standard in mainstream publishing, but it is also standard that the terms will be equal to or better than the original contract.

For example, Simon & Schuster's contract reads: *The Author grants the publisher an exclusive option to acquire the Author's next (i.e., written after the Work) full-length work of XXXX for publication* **on mutually satisfactory terms.**

And it gives them 60 days to make up their minds.

That "mutually satisfactory terms" is the key. An exclusive option or a first refusal that doesn't include that phrase basically means the publisher has the right to acquire your next work on any terms they choose.

Now, that could probably be taken to court and argued, but who has time, money, or energy?

This is a non-issue for most of the publishers in our field whether they include that clause or not. In fact, in all my years of publishing, I've only known one publisher try to slip past a contract where the terms had been changed to less favorable ones. Since any publisher of integrity is not going to quibble on this point, I'd like to see it made standard in the contracts of all our ebook and indie publishers.

Example:

If PUBLISHER extends an offer of publication on the new work, it shall be on terms no less favorable than in this Agreement. **If PUBLISHER does not accept for publication this additional WORK within 60 days of submission, it will be considered refused and the AUTHOR will be free to market rights to the new WORK without encumbrance.**

Better yet, I'd like to see all indie pubs waive the first refusal option as Carina Press and Samhain Publishing do.

Although moving forward I'll probably self-publish the major portion of my work, I will still continue to work with publishers. Why? Because sometimes it's a relief to just focus on the writing. But also because I feel that working with publishers has been more advantageous to my career than working completely on my own would have been. I like the safety net of good editors and I appreciate the fact that my publishers are willing to invest in me and my work. I like to believe that our relationship has been equally satisfying and rewarding—which is what partnership is all about.

That said, at this point, I earn more self-publishing than publishing through any publisher I've ever had. BUT would I still have the same visibility and credibility if I only self-published? Might my self-publishing earnings start to slide if I never showed up in a publisher's catalog again? It's very possible.

And while writing well is its own reward, and at the very least it's one sure way to have a never-ending supply of the kinds of stories you love to read, very few of us are content with an audience of one—no matter how appreciative. Something in the act of storytelling requires that the tale be shared.

Which brings us to the other half of this equation: persuading the publisher of your choice to make you an offer you can't refuse.

Although the majority of M/M publishing is happening online through e-publishers, the decimation of traditional publishing's "mid-list" has sent many former mainstream writers searching for new homes on the World Wide Web, and that means the competition for cyberspace and bookshelf is the fiercest it's ever been.

One of the most important things you can do for yourself is wait until your work is ready before you start sending it out.

Believe me, I know how hard that is. You've finished the first draft, you're thrilled, you *love* these characters and this story, you want to share it—you want people to read it and tell you how much they love it too—and you'd like to be paid for all that time and hard work you put into it.

All the same, put the story aside for *a minimum of two weeks*. Leave it alone and work on something else. Give it to your beta readers or trusted CP, hand it over to your critique group. Only when you can look at the writing with fresh eyes—meaning you don't anticipate what the next sentence is as you're reading through it—can you start revising in any meaningful way.

Raven McKnight, Loose Id: Readers are hungry for M/M, and authors know it. In the mad scramble to take advantage of that demand, there can be a tendency to rely on the subgenre, the M/M factor, to carry the whole story. (This applies to other in-demand story elements, too—vampires, BDSM, werewolves, etc.) An author should put into the story the time and effort and attention it deserves, the investment needed to produce a quality story, strong in all aspects. With stories that contain in-demand elements such as M/M, it can be easy to let yourself fall into the mindset of "Well, people are going to buy it anyway, simply because they want to read M/M. So I can skate by on some of the overall quality stuff." For one thing, that's not the attitude any self-respecting writer should have about themselves or their work. For another, it's no longer a true belief. Demand for M/M is very high—but supply is starting to catch up, which means the M/M story written by the author who puts in the time and effort is going to trump the story written by the author who decided to skate by on the "They'll buy it because it's M/M" belief.

Revise with the same care and attention you lavish on researching your sex scenes. (Yeah, I know *you!*) Revise with an eye to every single element, from story to semicolon. Pay attention to every detail.

And only when you have finally and thoroughly polished that manuscript are you allowed to start the submission process.

Secret Agent Man

There's a lot of talk in our little genre right now about the necessity of having an agent.

Do you need an agent? Short answer? If you're writing M/M fiction, probably not. Not just yet, anyway.

Long answer? Basically you need an agent for two reasons that remain unchanging. To open doors that are otherwise closed to you. And to negotiate better, smarter deals than you could get on your own.

Reasons NOT to get an agent: you think having an agent gives you credibility and clout. Even seven years ago, that was still true. Now? Now it depends on the particular agent—and the particular doors he can open for you. You do not need an agent who can get you a contract with Dreamspinner Press. An agent who can sell your male-male romance to HQN. Yeah. That's probably the agent you want.

Opening doors that are otherwise closed to you. Let's say that hithertofore you've been publishing with Schnooky-Nooky Press and you're hoping, for starters, to break into one of the bigger epubs. You figure if your submission is agented, you'll get a closer read. Maybe even a priority read. This is quite possible. Having an agent means someone besides you is willing to invest in your career, and that does count for something. Plus, your agent may have already done a lot of the groundwork by asking for revisions and edits on your manuscript before she ever agreed to take it on. That could be very helpful to you, again, depending on the agent.

Or this scenario. You're hoping to move up the publishing food chain and maybe place your work with a major player publisher. Unless we're talking Harlequin and a few other romance publishers, yes, you absolutely need an agent. No question. The catch here is that agents operate—as so much of publishing does—based on relationships. Access to HarperCollins does not occur simply by virtue of being an agent. You really want to look at who your prospective agent represents—and where he's selling their work.

To negotiate better, smarter deals than you could get on your own. Can an agent get you a better deal when most of the epubs and indies we deal with are working from boilerplate contracts? Maybe. Probably? It depends on how you define (and price) "better." Are more author copies or shaving a year off a lengthy contract worth $23,000 to you? It's not a rhetorical question. If you're earning 100K+ thanks to the efforts of your agent, yes, I would think that was worth it to you.

As for saving you from signing a bad contract? Yes, this is certainly true. Although it's hard to go too wrong in e-publishing provided you exert a little common sense. Oh, and watch and listen to what's going on with authors around you. If you've got long-range writing career plans, you need to educate yourself in your field, and that includes having a basic grasp of the rights you should not blithely hand over.

And even if you do sign a not-so-favorable contract (as I have done a couple of times since I swanned out on my own) the ramifications don't tend to be lasting. It's an ill wind that blows no good, and I can say that (in this particular genre) even contracts that I regretted have almost always, in the end, worked in my favor. Or at least not done me any serious and lasting harm.

Could an agent keep you from signing a bad contract? Yes. Absolutely. So could a lawyer. You could always consider joining the Author's Guild, which provides free legal advice for members.

That said, if you do want an agent—and you need an agent to submit to the major New York publishing houses—you go about it the same way you submit to a publisher. You put together a proposal or submission package.

The basic submission package consists of a **query letter**, an **outline** and/or **synopsis,** and the first three (opening) chapters of your novel—which usually works out to about fifty pages.

Most writing books contain information on putting together a book proposal or submission package. One of the most important things to understand is that publishers don't actually freak out over the exact width of your margins or whether you're using Times New Roman or Courier font. The main concern is that everything be easy to read, cleanly presented, and that your writing is the very best it can be. Follow the publisher and agent guidelines to the best of your ability, but don't have a panic attack if something seems a little vague.

If you're bound and determined to get an agent, buy yourself a copy of *Guide to Literary Agents* or *Jeff Herman's Guide to Book Publishers, Editors & Literary Agents*. And then follow up on www.agentquery.com.

It's very important that you pay attention to the publisher and editor guidelines. I can't stress this enough. Those guidelines exist for a reason. Don't send erotica to publishers who don't handle erotica. Don't send literary fiction to Harlequin and don't send category romance to Trident Media Group. Don't email chapters to agents who don't accept email queries. Don't snail mail a submission to Loose Id. No one is going to be swayed by your dazzling writing; they're going to be irritated that you don't know how to follow the simplest directions, and they're going to bounce you right out the door. Which means you've just shot one opportunity.

Read the guidelines. Follow the guidelines. Exactly.

Every house, every agent is a little bit different. That's because they're run by people, and people are all a little bit different. They have opinions, preferences, prejudices. You'll minimize your chances of rejection if you have a little respect for these differences. Pay attention to the details.

Now, I'm sure as you glanced over the components of a submission package, it occurred to you that you could submit your book proposal before your book is actually finished. If you've got three terrific chapters, why not polish up your outline, write a synopsis based on that, and start pumping out those query letters?

Don't do it.

Once you're published, once you've built a relationship with an agent, editor, or publisher, yes, you will commonly sell your work based on what is called "a partial." But when you're first starting out, publishers don't know you. They aren't going to buy your work based on a promising start. They're going to read your submission and—assuming it's good—request "the complete."

That means they want to read the rest of the manuscript, and that's excellent news.

Unless you haven't completed the rest of the manuscript.

Which happens *a lot*, which is why publishers want to see the complete before they make any decisions—and waste any more time.

Now if you've been hanging on my every word, you're going to have that polished and immaculate manuscript all ready to go.

Score!

And if you've been listening to your walkman and shooting spit wads from the back of the class, you're now sweating bullets as you attempt to complete twenty-to-seventy thousand words in two weeks. Yeah, two weeks to…maybe…a month. Any longer than that and the editor or agent could be long gone, and even if he or she isn't, they won't remember you or your sparkling prose.

Even if you do manage to complete the rest of the novella or novel within two weeks, it's going to be the first—rough—draft. It's not going to be an example of your best work. Unless that's pretty much typical of your best work, in which case, you might want to take up another hobby.

Okay, back to the proposal process. You need to take time putting together your query letter, but again, don't agonize. If the story sounds like something the editor or publisher is looking for, and the chapters are good, they'll ask to see the complete. Your flawless query letter is not going to change anything if the story isn't something that the publisher is interested in.

Understand also that everyone hates writing query letters, that they always sound stiff and phony. I've read all kinds of articles on writing snappy, sizzling queries. Personally, I prefer a straightforward, businesslike approach. State who you are, what your credentials are (previous publishing credits), and give a back cover-type blurb of the book. Save the snap, crackle, and pop for the actual writing of the book. Check the resource section in the back of the book for a sample query letter.

We talked earlier about putting together an outline, and if you did that, here's where it pays off again, because all you have to do is clean up that rough original draft so that it matches how the book actually turned out. Sample original outline in resource section.

From the outline you'll find it quite easy to write a synopsis. Some agents/publishers require outline and synopsis, some require one or the other; read the guidelines and give them what they want. Sample synopsis, resource section.

Judith David, Loose Id: Read the guidelines, yes. But, to really **internalize** them, read at least two RECENT books from the publisher. I say recent because, even two years ago, publishers with whom I work weren't taking—seeking out—the volume of M/M, BDSM, ménage and beyond, capture, dubious consent stories that they are now. In some instances, I find the bar is being raised SIGNIFI-CANTLY in terms of the expectations for the quality of writing in the initial manuscript and the level of heat. Unfortunately, I'm also seeing elsewhere a fall in standards for story, mechanics, and character, just to get the heat to a quick release date.

My point is that the market is moving fast. Writers need to be aware that publishers are trying to keep up with it, whether it's to cut back the pornography or ramp up the eroticism. Emotion is the key. Every sexual moment needs to advance the emotional stakes in some way.

You can submit directly to the list of publishers in the Resources section. You don't need an agent. Just take the time to match the right project to the right publisher.

We've also listed the main self-publishing providers. And following this chapter is a chapter by Jordan Castillo Price on self-publishing. Jordan covers pretty much everything you could imagine, so I'll just reiterate the obvious: If you do decide to self-publish, make sure you get your work **professionally edited.**

I can't think of a single more important piece of advice.

The Magic Formula

Yeah, I know you've been reading patiently, waiting for this moment. Well, Frodo, Luke, and Dorothy, I've already *told* you the secret. The secret sauce recipe is in your hands—and possibly on your clothes.

It's all about the quality of the writing. And the secret of quality writing lies in paying attention to the details.

Take time and trouble to craft realistic but loveable characters—first and foremost, really think about your characters. And then start working out a plot with enough depth and conflict to carry the story of those characters the necessary distance. Think about the arc of the relationship.

Pay extra attention to dialogue, to pacing, to your action scenes, whether they take place between the sheets or during a car chase. Give some thought to what your story is really about. Yeah, it should be fun, but that doesn't mean it has to be meaningless. And don't forget the possibilities to up the emotional ante through use of hurt/comfort and plausible angst.

And take the time to edit your work. Acceptance may not be quick and easy, but rejection is. Don't make it easy for editors and agents to pass on your work.

Describe Your Ideal M/M Submission

Angela James, Carina Press: My perfect submission in gay fiction really isn't any different than my perfect submission in any other genre fiction. I want characters I can fall in love with, cheer for, hope with. I want a story that captures my attention from page one and doesn't let go, even after I've read the last word. I want the author to be passionate about their career, be looking to build a relationship with a publisher, and be open to new ideas and change.

Deborah Nemeth, Carina Press: I love M/M fiction and I'm always looking to add more M/M authors to my list. My ideal submission grabs me from page one with a compelling voice and engaging protagonists that grow and change. It's polished, well paced, well plotted, builds to an exciting climax and a satisfying resolution, has a fresh premise and conflict strong enough to carry the story. The submission cover letter contains the genre/word count, author's credentials, and a blurb that hooks my attention.

Irene Williams, Loose Id: Authors who take their writing seriously and write good hot stories with at least some romantic elements in them.

Sasha Knight, Samhain Publishing: My ideal M/M author: One with unlimited imagination, who surprises me with the creativity in every submission. Writes clean, is easy to work with, accepts criticism and praise with equal grace. Writes characters I fall in love with, and stories that will stick with me for years to come. One who understands that promotion is as important as writing and recognizes that the best way to promote themselves is by writing their next book—and making it the best it can be.

Aleksandr Voinov, Riptide Publishing: Ideally, we want to acquire fiction that's honest, well-made in terms of craft (say, show, don't tell should be applied properly), with interesting characters that have that spark of life that makes you feel like you know them and want to spend the next few hours with them in your head. Of course the basic plot of a gay romance is "boy meets boy, boy loses boy, boy finds boy again", but interesting settings, great characters and subplots can still make that unique and interesting. The perfect case is a book that would stand up, writing-wise, with the best stories published in the mainstream. No story gets a free pass because it has gay content (or sex).

We are also acquiring trans, bisexual, and lesbian content, though currently most of what we're doing is M/M and gay fiction.

Trace Edward Zaber, Amber Quill Press: A manuscript (or an author who knows how to write such a manuscript) containing high emotion, an interesting plot, sizzling sex scenes (for erotica stories) and, the bottom line, a firm grasp of the English language! 99.9999% of all manuscripts we receive in our yearly contest are rejected based on misspellings, punctuation issues, grammar problems, sentence structure, etc. we find within the first few paragraphs. Authors need to learn their craft, and those who do not...well, the slush pile grows increasingly higher thanks to those individuals. No editor worth their weight in salt will deal with an illiterate author, especially one who acts like a prima donna and refuses to alter a single word, and unfortunately with e-publishers and small presses popping up every week (and run by owners who haven't a clue how to construct a proper sentence), these sort of authors are becoming the norm. Frankly, it's shameful.

Margaret Riley, Changeling Press: A short, hot, sci-fi or paranormal read that's got enough plot to stand on its own no matter what the sex of the primary characters, and enough sex to scorch your computer screen. And if we don't fall in love with your heroes on the first page, we're not interested.

Tina Burns, Liquid Silver Books: An ideal submission for anything would be a well-written/edited story, characters the reader can identify with, a story that keeps the reader glued to the pages, and an author willing to participate with us as a publisher.

Nicole Kimberling, Blind Eye Books: I only print a couple of books a year so I am very selective. My perfect submission is a manuscript with likable characters and an interesting plot. Everybody prob-ably says this, but "likable" and "interesting" are such highly subjective terms that it's more specific than it seems.

For me likable characters are ones who are ambitious and self-ac-tualized. Likable characters display emotional depth and intel-lectual life, while simultaneously displaying basic human empathy and understanding of the rights of others. Likable characters do not know they are the main character of the story, and if someone told them they were, they would wonder why. They do not need to be humble, but they do need to not think that they are the single most important being in the entire known universe—even if for a few minutes in the story, that's exactly what they are.

Interesting plots involve situations that could not have emerged from a random plot generator and that are integrated with the theme of the story as well as being in line with the character's stated goals. Interesting plots occur when the events of the story seem inevitable instead of contrived. Interesting plots in standalones chronicle the single most important time in a character's life. Interesting plots in series examine the twists and turns of life through the narrow lens of one set of characters.

WHAT GOES WITH A TOOL BELT?
SELF-PUBLISHING BY JORDAN CASTILLO PRICE

The author who wishes to self-publish has more resources to draw upon than ever before. The previous generation of self-publishers needed to purchase print runs of hundreds or thousands of books. They had to store those bulky, heavy boxes of books somewhere. They were responsible for handling the marketing and distribution of the title, after which, in an attempt to recoup their investment, they'd hope and pray that someone would buy all that stock that was curling and warping in the attic or garage.

Enter two new technologies: print-on-demand books, and ebooks.

And the whole game changed.

What is Print On Demand (POD)?

Most commercially available books, newspapers, and magazines are printed with a process known as offset printing. In offset printing, the image or page to be reproduced is transferred to a rubber roller via a photographic process, and paper is fed beneath the roller to receive an impression of the image. The setup is quite involved. Spreading the setup cost over several tens of thousands of books is economical, but with the small print run a new self-published author is likely to require, the high setup charge may make this printing method prohibitively expensive.

In 1993, a fully digital printing process was created that does away with the plates and rollers, and instead uses a technology more like the laser or inkjet printers on your home computer. This technology, which doesn't require the same elaborate setup as offset printing, allows books to be printed from digital files one at a time, as they are needed. On demand.

Print-on-Demand (POD) technology eliminates costly setup, thereby making small print runs viable. Most POD companies will also handle the distribution duties for the author, interfacing directly with online retailers, libraries and bookstores. POD technology became available to small presses and self-published authors in the early 2000s.

POD services cater to a range of author skill levels. Entry-level POD services, such as Lulu and CreateSpace, can help authors assemble their books via online templates. The more professional services like LightningSource require the customer to establish themselves as a publisher by purchasing their own block of ISBNs, and the files submitted must adhere to strict specifications, which typically require advanced software knowledge to create.

How Have Ebooks Evolved?

Print books have been digitized since the 1960s. Ebooks intended for consumers began appearing in the late 1990s, to be read either on the computer, on dedicated devices such as the Rocket Ebook Reader, or on other multipurpose devices like Palm Pilots. In the beginning, ebook selection was limited, and ebook formats went in and out of vogue as technology developed and changed. The ebook took off in earnest when Sony introduced the Reader in 2006 and when the Kindle came out in 2007. The first batch of Kindle devices sold out in less than six hours!

The end product of an ebook doesn't require any fancy printing presses or binding machines, or even any pricy software. A basic home computer and common software will allow you to produce the bare minimum quality files required to create an ebook. Even so, at the early stage of the game, self-publishing was not as common as it is today. In the mid-2000s, it was possible to create an ebook file, but distributing that file—getting it into consumers' hands—was complicated and time-consuming.

Since then, more and more distributors and online sellers have begun accepting ebooks from anyone, even a lowly self-published author with just a single title to sell. As long as your file is readable by the e-reader it's intended for, you're in business, and your ebook can be sold online right beside books produced by Big Publishing.

Quality: The Great Equalizer

Since your ebooks and your POD books are not relegated to a special "self-published" section at online booksellers, and since they will pop up just as readily on a title or keyword search as your professional competition's offerings, there is one way in which self-published books can make or break their own reputations: quality.

It Begins with the Cover

Cover art is just as important when selling books online as it is selling books in a brick-and-mortar store. The size is different; rather than browsing through a bookstore shelf and looking for book spines that catch their eyes, readers browse through cover art thumbnails to select which titles they'd like to examine more closely. Publishers provide cover art for their authors. As a self-published author, you will need to procure cover art yourself.

Product Description is Crucial

The book description or "blurb" is the next element that lures the reader down the path of purchasing your book. The story's genre must be conveyed here, and enough of the plot should be divulged to entice the reader to buy the work without giving away too much of the story and spoiling the book's critical reveals. Some M/M publishers write the blurb for a title, whereas some publishers require the author to submit their own. A clumsily worded blurb is a red flag to a potential reader that the book it represents may be less-than-professionally done.

Editorial concerns

Recently a new author was making his rounds on various lists talking about the wonderful new book he'd self-published. It was his first book, and he was very proud of it. I checked out the cover and it looked professional. I looked at the blurb and it seemed interesting. I bought the book...and I found editorial problems on the very first page. Not just there, either. Throughout the section I read—only one chapter, because I was too mortified for the author to go on.

There are several phases of editing: content editing, line editing, and proof-reading. Even if you are the most careful and grammatically correct writer in the world, you need editing for things as broad as forgetting to mention where your characters are (because, after all, you see it very clearly in your head), as mundane as changing someone's name mid-story, or as simple as dropping/repeating words or making typos. You can't do this yourself. You can try, but your brain will see only what you meant to write, not what you actually wrote.

Publishers provide editing and proofing services for you. Granted, some are better quality than others, but at the very least they bring fresh eyes or some house-style standards. When you self-publish, you must enlist this service yourself.

Typographical and Formatting Considerations

With a POD book, another potential pitfall is a book block that looks strange. Fonts are subtly different from one another in a way that an un-trained designer wouldn't notice. Times New Roman, for instance, is commonly used in office memos and POD books. However, this font was de-signed to be used across short column spans in a newspaper. Across the width of a whole page, it's fatiguing to read, and registers subconsciously to the reader as unpleasant and unprofessional.

In ebooks, the typography is often overridden by the style sheets inside the e-reader device. Plainer formatting is better, at least at the current stage of technology. Since ebook formats are constantly evolving, a push toward more typographic control in the final ebook product is underway. But even with a very plainly formatted ebook, there are still many technical consid-erations to address.

• Does the ebook file open?

• Does any of the type get garbled?

• Is the file size appropriate to the length of the book?

• Do the hyperlinks in the ebook work properly?

• Is there a functional table of contents?

• Is correct metadata attached to the file?

Publishers will create your POD or ebook formats according to their house templates and standards. When you self-publish, you'll need to hire someone to format your work or learn how to do it yourself. The learning curve is steep. And while it is possible to use common word processing software to format your books, a flawless file is difficult to achieve without professional design software.

Distribution

Finally, once your book is written, edited, and typeset, the POD books must be printed and shipped, and the ebooks must be made available for online purchase and download at vendors that readers wish to utilize.

Print Distribution

Your POD printer should handle distribution in the markets you choose: US, Europe, Australia, or worldwide, depending on which distribution channels you select. The amount of control you have over your distribution channels or the discount you offer wholesalers will vary. With services geared toward indie authors such as CreateSpace, there are only a few options available, and you'll need to choose the one that carries the least risk with the widest distribution. Other services geared more toward small publishers such as LightningSource entail greater upfront expense and require higher quality standards for the book cover and interior files. This initial hurdle is balanced by the capability of setting discounts so your profit is higher. There are also more options for size, paper, and cover finish in your final product.

Disturbingly, many "vanity presses" are presenting themselves to look like POD printers who offer additional editorial, design, and marketing services. Do your homework carefully before choosing a POD printer, particularly if you are purchasing services from them in addition to just printing/distribution. You may find that their design service amounts to dumping your content into a standardized template, and the marketing they provide has nothing to do with your intended audience.

Note that while POD printers theoretically make the titles available to brick-and-mortar bookstores, most physical bookstores do not carry POD titles. Why? Due to a practice set in place during the Great Depression, bookstores order large volumes of physical books, and then quickly return whatever they can't sell for 100% refund. Many of these buy-and-return cycles are so automated that some stores' systems are ordering more copies of a title even as their returns department are shipping new copies of that title back to the publisher for a full refund. The books are commonly destroyed rather than restocked. The system is so broken that producers of expensive hardcover books have begun including RFID chips in their bindings to prevent large bookstores from claiming full refunds on books that have never been produced, let alone purchased by them.

What this means for a POD self-published author is that if you elect to make your titles returnable, chances are the majority of the books you've paid to be printed will be returned and destroyed, or shipped to you at your expense in a condition too battered and shelf worn for you to even use as a promotional giveaway. Because the individual cost of a POD book is much higher than that of an offset printed book, every return represents a greater bite out of your potential profits. The return ratio for bookstores is so high, in fact, it is common for returnable POD books to show an overall loss rather than a profit.

Electronic Distribution

Currently, there are three main ways to distribute ebooks, and since there are advantages and disadvantages to each of them, there is no one "best way" to get your titles onto your audience's e-readers.

1. Direct to readers - The method of selling files directly to your readers has the potential for earning the highest profit per book, but it is also the most labor-intensive. When I established JCPbooks.com in 2008, there was no good method of selling non device-specific ebooks without creating a site, setting up a shopping cart, and establishing a payment method. Nowadays, there are ebook sellers willing to work with self-published authors, and they will handle these details for a percentage of your profit. I find the major drawback to direct sales is that I need to deal with customer service issues myself, or potentially hire and train someone to handle them. There is also no way to cross-promote my titles with similar authors. The only traffic my store sees is the traffic I send there myself. The benefit is that I'm able to create coupons, promotions, and product bundles.

2. Direct to etailers - Many large etailers such as Amazon, Barnes & Noble, and Apple will now deal directly with self-published authors. If you only have one or two titles, however, the administrative time spent setting up accounts with each of these businesses may be prohibitive. You may also run into tax and payment snags if you're based in a different country. In addition to these major outlets, there are also genre-specific ebook sellers who carry titles from many large and small publishers, and they are now willing to accept books from self-published authors as well. All of these sellers keep a percentage of the cover price in exchange for displaying the title and handling the sale. The percentage varies.

3. Hire a middleman - Some services such as BookBaby will distribute your titles to several etailers for an upfront fee per title. More commonly, publishing and distribution platforms such as Smashwords take their payment as a percentage of the sales price. Allowing the middleman to deal with multiple etailers saves considerable work on the author's end, but royalties are lower because more people are being paid, and there's more lag time between the purchase of the book and the payout. Like the "vanity presses" that masquerade as POD printers, some ebook creation services provide inferior to nonexistent design, editing and marketing services at a huge expense to the author that they are unlikely to recoup.

Common Self-Publishing Misconceptions

Self-publishing success stories are the flavor of the day, and it's natural to want to emulate the self-published authors who hit the bestseller list on their own talent, luck and ingenuity without the help of Big Publishing. But these stories are usually sensationalized, and they perpetuate misconceptions about what self-publishing really entails.

Wearing all the Hats

MYTH: When I self-publish I won't have to worry about an editor hacking my wonderful manuscript to bits.

REALITY: You need an editor. Period. Self-publishing a title should not mean you are now not only the author but the editor, cover designer, and typesetter. If you try to do all of these things yourself, your final product will look amateurish unless you are trained in each of these areas. (And even then, you need an editor.)

Skipping Steps

MYTH: Self-publishing is a lot easier than going through the process of rejections and revisions. I want my story out now!

REALITY: It is true that the time from the manuscript being complete to the time it goes on sale is much shorter when you publish it yourself. But as the publisher, you're not just sitting back and watching a process unfold. You're either doing the nitty-gritty technical work (and probably mastering a very difficult learning curve in the process) or you're researching and hiring other professionals to help you get your files ready. Also consider this: if your story is being repeatedly rejected, chances are it still needs editorial work.

Big Bucks!

MYTH: I'll make tons of money self-publishing because I get to keep all the profits.

REALITY: It's true that a publisher keeps a percentage of the profit from an author's book sales. But from that percentage, the publisher pays the editorial team, the technical staff, and the cover artist, as well as their other operating expenses. When you self-publish, these expenses are your responsibility. The mistaken idea that self-publishing should be free leads many self-publishers to cut corners. They attempt to work around the fact that they're not willing to buy and train on professional publishing software, and their book interior shows it. Homemade cover art is readily apparent in the bizarrely cobbled-together graphics crafted from public domain photos and the fonts that came with the computer system.

Self-publishing is definitely easier to do on a tight budget than it was ten years ago…but it isn't free. And the self-publishers who cheap out on their cover art and file formatting are much less likely to succeed than the authors who are willing to invest in a professional presentation.

Insta-Fame

MYTH: If I self-publish it, they will come.

REALITY: All the overnight successes you hear about have actually been building their fanbase for years by the time their self-published book hits big. The headlines tend to minimize that fact since it doesn't make for a very punchy story. "Self-Published Author Succeeds After Years of Building Own Platform" isn't exactly front-page material. Behind every "overnight success" is an author who has nurtured their own following, either by participating in fanfic communities, by attending conventions and making connections, by maintaining a successful blog, or by financing their own physical book tours.

While M/M publishers expect authors to do their own marketing by maintaining an online presence, being with a publisher does provide a very basic platform to a new author who's starting from scratch. At the very least the publisher will place your new release in their newsletters or other broadcast announcements, and it's likely they will send it out for reviews and provide opportunities for blog tours and giveaways as well.

Is it Worth It?

Self-publishing is not for everyone, and there is no one-size-fits-all answer as to whether self-publishing is right for you. If you enjoy a technical challenge and you're willing to invest in professional presentation, and especially if you already have an established fanbase, self-publishing may be a wonderful fit. But if you think of self-publishing as a shortcut to bypass traditional publishing, you'll end up doing a lot of work that may or may not reap any benefits. Start small, perhaps with a short story. Do your research. Most importantly, be prepared to invest time, energy and money, and you'll have a much better chance at success.

RENT BOYS
MARKETING AND PROMOTION

Yes. I know. You're a writer not a salesman. Not a promoter. Not a marketer. Not a prostitute. A WRITER. You hate promotion, marketing, flogging your wares. You hate knowing what BSP means—let alone being accused of it. (It means Blatant Self-Promotion, by the way.)

Get over it.

To start with, we ALL hate the promotion and the marketing. Believe me, you're not the only writer out there who took the gig thinking that it was strictly going to be about the creativity and the words. Every one of us longs for the good old days when publishers took care of that other tiresome stuff. Granted those days were before most of us were born, but still. Those were the days, eh?

Please quit whining about how unsuited you are to a life of promotion and marketing. You're not any more unsuited than anybody else. The simple truth is, if you want people to read and buy your books, you're going to have to sully your lily-white hands with a little promotion and publicity. These days it's as much a part of the job as learning proper punctuation and grammar. Unfortunately, you can write the best book to ever throw two guys into each other's arms, but if no one knows about it, you're not going to get the fame and fortune—or even the two hundred bucks of royalties that are rightfully yours.

In fact, it's actually reached the point where some publishers request a marketing plan as part of your manuscript submission. That's because the way that readers find out about your work is through marketing and promotion. It doesn't matter how good your book is if no one has heard of it.

And by that, I mean it doesn't matter to *you*, because you wouldn't have chosen to publish if you didn't want people to read your work. We write for ourselves. We publish for others. Let's not pretend otherwise.

So let's start with the basics.

"Josh Lanyon" is a pen name.

One of the first questions you'll want to ask yourself as you consider publishing your writing is whether you will write under your given name or a pen name.

I suggest you use a pen name. Three reasons: 1) You may eventually choose to write something besides romance and erotica (AKA known as "porn" by many potential mainstream publishers). You may want to write literary fiction, and you may want it under your real name, and when your deathless prose starts appearing, it may confuse and disappoint your previous loyal readership—just as your backlist may confuse and disappoint your new readership. I prefer to keep things simple for my readers.

2) There are a lot of nuts out there. I'm not suggesting you might end up battling your local school board over your fitness to retain your teaching position in a classroom full of minors, or that you'll pick up a persistent stalker or two, or that you'll be going to court with your ex to keep custody of your children, or entertaining impromptu visits from representatives of the local branch of Church of the Looney Tunes, I'm just saying I'd advise you to keep a strong firewall between yourself and the so-called real world.

And, 3) If you do get picked up by a large New York publishing house, your new publisher will take a look at your previous sales record, and unless the numbers are in keeping with sell-through on the typical mass market print run, you're going to find yourself with a new pen name (like it or not) anyway—and if your previous pen name was your *real* name…that's liable to be a little frustrating.

When choosing a pen name, I'd opt for something that sounds professional, is easy to spell and search, and that means something to you. I discourage using your "fandom" moniker or something that sounds like a failed porn star.

Beyond using a pen name, I leave it to you how much of a platform identity you want to construct. Since the final bolt was tightened on the first printing press, authors have devised elaborate and fictitious platform identities in order to sell their fiction. Or, heck, maybe you want to interact *as* fiction. Maybe you want to interact with readers in persona as the protagonist of your series. We're writers. It's second nature to make stuff up. Personally, I think keeping it simple is your best bet.

Either way, you can still promote on line and engage sincerely with readers while using a pen name. In fact, unless you're concealing your gender, you can still attend conferences and do book signings and promote exactly as you would under your own name. Assuming you like that kind of thing.

If you're concealing your gender, that's nobody's business but your own. However, I would advise the following: do not submit your work to female-only anthologies (if you are actually a male author), do not write nonfiction articles, essays, or memoirs about your experiences and struggles as a gay man (if you're actually a woman), and do not hire anybody to pose as you—let alone disguise yourself with false mustaches, bushy wigs and Groucho Marx glasses. I'm just *sayin'*…

These days the two big words in promotion and marketing are *Relationships* and *Discoverability*. We'll get to relationships in a minute. Discoverability is what makes you and your title—eventually all your titles—stand out in that yearly, monthly, weekly flood of new authors and new releases.

From the minute you appear on the scene, you will be working to establish something called Author Branding. Basically what this means is when readers—actually anyone in the genre—sees your name, they feel a sense of instant recognition. Successful branding is twofold. It has to do with what you write and also your online persona. Ideally these two things dovetail. Which is to say if you write dark, elegant, angsty stories but your online persona consists of posting pictures of nekkid men and pulling practical jokes on other writers, readers are going to experience a disconnect. It's going to take a while to associate your online brand with your writing brand. In fact, if it's too big a disconnect, you may find that your online presence is working against you.

What I'm telling you is, you'll want to control your author brand. You don't want your image defined by the random luck of what search engines might pull up or the contradictory messages of your various test runs. You need to give this concept of author brand your full consideration before you get out there and start making a fool of yourself in public.

Because...yeah. You will. We all do.

One tool for helping you determine your branding is to come up with a tag line, or "hook", that you use on your website, in social media, and maybe as the sig file in your emails.

For example, my tag line is "A distinct voice in gay fiction." It's the first line of my short bio, which is plastered over all my social media platforms.
L.B. Gregg's is "Frank, funny, and fresh."
Josephine Myles uses "M/M romance with lashings of English sauce."
L.C. Chase is tagged "Writing romance, man to man."
Kari Gregg is known for "A World More Extraordinary—Intense, Erotic Romance."

You get the idea.

If you're wondering what a sig file is, it's that three or four line little note you see at the bottom of author emails. (You'll also want an author email address and mail account.)

Your sig file should be no more than four lines long. **It's not your resume**; it's simply the title of your latest available work and your website address. Or maybe it's your tagline and blog address. Just keep it brief and to the point. Change your sig file around every month or so, because people grow used to it and it becomes invisible.

Website. If I have to explain what a website is, you're holding a seriously out-of-date copy of this book!

Yes, you do still need a website. No, Facebook and Goodreads have not taken the place of a website. The key to a good website is that it's easy to navigate and that you keep the content fresh. Meaning you update the site every time you've got a new story out, and you offer free fiction and/or contests on a regular basis. If that free story is good enough, it's the best possible sales pitch for the rest of your work. (And don't underestimate the simple pleasure of feedback from readers; besides, building a loyal fan base is what it's all about.)

Your website is like your business card. You have to have one. It needs to look professional: www.joshlanyon.com

The author email and website are the absolute bare minimum. Obviously there is a LOT more you can do to promote yourself and your work. But be realistic.

In the first edition of *Man, Oh Man*, I asked Allie McKnight, in charge of marketing and technology at Loose Id, a few questions about self-marketing for authors. It's interesting to me that while many things in publishing have changed, this advice remains as current as ever.

How important is promotion and marketing to an author's success?

Allie M.:   This is one of those catch-22 questions. Promotion and marketing expose an author's work to a broader audience. But no amount of promotion or marketing can make a poor book into a best-seller. The book itself must capture the readers, and the best marketing is word of mouth. It's my opinion that authors should focus on getting their book into as many hands as possible, while looking to cultivate positive impressions.

Name three essential things an author should/could do to promote her work.

1. Understand the story you're selling and reduce it down to a sharp premise and a clever hook. That is, spend most of your marketing time developing the book's "branding," i.e., something like, "She's a rich man's Cinderella, right down to her three-year-old Jimmy Choos, but her Prince Charming's more interested in pumpkins than pumps." It sounds silly out of context, but it contains key elements people will

remember, and from there you can call it a Cinderella story with a twist—riches to rags, or concentrate on the way the two characters are different from each other. Plus the tone says chick lit, especially with the mention of shoe types. Every promotional item—including the cover art—should ideally be designed around that theme.

2. Use professionals. Nothing turns readers off faster than promo you printed off your DeskJet. No swag is better than swag people are going to pitch. So, put your time and money into communicating your marketing hook to a professional or using a professional printing service, and think hard about whether the world needs one more pin, pen, or Post-It stack. Same thing with a website. Get it professionally designed. If you can't afford that, go with a low graphics solution and use a simple template. There are plenty of standard designs that come with software like WordPress. Anything's better than websites you have to scroll forever to read.

3. Have a website or blog that allows you some form of communication with readers. Readers like to express their opinions. They like to know about you and your next project. As above, use professionals, but be sure to update frequently with little tidbits of news or ideas, anything to keep them coming back frequently.

In your opinion, what is the single most effective promotional tool you've seen?

I've never seen a tool that works for everyone. If you're a blogger and you like blogging and you're good at it, blogs are an excellent tool. If you're not, they're worse than no blog. Email lists can be equally effective, if you like to distribute short stories or parts of your upcoming works in progress—though you can do that on a blog, as well.

I suppose I'd say a website is very nearly essential for promotion right now. But a bad website can't help you, and it can hurt you. Go for simple and add on as you see what you can reasonably maintain.

Anything else you want to add or say?

Right now, when you're planning your promotion, you're probably excited and eager. A bottomless font of energy. When your book comes out, that buzz will carry a week or two at most. Be honest with yourself. Plan promotion that you can do and maintain, that won't be a burden to you to do, and won't keep you promoting when you should be writing.

And finally, the best promotion is to write a good book. So focus your efforts there, and when you've sold the first one, get to work on the next.

To reiterate, whether you're self-published, indie-published, or traditionally published through a major New York house, the major portion of marketing and promotion will be your responsibility. It begins in earnest from the moment you contract your first story—and it never ends.

Now here's a tip. The number-one mistake most authors make is they promote and market to other authors. They blog How To Write posts, they tweet industry gossip, they fill their Facebook pages with memes and word games for other authors. Basically, they leave readers out. Oh, they don't *mean* to leave readers out. If readers show up, they'll be greeted warmly—and, yes, God knows half the readers in this genre are aspiring writers themselves—but there is no real *opening* in all this busy, busy, busy social media-ing for the plain old regular dedicated reader. The plain old regular dedicated reader can barely get a word in edgewise.

The key to really effective promotion and marketing is to build relationships with readers. READERS. You build those relationships one at a time. It takes energy and attention. The problem is, we're all falling into this social media mindset where we kid ourselves that tweeting three thousand people what we're reading or listening to is the same as building a relationship with them. It's not. A generic tweet to three thousand people is not a conversation.

The lure of social media is that we can reach thousands of potential customers in an instant. The danger is that you start thinking of people merely as potential customers.

When using social media, your goal is to add value to the conversation—not merely to fill up the silence. In fact, sometimes silence—retaining a little mystery, a little enigma—will take you further than making sure everyone knows you like oatmeal for breakfast and you're listening to Lifehouse. You want to share personal tidbits, yes, but mix it up with useful, value-added information like links to articles or essays or quotes or news related to your online or author persona.

And *think* before you speak. Don't squander your entire credibility budget on stupid things. If you're tweeting that something is really, really important and everyone needs to read it, it damn well better be something we'd all recognize as universally important. Otherwise, remember that story about the little boy who cried wolf? And I'm not talking shape-shifters.

Do add value to the conversation. If you're just urging people to buy your book, you're not adding value to the conversation. You're also not adding value to the conversation by simply blabbing all the time. If you're not contributing content to the discussion, you're adding to the white noise.

Invest in a couple of good books on promotion geared to writers. There are plenty out there. Just don't believe everything you read. Keep in mind that rude, stupid promotion is worse than no promotion at all. The idea of all publicity being good publicity was based on the theory that people would remember your name but not the reason for remembering. Now days one click on the Internet provides an instant refresher of why they hate your guts.

In addition to a website, you need a mailing list because even your most devoted fans don't visit your website every week or even every month. If you want them to buy your new work when it first comes out, you've got to make sure readers stay informed.

You can do fancy mailing lists—there are programs and software for that—or you can start cheap and simple with a Yahoo or Google group. I use Mail Chimp, mailchimp.com which is free until you hit 2000 members (and then it's still very cost effective).

You can start actual web discussion groups, which is great if you have the time and energy to moderate—and you can think of something to talk about besides yourself all the time.

You'll also probably need to consider a blog of some kind.

A blog is an online journal or weblog. It's used to interact with readers on a more regular and personal basis than a mailing list affords. Some people do daily updates, I try to do mine weekly. I have two: LiveJournal, jgraeme2007.livejournal.com and Blogger.com, joshlanyon.blogspot.com

So what do you blog about? Well, blog about stuff that would be interesting to readers. Promote yourself as an expert—assuming you have an area of expertise. Perhaps you have some area of knowledge that ties in with your fiction: the law or gardening or a particular period of history. Maybe you can talk about your day job, assuming you have some kind of interesting profession that ties in with your stories. You can talk about your journey to publication. That's personal and it's interesting without being strictly aimed at aspiring writers. I used to believe that all authors blogging writing advice was a good idea, but since everybody is now an author, and mostly an inexperienced author, the writing advice tends to be derivative. Plus…you'll do better to have people focused on your stories and content, not on your style and technique.

But while you need something interesting to talk about, don't get too personal or too revealing. Your marital problems and fights with other writers might be fascinating to some in the same way people slow down to gawk at traffic accidents, but they won't earn you respect and they won't persuade anyone to buy your work.

Again, there are lots of options for free blogging, or you can pay to have a blog professionally designed. The main thing, in my opinion, is to not subject visitors to a constant barrage of advertising. Nobody's going to keep tuning in for that. What you want to do is post about topics that interest you combined with opportunities for readers to respond, so that discussion builds from there.

If that doesn't sound like something you can manage, maybe you can try banding together with some other writers and do a group blog. That takes some of the pressure off. In fact, group promotions are one of the more painless ways to promote your work. Sharing expense and effort often has the added payoff of exposing your work to fans of your writing and promotional partners.

There are plenty of things you can do to promote your work that are free or inexpensive—beyond the investment of your time (and that actually is one of your most valuable assets, so spend it wisely).

When it comes to promotion, you're aiming for a cumulative effect. No one thing will be enough. You'll need to experiment until you figure out what works best for you—meaning what is both effective and comfortable enough so that you can sustain the effort. Yes, you will need to sustain the effort.

One of the easiest things you can do is take active part in a number of online communities and discussion groups. Joining a group you have a legitimate and genuine interest in, and then actively participating in casual conversation, offers a great way to reach potential readers. And it's good for you—writing is a lonely, self-absorbed business. It's healthy to communicate with people about something besides yourself and your writing. Remember that thing I told you about relationships?

But I caution you strongly: do not join discussion groups merely to spam them with announcements of your releases. Rude and oblivious writers have been doing that for years, and most Internet groups are highly sensitive to being used as an audience for your commercials. You won't convince people to buy your books, but you may very well convince them to *not* buy your book. Nobody likes a spammer.

Join groups that you really want to take part in—and take part. If your posts show you to be an interesting and intelligent person, odds are in your favor that people will begin clicking on your sig file and checking out your website. Then, if the writing excerpts on your site are good, people will start buying your work.

The following are a collection of tips and tricks that arose during a brainstorming session at the online group homopromo: groups.yahoo.com/group/homo Some cost nothing but your time. Some require financial investment. Some are more effective than others. Basically you try what appeals to you and see how it goes.

- Hold contests, scavenger hunts, and website giveaways (but be imaginative—offer things like naming a character in your next book, themed gift baskets, original artwork, etc.)
- Volunteer for guest blogs, for interviews, for anything going!
- Purchase professionally made bookmarks or other items to hand out at signings, mail to bookstores, give out at conferences
- Create and gift play lists for your books
- Post excerpts from new releases on mailing and discussion lists
- Buy Google AdWords
- Create your own downloadable bookplates
- Do a blog tour or a cyber launch party
- Exchange banners and links with other authors
- Buy banners and online ads at review and GLBT sites
- Give books away through Goodreads
- Buy ads through Facebook and/or promote posts
- Create reader guides for book clubs
- Buy print ads in GLBT or genre-specific venues
- Invest in audio books
- Invest in translations
- Commission an author app
- Build and maintain a consistent social media presence on sites like Pinterest, Tumblr, Twitter, Facebook
- Do your own podcasts
- Do character interviews
- Join an advertising co-op with other authors
- Enter your work for awards like the Eppies, Ritas, etc.
- Buy or make video trailers on websites and YouTube
- Socialize and be active on your publisher's lists
- Network on sites like Goodreads, Shelfari, Wattpad, Amazon Discussions, etc.
- Get your stories accepted by the larger and more prestigious e-publishers

- Attend conferences and workshops—taking part in panels
- Conduct online writing workshops and seminars
- Do book signings and live appearances
- Hire a publicist or promotional company
- Write op-ed pieces, nonfiction articles in your area of expertise or on the writing life
- Take part in online chats
- And—in my opinion the single most important thing you can do—keep writing and keep *branding yourself through your writing*

You may have noticed one thing I don't recommend is reviewing other authors' work. In fact, I strongly discourage it. Though it seems to mostly work in other genres, I have seen nothing but death and disaster for M/M authors reviewing each other. Okay, maybe not death. Not yet. I expect it daily.

Now, I completely understand why you think I'm wrong about this. You love to read and very often it was the process of analyzing and reviewing that inspired you to strike out and write your own stories. You've made friends through reviewing. You may even have built a loyal little readership based on your reviews. Maybe established a little bit of literary street cred? You're *good* at reviewing. Plus, there are so many STUPID books out there.

Sure. I get all that. And I'm not saying don't review. I'm saying don't review under your author name. Because if you review under your author name, you're obviously using reviewing as a promo and marketing tool, which means your reviews are tainted by the fact that you're no longer an unbiased observer, you're the competition. You're a rival. Now you may fondly imagine you're above all that, but nobody else does. And when you criticize the books of the competition, you're also criticizing the taste of the readers who love those books. Those are *your* potential readers, too. Reviewing another author negatively can cost you dearly in this genre—*unless* you're more interested in being a reviewer than a fiction writer.

Which brings us to…

PLAN B - Reviews

As wonderful as your book is, unless something in the blurb triggers a reader's interest, she or he probably won't buy it until they've either read enough tantalizing reviews or heard some positive word of mouth. That's why you want lots of reviews—why it's worth risking pirates and mailing electronic ARCs (Advance Review Copies) to the smallest and most obscure blogs, even worth investing in print ARCs when necessary (especially if you've self-published).

When I mentioned earlier that some marketing and promotion is done by your publisher? Well, arranging for reviews is often it. Which is okay, because reviews are one of the most effective promo tools out there.

Except…reviews aren't really promo tools.

Even though we all rely on them for promotion and marketing. Do you see why this can create considerable tension between authors and reviewers? We have different missions, though occasionally they overlap. The reviewer's goal is to match the right reader with the right book. Your goal is to get as many readers as possible to buy your book.

Anyway, ask your publishers where they send their M/M releases for review. Do your own research and check your publisher's listing against your own; new review sites are springing up all the time. And if your book has crossover potential, meaning you've written, for example, an M/M mystery, an M/M fantasy novel, or an M/M historical, check out genre-specific review sites as well. There are some great ones out there like Speak Its Name for historical GLBT novels, or Reviewing the Evidence for (print) mysteries. And don't overlook the hundreds and hundreds of blogs and bloggers. Many of these informal sites take their reviewer rep very seriously and do as in-depth and well-written reviews as the official review sites. Yes, it costs money to give books away. It's called *advertising*. Budget for it.

Few things stroke your ego more than a flattering critique from a sharp reviewer. But, gratifying though that is, the real value in reviews lies in the repetition of your name for readers, which means that good, bad, or indifferent doesn't matter as much as getting reviews in as many places as possible.

So when you get that first negative review—and you will—do not panic, do not freak out, and do not attack the reviewer. Your book is not doomed. Your career is not over.

Because a whole review culture now exists and it is crucial for every author to figure out how to best navigate those sometimes perilous waters, I invited a handful of well-known reviewers to a roundtable discussion. Thank you to Sunita Darnell, Jessewave, Josiegoodreads, Elisa Rolle, Mandi Schreiner, and Tom Webb for offering their insight and experience.

Why do you take the time and effort to review books in this genre?

__Mandi Schreiner (Smexy Books):__   Romance is the only genre I read, and I'm passionate about the M/M genre, and I love discussing the books I read. I find reviewing to be a great outlet for this. If I find a book I love, I want everyone to know it! And same if I find a book that wasn't for me. Readers spend a lot of money on books every year, and if they turn to me to get an opinion on a book, I like to be able to share that with the readers of my blog.

__Elisa Rolle, My Reviews and Ramblings:__   Of course I read and review gay romances since I like them, but I actually started to review them since at the time there was no one doing it seriously. Now I continue since I still receive positive feedback saying my reviews are helping readers selecting through the sea that is gay romance. In a way it's always my love for organizing things with an order that is pushing me.

__Josiegoodreads (Mrs Condit & Friends Read Books, Goodreads and Amazon):__   I started for friends and favorite authors. I think it's nice to help authors promote and get established.

__Tom "Bear" Webb (A Bear on Books):__   I'm a reader first and foremost. When I started reading in the genre, I kind of fell into it by mistake. I did a search, just for fun, on my Kindle for "gay cowboys" and the first book that came up was Bareback by Chris Owen. I read it and loved it. From there, I started looking for more books to read, and found some that were good and some that were...not so good. And the reviews were the same. Some I would read and they would be spot-on, but others were snarky, disrespectful of the author or work. In many cases, the review would be "good job" or "this book sucks". I work too hard for my money to waste it on books with such little support. Now, I did run across a lot of jewels that way, but they were like needles in a haystack.

So I wrote my own reviews. I thought, I can do this as well as some of the people I kept seeing. The response was almost instant; I was getting feedback from other readers thanking me for giving a book a nod, and then, surprisingly, a few authors who read contacted me and thanked me for taking the time to focus on the book itself and not the writer.

Long story short, a friend suggested I start my own review blog. So I did. I set the criteria as this—I only review books I like, and I focus on the work, not the author. The blog is mine, and while I am toying with the idea of opening it up to guest reviewers, I control all the content. This way, I can talk about books that move me or stand out to me in some way.

I love M/M romance, I read at least two books a week, and I care that great books by wonderful writers get attention.

Sunita Darnell, Dear Author: For me, reviews are an opportunity to share my likes and dislikes about books in the genre with other readers and to contribute to an ongoing conversation. In addition, I think that reviewing books that are categorized as "niche" on a general romance blog like DA offers the possibility to introduce new readers to books they might not otherwise read. The "niche" aspect of M/M is more a product of historical conditions than anything specific about the work. When I started reading M/M, I quickly realized that they were part of the romance genre I loved, just about two men rather than a man and a woman, and I've seen new readers go through the same mental process.

Wave, Reviews by Jessewave: My answer is very simple. I review books because I love to read and reviewing is a natural extension of that love. As for the genre, I love this genre and want to see it succeed beyond today's very narrow parameters. M/M appealed to me as I was repelled and offended by the heroines in het romances and had read books such as The Front Runner by Patricia Nell Warren, Magic's Pawn by Mercedes Lackey, A Single Man by

Christopher Isherwood, The Dreyfus Affair by Peter Lefcourt and many others that impressed me.

What qualifications, if any, do you believe are necessary for book criticism and reviewing? Do you feel reviewers have any particular responsibility?

Elisa: What you need to be is a book lover; if you have some literary background, it can be useful, but if you don't like the genre you are reading, your reviews are empty. So no, I don't think a professional reviewer is better than a simple reader, on the contrary they can be less believable. The main responsibility of a reviewer is to remember you are not the protagonist; it's not important to push your own personality into your reviews. You have to take a step back and don't let your likes or dislikes be the ones doing the reviewing. Sure, you have opinions, and you can state if something is your cup of tea or not, but if you really are not up to reading that book, then don't read it. And above all, you are reviewing the book not the author; you should forget who the author is, or if they are a friend. Probably, if you have some grudge with an author, you should avoid reviewing one of their books.

Josie: Reviewers need to be fair. I don't tend to criticize, I work on the basis if I have nothing nice to say, keep quiet. Qualifications are just a sense of fair play. Don't be nasty; if you need to say anything bad, then make it constructive criticism and give examples. Something the author can work from and look at.

Bear: That's a hard question to answer in many ways. This isn't a job, so anyone can do it. In order to be a successful critic or reviewer, though, I think there are a couple of qualities that are important. First, you have to love to read, and love books. Readers recognize each other; someone who dabbles and sticks their toe in the water to test the temperature will stick out like a sore thumb when trying to critique books. Those who have a passion and can articulate what they like about a book will rise to the top. And those are the people I listen to when I go looking for a new book to read. I don't stand on formality—just tell me what was good about the book and why I should read it.

Now, reviews do have a responsibility to be honest and fair, and to stay out of the silliness that sometimes rears its head in this genre. We are reviewing BOOKS, not personal lives or sales or gender. Stick to that.

Sunita: I don't think there are formal qualifications that we can specify for a reviewer. One of my favorite film reviewers, Pauline Kael, had no formal background in film or criticism and yet she became a great critic. I do think that reviewers who have read widely in a genre tend to provide more useful reviews, but a newcomer's assessment can also be enlightening because she doesn't take for granted the genre aspects that a veteran can overlook or ignore.

The important thing about reviewing is to be consistent and transparent in your approach to and evaluation of a book, and to support your points with examples. A reader doesn't have to agree with you, but if she can see how you arrived at your conclusions, she can find your review useful.

In terms of responsibilities, I think there are two critical responsibilities a reviewer has to keep in mind. First, review the book in front of you. Not the author, not the book you wish had been written, not the entire oeuvre (although placing the book in the larger context of the author's work is sometimes helpful). Think about what the author is trying to do in the book. Be generous, by which I mean, give the author the benefit of the doubt. That doesn't mean glossing over the flaws, but rather thinking about how the book succeeded or failed on its own terms.

Second, a review is for other readers. We say this all the time, but I think it bears repeating. The review is designed to provide information to people who might want to read the book. An honest, straightforward review that focuses on the book is the best justice you can do to it. Don't make the review a platform to show off your own skill with words, or analysis, or imagination, unless it's in the service of the review. If you want to dazzle people with your words, write your own book.

Wave: In response to the first question, I believe that reviewers should have some qualifications in order to review books, which could include a facility in English and a knowledge of books gained through extensive reading in different genres. In other words, it shouldn't just be "have computer, will review" or getting an "A" for book reviews in high school English. However, as far as I know there are no accredited courses either online or in brick-and-mortar schools leading to a degree or diploma in reviewing. On the other hand, there are many books available on reviewing, and I have used a few of them as part of my reference material such as: The Slippery Art of Book Reviewing by Mayra Calvani & Anne K. Edwards and Faint Praise: The Plight of Book Reviewing in America by Gail Pool.

In terms of personal hands-on life experience that might qualify someone to be a book reviewer, the reviewers on my site, reviewsbyjessewave.com, in addition to being avid readers, come from countries all over the world (currently Germany, Serbia, Russia, the Netherlands, Great Britain, USA, and Canada) and a wide range of age groups, education, skills, and varied careers such as (doctor, publisher, psychotherapist, lawyer, teacher, librarian, author, business consultant, stay-at-home retiree, busy moms, and business owner). We hope that by utilizing this broad spectrum of experience, backgrounds, and age that our reviews stand out from the rest by taking a different approach.

I should point out that while there are writing courses and countless books published on writing techniques, many authors have no formal writing credentials, and based on my personal reading experience, some of them seem to subscribe to the school of "have computer, will write".

I'm not sure how to answer the second question: Do you feel reviewers have any particular responsibility? Did you mean: Should reviewers have any responsibility towards the authors when they review a book? I think every reviewer should be responsible for the content of their reviews by ensuring they are accurate and honest. We don't review authors but the books they write.

Mandi: I don't think reviewers need to have any qualifications. They just need to have read the book. Which is silly to say but I've seen people criticize books they haven't even read yet. I think the only responsibility reviewers have is to be honest. Which seems like an easy thing to do, but I think reviewers struggle with this sometimes. You develop relationships with authors due to the atmosphere of social media. We are on Twitter and Facebook with authors. And I think sometimes reviewers feel bad or awkward if they post a negative review and then interact with them online. I think reviewers need to step back and really focus on the book they just read.

Should authors ever read their reviews? Do you feel there is anything a writer could learn from reading your reviews?

Josie: A writer could gain from mid-range reviews, if they read them constructively. Rave reviews just make them feel good and bad reviews knock their confidence.

Bear: Of course they should. Many reviewers see the whole picture, and can bring an impartial eye to a work and perhaps see something that the author may not. Readers want to buy good, solid books, and to make that happen, writers have to listen to what their audience is telling them.

Now, should they change their styles or content because one reviewer says he/she doesn't like it? No. But if the same critique keeps coming up, perhaps it's time to listen. I'm not an advocate of viewing the writer/reviewer relationship as anything other than a partnership. The writer trusts me with their work. I read it and appreciate the effort and hard work that goes into it. Does that mean I will like every book that I buy? I wish! I only review about ten percent of the books I read. But I try to walk away from every book with at least one nice thing I can say about it.

Can a writer learn something from my reviews? God, I hope so. I hope they can see I hear them. That I walk away with something that touched me, and they did a good job. I point out what works, so they can use that as a building block for the next book.

Sunita: I think each author should do whatever feels right for him or her. For some authors, even positive reviews are difficult to read. For other authors, if they don't read their reviews, they spend all their time wondering what's being said. Still others ignore reviews and are the better for it.

If an author can learn something from a review I've written, that's great. But that book is done and over, from the author's point of view, so I don't write with the expectation that the author can learn from it. I do try to be explicit about what does and doesn't work for me in the book, but that's for readers. That said, I do write with the knowledge in the back of my head that the author may be reading. I'm not good at snarky reviews, so I don't have to tone down my words much, but I try to be fair, if not always gentle.

Wave: If an author is going to suffer from depression or writer's block because of negative reviews, then I don't think she should read her reviews. However, if authors want to learn what they may be doing wrong, I believe they should read reviews by reviewers they trust. If one or two reviewers say something negative, an author can easily dismiss their comments, but if 4 or more reviewers say the same thing, there might be some validity to their comments. Of course my assumption is that authors want to improve their writing skills on an ongoing basis through whatever means are available, including reviews of their work.

Mandi: That is totally up to the author. I write my reviews solely for the readers of my blog. I don't write my reviews for authors.

Elisa: Yes, they should, and they should try to read them with a critical eye; of course in the previous question I stated that a reviewer should be also impartial, and so what they are writing in the review are advice and not attacks. If they are advice given with a good predisposition, then they can be useful to the author. An author should always consider the reader as an external and critical eye to their story; they should not trust too much relatives or friends.

Should writers ever respond to reviews, either to thank, clarify, or disagree with a reviewer?

Bear: Never publicly. And probably not privately. But I do have to be honest, I have had a lot of authors who write to thank me for reviewing their books. I have made some really nice friendships from these communications, but there is always the perception that it might flavor a future review. For me, it doesn't. I usually refuse to review friends. I have, and sometimes do, but it's only with those writers who know me well enough to understand "Reviewer Tom" is not "Friend Tom".

I don't care if a writer does it. It's not going to change me, my reviews or what I have to say. But if someone wants to clarify or disagree, it's the writer that will look bad every darned time, not the reviewer. Well, unless the reviewer is fool enough to answer back.

Sunita: There is so much disagreement about this. I enjoy having authors comment on my reviews. Jo Beverley once corrected a mistake I made; she did it very courteously and I was glad she did (it was a very positive review). But many readers feel that author comments shut down discussions on the book, both at blogs and at other sites. So I would say that while I personally don't mind, I think authors are better off staying away from reviews. Clarifications don't usually help, and disagreements get ugly very quickly (not necessarily on the author's part, either).

Wave: I think so, especially if it is a positive review and it's clear the reviewer spent a lot of time and effort on it.

Many authors email me to respond to both positive and negative reviews, and some of them do comment on the site, especially if the content is incorrect in some way. I believe everyone knows that we have a strict policy here about no flame wars, and we encourage authors to drop by. Even though this site is mainly for readers, as you know, we welcome authors and feel that they are an integral element of our success.

Mandi: No. And I know a lot of people disagree with me, but I feel very strongly that authors should not comment on a review. Not even to say thank you. Once someone sees a comment from an author, discussion usually stops because the audience is reminded the author is aware of what is being said. Honest discussion is harder to achieve if readers see the author pop in because I think they don't want to hurt feelings. So I think authors should stay out. If there is a mistake in the review or if they want to thank the reviewer, make contact privately.

Elisa: Yes, why not? Of course always with a positive confrontational attitude. They have the right to ask for clarification if a reviewer states something on their book they didn't understand. Moreover, if the review was positive, I think the reviewer would like to know. I always like when an author tells me I caught in their story something others didn't, or even better, neither of them understood was in the story. I have also had authors thanking me for a not-so-good review because they learned from my review something they were using for the next book.

Josie: Probably not.

Do you critique new writers more leniently than experienced writers?

Sunita: Yes and no. I don't grade them differently, but I'm gentler in the way I discuss the flaws. I assume there's still lots of room for improvement, and I tend to frame criticisms as issues that need work. I wonder if that comes across as condescending? I hope not. Here's an example: newish writers are often not very good at plot and pacing. I'll note the problems but not dwell on them. With veteran writers I figure if they haven't learned to plot after several books, it's probably not going to happen, and I'll point it out as a recurring issue.

Wave: On this site we make a point of reviewing books by new writers whenever we can because we realize how difficult it is to get a book reviewed in this oversaturated genre, especially if you're unknown or have no fans.

I do try to be more lenient if I know that the book I'm reviewing was written by a new writer, but sometimes it's difficult to tell. A few new writers have blown me away recently with such exquisite writing that I have difficulty reconciling their talent with the fact that the book might be their debut novel, so I try never to make assumptions that new writers are not as talented as established authors.

If a book written by a brand-new writer is really terrible and should never have been published, then of course I would be honest, but I would also try to find something positive to soften my review.

Mandi: No, I think I hold each book up to the same standards.

Elisa: Not more leniently, but I give them priority on my reading list; it's both for me and for them. Reviewers tend to ignore new authors until someone else takes the effort to read their book, and so, basically, there is not much available on them for a new reader to decide if they would like to pick up that particular book rather than others from best-known authors. But aside from having more chances to be read by me, I'm not any different when reviewing them than if I'm reading the 10th book from the same author. New authors tend to listen to you more than others; sometimes I have the feeling that some reviewers spoil authors: if you are friends with a reviewer, it's unlikely that reviewer will give you an honest review, it will be always a starred one, and so you, as an author, will tend to not listen to an opposite voice. I, as a reader, tend to not read or trust a perennial 5 star from the same reviewer to the same author.

Josie: I treat all authors the same.

Bear: No. There are new writers who write so much better than some established ones, so I judge the book on its own merits. I might point out that this is the debut work and I look forward to more from him/her, but it's all about the book with me, not the writer.

Do you feel that male writers have an edge in this genre?

Wave: I'm not sure that male writers per se have an edge in this genre, but I think that gay male writers have an advantage because of their perceived credibility, the believability of their plots and characterizations, as well as the realism of the sexual relationship between their MCs. When some gay male authors write certain scenes, the authenticity comes through, while I think some female authors don't do the necessary research. (Would you believe that many female writers refuse to watch gay porn, which I'm told is a great research tool, and stick to tab A into slot B?) On the other hand, the emotional content of some of the books written by a few gay male authors is probably not as well developed as books written by female authors. Each gender has advantages and disadvantages, and as a reader I want a balance of both perspectives, but that doesn't happen often.

I try not to generalize as there are authors of both genders who surprise me because intuitively, as writers, they can take the reader inside their characters' heads and emotions effortlessly. That is called writing. I just wish our authors, regardless of gender, would think outside the box on a regular basis when they develop their plots and characters.

Mandi: I haven't noticed this.

Elisa: Male writers are different from female writers in most of the cases. There are exceptions—there are females that are able to write as male and vice versa—but in general, men are more direct, erotic bordering on erotica, women are more romantic, erotic bordering on romance (of course if we are speaking of romance). It's not a question of not being able to write male characters with realism if you are not a man, it's something less physical than that.

In a way men have more freedom with their characters since, if they make fun of some male faults, there is no one accusing them of not being realistic; if a man writes about a flamboyant gay man, no one will tell him he is not realistic since his character is too feminine, but a woman doesn't have the same freedom. Once I read about a polemic since there was a woman writing about gay Afro-American men, and she was using the word "chocolate". Everyone was saying how she was racist, how she wasn't realistic, and so on...and at the same time I was reading a book by Terrance Dean, who is gay and a man, and he was using the same exact word. When I told that in the forum, they told me he could since he was Afro-American and gay, so he was "allowed".

Josie: No. To be honest, I prefer female authors as I think they make the characters more emotional, which is something I like.

Bear: Yes. I think they have a certain cache that gives them an initial edge. Let me qualify this with two statements, however.

1. If the book is junk, they lose whatever edge their gender gave them. The quickest way to lose an edge is to fumble the ball. The majority of readers in this genre are straight females, and they are smart and know what they want. Fail to deliver, male or female, and they will leave you in droves.

2. I find some male writers get the emotional connections and sex "right". I'm a gay male myself, and who better to know what I like than another gay male. However, see the point I made above. The audience isn't gay males. And what's important to me may not be what's important to my friend Laura.

Sunita: Not in quality but definitely in visibility. I've read good and bad, believable and eyebrow-raising books by male writers. I haven't seen any systematic differences between women and men, perhaps because both are writing for an audience that is majority female and in large part looking for the same kinds of payoffs in their reading experiences. But I do think male writers get treated as if what they write is somehow more "real" than what women writers produce. And at least some male writers seem to develop a fan base that women writers do not. If I look at my keeper shelves, I see books written by men and women, straight, gay, bi, and trans*, and the quality and style of the books don't follow any obvious pattern.

Are there any elements or tropes you feel have been overdone?

Mandi: Sometimes when I read a book I get that "here we go again" feeling and I think how many times can we read a Best Friends to Lovers trope, or a Gay For You trope. But then I'll pick up a book and it will have that something special. It will have a character or a situation that really impacts me emotionally. And the book will have the same trope as the 100 others I've read, but at the same time the author somehow portrays it in a way that makes it special. I don't know how authors do this, but this is why I read and read and read. To find those amazing books that stick with me for a long time.

Elisa: To me no, but I heard complaints about the Gay For You theme, especially from gay authors; they think it is even dangerous, since young gay men reading these romances can have the impression that it is possible to turn a straight man with "love", and maybe they are flirting with danger instead. Truth be told, I'm not really fixated with a theme or another, so I don't feel anything as overdone since I don't read all novels available on that theme.

Josie: No.

Bear: God, yes. Shifters where the big bad Alpha has the twink sub mate. Instalove. Gay For You where the straight male suddenly remembers his high school teammate/best friend or college roommate he had sex with one time and conveniently forgot about. Cowboys, to some extent. I'm getting there with closeted firemen and police officers. Hateful parents. Redneck haters. Shrill women.

Sunita: I'm on record multiple times as disliking Gay For You and Out For You tropes. I understand that it's a popular fantasy trope (fantasy in the sense that readers who enjoy it understand that it's a trope, not a representation of common experience). But while I enjoyed it when I first started reading M/M, now I avoid it like the plague. It sets up an extremely predictable conflict and storyline that then resolves in an HEA or HFN that I find utterly implausible, as a rule. I read romance to read about an emotional journey that ends in a believable resolution. Gay For You does not satisfy that for me.

I am also not a fan of what has been called Homo OK, the M/M equivalent of small-town romance, where everyone is thrilled at these two men who are either out or closeted and then out, and all that is really left is to get them together. The entire town conspires to bring this about. Really? I don't think so.

Wave: Books with over-the-top, overwhelming angst. I think some authors are just lazy and use angst as a means to hook readers, instead of developing their stories and characters by making them believable. I want to read a story that stirs my emotions but not to the extent that I have a continual knot in my stomach which makes me feel ill, but I'm probably in the minority since a lot of readers love major angst, so who am I to deprive them?

Moving on…the idea that there are only 5 or 6 original plots from which all romance stories flow seems to be accepted in the romance genre more than anywhere else. This makes it easy for authors not to dig deeper and engage those grey cells as they use this as an excuse to continue with the same old tropes. I maintain that there are many original ideas out there in this big old world of ours just waiting to be parlayed into a story. If our innovators and inventors had believed in the old recycled ideas, we would still be reading by kerosene lamps, as an example.

We seem to have given stalkers and kidnappers a rest for the time being, which is a good thing, but here are a few tropes that I personally am tired of reading:

Homophobic parents or churches = runaway teens = hookers

Overemphasis on homophobic police precincts and cops. I know they exist in some cities/states/countries, but can we turn the page? There have been advances recently in a lot of precincts, LAPD being one of them, but writers do not do the research and continue with the same theme that every straight cop is a homophobe.

Rape. It seems that every other gay man in M/M romance gets viciously raped. I'm still trying to figure out why this is.

Sex workers. Seems like all gay teenagers who have been kicked out of their homes by their parents only survive by becoming sex workers.

Poorly written BDSM books. With the runaway success of Fifty Shades of Grey there is now a flood of BDSM books, which is dangerous because many authors write about a lifestyle that they do not know and haven't researched properly.

Gay For You. One author said that the terminology should be Out for You, which I think is more believable.

Insta Love. 'Nuff said.

Hangings in Historical Romances. The prevailing threat or sense of doom in these books that the MCs will be hanged if caught. Do we need to be hit over the head with this in every single book?

The Big Misunderstanding. MCs don't communicate with each other, ever, leading to a separation of even decades before the HEA. Apparently most men don't communicate in real life?

Facile HEAs. I like shorter books such as novellas, but the insistence of HEAs in this genre leads to rushed, unbelievable, facile HEAs.

Best friends turned lovers. While I do like these books, half of the last ten books I read recently have this theme. Must be a new trend.

Are there any elements or tropes you feel are under explored?

Elisa: Gay men dealing with marriage and family; now that few states allow gay men to marry, I'd like to read romance with that spin, even dealing with having children (surrogate mother or adopting); in an alternate future dealing with artificial pregnancy, why not? But most of all I'd like to read about the day-to-day challenge of building and maintaining a family. And not since they are forced by an unexpected event (like relatives or friends dying, leaving them unexpected parents), but since they actually chose to embark in this adventure.

Josie: Military service in war and peace time probably. Sailors. Submariners.

Bear: Realistic sports stories. Gay men who have good and solid family relationships. Men who are over the age of thirty need love too. And the books about those over forty or fifty? Almost nonexistent. Solid biracial relationships. Bittersweet stories where the ending may not be a HEA.

Sunita: Grownup men in grownup romance, perhaps. Ones where the same types of conflicts that keep het couples apart (careers, families, cultural differences, for example) keep two men apart. Gay lit has tended to emphasize the difficulties of being gay, coming out of the closet, and coping in a prejudiced world. A lot of M/M goes to the other extreme by creating fantasy worlds. I want more stories set in the middle.

Wave: Looking through the blurbs for many recent books, I'm struck by their sameness and monotony, so when I see something different I snap it up, not because it might be the best book ever written, but because the author actually put some thought into the blurb and, hopefully, the plot, and tried to move away from the usual themes. I would like books that have more frotting because I love it—but that's not a theme just a personal wish.

I want to read books that explore the following themes:

Well written urban fantasy/dystopia stories such as Mind Fuck by Manna Francis

Original steampunk stories such as Wicked Gentlemen by Ginn Hale

Excellent murder mysteries which are actually mysteries

MCs whose ethics or morals are ambiguous—again, Mind Fuck is an excellent example

Books with substantial internal conflicts that test the MCs relationships, integrity, and loyalty

More books about sports but please, no more hot high school quar-
terbacks, and authors, for the benefit of fans, research the sport
you're writing about

Books that are outside the lines (e.g. Sean Kennedy's Tigers &
Devils)

More books with MCs who work in complex and unusual career fields
and have to cope with major job stress (The Rare Event by P.D.
Singer is one example)

Paranormal books that aren't about werewolves and vampires. Give
us different types of shifters

More well-written fantasy books like Irregulars

Unusual sci-fi themes such as J.L. Langley's Sci-Regency series

Plots ripped from the headlines

More romantic comedies

Mandi: I'm always on the lookout for books featuring a virgin
hero. I find when paired with an experienced woman, that dynamic
is an exciting one. I also seek out courtesan heroes, especially
in contemporary settings. I love to discover what has happened
in their past to bring them to that profession, and then how they
are able to give up that profession for their one true love.

Are there any elements or tropes you personally will not read?

Josie: I don't read horror, and anything to do with circuses freak
me out.

Bear: Slavery and forced sex are big no-no's for me. Child
exploitation. Heavy BDSM.

Sunita: Not really. In the hands of the right author, any trope
can work. I don't seek out hurt/comfort, but many of the authors

I like write it well. I don't like books with wall-to-wall sex, but I can name several exceptions on my keeper shelf. I generally don't read shifter books and other fantasy books, but that's not unique to M/M.

I shy away from books set in current war zones. There aren't many M/M authors who can write a believable South Asian or Middle-Eastern Muslim. Now that I've said that, though, I probably have a recommended read with one on my shelf!

Wave: Books where rape victims are re-victimized when the author makes them apologise to the rapist for being viciously sexually attacked, and ultimately fall in love with their abuser in order to achieve a HEA. Similarly, a book where an MC is so viciously physically abused in a relationship that he ends up in hospital due to his life-threatening injuries, but the book ends with a HEA between the abuser and the victim.

Mandi: I'm pretty much open to anything. I guess I do draw the line at incest, or brothers who fall for the same woman in a menage type story. But otherwise, if written well, I can handle most themes.

Elisa: It's not an absolute veto, since I read books on that theme, but sincerely I don't like very much extreme BDSM; I really don't understand the appeal of pain linked to pleasure, and until it's light, I can see it as a game, but when it becomes heavy, then sincerely I don't understand it and I prefer to not read about it.

How important do you believe the role of book reviews are in any given book's success?

Bear: They can add sales, but I think word of mouth is a much bigger indicator of success. There are "name" reviewers who can make a book have a sales spike, but if the readers actually read it and it is horrible, it's like a movie that hits big for one weekend then fades away.

Having said that, I also know from personal experience of two books that sold VERY well after I gave them a review. I started the ball rolling, but these books were just begging to be discovered, and when they were, nothing could stop them. I think that is a more typical role that a review plays. How many times have we seen a media darling bomb in the popular court of opinion? The fact is, you can't make someone like something that they don't like. But if you present it in a way that they discover it for themselves and it's good...if you build it they WILL come.

Sunita: They seem to help with visibility, in that they alert potential readers to their existence. But I think word of mouth is probably more important, especially in a niche genre. For less well-known authors reviews are useful, and perhaps also for established authors who hope to be discovered by new readers. But really, it's all about visibility.

Wave: Like any product such as wine, movies, or live shows, books are one more product in a long line that are reviewed as a matter of course so that purchasers have a heads-up before they buy. Since everyone's taste is different I always keep in mind that what one reviewer likes may be anathema to another reader. The trick is not to take your role as a reviewer too seriously.

I can only repeat what I'm told by authors, especially new authors. On many occasions I receive emails from them indicating that a review of their book on this site helped to launch their writing career(s). Recently at GayRomLit 2012, several authors came up to me to thank me for reviewing their books and sending their sales through the roof. Even those authors whose books received negative reviews on the site actually thanked me or the guest reviewers since they feel that any publicity is good publicity.

I think a mix of a great book together with excellent reviews and a good marketing strategy may be the real keys to success. However, I would draw your attention to the runaway success of Fifty Shades of Grey whose plot was stolen from Twilight, and which earned 4500-1 star and 1300-2 star reviews on Amazon and apparently was awful and in need of an editor, any editor. This book has spawned a movie and two other poorly written sequels that female readers apparently can't get enough of, despite the reviews. Fifty Shades was a Goodreads Choice Awards Finalist for Best Romance this year. Go figure.

The short answer to your question is—your guess is as good as mine.

Mandi: I think more than ever, book bloggers can play a key role in getting the word out about a book. But not only through book reviews. I think talking about a book on Twitter (where I get a ton of my own recommendations) is really where you "sell" a book. It's instant interaction and I just really like that venue.

Elisa: Maybe it's the starting push, but then if the book is no good, they are not so important and actually they can even revert against the reviewer (disappointed readers can be dangerous). The same for a negative review. Actually I don't really trust very many negative reviews since if they are so bad, I always have the feeling who is writing them has an hidden agenda, probably since, from my point of view, I would not write a review of a book I really didn't like. It was worse for a book to not have reviews at all than having a bad one.

Josie: Book reviews are exposure, and ultimately that has to be a good thing, unless it's a really awful review.

What are the elements that really get you excited about a new book or a new author?

Sunita: A recommendation from someone whose tastes I trust. A review that tells me an author has a fresh spin on an old story. An author with a distinctive writing style and voice. A historical set in an underused place or time period.

Wave: I like authors who take risks, use their imagination and try something new instead of writing a book using old tropes that have been overused. Authors constantly say that there's nothing new in the romance genre, and while that may be true to some extent, I have read books where the plot does not revolve around old tropes like boy meets boy, they fall in love, they have a Big

Misunderstanding, and years later they get back together and have their HEA.

I would like to read content-rich stories with flawed characters and strong, romantic themes with plots in other genres such as noir mystery, as well as the other themes mentioned above. Books that are set in different locations/backgrounds rather than Anytown USA. This requires research and time, but the investment of time and effort makes the stories richer and results in books that you can't put down once started. That to me is what writing (and reading) is all about.

I love authors who can weave a story from almost nothing even, dare I say, an overused trope much as I don't like them, and make it into a great book. The key is the writing, but that takes a lot of skill and talent to achieve.

Mandi: This is a tough question because I get excited about a lot of things. Currently, I get excited if it is a motorcycle club book, an assassin heroine, a dark and emotional erotic contemporary, or any type of contemporary male/male book. I really need the blurb (and I'll admit sometimes the cover) to catch my eye. I am very eager to try new authors, as it is fun to discover that gem of new writing talent.

Elisa: Some point of originality, like a new spin in the story, or something that gives me a shot of adrenaline while reading it. Being original is complicated but not impossible, so my suggestion to an author is to trust their guts more than some heavy-handed editor, and above all, if they heard the sentence, the readers are expecting this, then run away, because giving to the readers what they are expecting is the sure way to be ordinary and forgettable.

Josie: A good, fast-paced, tight, suspenseful storyline, something that makes me not want to put the book down.

Last time I experienced this was with your Armed and Dangerous series, which I first read late this year, S.A. Meade's Stolen Summer and J.A. Rock's Wacky Wednesday.

Bear: A unique voice. A coherent storyline. Characters that have depth and texture. A new take on an old formula. Keeping it simple and telling a story. I hate it when an author thinks he's the next arbiter of what's cool, and the book is chock-full of snark or smarm. Give me a writer who can string a few sentences together and paint a picture for me, and I will cook you dinner and rub your feet.

Build me a world I can escape in, and populate it with interesting people who I might know in my real life. Even sci-fi/fantasy books that take place in Middle Earth or Transylvania or Mars have a nosy neighbor, a friend who will tell you the truth no matter what, and a hot guy who I want to cheer for.

Do you have any advice for authors?

Wave: Make your stories content rich, exciting, and fresh. Be as original as you can be by trying something new and different, and don't copy someone else's bad ideas. Take risks. Stretch. If you have a good editor, respect her/his opinions—he/she may actually know what they are talking about.

Mandi: Coming from a book reviewer and reader—Have a strong online presence, but don't drown us with book promotion. Take care to answer reader email and tweets. Keep your website up to date and always tell us about your next book and what you have planned for the future.

Elisa: Try to be as original as possible, writing what you like not what you think will sell, believe in your story and your characters. Have a positive attitude, and be careful who you trust on the net. Remember that very few people are doing it out of love for the books.

Josie: Get a decent editor and proofreader, get the book beta'd, and don't always rely on a publisher's editor to catch everything. Check it out yourself even if you send the prerelease proof to a beta just before release for a final check.

Bear: Write from your heart. Tell a story like you would want to read. Trust your vision of your work. Have faith in your readers.

Don't condescend or get cutesy. Don't get caught up in dazzling me with your technical knowledge of the Style Manual—that's what an editor is for. Get yourself two or three good beta readers who won't kiss your butt, and listen to them.

Dare to write that secret story in your heart. If you can think it, dream it, envision it, then tell it.

Sunita: Write what you want to write. In this era of self-publishing and enormous flux in the industry, there is likely to be a readership for it.

Don't get hung up on social media. If you're on it, be yourself. Some people won't like you but others will like you even more.

Interact with readers as a reader, as someone who loves books. We know you're an author. But if we know you as a person, that's far more valuable to you.

Any other thoughts you would like to share?

Elisa: You catch more flies with honey than vinegar, so my suggestion, for both reviewers and authors, is to avoid those venues where people are pushing for polemics. In the long run, it doesn't help you or your blog/books.

Josie: No. Just I love M/M and couldn't imagine ever reading mainstream fiction again.

Bear: I'd like to thank all the wonderful writers in this genre. There are some truly talented people who put out books, and they aren't given nearly the amount of credit that they deserve. If some of the books had a traditional "het" theme, they would be bestsellers.

With the success of Fifty Shades of Grey, I think it's just a matter of time before a mainstream M/M story catches fire and hits big. I hope I get to review it!

Wave: The genre is now 10 years old, so perhaps we should stop importing romance tropes from het and focus on developing our own original ideas that don't revolve around some of the topics mentioned earlier. Also, if there is one bit of advice I can offer: authors make your male characters believable.

Like any other business (and writing is a business), if this genre doesn't evolve and change, it won't grow but will become stunted or stale, and horrible as the thought is, it could wither and die. The injection of new ideas is always critical to the success of any business. Authors can't continue to offer the same clichéd, overused tropes in their books and expect to grow their readership. We live in a global market, and these books are read all over the world. Dreamspinner is investing a lot of money translating its books into many different languages—obviously this publisher is thinking strategically and sees the potential of the global market. Discerning readers in other countries have different expectations than their mothers or grandmothers who used to read romance novels back in the day. The profile of the typical reader today is someone who is reading on his/her Kindle, iPhone, or iPad and checks reviews on Twitter; you'll find that he or she is much younger than the romance reader of 20 years ago—a new breed with different expectations. If this genre doesn't keep up, authors will find that they are yesterday's flavour. Even Star Trek evolved with the times.

You can't underestimate the importance of book blogs and review sites, which are the modern or maybe cyber equivalent of book clubs. Word of mouth spreads by way of review and blog sites. Some of these sites are small and casual and just for fun. Some are large, highly organized, and academic in nature. Some are influential. Some are purely for the amusement of the site owner. But in all cases, people are reading and talking about books. And that could never be anything but a good thing.

TIPS FOR MARKETING AND PROMOTION

Adrianna Dane: Ah, marketing and promotion. There's so much to be said on that subject. I do a variety of things and don't spend all my time in strictly one direction. I'm not generally an extrovert, so it does take work. This is an area where I need to challenge myself. I sometimes participate in loop chats, I blog,

I create bookmarks and postcards, I attend at least one convention per year, sometimes more, I maintain a website or three, I do some podcasting, I do interviews, and I've just started to participate in panels and workshops. I try to be cost effective in what I choose to do, and I am always looking for new ways to reach readers. If I can think of a way to approach it that will work for me, even if it means I'm outside of my comfort zone, I'll see about giving it a try. I look at and study what others have done, but just because it works for them, doesn't mean it will work for me. I have to put my own spin on things. Creativity is just as important in marketing as in writing.

Author of *Mariposa Soul, The Seductive Tale*, **etc.**

Kayelle Allen: The biggest thing for me is to involve other authors. I have learned that while others are indeed my competition, we are all in this together. I regularly invite others onto my personal group to do promos, author chats, featured author days, and contests. I partner with others when my new books come out. Why? Their readers are now suddenly aware of me. They tell their readers to come over and visit on my site. My personal group on Yahoo doubled within a year, and then doubled again. Sales increased. I'd say being open to others has been my biggest success, and the bonus of it is that I have gained many wonderful friends.

Author of *Wulf, Jawk*, **etc.**

T.A. Chase: The one thing that works best for me, besides finding a co-op of like-minded authors to join and cross-promote, is my blog. I've found readers like to know what's going on in their favorite authors' lives. Whether it's a movie I've gone to see or a song I've found particularly enjoyable. I do a quick update every day. If you're regular about when you do your update, whether it's once a day or once a week, readers will come to check you out, and it's a good way to get them interested in your books without having to chase them down.

Author of *Here Be Dragons, No Going Home*, **etc.**

Josh Lanyon is a pen name and Josh Lanyon is a brand. After reading this far, my faithful readers, you know what to expect in a Josh Lanyon novel and you know what to expect from the Josh Lanyon brand. If you don't like my work, you would call this writing predictable. If you do like my work, you'll find it reliable and consistent. Consistency is the name of the game in promotion and in writing.

Whatever you commit to in terms of promotion, make sure you keep at it in a consistent fashion. Do not blog every day for a month and then disappear for six months. Do not set up a Twitter account, collect 1000 followers, and never show up again. Do not leave your website with out-of-date announcements of book releases that happened years ago. Do not forget to post updates on your Facebook or contribute to the Goodreads groups you joined.

As for your writing—your writing defines your brand—no matter how much you write, your work has to stay at the level of excellence and originality that your core readership expects from you. You can never take those readers for granted. If you offer them quantity in place of quality, your brand name becomes crap.

I can only imagine what your logo will look like.

One final thought about promotion: I made a conscious decision a long time ago that I would never spend so much time and effort promoting that it cut into the quality of my work. That's the risk. You can lose entire days to loops and chats and blogging and interviews and before you know it, you've got a deadline crashing down on you.

I try to do three things toward promotion each day. It may be nothing more than posting an excerpt on a discussion list, responding to comments on my blog, and taking part in a live chat in the evening, but it all adds up.

Different techniques work with different books and different authors; no one thing works all the time with every reader except writing a terrific book. *That's* the best marketing tool around.

MIND YOUR MANNERS
Author Etiquette

Some authors are better at branding than they realize. That's not always a good thing. You do not want to be the author that readers hate to see in their news stream. Or, in the words of *Romper Room* (which is what it feels like out there sometimes), Do be a DO BEE, Don't be a DUMB ASS.

I think that's how it went?

I casually threw the question of Authors Behaving Badly out to my Facebook page. I asked readers what kind of author behavior was a turn-off, and I asked authors what were some of the things other authors did that they considered rude.

Two days later people were still responding.

Some of the things readers actively disliked were unsurprising. Spamming them with promotion and marketing. Attacking reviewers. Being rude about differing political opinions (for the record, nobody's talking about **NOH8**). Other things were surprising. For example, the fact that readers consider lack of editing and lousy formatting to be disrespectful.

Sometimes we authors forget that we're not operating behind a force field. Readers are here with us. And our interactions with them—and with each other—influence their decision whether to buy our work or not. Because rudeness is as often ignorance and lack of experience as it is obliviousness to the feelings of others, I thought it might be useful to share some of those reader comments.

Aniko Laczko: Authors who have a go at another author's fans. I've seen some authors who have called fans of an author whom they for whatever reason don't like, all sorts of derogatory names. Not cool.

Barb Gilmour: When writers whinge and whine about stuff in their personal life on their public forum. I couldn't give a damn about how much of an arse the hubby is—I don't buy *his* books. Any airing of dirty laundry is a turn-off to me. If they need to vent, do so on another account.

Sammy Goode: This actually happens in any writing arena—it has happened numerous times in the script-writing field I am in, and each time it both saddens me and disgusts me. When two authors release work that have a similar theme or a similar plot arc or resolution, I have been continually shocked to see an author's fans leap on that other author and begin to accuse them of plagiarism or worse yet, outright stealing due to a supposed "lack of talent and integrity." So often, the author's fans encourage the author to speak out against his fellow writers and they seem eager to do so. This begins a free for all, with other authors who are friends with the initial accusing fans and author jumping into the fray to knock this supposed "stealing hack author" down a few more pegs. And why? Why all this hateful speech and attack? Because that "hack" author's book is doing just a bit better in the ratings—has sparked more interest than the other guys. I find this so very sad and so despicable. We should be supporting each other—not tearing each other down. There are more than enough fans to go around.

Tricia Ahls Moorehead: Outing another writer's "real" identity and slaughtering them for being M/F or Other.

Lizabeth S. Tucker: A writer implying that they are just writing the books because they are "easy money". I've actually heard one writer say that in an interview. An incredible lack of respect for the readers or the community in general.

Carli Cmdm: Don't create special groups for book launches, do it from your author pages. It's more inclusive and will get you a better result because more readers will see it. What I don't like is for the author to be a no-show in his/her page for months until there is something to sell. Believe it or not, we like authors and enjoy some interaction. Doesn't have to be daily, but check in awhile to say hi. We appreciate it!

Whitney Watkins: I find it kind of annoying when authors get cliquey. Like they only respond to other authors' posts. I get that they are friends too, but this is social media and your fans buy your books. Treating them less important because they aren't an author is a little rude.

Marilyn Blimes: Authors who only talk to other authors…uh…that other author may beta your book, but I'm going to buy it. Don't act like I'm not here.

Dianne Thies: If an author is going to have a FB page, they must spend time interacting with fans. I've seen some quite popular authors on FB who rarely respond to fan questions or even acknowledging fans who post that they love the author's work. If it's a case of too many social media accounts, trim them to 2 or 3 that seem the most important and keep up. A few words can go a long way.

Kathleen Charles: I lose all respect for any author who speaks poorly about another author. I find it an unforgivable character flaw. I have quit reading authors for this behavior.

Amanda Ribeiro: The biggest complaint I have is when one author rips apart another for no reason. You don't like them, fine, but that is no reason to go after their writing, or their fans. It is also not cool to encourage or ask your fans to go after their fans. It comes across as petty, jealous, immature behavior.

Lori Oglesby Johnson: One thing that really bothers me (as a fellow writer and as a reader, too) is when authors trash other books or authors via social media or blogs. If you're talking to your best friend over coffee, it's fine to say you don't like a certain book. But to multiple blog posts analyzing lines of text and making fun of dialogue? I think it's too much.

I've seen this done with some of the recent really popular books or series. (Think 50 Shades, etc…) Now, maybe these books really are bad or poorly edited, etc. However, to me, it still looks like you're extremely jealous of the popularity of the books when you spend so much time putting them down.

Katelyn Sweigart: Having multiple social media platforms. There are two things that end up happening: 1) They don't treat all platforms with the same content, so interesting content may be favored on one platform while all others get a bland experience. And 2) They end up rehashing the same content for every platform. I know these seem unavoidable, but having to jump between five-six different social media platforms to get the full experience or just not following the right platform to get the unique one. Also, authors will end up getting burnt out on having multiple accounts to check. Stick to three at most, rehashing some material, but utilizing the platform in a way that best highlights its strengths. If you want more than three, make sure you use the platform the way it was meant to be used. There are big differences between Facebook, Twitter, Pinterest, Tumblr, etc.

Susan Ford: I bet you I am the ONLY person to suggest this, but I am TIRED of the naked-men pictures! No really, I am. If I'm on a website, I want to read the content. There are tons (and tons and tons) of places I can go to look at naked-men pictures. When I'm web browsing, I want to read an interesting article, a review, read about your next book, your last book. You get the picture. I'm very far from prudish, but a penis is just not that interesting to me if I can't just reach out and grab hold of it myself, ya know?

Lisabeth S. Tucker: I've seen a few erotic authors who use relatively tasteful naked photos on FB and with Twitter. Others go farther. Neither is a good choice. It doesn't brand you as an erotic writer, it smacks of spam dating/hooker/escort/stripper/porn. So let your bio and your books tell the story.

Rose Wynne: I myself don't follow much social media, no time really. The authors I friend on Facebook are few. I follow them because they are informative, funny, and interact with their fan base, they post interesting links, little snippets of their personal life, without going overboard, and give details of when their books are coming out or how they are going with projects that are ongoing. In other words, they care enough about their readers to give a little of their time to interact and share a little of themselves, as well as promoting their work. I don't expect them to give undivided attention to every post, because I kind of would like them to write too. I have had a couple of friend requests from new authors that I don't know, and well…no. Unless someone says who they are and why they would like to friend me, then I am not interested. I will go and look at their work, see it for myself, and only if it's something that really grabs me, then I will add it to my read list.

One of the things that I look a lot at are author sites. My pet peeves with these are dead links. Also poorly set out pages and page links that are hard to read and follow. I go to these to see what an author has on offer, to read the blurb on a book and possibly an excerpt. I like to see what's maybe coming up next too. I don't mind if the site has been quiet for a while, but I do expect the information on past works to be up to date and relevant. Blogs and journals are similar. They tend to have more of an author's opinions and some interesting articles and information, and I love reading these when I get the chance. But you are promoting a product too, so make sure that product is easy to obtain and it's information, is informative, easy to follow, and make sure your links to sellers work.

Kristel Santelli: I hate it when authors share their new releases on other author's web pages. If that author whose fan page it is wants to talk about it and is the one to post it, great. But don't go there yourself. It looks pathetic. Even if those two authors are friends and share some of the fan base. And tagging another more popular author while you boast about your new release is the same thing. You don't fool anybody!

Suzanne Edmonson: Posting a link to a 1-star review, either to get sympathy posts in response or to send your fan base out to defend your book. Even if the review is completely unfair, it still strikes me as a manipulative way of publicizing.

Tom Webb: One of the rudest things I have seen a writer do is discount and mock what a reader had to say on his/her FB wall. To post, verbatim, a comment a reader sent in private, saying they were disappointed in the way the writer posted mean and sarcastic comments on his/her public wall, and felt it was disrespectful and then say she would not be buying any other of his/her books. Then this writer posted the comment on his/her wall and proceeded to, in my own opinion, viciously mock the reader and basically encourage others to do the same.

As a reader, I will never buy another of this writer's books, even though I adore his/her writing. My dollars pay for this writer's works and living, and I vote with them. I won't spend my money on someone I can't personally respect.

Angela Middaugh: Oh, yes. My two pet peeves: when you friend me with no motive other than to promo four or five times a day, and when your book is poorly edited. I'm poor. It pisses me off to spend six, seven, sometimes even eight ninety-nine for a manuscript full of typos and mucked-up punctuation... Although, when the story is coming from an actual publisher as opposed to being self-pubbed, my ire is directed at the publisher.

That Thing You Do

By now you're probably seeing a pattern. I'm also guessing that none of those reader comments came as a complete shock to you. We all know these are rude and silly things to do. Things more than likely to backfire. But in our desperation to succeed, we kid ourselves that these bad behaviors aren't really *that* bad, that everyone else is behaving like this—or that readers won't notice.

But everyone *isn't* behaving like this and readers *do* notice. They notice all of it. I could go on and share what they said about books—everything from overpricing to lack of editing—but I don't want to overwhelm anyone. Besides, we've still got to wade through what our fellow authors had to say.

David Steffen: Invasive self-promotion. Don't get me wrong, I know you have to get your name out there, but don't invite me to your book reading on the opposite side of the world, don't private message me with a link to your book, etc.

Jessica Freely: I will say that I don't like it when I friend or follow someone and immediately get a promo DM from them. That will often lead to an immediate unfriending or unfollowing.

Josh Lanyon: Obvious passive-aggressive behaviors. Tagging or copying another author into a critical post and then pretending it's just a friendly conversation—can't they take a joke?! Or claiming the author "barged into" a private discussion. Snotty hash tags such as #headdesk, #hackwriters, etc. Posting under your author name and then trying to play the I Was Speaking as a Reader! card. If you don't want a war, don't fire the first shot.

Becky Black: I'd say for me one thing I hate is when they act superior and too good to give the time of day to new writers. We're all just folks on the same journey, some at different stages, all trying to achieve the same thing in the end. Fellow writers have helped me get where I am, with advice, with critique, with support, and I'll bet that's the case for most writers. I think they should make sure to give back to the community that's helped them, not act like they are now above it.

Anonymous: One of my pet peeves is agreeing to exchange crits, and spending oodles of time and effort on someone's manuscript, then having them spend virtually no time reading yours or never finishing it. Big irritation. As I have no local writer's group or crit group, I've only exchanged crits online with people I've met online in various capacities; I imagine there's more accountability in a face-to-face setup. Oh, and update your website. I've seen some authors who are quite prolific but are still announcing the 2007 release of their latest book!

Anonymous: Sending out fab offers for free books in exchange for reviews (or swapping reviews!) is asking a HUGE favor. As an author, writing a review effectively endorses that book/author to the readership we have worked so hard to build. Blind emails and GR messages from total strangers (or people I've just met/barely know) asking me to pimp their work is just insulting. You do that for a friend. Maybe. You don't do that for every jackass who knows how to send a private message or harvest an email. Presumptuous much? It's infuriating.

Katherine Johnson: My biggest issue is when an author feels the need to berate and belittle others in the same genre. There isn't a shortage of ideas, and we aren't going to run out of readers. If an author isn't selling as well as another, it should be something to learn from—not something to trash the other author about at every turn and in every venue. Another pet peeve: Pitching a fit over bad reviews. Reviews are for readers, not the authors. It goes back to the saying: You can't please everyone. Some authors need a reminder that not every book is going to appeal to ALL readers, and that's okay.

I (and several of my fellow authors) identify as either trans or genderqueer. It has absolutely NOTHING to do with our writing, yet I've seen people either out or run someone's name through the mud for just that.

Lou Harper: Creating a puppet account on GR and spamming book recommendations. Personal attacks, excessive display of ego, fake reviews.

Kari Gregg: When a fellow author signs me up for newsletter/promo blasts uninvited, I am exceedingly vexed. Authors should treat one another as colleagues, not potential customers.

Joanna Chambers: For me, it's the self-promo. I don't even go on Twitter much anymore (which is a shame when it's so good for a feeling of relative conversation) because I feel quite drowned by all the promo tweets. My fault actually, for following pretty indiscriminately.

Kate Aaron: Genre snobbery. Hate it. Sockpuppets. Spamming Facebook, Twitter, and Goodreads with PMs and recs for their own books without even saying hello or taking the time to see if it might be something I'm actually interested in. Asking for feedback when what they really want is praise. Assuming publishing is easy and not wanting to put in the effort to learn their trade or craft. Author meltdowns. Aggressive or patronising responses to readers who don't fawn over their stuff. I could go on... Expecting other authors to fix their books for them for free without giving anything in return. That one most of all. Want an editor? Pay one. Don't come running to me to do it for nothing.

Sue Holston: Not acting in a professional manner at conventions. It's one thing to have a good time, drink with your friends, and party hard. It's another to see your favorite author sloppy drunk, staggering around or God forbid being escorted out of the establishment because they are so wasted they cannot stand upright. (I've seen this at plenty sci-fi cons by actors, but it's not good in ANY professional setting).

Taylor V. Donovan: This is more of a behind-the-scenes issue, but joining crit groups and appropriating ideas and storylines from fellow authors' WIPs.

Taylor Gibbs: Outing someone who is gender neutral as male (or female) is a big one, for me. If it happens, I look at the author who outed the colleague differently. The assertion that only one type of person can write "authentically." The assertion that gay genre fic is much more superior to M/M genre fic.

Anonymous: I hugely resent being made to feel like I have to defend my right to write M/M. I've also had fellow authors take potshots at me over religion. (I'm a Christian. Yes, I believe in the Bible. No, I don't think all homosexuals are automatically going to hell.) Another thing I've had it up to here and beyond with is my fellow authors mutual love fests. Of course not all of them, and not all the time, but holy geeze, how much stroking off do we really need to give each other? This kind of falls in with the whole incessant-promo thing. The same dozen or so authors incessantly tag each other in the 7-7-7 thing, or for each other's blogs, or posting fabulous reviews on each other's timelines, or whatever. Yeah, it's great to pimp your friends, but there are more than a dozen really awesome writers out there. I guess it gets to me in particular because it reminds me too strongly of high school I was painfully unpopular and uncool. I kind of feel like that as an M/M author I'm once again not cool enough for the in crowd. You know, the ones endlessly tagging each other with cute little in-joke hashtags.

Max Vos: For me…being snubbed by other authors just because you're a newbie, i.e. don't have 10 published books. You don't have to be an ass about it.

Ethan Stone: I get annoyed by arrogance, i.e. authors who twat (as Kathy Griffin says) about what an AMAZING author they are. Also, I am offended when authors say things like "Third person is the ONLY POV that should be used. Why would anyone ever use first person?"

Sarah Madison: Twitter feeds set up to auto-tweet promos all day with no interaction with any live person at all. Using cutesy fonts on Twitter that make my eyes bleed. Those are just nit-picky though. My biggest peeve is the notion that there is not room enough for all of us as writers within a given genre. That somehow there is only enough room for a chosen few and that the rest should just get out of the way. Readers read. Sure, most people have a financial limit and might have to pick and choose what to buy this month—but there is always next month for a reader. And the person who likes the bestsellers might just like my stuff too. (There is no accounting for taste!)

The fact that I'm out there in the genre too doesn't mean I'm actively taking sales away from someone else. I really hate this whole notion of "competitive authorship".

Adara O'Hare: I don't think anyone here is saying "self-pro-moting" is a bad thing (though I could be mistaken). It's the "self-promoting to the point of annoyance" that bothers most peo-ple. Authors need to remember that if someone has chosen to follow/friend you, it's because they already like you and find you worth following. That's not the base of people where you need to concentrate your efforts, because most of them will already be primed for more from you. The vigorous self-promoting needs to be outside of your fan-base, to get new fans in, not annoying your current base with too many tweets about something we already saw 5 times in the last 2 days.

Charlie Cochrane: Adding my two penn 'orth. People defaulting on what they said they'd do. Not sending you a blog post they promised or not turning up for a chat they said they'd do with you, and the like.

Monika De Giorgi: The most annoying thing a fellow author did was writing me an email (I didn't even know her), in which she told me that she did seminars on writing (not teaching but took them) and now read the excerpt on my blog and didn't like it. She then gave me a few examples how she would have written it better in a very haughty way, told me she thinks I was a fan-fiction writer (I never wrote any fan fiction) and in the end had the nerve to ask me if we could start kind of a "writing group". Errm... The best thing was, she didn't even do her research. The excerpt she read was from a book I wrote at age 18. I'm now over 30.

Shae Connor: Constant promo is the biggest one for me. I don't have anything at all against promotion; it's part of being a writer, and I certainly do it myself! But it shouldn't be the first thing I think of when I see your name: "Oh, s/he floods my Twitter/FB/etc. with BUY MY BOOK links all the time." Be a real person, not an advertising machine.

Michael Barnette: When authors refuse to follow the rules of a group and post daily—or more—with their promotions when the rules clearly give a day or number of allowable posts. Seriously, one post a week on a group is quite sufficient. More than that becomes irritating to readers and the owner of the group. Also, authors who try and argue with the group's host about how their book is very special and should get better treatment—more promo opportunities—than those of other authors, be they new or established.

Your book is no more special than any other book, deal with it and follow the rules.

A.B. Gayle: For a negative, if I guest an author on my blog with an interview, I do think they should take the time to respond to any comments people make. I realize that authors are busy people, but if you haven't got time to do that, don't accept the request. Fair enough if someone comments months later, but short term, check them out and respond.

KZ Snow: My answer to your question can probably be summed up in one word: ego. Of the inflated variety. When writers get too full of themselves, they start exhibiting distasteful (e.g., insensitive, condescending, exclusionary) behavior toward their peers. This is something I think we all need to guard against.

Belinda McBride: I can turn a blind eye to a lot, whether it's adding me to groups, spamming my wall, or whatever. But when authors bring their personal drama to a public forum, I tend to take them out of my news feed. Life is tough enough, people don't need to see our ugly laundry. Also, I HATE when authors attack other authors on public forums, blogs, review comments, and so forth. It's cannibalistic. Back when I first stumbled on some of the big romance review sites, my jaw dropped at the horrible behavior of reviewers, readers, and authors alike. I rarely visit those sites, and my first personal commandment of behavior is "Thou shalt not comment."

Brenna Lyons: Groups of authors who spam each other's promos the day or two after the original author did it on a group. Seriously… Author A posts a promo about a book release or review or contest win, and over the next week, the exact same promo is posted by three other friends of the author on the same precise groups, in an attempt to bypass the single promo rule on the list. It's annoying to readers and turns them off of reading ANY promos on list.

What do authors consider bad behavior on the part of other authors? Pretty much the same stuff readers do. Don't do that stuff.

It's really simple. Treat readers and other authors like *you* would want to be treated.

IT'S NOT JUST A JOB;
IT'S AN ADVENTURE
PUTTING TOGETHER THE WHOLE PACKAGE

A skilled and disciplined writer can pretty much write anything. It's like training to a certain level. Once your muscles are strong and flexible enough, you can rely on them to carry you the distance. That doesn't mean everything you write will be accepted, but the passes will be based almost strictly on the needs of a publishing house versus your writing ability.

In the early part of your writing career, that's not the case. Most of the rejections you receive will be based on execution. It's difficult to believe this, especially in a genre such as M/M where it's very easy to get published, ready or not. But if you want to get smacked back to reality fast, try submitting your work to a mainstream publisher—or even an indie publisher outside this niche genre.

I don't say this to be unkind. I say it so that you will continue to hone and polish your craft. I say it so that you will not rush to publish before your work is ready. Once upon a time almost nobody had their first novel—or even first few novels—published. The fact that that's no longer true is due to technology not accelerated genetics in beginning writers. Now days a lot of authors learn their craft in public. Some of them—the ones with stories so original and inventive they supplant the amateur writing—go on to fame and fortune. Most fizzle into the strata of invisibility which forms the new digital mid-list. I've been publishing since I was sixteen, and I'm still learning all the time.

If you're convinced your work really *is* all that and a box of Cracker Jack, but you're just not getting anywhere in your writing career, take a good hard look at the way you interact with readers and other authors. Sometimes the fault is in our stars. Sometimes the fault is in us and our bad manners and lousy attitude.

The bottom line is you don't have to be a good person or a brilliant writer to sell M/M stories. You don't need to be subtle or sensitive. You can have a successful publishing career based on nothing more than a crafts-man-like approach. Hell, you can probably be successful with a techni-cian's approach—assuming you're a good enough technician and you've got a thesaurus handy.

If you're just in it for the money, well, there's money to be had. Not riches, mind you, but this is a lucrative corner of publishing right now, which means that all kinds of writers who generally have zero interest in M/M fiction are trying to cash in.

That isn't wrong. It's logical. We're all trying to survive; we all have to earn a living; and we're all competing for publishers and readers. But the reality is, the entire book industry is in flux thanks to the twin juggernaut of ebooks and self-publishing. Authors are now competing with indie authors, main-stream authors, the entire backlists of those authors, everything in public domain, and hundreds of thousands of ambitious new authors self-publish-ing their own work. That's *a lot* of competition. More competition than any writers have faced in the entire history of publishing.

As I mentioned earlier, the new name of the game is "discoverability." But before you can be discovered, you have to get published, and with dwindling demand and so many quality writers and manuscripts to choose from, pub-lishers become increasingly selective. Which is a very bad thing if you were only getting published because the original demand for M/M stories was so great.

I know what you're thinking. *Wait! Did I hear you say d-d-dwindling de-mand?*

Yep. You did. In addition to the most competitive publishing environment in the history of the planet, we're well into what is known as a glut. A glut is the natural end result of the old publishing paradigm of supply and demand. Four years ago I predicted this glut, and my prediction has been borne out by the torrent of god-awful crap now flooding the market and bringing reviewers, and even some readers, close to the breaking point.

How does a glut occur, and what's the future look like once a market has been glutted? Well, it begins when publishers see that there is an urgent demand for M/M fiction. They send out calls and they begin aggressively acquiring like there's no tomorrow. Then tomorrow arrives and the market is flooded with inferior stories and writing. Readers tire of the novelty, the demand wanes, and the supply of backlogged manuscripts exceeds the needs of the market. Sales begin to fall. Publishers stop buying in bulk and writers scramble to sell their work.

I'm not trying to discourage you; I'm explaining why you need to constantly strive to improve your writing—even if you're getting published now. And if you're trying to break into a competitive market, you have to be at the peak of your abilities, not kid yourself that because some so-so books get published, you can succeed merely by showing up.

Some people have a knack for writing, just as some people are natural athletes or are born with perfect pitch. Those folks have a natural edge. But every element of writing that we've discussed thus far is something that you can control. You can learn to create stronger characters and complex plots. You can heighten sexual tension, tighten pacing, and bolster the thematic elements of your work. If you don't have a sense of humor, you can still write focused and snappy dialogue. If you don't have a lot of imagination, you can still come up with commercial and interesting story hooks.

The only thing that really can't be taught is heart. If you don't genuinely enjoy M/M or GLBT fiction, if you're only doing this for money, there's no faking it. Your stories will lack that emotional center that means the difference between an okay book and a book readers love. If you write books that readers love, they'll buy everything you write, and even when you turn out the occasional clunker, the odds are good that they'll forgive you and keep on buying your work.

Even more important than writing what you know is writing what you *love*.

Laura Baumbach, MLR Press: I think it shows in the writing when something isn't someone's genre. Not that there aren't some writers who have been successful with it, but the vast majority fail if they are just in it to cash in on the popularity. They fail because they change their character's name to a masculine noun but not anything else about them. They don't successfully write two men in a relationship. They don't recognize the differences in the sexual needs or the reactions of men. It's not the same as a heterosexual couple with the tab and slot names changed. The emotion of love is the same, yes, the desires and physical want the same, but men act and react differently with other men. I don't mean they don't want or like romance, either; they do. It's a complex dynamic that not everyone grasps. And if M/M isn't a genre that calls you to it for itself, because that's what you have to write, the writer usually fails to write it convincingly. Readers will know, especially the male ones.

Oh yeah, *them*.

There's a reason not too many men are involved in fan fiction, and it's partly the same reason that so many gay male readers have yet to be won to M/M literature. Despite the hot sex and the imaginative plots, despite the fact that plenty of men read and enjoy romance, a lot of the writing is just too…feminine. But not feminine in a real-life way. No, bewilderingly, these stories are feminine in the same painful romantic cliché way that drove so many of these female writers (and readers) from heterosexual romance. In fact, I'm not sure feminine is even the word, given that—bizarrely—some of the biggest culprits are male authors! The characters, the dialogue, the contrived plots, and overblown sex scenes read like they were written by teenage girls.

That's not to say these books don't sell. They clearly do appeal to a significant segment of this reading demographic. But if you're interested in broadening your appeal, in expanding your readership to include more members from the other half of the species, you'll work to make your male characters a little more realistic, a little less of a strictly adolescent fantasy.

Occasionally I read an M/M story either so sappy or so planar—the characters either emasculated or too testosterone-bound to feel anything—that I wonder whether the writer actually ever met a man she didn't hate. If you don't like men or writing about men, your readership is going to be limited—and you're not going to have a lot of fun. And since the money is not *that* good—and will not be getting any better for most of us…

Writing is hard work. Don't kid yourself. If you're going to write the kind of thing you don't enjoy, you might as well keep the day job.

I'm not a fan of creative writing exercises. If you're going to do character studies and plot arcs, do them for stories that you plan on writing and selling. Invest time in your writing, but invest wisely.

The best advice I can give you is to write and read a lot. Constantly, in fact. Read in this genre—yes—but read outside as well. Push yourself all the time to write outside your comfort level. Try devising different kinds of characters, try constructing more complex plots. Don't settle for the first ideas that come to you, keep working them, keep refining. Your first draft is *not* good enough. I don't care what your friends tell you. Or the fact that Schnooky Nooky Publisher is willing to give you a contract. Because, in case you failed to notice, they will give ANYONE a contract.

WHAT'S MY MOTIVATION?

I mean, besides filthy lucre. Even now, when having a roof over my head and food in the microwave depends on my writing every day—writing publishable-quality deadline-driven prose *every day*—I still have days when I feel…unmotivated.

When it is hard as hell to crank out the words.

At some point in every project, I suddenly run out of steam. I start wondering what I liked about this idea to begin with, the writing seems stiff and clunky (even as I remind myself that I write a very ugly first draft). The characters feel unknowable and removed. I've learned the hard way that this means absolutely nothing. It's totally me, and nothing to do with the work at all. I know this because I've gone back months and years later to take a look at those half-starts, and without fail, they're all as strong as anything I went ahead and finished. In fact, many of them I *have* gone ahead and finally finished.

Finish your first draft.

If the idea was worth starting, it's worth finishing. This is assuming that you took a few minutes to think through the initial idea and jot down a rough outline so that you knew before you started that you had enough plot to carry you the distance. Don't fall into the bad habit of starting and abandoning projects for new and better ideas. The odds are good that your new idea isn't any better than the old idea.

It's kind of like falling in love. The new idea is full of romantic promise. It's an attractive unknown. You haven't had time to see its faults, its flaws. You haven't seen it drunk off its ass or snoring with its mouth open. It hasn't stuck its tongue in your ear when you're trying to sleep, or wrestled you for the remote control. But after you've spent some time with the new idea—putting in the work required of an actual *relationship*—you start to see that it has its flaws too, and its socks are just as smelly when strewn across the living room floor as the old idea's socks were.

Finish the first draft. Write all the way through to the end, skipping over the rough parts, the parts that just won't come, the parts that you hate, just write 'til you get to the end. That's the first and most important step.

Whether you sell that book or not, the very act of writing it, of working through it, is a big part of your training and education. No time spent writing is ever time wasted.

Write every day. As near as possible. If you can't manage to write, then edit and revise, do research—or work on another project. I always have several projects going at once, so even if I get a little bored or feel like I need distance from one manuscript, I keep my momentum going. A writing career isn't about one book; it's about consistently producing quality stories that readers can't wait to read. You have to take the long-range view when it comes to your writing career.

Read. You started out as a reader. Keep reading. On the days when you really just can't write, read. It takes a hell of a lot of writing and reading—and more writing—to develop whatever is the literary equivalent of an ear for music.

Set goals and stick to them. If the plan is to finish a book by the end of the year, figure out how many words a day you need to write in order for that to happen, then take a look at your calendar and figure out how you're going to make that work. But be realistic. Be practical. Set goals you can reach without killing yourself or burning out.

It's not hard for me to stay motivated. My financial survival depends on it. But even when it didn't...writing is my passion. I love it—even when I hate it. It's what I do. It's what I am. I am a writer. You're not a writer if you don't write.

Remind yourself of that when the going gets hard—remind yourself that writing two hundred and fifty or whatever words a day isn't a punishment, it's what you *want* to do.

Irene Williams, Loose Id: Write it. Finish it. Make us believe it.

BEST ADVICE YOU HAVE FOR ASPIRING WRITERS

Anne Tenino: Keep trying. You've heard all the stories—abysmal books that become bestsellers (I'm sure you can think of a name or fifty) and wonderful books that were rejected fifty-odd times (such as the Harry Potter series—also eventually all bestsellers). The point is that success is an alchemy of timing, hard work, talent, and luck, and the only sure thing is that you'll never be published if you aren't writing and submitting.

My other piece of advice that I live by (and is to me more important to keep in mind than the above): Not everyone can love your work. Remember this even in those times when you feel like everyone does, because it will keep you humble (this is important when you begin to write your next book). Remember the reverse is true when you feel like everyone thinks you're a hack. Keep evidence around—copies of good reviews and emails from readers—to convince yourself you don't suck on those days when you're pretty sure you do.

Author of *Too Stupid to Live, Frat Boy and Toppy,* **etc.**

Ally Blue: For me, the very best motivation is simply to keep writing. Write a little every day, even if it's only for a few minutes. You've heard this before, but it really is the most important, most helpful thing you can do. I also like to go out and people-watch. Downtown areas are my favorite places to people-watch, but you can do it anywhere. Find a person who catches your eye or captures your imagination, for whatever reason, and make up something about that person's life. Once you get started, it's hard to stop. I've ended up with some wonderful ideas that way.

Exercise. Seriously. Going for a three-mile run ups my energy level and gives me a sense of accomplishment, and that carries over into my writing. You could apply that basic theory toward anything, really. Meeting one goal makes you feel good and gives you confidence to meet the next one.
Author of the Mojo Mysteries and the Hellscape series, etc.

Kayelle Allen: I have a workroom with a door that shuts and locks. I post a sign on the outside when I can't be disturbed. Otherwise, family is free to knock and enter. Knowing the door is shut (and I can see it from my desk) reminds me that it's important to finish, since it's keeping me from my family. That visual cue also helps my family remember not to disturb me unless it's a real emergency.

Music is a huge motivator for me. I love music and need it to work. With each royalty check, I purchase an iTunes gift card. If I want new music, I have to earn it by writing!
Author of *Wulf, Jawk*, etc.

Lou Harper: When starting up: Find yourself a beta reader and/or crit partners. They should be people who are roughly on the same wavelength as you, so they can help you to get where you want to go, as opposed to where they think you should go. They must be people who will honestly tell you when something you're writing is not working. Those who only give compliments are useless.

Listen to constructive criticism. You're not perfect.

Hone your craft. Don't start your writing career with that 150k word epic saga. Write short stories, novelettes, novellas.

Shoot for the moon. Research the publishers and submit to the one on top of your list. They may reject you, but may not.

Be patient. Do not submit to bargain-basement publishers just because they'll accept your MS without reading it and will publish it within a few months.

Don't compare yourself to other authors, especially those who have been in the business much longer than you.

When submitting your manuscript, make sure it's formatted according to the publisher's specification. For some editors an incorrectly formatted MS means automatic rejection.

Author of *Last Stop, Dead in L.A.*, **etc.**

Anthony Bidulka: There is a lot of advice out there for people wanting to write. I can only offer my slant. First, I feel it's important to know what kind of writer you want to be. What is your definition of being a successful writer? Is it to see your short story or poem in print? Is it simply the act of making the time to sit down and put pen to paper? Is it to show what you can do to family and friends? Is it to become published and sell lots of books and make money? Is it to educate? Is it to entertain? Is it a career? A hobby? A love affair that is hot and quick, never meant to last forever?

Second, set reasonable goals, achieve them, celebrate (more on that later), set new goals.

Third, communicate with other writers. Spend time with writers. Take a class. Join a local or provincial or national writers group. Meet people who see the world the way you do (or maybe not), who can dispense personal "how to" advice. Try to understand how the writing life fits with your own.

The fourth and last piece of advice I have is for if and when you do become a writer, in whatever way, shape or form: never forget to be grateful and celebrate. To this day, for even the slightest achievement or milestone, for every good book review, or the first time I see the cover art for a new book, for every bookseller who invites me to read in their store, I am grateful and I celebrate. I celebrate being a writer. It's what I do, it's who I am, it's

me.
Author of *Amuse Bouche, Sundowner Ubuntu,* **etc.**

Laney Cairo: Is there anything I can say that doesn't sound pretentious? Write, write, write. Doing a college degree in writing
isn't necessary, it might even put you off writing completely,
but the occasional class on the technical side of writing can only
improve the writer's skills.

In an interview, Neil Gaiman said, "Somebody like Ray Bradbury
once said something like, you have a million words of crap in you
and you have to get them out before you get to the good stuff."

Neil's right. Write your million words of crap, which shouldn't
take that long, really. Then write some good stuff that other
people might want to read.
Author of *Fand, Undercover Blues,* **etc.**

T.A. Chase: Motivation, for me, is simply wanting books that I
can relate to or want to read. I keep writing books that fit my
taste. If aspiring writers do that, they'll never stop writing,
no matter how long it might take to get published.
Author of *Here Be Dragons, No Going Home,* **etc.**

Chris Owen: I often create little rewards for myself to make
sure I sit and write when I'd rather go and work on one of my
hobbies, but for the most part I don't worry about being motivated.
Writing is my job, and if I want to get paid, I need to write.
It can be pleasant to know that at the end of the current page I
can take twenty minutes to do something fun like organizing the
kitchen, but as I really enjoy telling stories, motivation to get
the work done isn't a huge problem. My trouble is more one of
time management—there's simply not enough hours in a day to get
to all the fun things I like to do.
Author of *Bareback, An Agreement Among Gentlemen,* **etc.**

L.C. Chase: Rejections are like badges of honor. You're paying
your dues. Each one should be motivation to keep writing, keep
learning the craft, keep improving. Sure, take a day to drink

too much wine and wallow. But the next day get back up more determined than ever and make your story better. And something else to keep in mind, an editor once told me, when he rejected one of my pitches: "I'm just one editor at one publisher."
Author of *Riding With Heaven, Long Tall Drink,* **etc.**

ONCE AROUND THE BLOCK

Once in a while you may run into a creative wall. I don't mean you feel unmotivated to write; rather you can't manage it at all. This is generally referred to as writer's block.

I think there are two kinds of writer's block. The first happens when you're blocked about a particular, specific project. You can't see your way, the words won't come, and if you force the words, you can tell you're spinning your wheels, digging deeper and deeper into the mire.

This usually indicates you've gone off track with the characters or the plot.

You fix it by tracing back to the last point where the story felt like it was flowing properly, and you delete everything from that point on. You stick the deleted bits in a special file where you keep all such fabulous writing—and it usually is really fabulous writing that unfortunately didn't advance the plot an iota—for cannibalizing at a later date. You return to the manuscript and you start fresh from the last point where everything was working.

Brutal, but effective. Take it from me, this works.

The second kind of writer's block is when you have no energy or interest in writing anything at all. Maybe you're too stressed to feel creative. Or maybe you just feel burned out. Maybe you've been ill or there are things happening in your personal life that require all your energy and focus.

Guess what? Those are all legitimate excuses for not writing.

If you're ill or stressed with personal obligations or commitments—and you're working to a deadline—communicate with your editor as soon as possible. Let her or him know what's going on. This stuff happens, and you're not the first writer to miss a deadline—not that you'd want to make a habit of it, but adding guilt to the existing stress load isn't going to make you more creative or productive.

If you're not working to a deadline, allow yourself a reasonable amount of recovery time. And then get back to work.

If the problem is burnout, that's a little different. Basically your creative well has run dry, and you need to refill it. Dr. Lanyon—who ended up needing a year to recover from his own case of burnout—prescribes reading, watching films, spending time with friends, taking a trip, taking a class, taking a walk. But, it can't be the same old stuff you usually do when you need a break. Read in a genre you don't write in, rent foreign or silent or animated films, visit a museum, call friends you haven't talked to in ages, listen to music you don't ordinarily listen to. Try a new restaurant, read poetry, look through art books. Fill your brain with new images, new sounds, tastes, smells. Kick-start your senses. Stimulate your brain.

If you feel like jotting down some ideas, great, but no pressure. When the well is full again, you'll be eager to write.

WORKING THROUGH WRITER'S BLOCK

Adrianna Dane: I have moments when I'm not sure which direction to go in and I freeze. In order to clear the way, I have a folder of writing prompts, and I'll usually pick something random and do a stream of consciousness writing session. It could even be a character and I just start fleshing out a quick character study. It may not even be related to the story I'm working on. I have been known to just look out the window and start describing the tree in minute detail. Or I'll use the old standby of "I remember…" and take it from there. That will usually get me going. I remind myself that no one has to see what I write, and I work to turn off the self-editor simply to get the words down. If I can turn off the editor, the muse usually gets back to work, and I get down to writing.
Author of *Mariposa Soul, The Exile: A Seductive Tale*, **etc.**

Ally Blue: I'm not sure I've ever had REAL writer's block, but I've had times when I was disenchanted with what I was writing and that made it extremely difficult to get the words out. In those cases, I take a break. Either I take a day or two and don't write at all, or I take a day or two and write something completely different. Fan fiction is a wonderful way to get your groove back. You don't have to submit it anywhere, or even let anyone else read it, but for me writing it helps unblock the creativity flow. With fanfic, you don't have to worry about making up characters (they're already there!), you don't have to worry about proper punctuation or grammar or even whether the story makes any sense. Just write whatever comes to you. Let yourself write something stupid, or nonsensical, or just plain bad. It's very freeing, and I find that I can then get back to my contracted work with more energy and more ideas, and be excited about it again.

Author of *Willow Bend, Love's Evolution*, etc.

Kayelle Allen: I get it with every book. If I let it defeat me, I'd never be published. Knowing it will be there and that it will pass helps me deal with it. I do several things to overcome it.

One is to write something else related to the book. I might create a press release, for example. I also edit other parts of the book that I've already finished. Reading the book from start to wherever I happen to have run out of steam gives me a new view of the story as well. Also, I keep emails from beta readers (or crit buddies) who have looked over my work and see what their responses have been. The excitement they feel often generates into renewed personal excitement.

I always write the synopsis before I write the book. It might be only three or four paragraphs, but the overall concept of the story is there. When I get stuck, I go back and see if I'm heading in the right direction. Often, the block has come because I've changed the storyline. If necessary, I change the synopsis to suit the changes. Sometimes, I have to tear out stitches and rewrite the piece I just finished because it didn't go where it needed to go. However, I always save things I cut. Several of those have ended up in other books.

That said, I once spent a year on a book that I finally had to set aside. I later discovered why, but at the time, my dogged determination to complete it had me spinning my wheels. Once I put it aside and worked on something else, I turned out two books within six months. The book I set aside has provided the basis for five other books, however. Sometimes, you need to say enough is enough and move on.

Author of *Wulf, Jawk*, etc.

William Maltese: Knock on wood, and give credit to a possibly overactive imagination, but I can't recall ever having had writer's block in the stereotypical—sitting for hours in front of a blank computer screen, trying to write something, anything—sense of the term. What I do experience are periods of time when I just have to quit writing altogether and go off and do something entirely unrelated, like just stripping down for a lie in the sunshine, or reading a good book (other than one I've written), or spending a couple of days doing absolutely nothing but being a couch potato. I find such respites rejuvenating, and they invariably leave me, sometimes sooner than expected, anxious to get back to my neglected creative-writing routine.

If, for whatever the reason, I'm in the middle of a project, and a problem in the plot line arises that I'm not immediately able to figure out, I usually find that by taking the problem to bed with me and going over and over it in my mind, each and every time I regain even partial consciousness, that the problem usually has a solution, come morning (no pun intended).

Author *of Love Hurts, Diary of a Hustler*, etc.

T.A. Chase: Every writer has experienced writer's block at some point in their writing life. Especially if a particular story or character isn't talking at the moment. How I combat that is simple. I just go to work on a different story. There's always a plot or character who will talk to you and get the creative process working again. After that happens, I can go back to the story that created the block in the first place and start working on it again.

Author of *Here Be Dragons, No Going Home*, etc.

Chris Owen: I don't think I've ever been blocked. There have been long periods of time when I didn't write—months long—but I never thought of it as being blocked. I knew that the ideas would come back and that I would write again, and I never got upset about it. I tend to follow my passions through life, and I've learned that they can come and go and come back even stronger. When I'm not writing, I'm more than likely off doing something else I love or taking a class to learn something new. The words will come back, the ideas will come back. I don't fear the loss of writing; it's too much a part of who I am to be something that I can't find again.

Author of *Bareback, An Agreement Among Gentlemen,* **etc.**

FAMOUS LAST WORDS

If you give ten writers the same plot blurb and put them to work, I guarantee that you'll get ten totally different stories with ten sets of totally different characters. Sure, there will be similarities, but we all bring our individual background, unique perspective, and particular brand of imagination to the work.

You can memorize every single thing I've said about writing, and you can put it all into practice, but your stories will remain your own. The thing that makes the oldest tale in the world seem fresh and new has to do with that inimitable something the author brings to it—and no two authors bring the same thing.

Not everything that works for me will work for you. That's one reason I enlisted the help of so many other talented writers—not to mention reviewers, editors, and publishers. There is no one way to write a book or tell a story. The only certainty is that good writing is hard work—and that hard work generally pays off.

I hope you'll find most of the opinions and information gathered here of use. If you take nothing else away, remember that there is no such thing as a born writer. Some people may be gifted with a certain knack, but writing skill is something that develops with time and practice. Persistence and discipline are every bit—if not more—important than raw talent.

If this is what you want to do, there's nothing to stop you. It's up to you now.

ALL SHE WROTE

Sasha Knight, Samhain Publishing: Familiarize yourself with a variety of the published work currently available. Do your research. When you're interested in submitting to a publisher, read some of what they've already published. Find critique partners who are comfortable with the genre and, after you've gone over the manuscript until you can't see straight, have them go over it with a fine-tooth comb as well. Submit the most polished product you can.

Pay attention to submission guidelines at the publishers. Be professional and courteous. Treat your writing as a job, treat the publishers as professionals—and expect to be treated the same in return. Publishing is a business—never forget that.

That said, love what you do, really love it, because writing is a difficult job, but the more you love it, the more that will come across in your writing. Don't give up, but also don't expect to contract the first book you write to the first person you submit it to. Part of the writing job includes rejection. Consider the rejection, and any feedback you receive, and see what you can learn from it. Then move on. Revise. Or don't. Keep writing. Keep moving forward. Keep learning and growing as an author. And celebrate when you finally get that contract.

And then start the writing process all over again.

Trace Edward Zaber, Amber Quill Press: These days, it's very easy to get published. With the Internet consuming our lives, many people who write a blog or send an email also assume they are authors. Wrong! Unfortunately, many publishing houses are also being formed by these very same individuals. So first, authors must be aware of this and they must learn their craft! No doubt about it! Learn punctuation, learn sentence construction, etc. These are the tools of the trade, so no skimping can be done here, unless an author doesn't care about quality. Then an author must read every how-to-write book on the shelves at their local library, and even join a critique group to learn how to deal with rejection and criticism. And finally, if an individual still yearns to write after all of that, they must research every single company and its history before submitting a manuscript. Too many authors in the past few years have been duped by hitching their wagons to the newest hot e-publisher or small press star based on word of mouth, only to wonder why the company "forgets" to pay royalties or folds within a year's time. What many authors don't seem to realize is that many new publishers were formed by frustrated authors, and many of these individuals have never run a successful lemonade stand, let alone a quality—not to mention, profitable—publishing house! Research is the name of the game these days, especially with so many fly-by-night companies popping up. Therefore, authors owe it to themselves to invest time in this endeavor. If not, they will be sorry in the majority of cases.

Tina Burns, Liquid Silver Books: Really, no matter what genre you're writing there are some key things you want to make sure your story does:

1 - Makes sense. You'd be surprised at how many stories don't.

2 - Well-developed characters. That doesn't mean a ton of back-story, but try to write 3-dimensional characters.

3 - Make sure it's critiqued. And not by someone who doesn't know how to write and just gushes over it. A publisher can tell which authors have those type of critique partners.

4 - Find the right publisher for your story. Research. If you've written a mainstream M/M mystery, then submitting to an erotica publisher will not get you published. Make sure the publisher is solid in their business practices.

5 - And probably the most important, have fun. Write what you love, not what's the HOT topic. Trust me, publishers and editors can tell when you've written a story to sell vs. from your heart.

S.A. Clements, Torquere Press: Research your market. If you write soft romances with no sex, you're looking for a different publisher than you are if you write traditional gay male erotica. If you write threesomes with men and women, your market is different than if you write erotic M/M only romance. Query your potential publisher to see if they're right for you, which will save a lot of rejection in the long run.

Be professional. Read the submission guidelines. Send us an interesting synopsis and query letter.

Write us a good story.

JUST DO IT!

One final thought. In order to write, you have to have something to write *about*.

Everybody needs to unplug once in a while. I mean that literally. Turn off the computer and go spend some time with real people. Not only is that good for *you*, it's good for your writing. The people in our stories behave in a way that suits the plot. Real live people aren't so accommodating, and it's helpful to remind ourselves of that now and then. Don't hone your craft at the expense of the people in your life. Stay involved and stay engaged in the world around you. If you have to choose between being a great writer and actively participating in your own life, something's wrong.

Choose life and you'll always have something to write about.

GLOSSARY

Alpha male - The leader, always in control. Aggressive, dynamic. A Top.

Beta male - Combines qualities of Alpha leadership with sensitivity of Omega. Independent, communicator. Sometimes can be a former Alpha or an Alpha on the rise. Can play Top or bottom.

Beta reader - Fan-fiction term for a critique partner who checks mostly for spelling, grammar, punctuation, and canon inconsistencies.

BDSM - Bondage, Discipline, Dominance/submission, and Sadomasochism. An acronym for erotic and non-erotic practices in a consenting adult relationship. Those practices include a variety of interpersonal dynamics. Restraint, sensory stimulation, role-playing, etc. are common.

Fan fiction - Stories made up by fans of television, movie, or other media characters. There is also real-person fiction. Don't ask.

Genre fiction - Fiction written to fit into a specific literary genre or category (in fact, it is also sometimes called "category or commercial fiction") like mystery, western, romance, etc.

HEA - Happily Ever After

HFN - Happy For Now

Male/Male Fiction - A subgenre of romance featuring a love story between two (sometimes more) gay men.

Omega male - The polar opposite of the Alpha male—subservient to Alpha *and* Beta—always a follower. Passive, submissive, sensitive. A bottom.

Slash - Fan fiction where the typically heterosexual canon protagonists engage in same-sex relations and romance with each other. The classic example is *Star Trek*'s Kirk and Spock or K/S. "Slash" actually refers to the slash mark.

UST - Unresolved Sexual Tension - A trope in television and literature whereby two people are madly attracted to each other but kept apart by circumstances either reasonable or contrived.

Yaoi - Japanese term for explicit sexual and romantic love between men as portrayed in anime (cartoons) and manga (comic books). Artwork, themes, and roles in Yaoi are strictly defined.

THE HELL YOU SAY
ORIGINAL NOTES

Professor Guy ?? - 50ish, a handsome Professor Sneed, socks with sandals, coal black hair, a cape. A pipe and can blow smoke rings. Teaches demonology. An expert on all things mystical and magical. Strong and eccentric, liberal. A possible romantic partner to Adrien. As strong and attractive as Jake, but different.

TV's BARNEY IS THE ANTICHRIST?

Proof that Barney, the cute purple dinosaur, is Satan can be ascertained with a little numerical study of his name and description.

Given: Barney is a cute purple dinosaur.
Step 1: Extract the Roman numerals from the given.
(Remember since the Romans had no letter 'U', we must replace each instance of 'U' with a "V")
Initial conversion: CVTE PVRPLE DINOSAVR
Numerical extraction: CV V L DI V
Step 2: Add them: $100 + 5 + 5 + 50 + 500 + 1 + 5 = 666$
And you thought that PBS was safe!

Note: darker, edgier than ADT

It's Christmas time and the dark side is catching up with Angus, Adrien English's college student employee and "resident warlock." When he begins to receive death threats at work, Adrien decides on a quick fix, and gives

Angus a cash Christmas present with instructions to take a little "holiday" with new girlfriend Wendy (whom Adrien refers to as Wanda Witch).

"Listen, Harry Potter, do us both a favor..."

(Why is Angus in trouble with the coven? How does Adrien get him out of it? Has he witnessed something? What do we know about Angus?)

Meanwhile, Adrien's mother Lisa has finally decided to remarry—not that Adrien has a problem with this but it's unexpected and jars him a little—or maybe it's just the holidays and the melancholy feeling they trigger for those alone. Still, he braces up to his equally wacky father-in-law to be who is taking an uncomfortable interest in his new "son." (Does he have a useful extended family for Adrien to play off?)

Her upcoming nuptials trigger Lisa to...?

Adrien goes to UCLA to check out Angus's professor of all things mystical and mythological, the man who Angus believes is behind all his trouble (Angus is his teaching assistant?). Guy ??????? Is a handsome 50ish Professor Sneed type, eccentric but charismatic—and gay. He fences with Adrien and clearly knows more than he pretends.

Shortly after, Adrien is harassed by punk Goth kids. Adrien, as usual, is sarcastic and to the point, very much parent to child; but though Adrien is tough-minded and courageous, the threat against him is real, and he is physically vulnerable.

Jake, meanwhile, is investigating the mysterious deaths of UCLA college kids in the Goth underground. Devil worship, etc. seems to be involved.

Though their recent experiences at Pine Shadow Ranch (see A DANGEROUS THING) deepened their friendship, Jake's increasing tension over the fear of being "outed" puts strain on their relationship. He's a bit more snappish and brusque with Adrien who, despite his feelings for Jake, won't put up with any crap. This tension will carry into their "case."

"What part of stay the fuck out of it, don't you understand?"

To Adrien's exasperation, Angus and Wanda return, just in time to get accused of murder. (Whose?) Now Adrien is involved whether he wants to be or not, because no one is interested in helping Angus.

Professor Guy comes to warn Adrien that a spell has been cast on him. Adrien scoffs, but he is having a weird run of bad luck, including a fender bender, handles come off in his hand, food is spoiling, etc.

A chance encounter with Jake (accompanied by his cop girlfriend Kate and his nieces and nephews) results in Jake snubbing Adrien. Later he apologizes and tries to make it up, but the truth is, Jake still desires children and a "normal" life. On Christmas Eve he decides to marry Kate and renounce his dual sexuality.

Nonetheless, Jake will still provide Adrien's "back up" (albeit unwillingly) when he tackles…WHO??? Jake's case is heart of the mystery and Adrien's involvement is tangential. Who is murdered and why?

Other smart-ass pop cultural references: *Lord of the Rings*, Magick, Dungeons and Dragons, the devil, etc.

Angus free, the promise of a new relationship, the close of one year and the beginning of another brings Adrien to accept the fact that Jake is a lost cause. Adrien catches his flight (symbolic) to Brittany on his own.

THE HELL, YOU SAY
Original Outline

CHAPTER ONE — Phone death threats to Angus; Adrien sends Angus on holiday. Jake mentions recent discovery of possible ritual murder. Book signing with Gabriel Savant, and Savant's announcement of cult exposé. Brunch with Lisa—Lisa announces marriage plans.

CHAPTER TWO — Brunch with Lisa cont. Jake further discusses cult scene and the discovery of a second body. Adrien visits UCLA and Professor Guy Snowden—attractive but can he be trusted? Bob Friedlander stops by bookstore looking for missing floppy disc.

CHAPTER THREE — Dinner with Adrien's new and slightly overwhelming "family." Someone lurking in back alley of shop? Pentagram on the shop doorstep.

CHAPTER FOUR — Jake patronizing Adrien—and warning him off case; Adrien visiting Dragonwyck witchcraft shop; Adrien reading news story details on second murder victim.

CHAPTER FIVE — Partner's In Crime writing group; indication of Jake's ambition; call from Guy Snowden; ongoing trouble getting coverage in shop; Jake and Adrien "at home."

CHAPTER SIX — Gabriel Savant still looking for disc and acting weirder and more paranoid than ever—first mention of *Blade Sable*; lunch with the attractive but secretive Professor Snowden; Jake injured in hit and run.

CHAPTER SEVEN — Visit to Jake clearly underlining the two separate sides of Jake's life; computer research on Wicca, etc; call from Jake; lunch with Lisa; Adrien joins Dark Realm and begins asking about *Blade Sable;* Gabriel Savant is missing.

CHAPTER EIGHT — Adrien hires Velvet Snow; more threats from the dark side; dinner with Lisa's Councilman. Visit from *Blade Sable* girls; Jake with news of Kate's pregnancy.

CHAPTER NINE — Phone call from Angus; visit to Angus's house and discovery of the body in the bedroom.

CHAPTER TEN — Jake's decision to conceal Adrien's role in discovery of the body; phone call from Snowden; Angus arrested; official visit from Jake and Detective Rossini.

CHAPTER ELEVEN — Snowden indicates a personal interest in Adrien and introduces Adrien to Oliver Garibaldi; no word from Jake; Velvet Snow going through Adrien's desk; Super Bowl Sunday at the Dautens'.

CHAPTER TWELVE — Visit from detectives working for Angus's attorney; first nibble at Adrien's *Blade Sable* Internet query; Bob Friedlander pumping Adrien for information at bar. Jake canceling dinner plans.

CHAPTER THIRTEEN — Visit to Snowden at UCLA and recognition of second *Blade Sable* girl. Unsuccessful effort at tracking student—is Snowden really trying to help? Names of other students in Angus's "coven."

CHAPTER FOURTEEN — Police questioning Adrien's role in Savant's disappearance. Wiccans arrive to perform cleansing ritual just as Adrien's new sisters make a surprise visit to Cloak and Dagger books.

CHAPTER FIFTEEN — Adrien pursues Wicca lead and visits the hedgewitch. Believes he is being followed by Velvet Snow.

CHAPTER SIXTEEN — Meeting with Internet contact who turns out to be Oliver Garibaldi. Garibaldi fills Adrien in on street rep of *Blade Sable* and invites Adrien to explore spiritual possibilities. Jake tells Adrien he is going to marry Kate.

CHAPTER SEVENTEEN — Detective Rossini visits without Jake—clearly suspects something. Adrien pursuing suspicions of Friedlander's role in Savant's disappearance (makes connection that Friedlander writes the books and Savant is the public persona).

CHAPTER EIGHTEEN — Adrien attends social gathering at Garibaldi's and bumps into Guy Snowden—and Velvet Snow.

CHAPTER NINETEEN — Following up on questioning students who knew Angus and Tony Zellig.

CHAPTER TWENTY — Questioning Garibaldi regarding Savant's disappearance.

CHAPTER TWENTY-ONE — Adrien and Snowden go to Goth club and nearly get run down by hit-and-run driver.

CHAPTER TWENTY-TWO — Snowden and Adrien "investigating" infuriates Jake who shoves Adrien down and warns him to keep out of case.

CHAPTER TWENTY-THREE —

CHAPTER TWENTY-FOUR — Adrien sneaking into Blade Sable "church" and cutting Savant loose. Phone call to Snowden asking him to take credit for solving Savant's disappearance and to keep Adrien out of it.

CHAPTER TWENTY-FIVE — Loose ends tied up. Angus free and a final wordless encounter with Jake. Snow in Los Angeles? Christmas with the Dautens (like being trapped in a Perry Como special). A phone call from Snowden.

"Oh well. What the hell."

THE HELL, YOU SAY
SYNOPSIS

Mystery writer and Los Angeles bookseller ADRIEN ENGLISH (POV) is an attractive, successful, thirty-something gay man with a knack for playing amateur sleuth—much to the disapproval of his on-again off-again lover, closeted LAPD homicide detective JAKE RIORDAN.

In the third book of the series, it's Christmas time, and the dark side is catching up with ANGUS, Adrien's college student assistant (and "resident warlock") at Cloak and Dagger Books. After Angus receives death threats at work, Adrien decides on a quick fix, and gives Angus and his girlfriend WANDA a Christmas bonus with instructions to take a little holiday. Adrien is certain he can resolve the situation by contacting Angus's former professor, DR. GUY SNOWDEN, an expert in the occult. Jake is none too pleased with this intervention as he believes Angus may know something that would help his current investigation of what appear to be a number of ritual murders occurring over the past decade.

After a trip to UCLA and an interview with the unexpectedly attractive Dr. Snowden, Adrien is hopeful that Angus's harassers will find someone else to terrorize—although he doesn't quite trust the enigmatic professor.

A book signing for best-selling author GABRIEL SAVANT leads to a public announcement that the flamboyant writer's next work will be a non-fiction exposé of the local cult, Blade Sable. When Savant disappears after showing up at Cloak and Dagger Books (ostensibly searching for a missing disk with some mysterious research notes), it appears Jake's suspicion that his murder case may be tied to the local occult scene could be correct.

Meanwhile, LISA ENGLISH, Adrien's overprotective society matron mother, announces that she is remarrying. Adrien does not have a problem with this, however Lisa's machinations to get Adrien to bond with his new "family" serve to underscore his loneliness and desire for something more permanent with Jake—as well as his uneasy instinct that Jake is slowly and subtly withdrawing from him. Jake has never made any secret of his desire for a "normal" life. When Jake informs him that his "cover" girlfriend is pregnant, Adrien realizes it's only a matter of time before Jake ends their fragile relationship.

If Dr. Snowden has followed through on his promise to speak to Angus's harassers, there's no sign of it—in fact, after a bloody-looking pentagram is scrawled on the doorstep of Cloak and Dagger Books, it appears that Adrien may now be a target. Never one to leave well enough alone, Adrien begins to investigate in earnest. He encounters local Wiccans, the Hedgewitch of Hollywood, and—through the reluctant Snowden—wealthy and enigmatic OLIVER GARIBALDI, a local expert and writer on the occult.

Not only does Garibaldi seem to know Adrien's stepfather-to-be, but he seems well acquainted with VELVET SNOW, Adrien's new bookstore assistant, who Adrien discovers searching through his private belongings and listening at keyholes.

Adrien believes he has a solid lead when two of Angus's friends try to raise a little hell at the bookstore, but the lead turns (literally) into a dead end when he finds one of the girls murdered at Angus's house.

Angus is arrested for the murder. Adrien believes Angus is innocent—so does the PI Angus's defense attorney hires, who suspects Adrien is hiding something. Adrien *is* hiding something: his relationship with Jake, the police detective investigating the girl's murder. Threat of exposure widens the gulf between Adrien and Jake, which at last erupts into near violence when Jake discovers Adrien is still poking his nose into Jake's business.

With Jake effectively out of the picture, Adrien is on his own pursuing his inquiries through the Internet and around the Los Angeles occult scene. He turns to Guy Snowden for help. They are nearly run down outside a Goth club.

Adrien also investigates the possibility that Savant is the victim of some non-occult force. Could his assistant (and secret writing partner) Bob Friedlander have played a hand in the celebrity author's disappearance?

With Snowden's help Adrien at last finds and rescues the missing author Gabriel Savant. Savant has been kidnapped by Oliver Grimaldi, leader of Blade Sable. Garibaldi plans to slay Savant during a Satanic Mass on Christmas Eve.

With Angus free and the murderous Garibaldi brought to justice, Adrien has no excuse not to spend Christmas with his new "family." A surprise last-minute phone call turns out not to be from Jake but from Guy Snowden.

Sample Query Letter
Death of a Pirate King

Josh Lanyon
1234 My Street
Apt. A
Anywhere, ZZ 12345-1234
Joshlanyon@myemail.com
(123) 123-4567

April 6, 2007

PUBLISHING HOUSE 'R' US.
John Smith - Editor-in-Chief
123 Bright Lights Avenue
New York, NY 10022

Dear Mr. Smith,

I'm Josh Lanyon, the author of the Adrien English mystery series, previously published by the now-defunct Gay Men's Press in Britain. I'm currently at work on the fourth book of the series, DEATH OF A PIRATE KING (estimated word count 75 - 80,000), and am submitting sample chapters and outline for your consideration.

In the fourth book of the series, Adrien is asked by hunky bisexual film star Paul Kane to look unofficially into the murder of a movie producer—something Adrien is hesitant to do with hostile ex-lover, closeted LAPD lieutenant Jake Riordan, overseeing the case.

I am able to provide sales figures on the first two books in the series (which have now been retooled and re-sold to electronic and print publishers who are marketing them toward the rapidly expanding M/M audience). The third book is currently short-listed for a Lambda Literary Award in the Gay Mystery category.

In June I won a Mystery Writers of America grant for the series. The terms of the grant require submission of DEATH OF A PIRATE KING to six traditional publishing houses, but having read interviews with you over the years—and being a great fan of so many of the books you publish—I wanted to start with PUBLISHING HOUSE 'R' US and yourself.

I've enclosed an SASE for your convenience. It is not necessary to return sample chapters or outline. I appreciate your time and consideration, and sincerely hope that you will decide the Adrien English series belongs at PUBLISHING HOUSE 'R' US.

Sincerely,

Josh Lanyon

TABLES

Table One: Writing Contests

Name	Link	General Information
Gival Press	www.givalpress.com	Fiction: The Gival Press Short Story Award The Gival Press Novel Award
The EPIC Awards "EPPIES"	epicorg.com/competitions.html competitions@epicorg.com for questions	The Electronic Publishing Industry Coalition (EPIC™) is an organization of electronic publishing professionals. The EPIC Awards are given annually to recognize outstanding achievement in e-publishing.
Cupid and Psyche Awards "CAPA"	www.theromancestudio.com/capa.php	Awards given by The Romance Studio (TRS) for excellence in romantic fiction. Only books reviewed by TRS are nominated and considered.
Independent Publisher Book Awards "IPPY"	www.independentpublisher.com/ipland/ipawards.php jimb@bookpublishing.com for questions	Independent authors & publishers awards program, which is open to all members of the independent publishing industries.
Passionate Ink "Passionate Plume Awards"	passionateinkers.blogspot.com/ or passionateink.org	Passionate Ink is the Special Interest Chapter of Romance Writers of America (RWA) for erotic romance writers.
The Lambda Literary Awards "LAMMYS"	www.lambdaliterary.org/awards/awards-guidelines/ Contact Kathleen DeBold at kdebold@lambdaliterary.org for questions	Lambda Literary Awards are open to all authors regardless of sexual orientation or gender identity with the exception of three awards: The Betty Berzon Emerging Writer Award, the Jim Duggins Outstanding Mid-Career Novelist Prize, and the Pioneer Award. Submission fee required.

Table Two: GLBT friendly & M/M Review sites

NAME	WEB ADDRESS
Attention is Arbitrary	attentionisarbitrary. blogspot
A Bear on Books	tom-webb.blogspot.com
Bitten by Books	bittenbybooks.com
Blackraven's Reviews	blackravensreviews.com
Brief Encounters	briefencountersreviews.com
Cryselle's Bookshelf	cryssellescraziness.blogspot. com
Dark Divas Reviews	darkdivasreviews.com
Dear Author	dearauthor.com
Elisa Reviews and Ramblings	reviews-and-ramblings.dreamwidth.org/
Fiction Vixen	fictionvixen.com
GayListBookReviews	gaylistbookreviews.wordpress .com
GLBT Bookshelf	bookworld.editme.com/
Hearts on Fire	heartsonfirereviews.com
Infinite Love	victoriazagar.com/
Jeannie Zelos Book Reviews	jeanniezelos.wordpress.com/
Joyfully Jay	joyfullyjay.com
Joyfully Reviewed	joyfullyreviewed.com
Library Thing	www.librarything.com
Live your Life, Buy the Book	liveyourlifebuythebook.wordpress.com
Love Romances and More	loveromancesandmore.blogspot.com
Mamba's Lair	amaras-place.blogspot.com
MM Good Book Reviews	mmgoodbookreviews.wordpress.com
MM Romance Reviews	mmromancebookreviews. blogspot
Mrs Condit & Friends Reads Books	mrsconditreadsbooks.com
Pants Off Reviews	pantsoffreviews.blogspot.com
Rainbow Reviews	rainbow-reviews.com/
Rarely Dusty Books	Rarely Dusty Books
Reviews by Jessewave	www.reviewsbyjessewave.com/
Romance Around the Corner	romance-around-the-corner.blogspot.com
Scattered Thoughts	scatteredthoughtsandroguewords
Sid Love	sidlove.wordpress. com/
Smart Bitches Trashy Reviews	smartbitchestrashybooks.com
Smexy Books	smexybooks.com
Speak its Name	speakitsname.com
Stumbling Over Chaos	www.stumblingoverchaos.com

The Armchair Reader	coleriann.com
The Dancing Dove	dancing-dove.blogspot. com/
The Naughty Bits	teddypig.com
The Romance Reviews	glbt.theromancereviews.com
The Romance Studio	theromancestudio.com/
three am	kassa011.wordpress.com
Top 2 Bottom Reviews	top2bottomreviews.wordpress.com
Tracy's Place	ahhhhhromanc e.blogspot. com/
Well Read	jenre-wellread. blogspot. com/

Table Three: Publishers that have published M/M 03/31/13

Self-Publishing sites are noted in italics

(Please note: this listing is not a recommendation or an endorsement of the following publishers.)

NAME	ADDRESS	EMAIL	WEBSITE
Amazon KDP			kdp.amazon.com
Amber Allure An imprint of AMBER QUILL PRESS, LLC	NA	Submissions by invitation only	www.amberquill.com
Arsenal Pulp Press	Arsenal Pulp Press #101 - 211 East Georgia Street Vancouver, BC, Canada V6A 1Z6	info@arsenalpulp.com	www.arsenalpulp.com
Beau to Beau Books	NA	info@beautobeau.com	beautobeau.com
Blind Eye Books	Blind Eye Books 1141 Grant Street Bellingham, WA 98225	editor@blindeyebooks.com	www.blindeyebooks.com
Bold Strokes Books	Bold Strokes Books P.O. Box 249 Valley Falls, NY 12185	submissions @boldstrokesbooks.com	www.boldstrokesbooks.com
Carina Press (digital-first imprint from Harlequin)	NA	submissions@carinapress.com	ebooks.carinapress.com

Casperian Books	Casperian Books LLC PO Box 161026 Sacramento, CA 95816-1026	submissions @casperianbooks.com Please do not send unsolicited manuscripts.	casperianbooks.com
Circlet Press	Circlet Press, Inc. 39 Hurlbut Street Cambridge, MA 02138	circletintern@gmail.com	www.circlet.com
Cleis Press Inc	Attn: Brenda Knight Cleis Press and Viva Editions 2246 Sixth Street Berkeley, CA 94710	bknight@cleispress.com	www.cleispress.com
Cobblestone Press	NA	submissions@cobblestone-press.com	www.cobblestone-press.com
Dreamspinner Press	Dreamspinner Press 5032 Capital Circle SW Ste 2, PMB# 279 Tallahassee, FL 32305-7886	submissions @dreamspinnerpress.com	www.dreamspinnerpress.com
Ellora's Cave	Ellora's Cave Publishing Inc. 1056 Home Ave. Akron, OH 44310-3502	submissions@ellorascave.com	www.ellorascave.com
Forever Yours (digital imprint of Grand Central Publishing)		ForeverYours@hbgusa.com	www.forever-romance.com/about-forever-yours/

Green Candy Press	Green Candy Press 601 Van Ness Ave, E3-918 San Francisco, CA 94102	editorial @greencandypress.com	www.greencandypress.com
In Group Press	NA	query@ingrouppress.com	www.ingrouppress.com
iUniverse (self-publishing)	iUniverse 1663 Liberty Drive Bloomington, IN 47403 1-800-AU-THORS		www.iuniverse.com
Kensington Publishing Corp	Kensington Publishing Corp. 119 West 40th Street New York, New York 10018 1-800-221-2647		www.kensingtonbooks.com
Lethe Press	Lethe Press 118 Heritage Ave Maple Shade, NJ 08052	editor@lethepressbooks.com Rarely considers unsolicited manuscripts.	lethepressbooks.com
Liquid Silver/Molten Silver Division	Liquid Silver Books Imprint of Atlantic Bridge Publishing 10509 Sedgegrass Drive Indianapolis, IN 46235	submissions @liquidsilverbooks.com	www.liquidsilverbooks.com

Loose Id	Loose Id LLC 1802 N. Carson Street, Suite 212-2924 Carson City, NV 89701	submissions@loose-id.com	www.loose-id.com
Lulu.com (self-publishing)	Lulu Enterprises, Inc. 3101 Hillsborough Street, Suite 210 Raleigh, NC 27607-5436		www.lulu.com
MLR Press LLC	MLR Press, LLC 3052 Gaines Waterport Rd. Albion, NY 14411	mlrpress. submissionandqueries@gmail	www.mlrbooks.com
Mojocastle Press	Mojocastle Press LLC PO Box 290 Haymarket, VA 20168	mojocastlesubmissions @gmail.com	www.mojocastle.com
NeWest Press	NeWest Press #201, 8540 - 109 Street Edmonton, AB T6G 1E6 Canada	info@newestpress.com	www.newestpress.com
Phaze Division of Mundania Press	Mundania Press LLC 6470A Glenway Avenue #109 Cincinnati, OH 45211	books@phaze.com	www.phaze.com

Regal Crest Enterprises	Regal Crest Enterprises, LLC 229 Sheridan Loop Belton, TX 76513	web@regalcrestbooks.biz	www.regalcrest.biz
Riptide Publishing	NA	www.riptidepublishing.com /contact	www.riptidepublishing.com
Rooster Fish Press, an imprint of Windshift Press (self-publishing)	Rooster Fish Press: A Division of the Windshift Press Group 81 Jamieson Road Bowser BC V0R 1G0 Tel: 250 757 6801 Fax: 250 757 6802		www.windshift.bc.ca
Samhain Publishing, Ltd.	Samhain Publishing, Ltd. 577 Mulberry Street, Suite 1520 Macon, GA 31201	editor @samhainpublishing.com	www.samhainpublishing.com
Seventh Window Publications	Seventh Window Publications P.O. BOX 603165 Providence, RI 02906-0165	Contact Us link on website	seventhwindow.com
Smashwords (self-publishing)	Smashwords, Inc. 15951 Los Gatos Blvd., Ste 16 Los Gatos, CA 95032		www.smashwords.com

Star Books Press	STARbooks Press Mailing PO Box 711612 Herndon VA 20171	publish@starbookspress.com Will not consider unsolicited manuscripts	starbookspress.com
Storm Moon Press	NA	submissions @stormmoonpress.com	stormmoonpress.com
Torquere Press Publishers	Torquere Press Publishers PO BOX 2545 Round Rock, TX 78664	submissions @torquerepress.com	www.torquerepress.com
Total e-bound Publishing	NA	submissions @totalebound.com	www.total-e-bound.com/
Untreed Reads (self-publishing)	NA	submissions @untreedreads.com	www.untreedreads.com
Xlibris (self-publishing)	Xlibris Corporation 1663 Liberty Drive, Suite 200 Bloomington, IN 47403	publishtoday@xlibris.com	www2.xlibris.com